GREAT COMPOSERS

Through the Eyes of Their Contemporaries

Great Composers

THROUGH THE EYES

OF THEIR

CONTEMPORARIES

Edited by

OTTO ZOFF

Translator and Assistant Editor
PHOEBE ROGOFF CAVE

New York
E. P. Dutton & Company, Inc.
1951

INDIVIDUAL COPYRIGHTS

For selections from Ira Gershwin's "My Brother's Childhood" and Rouben Mamoulian's "He Liked To Be Gershwin," from "George Gershwin," edited and designed by Merle Armitage, copyright 1934 and published by Longmans, Green & Co., London, New York, Toronto.

For selections from "The Man Liszt" by Ernest Newman, copyrighted and published by Cassell & Company, London.

For selections from "How Chopin Played" by A. J. Hipkins, copyright 1937, and from "Schumann" by Joan Chissell, copyright 1948, published by J. M. Dent & Sons, London.

For selection from "Gluck" by Martin Cooper, copyrighted and published by Chatto & Windus, London.

For selections from "My Life" by Richard Wagner, copyright 1911, 1939, and from "The Life and Letters of Tchaikovsky" by Modeste Tchaikovsky, published by Dodd, Mead & Company, Inc., New York.

For selections from "A Smattering of Ignorance" by Oscar Levant, copyright 1939, 1940 by Oscar Levant, published by Doubleday & Company, Inc., New York.

For selections from "Modeste Musorgsky's Last Hours" by Serge Bertensson (July 1941 issue) and from "Richard Strauss and His Works" by William Armstrong (December 1903 issue) by permission of Etude, the music magazine. Copyright 1903 and 1941 by Theodore Presser Company, Bryn Mawr, Pennsylvania.

For selection from "Gustav Mahler" by Bruno Walter, 1941. Greystone Press, New York. Permission granted by Mr. Bruno Walter, Beverly Hills, California.

For selections from "Giuseppe Verdi" by Francis Toye, and from "Brahms" by Walter Niemann, copyright 1946 and published by Alfred A. Knopf, Inc., New York.

For selection from "Richard Wagner und Bayreuth," published and copyrighted by Knorr und Hirth, Muenchen.

For selections from "Recollections of Tchaikovsky" (April 1940 issue) and from "Recollections of Beethoven" (January 1923 issue), Music & Letters, London.

For selection from "Debussy and Brahms" by Andrew de Ternant (July 1, 1924 issue), The Musical Times, Novello and Co., London.

For selections from "The Schubert Reader" by Otto Erich Deutsch, copyright 1947, from "The Musorgsky Reader," translated and edited by Jan Leyda and Sergei Bertensson, copyright 1947, from "The Bach Reader" by Hans David and Arthur Mendel, copyright 1945, from "Haydn, A Creative Life in Music" by Karl Geiringer, copyright 1946, and from "Memoirs of Malwida von Meysenbug, Rebel in Bombazine," copyright 1936, published by W. W. Norton & Company, Inc., New York.

For selections from "Souvenirs d'Achille Debussy" by Gabriel Pierné and from "Debussy à Dix-Huit Ans" by M. Vasnier (May 1, 1926 issue), La Nouvelle Revue Française, Librairie Gallimard, Paris.

For selections from "The Letters of Mozart and His Family," chronologically arranged, translated and edited by Emily Anderson, Volume II, copyright 1938, from "Music Study in Germany" by Amy Fay, copyright 1896, and from "Clara Schumann, An Artist's Life" by Berthold Litzmann, published 1925 and copyrighted by The Macmillan Company, New York.

For selections from "Gilbert, Sullivan and d'Oyly Carte" by François Cellier and Cunningham Bridgeman, copyright 1927 and published by Pitman & Sons, New York.

For selection from "Beloved Friend" by Catherine Drinker Bowen, copyright 1937, by Random House, Inc., New York.

For selections from "Claude Debussy, Souvenirs" by Pasteur Vallery-Radot (May 15, 1938 issue), Revue des Deux Mondes, Paris.

For selection from "Arthur Seymour Sullivan" by Henry Saxe Wyndham, copyrighted and published by Routledge & Kegan Paul, Ltd., London.

For selections from "Johannes Brahms" by Guido Adler (April 1933 issue) and from "Claude-Achille Debussy" by J. G. Prod'homme (October 1918 issue), the Musical Quarterly, copyrighted and published by G. Schirmer, New York.

For selections from "Richard Strauss und die Wilde Gung'l" by Franz Trenner and from "Letzter Besuch bei Richard Strauss" by Rudolf Hartmann (September 1, 1950 issue), copyrighted and published by Schweizerische Musikzeitung, Revue Musicale Suisse, Zuerich.

For selection from "George F. Handel" by Newman Flower, copyright 1948 and published by Charles Scribner's Sons, New York.

For selections from "Gustav Mahler" by Guido Adler, copyrighted and published 1916 by Universal Edition, Wien and Leipzig (Associated Music Publishers, New York).

For selections from "Gustav Mahler, Memoirs and Letters" by Alma Mahler, copyright 1946 and published by the Viking Press, New York.

ACKNOWLEDGMENTS

I wish to express my thanks to those who have so kindly assisted me in the research work for this book. I am particularly indebted to Mr. Sigmund Bloch, New York; Mr. Richard Capell, London; Mr. Edward Fendler, Brooklyn, New York; Mr. Simon Goldberg, New York; Dr. Willi Schuh, Zuerich; and to the staff of the Music Room of the New York Public Library.

I am grateful to the various publishers for permission to reprint the many selections listed on the copyright page.

CONTENTS

Frederic François Chopin 241

Franz Liszt 260

Richard Wagner 280

Giuseppe Verdi 307

INTRODUCTION

THIS BOOK is a collection of reminiscences of actual conversations and experiences with great composers as recorded by their contemporaries.

We see Beethoven, for instance, through the eyes of friends, students, reverent callers, enemies, chance acquaintances. Some describe the boy, a precocious little piano virtuoso; others tell of the lonely hermit in his modest valley house near Vienna, or of the deaf conductor who threw his orchestra and his public into embarrassed confusion; still others recall the teacher, or the philanthropist, or the revolutionary. And some tell of the master's dying and his death.

All the written memories of Beethoven, if put together without selection, would fill many volumes, but only the merest fraction of these reminiscences gives us the giant in his most characteristic moods and actions. It is necessary to pluck carefully, two pages here, four pages there, if we are to paint for ourselves a clear and significant portrait of his personality.

Or take Chopin: He was adored; women, artists and priests milled around him incessantly, until his last hour. Many have committed to paper every syllable he uttered (or they thought he uttered); they have described his behavior down to the minutest mannerism, every bat of his eyelash, whether in society, during piano lessons or on his sickbed. Unfortunately these records are rarely reliable; many are no better than hysterical phantasy. And these rememberers are unable to distinguish between the essential and the non-essential. Myriad lights and shadows, falling on the mirror from all directions, clash and contradict and confuse one another, so that not one contour is clean and sharp.

Ever since Rembrandt painted we have understood that the fine portrait need not reproduce every detail of physical structure, of dress, or even of character. On the contrary, the best portrait picks out only a few of the many traits that lie in every face, isolates and highlights the dominating features. There are portraits of Rembrandt, Titian, Goya, Van Gogh that concentrate exclusively on the eyes and the hands, and these are among the masterpieces of all time.

In putting this book together, therefore, I have had to choose carefully — and choosing involves rejecting. I have had to omit pieces of charm and interest and poignancy simply because they would have blurred the picture or in some way spoiled the proportions.

It is a strange fact that many music lovers who have for years admired, or even played, the work of some master know little or nothing about the man who created it. Verdi worshippers are apt to show surprise when you refer to the bitter misery of his early years, or to the tragedy that overtook him during his hardest period—the death of his wife and two children in an epidemic—or to his active participation in his country's revolutionary struggle to free itself from the Austrian yoke. Friends of music rarely have the time or patience for reading thick biographies, which are too often overgrown with the moss of scholarship.

Artists live on a higher plane—and while they labor they

are in a sense dead to the world. But they are not utterly
cut off from other men; they cannot float perpetually in the
heaven of creation. They must share in the sufferings and
ordeals of ordinary mortals, and all too often they are
forced to descend to the lowest level of human existence.
And of course their participation in the everyday affairs of
earth has its effect on their work, which cannot be born in
a vacuum. No two of these creators are alike. If we try
hard to discover and understand their diverse and innumerable roots—if we learn something of their temperaments and their minds, utterly unique, of their frustrations
and their triumphs, their friends, lovers, neighbors, em-
ployers, enemies, of the little and the big events that
moved their times, of the ancestors who had a word to
say—perhaps then we will better comprehend the music
they made.

It is regrettable that there are so very few personal
reminiscences of the early masters. Almost nothing has
been written by contemporaries on such personalities as
Domenico Scarlatti and Claudio Monteverdi, for example.
They are more important composers, I believe, than some
nineteenth century figures on whom volumes have been
penned. It is a sad loss for us that in the renaissance and
baroque eras the individual was regarded only through
his work; it was the work itself that the public loved and
venerated, its creator was just a humble human creature
who transmitted what he received from a higher source.
A Voice made him its instrument; and he was that instrument, nothing more.

It has thus been necessary to leave out Scarlatti and
Monteverdi. And in some others cases — Purcell and
Handel among them — hearsay reports have had to be
accepted. But the secondhand accounts are the exception

in this book and resorted to only where firsthand witnesses are impossible to find. The chapter on Bach is shorter than that on Liszt only because fewer of Bach's contemporaries were inclined to record their memories of him. As to the selection and omission of other composers, it must be kept in mind that our volume offers us limited space. It has therefore been needful to make what may sometimes strike the reader as an arbitrary choice, but I believe the selection is on the whole fair and full.

Music has her countless friends, and since the book concerns not one composer but many of the greatest, it should serve a worthwhile purpose—that of bringing new knowledge of the music makers to a wide public. I have tried to make this a collection of memories of interest and delight to anyone who responds to music; not only musicians and musicologists but for students and concertgoers and amateurs; for every serious and receptive listener.

GREAT COMPOSERS

Through the Eyes of Their Contemporaries

HENRY PURCELL

> Born: London, England
> ca. 1659
> Died: London, England
> November 21, 1695

HENRY PURCELL ranks as the greatest composer of English birth, yet real testimony concerning the man and his way of working is sadly lacking. This is the more surprising when we consider that even in his lifetime he was recognized as a genius.

He began composing very young indeed. Tradition has it that he wrote his song *Sweet Tyranness* when he was nine, that he became a chorister at the Chapel Royal of London when he was only six.

He had hardly reached his twenties when he was appointed organist at Westminster Abbey, and two years later he assumed the same post at the Chapel Royal.

Purcell's music is a happy mixture of Italian and French influences with a very personal strain. The formalism of his forerunners has evolved into something dark, dramatic, sometimes mysterious, rather reminiscent of Shakespeare. He wrote exquisite chamber music for the church, songs, and odes, and during his last five years he busied himself much with theatrical composition. His only real opera, *Dido and Aeneas,* was produced in 1688 or 1689.

He lies buried in the north aisle of Westminster Abbey. His burial tablet well expresses his contemporaries' estimate of his worth:

> Here lyes Henry Purcell, Esq., who left his life, and is gone to that blessed place where only his harmony can be exceeded.

Lord Chamberlain

Record of 1661

Purcell grew up in an ideal environment. His father, Thomas Purcell, was a professional musician who made a distinguished career for himself. He thought his son promising and got him into the choir of the Chapel Royal. Henry was then six years old. The children of the Chapel had their official uniform; the description of that uniform is the first picture we get of the boy.

FOR EACH OF THEM, one cloak of bastard scarlett cloth lyned with velvett, one suit and coat of the same cloth made up and trimmed with silver and silk lace after the manner of our footmen's liveries, and also to the said suit three shirts, three half shirts, three pairs of shoes, three pairs of thigh stockings, whereof one pair of silk and two pair of worsted, two hats with bands, six bands and six pairs of cuffs, whereof two laced and four plain, three handkerchers, three pairs of gloves and two pieces and a half of rebon for trimming garters and shoestrings.

And at Easter, for their summer liveries, for each boy one cloak of bastard scarlett lined with sattin and one doublett of sattin with bastard scarlett trunk hose made and trimmed up as aforesaid, with three shirts, three half shirts, three pair of shoes, three pair of thigh stockings, whereof one pair of silk and two pairs of worsted, two hats with bands, etc.

Sir John Hawkins

Achievement and Character

Sir John Hawkins, the great eighteenth-century historian of music, of whom we shall say more in connection with Handel, never saw Purcell. All he related he had from hearsay. But in view of the lack of contemporary records concerning Purcell, we are forced to accept what we are told by men who inquired of his friends and acquaintances and wrote down what seemed to them interesting.

Hawkins was a man of great reputation; his *General History of the Science and Practice of Music* (five volumes), published in 1776, is still the most authentic source for the lives of earlier composers.

What he tells us is a plain, unvarnished tale: the positions Purcell held, his astonishing industry, and certain not too flattering details of his character. All his contemporaries held it much against him that he always worked for the political party that happened to be in power.

THE SEVERAL WORKS above-mentioned were composed with great labor and study, and with a view to the establishment of a lasting reputation; but there are others that is to say, hymns, in the *Harmonia Sacra,* and single songs and ballad tunes to a very great number, in the printed collections of his time, which alone show the excellencies of Purcell in vocal composition; even his rounds and catches, many whereof were composed and sung almost at the same instant, have all the merit which can be ascribed to that species of harmony. And here it may not be improper to mention an anecdote respecting one of them, which the communication of a friend to this work has enabled the author to give. The Reverend Mr. Subdean Gostling played on the viol da gamba

and loved not the instrument more than Purcell hated it
[sic]. They were very intimate, as must be supposed, and
lived together upon terms of friendship; nevertheless, to
vex Mr. Gostling, Purcell got someone to write the following
mock eulogium on the viol, which he set in the form of a
round for three voices.

> Of all the instruments that are
> None with the viol can compare:
> Mark how the strings their order keep,
> With a whet whet whet and a sweep sweep sweep;
> But above all this still abounds,
> With a zingle zingle zing, and zit zan zounds.

Though the unsettled state of public affairs at the time
when he lived obliged practically every man to attach himself to one or other of the two contending parties, Purcell
might have availed himself of that exemption which men
of his peaceable profession have always a right to insist on,
but he seemed not disposed to claim it. In James II's time
he sang down the Whigs, and in that of William, the Tories.
It is true he did not, like William Lawes, sacrifice his life to
the interests of a master who loved and had promoted him,
but he possessed a kind of transitory allegiance; and when
the former had attained to sovereignty, besides those gratuitous effusions of loyalty which his relation to the court
disposed him to, could as easily celebrate the praises of William as James.

> His billet at the fire was found,
> Whoever was depos'd or crown'd.

This indifference is in some degree to be accounted for
by that mirth and good humor, which seem to have been
habitual to him; and this perhaps is the best excuse that can
be made for those connections and intimacies with Brown
and others, which show him not to have been very nice in

the choice of his company. Brown spent his life in taverns
and alehouses; the Hole in the Wall in Baldwin's Gardens
was the citadel in which he baffled the assaults of creditors
and bailiffs, at the same time that he attracted thither such
as thought his wit atoned for his profligacy. Purcell seems
to have been of that number, and to merit censure for having
prostituted his invention, by adapting music to some of the
most wretched ribaldry that was over obtruded on the world
for humor. The house of Owen Swan, a vintner, in Bartholo-
mew Lane, humorously called Cobweb Hall, was also a place
of great resort with the musical wits of that day; as also a
house in Wych Street, behind the New Church in the Strand,
within time of memory known by a sign of Purcell's head,
a half length; the dress a brown full-bottomed wig, and a
green nightgown, very finely executed.

But notwithstanding the intimacies above-mentioned, he
had connections that were honorable. The author of the
Life of the Lord Keeper North, speaking of his lordship's
skill in the science, and the delight he took in the practice
of music, says, that at his house in Queen Street his lordship
had a concert, of which Mr. Purcell had the direction; and
at that time of day concerts were so rare, that it required
the assistance of no less than a master to keep four or five
performers together: his scholars were the sons and daughters
of the nobility and principal gentry in the kingdom, a circumstance which alone bespeaks the nature of his connections,
and the rank he held in his profession. . . .

Purcell died on the twenty-first day of November 1695.
There is a tradition that his death was occasioned by a cold
which he caught in the night, waiting for admittance into
his own house. It is said that he used to keep late hours, and
that his wife had given orders to his servants not to let him
in after midnight; unfortunately he came home heated with
wine from the tavern at an hour later than that prescribed
him, and through the inclemency of the air contracted a

disorder of which he died. If this be true, it reflects but little honor on Madame Purcell. . . .

It seems probable that the disease of which he died was rather a lingering than an acute one, perhaps a consumption, and that, for some time at least, it had no way affected the powers of his mind, since one of the most celebrated of his compositions, the song "From rosy bowers," is in the printed book said to have been the last of his works, and to have been set during that sickness which put a period to his days. He was interred in Westminster Abbey.

Charles Burney
The Darling of the Nation

The two great historians of music of the eighteenth century, Charles Burney (1726-1814) and John Hawkins, must be reproached for the same failure: they had many opportunities of obtaining authentic material—but they neglected to gather the Purcell lore so accessible to them. Valuable facts have thus been lost to us forever.

This is especially puzzling in the case of Dr. Burney. His father knew Purcell well; it would have been easy for him to get interesting details that would have enriched the meager store of tales handed down to us.

The following lines reflect the high esteem in which Purcell was held even during his lifetime, and reflects also his position as a musical revolutionary who broke the chains of tradition.

PURCELL is said to have profited so much from his first lessons and close application, as to have composed, during the time of his being a singing boy in the chapel, many of his anthems which have been constantly sung in one cathedral ever since. Eighteen was a very early age for his being appointed organist; that is *maestro di cappella* of Westminister Abbey, one of the first cathedrals in the Kingdom, for choral compositions and performance. It was not likely he would stop here: the world is, perhaps, more partial to promising youth, than accomplished age; and at twenty-four, in 1682, he was advanced to one of the three places of organist of the Chapel Royal. . . .

After this, he produced so many admirable compositions for the church and chapel of which he was organist, and where he was sure of having them performed better than elsewhere, that his fame was soon extended to the remotest parts of the Kingdom.

From this time, his anthems were eagerly procured, and heard with pious rapture wherever they could be performed. Nor was he suffered long to devote himself totally to the service of the church. He was, very early in his life, solicited to compose for the stage, and chamber, in both which undertakings, he was so superior to all his predecessors, that his compositions seemed to speak a new language; yet, however different from that to which the public had been long accustomed, it was universally understood. He produced the overture and act tunes for *Abdelazar,* a tragedy written by Mrs. Behn, and acted at the Duke's Theater, in 1677, when he was only nineteen; to *Timon of Athens,* altered from Shakespeare by Shadwell, when he was twenty. His songs seem to contain whatever the ear could then wish, or heart could feel. My father, who was nineteen years of age when Purcell died, remembered his person very well, and the effect his anthems had on himself and the public at the time that many of them were first heard; and used to say, that "no other vocal music was listened to with pleasure, for near thirty years after Purcell's death; when they gave way only to the favorite opera songs of Handel."

The unlimited powers of this musician's genius embraced every species of composition that was then known, with equal felicity. In writing for the church, whether he adhered to the elaborate and learned style of his great predecessors Tallis, Bird, and Gibbons, in which no instrument is employed but the organ, and the several parts are constantly moving in fugue, imitation, or plain counterpoint; or, giving way to feeling and imagination, adopted the new and more expressive style of which he was himself one of the principal inventors, accompanying the voice parts with instruments, to enrich the harmony and enforce the melody and meaning of the words, he manifested equal abilities and resources. In compositions for the theater, though the coloring and effects of an orchestra were then but little known, yet as he employed them more than his predecessors, and gave to the voice a melody more interesting and impassioned than, during the last century, had been heard in this country, or perhaps in Italy itself, he soon became the delight and darling of the nation.

JOHANN SEBASTIAN BACH

> Born: Eisenach, Germany
> March 21, 1685
> Died: Leipzig, Germany
> July 22, 1750

JOHANN SEBASTIAN BACH, many believe, takes first place among the musical immortals or at least shares it with Mozart and Beethoven. Although highly esteemed during his lifetime, he was far from being recognized as the giant he was.

He was born in Eisenach, the capital of the little Duchy of Saxe-Eisenach. His father was a musician and the descendant of a tribe that had made music for seven generations.

After years of hard work, hard study and hard travel—Ohrdruf in the Thuringian Forest, Lueneberg, Weimar, Arnstadt, St. Blasius, Coethen, and other places—he finally settled down with his family in Leipzig in the year 1723. Here at the age of 38 he served as cantor at the Thomasschule, the most famous music institution of Central Europe. He kept this post until the end of his life.

The most stupendous miracle in all music—was Wagner's description of him. Bach expressed the spirit of his age, the passionately Christian spirit. And the master did more: he created a beauty unsurpassed, manifold, eternal. His works fall into six categories: organ, clavier, orchestral, chamber, masses and oratorios, cantatas and motets. The most famous are his *passacaglia* and Fugue in C Minor; the Toccatas; the *Well-Tempered Clavichord;* the *Art of Fugue;* the six *Brandenburg Concertos;* the *St. John Passion;* the *St. Matthew Passion.*

Johann Friedrich Agricola
and
Philip Emanuel Bach

When Bach Was Not Quite Ten

We have very few stories about Bach from first-hand witnesses; public interest in the person of an artist was too slight in the eighteenth century to induce friends or visitors to record their experiences. The little written at this time was intended mostly for musicians and musicologists.

One of Bach's former pupils, Lorenz Christoph Mizler (1711-1778), was publisher of the musical periodical *Lorenz Mizler's Musikalische Bibliothek.* The last issue that ever appeared, in 1754, contained an obituary of Bach. It was written by Bach's son, Philip Emanuel, a great composer in his own right. The account is thus given from intimate knowledge. Philip Emanuel wrote it with the help of Agricola, one of Bach's pupils.

JOHANN SEBASTIAN was not yet ten years old when he found himself bereft of his parents by death. He betook himself to Ohrdruff, where his eldest brother, Johann Christoph, was organist, and under his brother's guidance he laid the foundations for his playing of the clavier. The love of our little Johann Sebastian for music was uncommonly great even at this tender age. In a short time he had fully mastered all the pieces his brother had voluntarily given him to learn. But his brother possessed a book of clavier pieces by the most

famous masters of the day—Froberger, Kerl, Pachelbel—and
this, despite all his pleading and for who knows what reason,
was denied him. His zeal to improve himself thereupon gave
him the idea of practicing the following innocent deceit.
The book was kept in a cabinet of which the doors consisted
only of grillwork. With his little hands he could reach through
the grillwork and roll the book up (for it had only a paper
cover). He would slip the book out at night, when everyone
had gone to bed, and, since he was not even possessed of a
light, copy it by moonlight. In six months' time he had completed these musical spoils. Secretly and with extraordinary
eagerness, he was trying to put them to use, when his brother,
to his great dismay, discovered it, and without mercy took
away from him the copy he had made with such pains. We
may gain a good idea of our little Johann Sebastian's sorrow
over his loss by imagining a miser whose ship, sailing for
Peru, has foundered with its cargo of a hundred thousand
thalers. He did not recover the book until after the death
of his brother. But did not this very passion to improve himself in music and the very industry displayed in his laborious
copying of the book perhaps provide the first basis for the
cause of his own death as we shall hear later.

After the death of his brother, Johann Sebastian betook
himself, in company with one of his schoolfellows, named
Erdman, who not many years since departed this life as Baron
and Imperial Russian Resident Minister in Danzig, to the
Michaels-Gymnasium in Lüneburg.

In Lüneburg our Bach, because of his uncommonly fine
soprano voice, was well received. Some time thereafter, as
he was singing in the choir, and without his knowledge or
will, he sang with the soprano tone which he had to execute,
the lower octave of the same note. He kept this quite new
species of voice for eight days, during which he could neither
speak nor sing except in octaves. Thereupon he lost his
soprano tones and with them his fine voice.

Johann Mathias Gesner

Bach Playing and Conducting

We know that during the second half of his life Bach served as cantor at the Thomas-Schule in Leipzig. This position was one of the most prominent in the Lutheran world, more or less corresponding to that of *maestro di Cappella* at St. Mark's in Venice. The second of the directors under whom Bach had to work was Johann Matthias Gesner (1691-1761), a warm admirer of the composer's musicianship. In an edition of *Quintilian* he inserted a footnote describing Bach as organist and conductor.

You WOULD think but slightly, my dear Fabius, of all these accomplishments, if, returning from the underworld, you could see Bach (to mention him particularly, since he was not long ago my colleague at the Leipzig Thomas-Schule), either playing our clavier, which is many citharas in one, with all the fingers of both hands, or running over the keys of the instrument of instruments (*organon organorum*), whose innumerable pipes are brought to life by bellows, with both hands and, at the utmost speed, with his feet, producing by himself the most various and at the same time mutually agreeable combinations of sounds in orderly procession. If you could see him, I say, doing what many of your citharoedists and six hundred of your tibia players together could not do, not only, like a citharoedist, singing with one voice and playing his own parts, but watching over everything and bringing back to the rhythm and the beat, out of thirty or even forty musicians, the one with a nod, another by tapping with his foot, the third with a warning finger, giving the right note to one from the top of his voice, to another from the bottom, and to a third from the middle of it—all alone, in the midst of the greatest din made by all the participants, and, although he is executing the most difficult parts himself, noticing at once whenever and wherever a mistake occurs, holding everyone together, taking precautions everywhere, and repairing any unsteadiness, full of rhythm in every part of his body—this one man taking in all these harmonies with his keen ear and emitting with his voice alone the tone of all the voices! Favorer as I am of antiquity, the accomplishments of our Bach, and of any others that there may be like him, appear to me to effect what not many Orpheuses, nor twenty Arions, could achieve.

Constantin Bellermann

The Master's Playing on the Pedals

Constantin Bellermann (1696-1758) was Rector at Minden. He was a well-known lutist, though a mediocre composer, who wrote operas and oratorios as well as music for his own instrument. He met Bach when the latter was visiting Cassel in September 1732.

BACH, of Leipzig, author of profound music, is not inferior to those mentioned above, Mattheson, Keiser, Telemann. Like Handel among the English, he deserves to be called the miracle of Leipzig, as far as music is concerned. For if it pleases him, he can by the use of his feet alone (while his fingers do either nothing or something else) achieve such an admirable, agitated, and rapid concord of sounds on the church organ that others would seem unable to imitate it even with their fingers. When he was called from Leipzig to Cassel to pronounce an organ properly restored, he ran over the pedals with this same facility, as if his feet had wings, making the organ resound with such fullness, and so penetrate the ears of those present, like a thunderbolt, that Frederick, the legitimate hereditary Prince of Cassel, in his admiring astonishment drew a ring with a precious stone from his finger and gave it to Bach as soon as the sound had died away. If Bach earned such a gift for the agility of his feet, what, I ask, would the Prince have given him if he had called his hands into service as well?

Johann Nikolaus Forkel

Bach's Character

Forkel (1749-1818,) organist of the University Church in Goettingen, was the earliest of the German musicologists; he displayed great energy in amassing his materials. Probably his finest piece of writing is his biography of Bach, the first of its kind and absolutely trustworthy, since he obtained the material from two sons of Bach, Philip Emanuel and Wilhelm Friedemann. They told him nothing they had not witnessed themselves or heard reported by honest witnesses. The care with which Forkel used every bit of evidence received from Bach's sons becomes clear from an examination of Philip Emanuel's few letters to him.

As an artist, he was uncommonly modest. Notwithstanding the great superiority which he had over the rest of his profession, and which he could not but feel; notwithstanding the admiration and reverence which were daily shown him as so outstanding an artist, there is no instance of his having ever presumed upon it. When he was asked how he had contrived to master the art to such a high degree, he generally answered: "I was obliged to be industrious; whoever is equally industrious will succeed equally well." He seemed not to lay any stress on his greater natural talents.

All the opinions he expressed of other artists and their works were friendly and equitable. Many works necessarily appeared to him trifling, as he was almost always employed exclusively on the sublimer branches of the art, yet he never allowed himself to express a harsh opinion, unless it were to one of his scholars, to whom he thought himself obliged to speak the pure and strict truth. Still less did he ever suffer himself to be seduced by the consciousness of his strength and superiority to display a musical bravado, as is so frequently the case with performers who think themselves strong, when they believe they have an inferior listener before them. His modesty in this respect went so far that he never spoke voluntarily even of his musical contest with Marchand, though he was not the challenger in this case, but the challenged. The many, sometimes adventurous pranks that are related of him, as, for example, that occasionally, dressed like a poor village schoolmaster, he went into a church and begged the organist to let him play a chorale, in order to enjoy the general astonishment excited in the persons present by his performance, or to hear the organist say he must be either Bach or the devil, are mere fables. He himself would never hear of anything of the sort. Besides, he had too much respect for the art thus to make a plaything of it. An artist like Bach does not throw himself away.

In musical parties where quartets or fuller pieces of instrumental music were performed and he was not otherwise employed, he took pleasure in playing the viola. With this instrument he was, as it were, in the middle of the harmony, whence he could best hear and enjoy it, on both sides. When an opportunity offered, in such parties, he sometimes also accompanied a trio or other pieces on the harpischord. If he was in a cheerful mood and knew that the composer of the piece, if he happened to be present, would not take it amiss, he used, as we have said above, to make *extempore,* either out of the figured bass a new trio, or out of three single parts a quartet. These, however, are really the only cases in which he showed off to others how strong he was. A certain Hurlebusch of Brunswick, a conceited and arrogant clavier player, once visited him at Leipzig, not to hear him, but to let himself be heard. Bach received him kindly and politely, listened to his very indifferent performance with patience; and when Hurlebusch, on taking leave, made his eldest sons a present of a printed collection of sonatas, exhorting them to study them diligently (they who had studied very different things), Bach only smiled to himself and did not at all change his friendly behavior to the stranger.

He was fond of hearing the music of other composers. If he heard, in a church, a fugue for a large body of musicians, and one of his two eldest sons happened to stand near him, he always, as soon as he had heard the first entries of the theme, said beforehand what the composer ought to introduce, and what possibly might be introduced. Now if the composer had performed his work well, what Bach had predicted happened; then he was delighted, and jogged his son to make him observe it. This is a proof that he valued, too, the skill of others.

The composers whom he studied, esteemed, and loved in his youth have been already mentioned. At a more advanced age, when his judgment was fully matured, he had other favorites. He then had a great esteem for the Emperor's first Kapellmeister, Fux; for Handel, Caldara, Reinh, Kayser, Hasse, the two Grauns, Telemann, Zelenka, Benda, etc.; and, in general, all the most distinguished musicians at that time living in Dresden and Berlin. He was not personally acquainted with the first four, but with all the rest. In his youth he had frequent converse with Telemann.

He had a very great esteem for Handel, and often wished to be personally acquainted with him. As Handel was also a great performer on the clavier and the organ, many lovers of music at Leipzig and in its neighborhood wished to hear these two great men confronted. But Handel never could find time for such a meeting. He came three times from London to Halle, his native town. On his first visit, about the year 1719, Bach was still at Cöthen, only four German miles from Halle. He was immediately informed of Handel's arrival, and lost not a moment in paying him a visit; but Handel left Halle the very day of his arrival. At the time of Handel's second visit to Halle, between 1730 and 1740, Bach was at Leipzig, but ill. As soon, however, as he was informed of Handel's arrival at Halle, he immediately sent his eldest son, William Friedemann, thither, with a very polite invitation to visit him at Leipzig. But Handel regretted that he could not come. On Handel's third visit, approximately in 1752 or 1753, Bach was dead. Thus his wish to be personally acquainted with Handel was not fulfilled any more than that of many lovers of music who would have been glad to see and hear him and Handel together.

At the time that Hasse was Kapellmeister in Dresden, the orchestra and the opera there were very brilliant and excellent. Bach had had there even in his earlier years many acquaintances, by all of whom he was much honored. Hasse and his wife, the celebrated Faustina, had also come several times to Leipzig and admired his great talents. He was therefore always received in an exceedingly honorable manner at Dresden, and often went thither to hear the opera. He generally took his eldest son with him. He used to say in jest, some days before his departure: "Friedemann, shan't we go again to hear the lovely Dresden ditties?" Innocent as his joke was in itself, I am convinced that Bach would not have uttered it to anybody except this son who, at that time, already knew what is great in art and what is only beautiful and agreeable.

Bach did not achieve what could be called a brilliant success in this world. He had, on the one hand, a lucrative office, but he also had numerous children to maintain and to educate. He neither had nor sought other resources. He was too much occupied with his business and his art to think of pursuing those ways which, perhaps, for a man like him, especially in his times, would have led to a gold mine. If he had thought fit to travel, he would (as even one of his enemies has said) have drawn upon himself the admiration of the whole world. But he loved a quiet domestic life, constant and uninterrupted occupation with his art, and was, as we have said of his ancestors, a man of few wants.

Moreover, he enjoyed during his life manifold proofs of love and friendship, and of great honor. Prince Leopold of Cöthen, Duke Ernest Augustus of Weimar, and Duke Christian of Weissenfels had a sincere attachment to him, which must have been the more valuable to the great artist as these princes were not mere lovers of music but also connoisseurs. At Berlin and Dresden also he was universally respected and honored. If we add the admiration of the connoisseurs and lovers of music who had heard him or were acquainted with his works, we shall easily conceive that a man like Bach, "who sang only for himself and the muses," had received from the hands of fame all that he could wish, and it had more charms for him than the equivocal honors of a ribbon or a gold chain.

Heinrich Nikolaus Gerber

As a Teacher

Heinrich Nikolaus Gerber (1702-1775) claims first place among the pupils of Bach. His veneration for Bach was so intense that it took him a year to summon up enough courage to approach him.

Gerber left Leipzig after three years of hard study and only once returned there—to see his beloved master. He became court organist at Sondershausen and did his eminent teacher honor as an artist. His biography was written by his son Ernst Ludwig Gerber, also an organist (1746-1819).

When there was nothing left for my father to draw from the sources in Sonderhausen, he went to Leipzig, partly to study law, and partly to study music with the great Sebastian Bach. My father was received there as a student in the University, under the Rectorate of Dr. Boerner, on May 8, 1724. In the first half-year, as he arranged his courses, he had heard much excellent church music and many a concert under Bach's direction; but he had still lacked any opportunity which would have given him courage enough to reveal his desires to this great man; until at last he revealed his wish to a friend, named Wilde, later organist in Petersburg, who introduced him to Bach.

Bach accepted him with particular kindness because he came from Schwarzburg, and always thereafter called him *"Landsmann."* He promised to give him the instruction he desired and asked at once whether he had industriously played fugues. At the first lesson he set his *Inventions* before him. When he had studied these through to Bach's satisfaction, there followed a series of suites, then the *Well-Tempered Clavier.* This latter work Bach played altogether three times through for him with his unmatchable art, and my father counted these among his happiest hours, when Bach, under the pretext of not feeling in the mood to teach, sat himself at one of his fine instruments and thus turned these hours into minutes. The conclusion of the instruction was thorough bass, for which Bach chose the Albinoni violin solos; and I must admit that I have never heard anything better than the style in which my father executed these basses according to Bach's fashion, particularly in the singing of the voices. This accompaniment was in itself so beautiful that no principal voice could have added to the pleasure it gave me.

Having spent two years in Bach's school, with an industry appropriate to the excellence of such a teacher, and having finished his courses at the University, he returned to his father in the country. Here he employed two years of leisure to put into order and apply the manifold good and beautiful things he had brought with him from Leipzig.

Philip Emanuel Bach
(as told to Forkel)
Bach and Frederick the Great

Frederick the Great, famous King of Prussia (1712-1786), was a talented composer himself as well as a fine flutist. He gave a concert every evening in his Potsdam palace. Bach came to Potsdam accompanied by his eldest son William. This was his last journey; it was the most colorful episode in his rather uneventful career.

Philip Emanuel dictated to the first Bach biographer of importance, Johann Nikolaus Forkel (1749-1818,), the story of this strange and triumphant visit. It is regrettable that he himself did not write it down; the account would certainly have been more detailed and circumstantial.

Forkel concludes his story with the great man's death; here again Philip Emanuel gave him the facts.

HIS second son, Charles Philip Emanuel, entered the service of Frederick the Great in 1740. The reputation of the all-surpassing skill of John Sebastian was at this time so extended that the King often heard it mentioned and praised. This made him curious to hear and meet so great an artist. At first he distantly hinted to the son his wish that his father would one day come to Potsdam. But by degrees he began to ask him directly why his father did not come. The son could not avoid acquainting his father with these expressions of the King's; at first, however, he could not pay attention to them because he was generally too much overwhelmed with business. But the King's expressions being repeated in several of his son's letters, he at length, in 1747, prepared to take this journey in company of his eldest son, William Friede-mann. At this time the King used to have a private concert every evening, in which he himself generally performed some concertos on the flute. One evening, just as he was getting his flute ready and his musicians were assembled, an officer brought him the written list of the strangers who had arrived. With his flute in his hand, he ran over the list, but immediately turned to the assembled musicians and said, with a kind of agitation: "Gentlemen, old Bach is come." The flute was now laid aside; and old Bach, who had alighted at his son's lodg-ings, was immediately summoned to the palace. William Friedemann, who accompanied his father, told me the story, and I must say that I still think with pleasure on the manner in which he related it. At that time it was the fashion to make rather prolix compliments. The first appearance of J. S. Bach before so great a king, who did not even give him time to change his traveling dress for a black cantor's gown, must necessarily be attended with many apologies. I will not here dwell on these apologies, but merely observe that as William Friedemann tells the tale, they were the basis for a formal dialogue between the King and the apologist.

But what is more important than this is that the King gave up his concert for this evening and invited Bach, then already called the Old Bach, to try his fortepianos, which stood in several rooms of the palace. The musicians went with him from room to room, and Bach was invited everywhere to try them and to play unpremeditated compositions. After he had gone on for some time, he asked the King to give him a sub-ject for a fugue in order to execute it immediately without any preparation. The King admired the learned manner in which his subject was thus executed *extempore;* and, probab-ly to see how far such art could be carried, expressed a wish to hear a fugue with six *obbligato* parts. But as not every subject is fit for such full harmony, Bach chose one himself and immediately executed it to the astonishment of all present in the same magnificent and learned manner as he had done that of the King. His Majesty desired also to hear his performance on the organ. The next day, therefore, Bach was taken to all the organs in Potsdam as he had before been to the fortepianos. After his return to Leipzig, he composed the subject which he had received from the King in three and six parts, added several intricate pieces in strict canon on the subject, had it engraved, under the title of *Musicalisches Opfer*, ("Musical Offering") and dedicated it to the inventor.

This was Bach's last journey. The indefatigable diligence with which, particularly in his younger years, he had frequently passed days and nights, without intermission, in the study of his art, had weakened his sight. This weakness continuously increased in his latter years till at length it brought on a very painful disorder of the eyes. By the advice of some friends who placed great confidence in the ability of an oculist who had arrived at Leipzig from England, he ventured to submit to an operation, which twice failed. Not only was his sight now wholly lost, but his constitution, which had been hitherto so vigorous, was quite undermined by the use of possibly noxious medicines in connection with the operation. He continued to decline for full half a year till he died on the evening of the 22nd of July, 1750, in the sixty-sixth year of his age. On the morning of the tenth day before his death, he was all at once able to see again and to bear the light. But a few hours afterward he was seized with an apoplectic fit; this was followed by a high fever, which his enfeebled frame, notwithstanding all possible medical aid, was unable to resist.

GEORG FRIEDRICH HANDEL

Born: Halle, Germany
February 23, 1685
Died: London, England
April 14, 1759

GEORG FRIEDRICH HANDEL was a German who became England's greatest composer. He received his entire education in Germany. At nineteen he brought out his first theatrical work, *Almira*, in Hamburg, where he was engaged in the opera orchestra of that city. For some years after this he studied in Italy, then returned to Germany.

He first visited England in 1710. Two years later he came back and this time he stayed; the Queen paid him a substantial allowance of two hundred pounds a year. From 1715 to 1718 he lived with the Earl of Burlington, then entered the service of the Duke of Chandos, who employed him as chapelmaster to the choir in Cannons, an excellent one. In this post Handel discovered that his true calling was that of church composer. He now matured rapidly and was the mainstay of England's musical zenith.

His life did not settle into dull placidity for with his founding of a rival operatic company in London, a long war commenced. Handel turned out operas one after the other, at least twenty-one in all. He also tried his hand at oratorios. His first efforts (*Esther, Deborah*) met with highly encouraging approbation and he continued, crowning his success with his most famous oratorio, *The Messiah,* which was performed in Dublin in 1742. The first performance in London was celebrated as a holiday by the general public.

In spite of the blindness which overtook him in his later years, he continued to compose with great success.

John Mainwaring

Childhood of Handel

John Mainwaring (1735-1807) is the author of the first biography of Handel in English. His *Memoirs of the Life of the Late George Frederic Handel* was published in 1760, one year after the composer's death.

The earlier portion of the book comes substantially from Handel himself; there are a number of details which he alone could have known. And we have no reason to believe that Mainwaring consciously invented his facts. Handel's father, a barber-surgeon in Halle, Lower Saxony, disapproved of music and wanted Georg Friedrich to become a lawyer. A friend smuggled a clavichord into the attic and on this instrument, which is inaudible behind closed doors, the little boy practiced secretly. So began his astonishing career. Mainwaring collected his data during the last ten years of Handel's life; he also obtained much information from Christopher Smith, Handel's secretary.

George Frederick Handel was born at Halle, a city in the circle of Upper-Saxony, the 24th of February 1684, by a second wife of his father, who was an eminent surgeon and physician of the same place, and above sixty when his son was born. He had also one daughter by the same wife. Handel always retained the strongest affection for this sister, to whose only daughter, i.e., his niece now living, he bequeathed the greatest part of his ample fortune.

While he was yet under seven years of age, he went with his father to the Duke of Saxe-Weissenfels. His strong desire to pay a visit to his half-brother, a good deal older than himself (for we have before observed that he was the issue of a second marriage) and at that time *valet de chambre* to the Prince, was the occasion of his going. His father intended to have left him behind, and had actually set out without him. He thought one of his age a very improper companion when he was going to the court of a prince, and to attend the duties of his profession. The boy finding all his solicitations ineffectual, had recourse to the only method which was left for the accomplishment of his wish. Having watched the time of his father's setting out, and concealed his intention from the rest of the family, he followed the chaise on foot. It was probably retarded by the roughness of the roads, or some other accident, for he overtook it before it had advanced to any considerable distance from the town. His father, greatly surprised at his courage, and somewhat displeased with his obstinacy, could hardly resolve what course to take. When he was asked how he could think of the journey, after such a plain refusal had been given him, instead of answering the question, he renewed his entreaties in the most pressing manner, and pleaded in language too moving to be resisted. Being taken into the chaise, and carried to court, he discovered an unspeakable satisfaction at meeting with his brother above-mentioned, whom till then he had never seen.

This was not the first instance of the father's ill success, when he judged it expedient to oppose or overrule his son's inclinations. This matter demands a more particular explication before an account can properly be given of what afterward passed at the court of Weissenfels.

From his very childhood Handel had discovered such a strong propensity to music, that his father, who always intended him for the study of the civil law, had reason to be alarmed. Perceiving that this inclination still increased, he took every method to oppose it. He strictly forbade him to meddle with any musical instrument; none were allowed to remain in the house. All this caution and art, instead of restraining, did but augment his passion. He had found means to get a little clavichord privately conveyed to a room at the top of the house. To this room he constantly stole when the family was asleep. He had made some progress before music had been prohibited, and by his assiduous practice at night he had made such great advances. . . .

We left our little traveler just on his arrival with his father at the Duke of Saxe-Weissenfels. In such a situation it was not easy to keep him from getting at harpsichords, and his father was too much engaged to watch him so closely there as he had done at home. He often mentioned to his friends this uncontrollable humor of his son, which he told them he had taken great pains to subdue, but hitherto with little or no success. He said it was easy to foresee that if it was not subdued very soon, it would preclude all improvements in the science for which he intended him, and wholly disconcert the plan that had been formed and agreed on for his education.

The reasonableness of such apprehensions every one admitted, in case it was determined to adhere to the scheme above-mentioned. But the prudence of adhering to it was doubted by many. It was observed with reason, that where nature seemed to declare herself in so strong a manner, resistance was often not only fruitless, but pernicious. Some said that, from all the accounts, the case appeared so desperate that nothing but the cutting off his fingers could prevent his playing; and others affirmed that it was a pity any thing should prevent it. Such were the sentiments and declarations of the doctor's friends in regard to his son. It is not likely they would have had any great effect, but for the following incident, which gave their advice all the weight and authority it seems to have deserved.

It happened one morning, that while he was playing on the

organ after the service was over, the Duke was in the church. Something there was in the manner of playing which drew his attention so strongly, that His Highness, as soon as he returned, asked his *valet de chambre* who it was that he had heard at the organ, when the service was over. The valet replied that it was his brother. The Duke demanded to see him.

After he had seen him, and made all the inquiries which it was natural for a man of taste and discernment to make on such an occasion, he told his physician that every father must judge for himself in what manner to dispose of his children; but that, for his own part, he could not but consider it as a sort of crime against the public and posterity, to rob the world of such a rising genius.

The old doctor still wished him to study civil law. Though he was convinced it was almost become an act of necessity to yield to his son's inclinations (as it seemed an act of duty to yield to the Duke's advice and authority), yet it was not without utmost reluctance that he brought himself to this resolution. He was sensible of the Duke's goodness in taking such notice of his son, and giving his opinion concerning the best method of education. But he begged leave humbly to represent to His Highness, that though music was an elegant art, and a fine amusement, yet if considered as an occupation, it had little dignity, as having for its object nothing better than mere pleasure and entertainment; that whatever degree of eminence his son might arrive at in such a profession, he thought that a much less degree in many others would be far preferable.

The Duke could not agree with him in his notions of music as a profession, which he said were much too low and disparaging, as great excellence in any kind entitled men to great honor. And as to profit, he observed how much more likely he would be to succeed, if suffered to pursue the path that nature and providence seemed to have marked out for him, than if he was forced into another track to which he had no such

bias, nay, to which he had a direct aversion. He concluded
with saying that he was far from recommending the study of
music to exclusion of the languages, or of the civil law, provided it was possible to reconcile them: what he wished was,
that all of them might have fair play, that no violence might
be used, but the boy be left at liberty to follow the natural
bent of his faculties, whatever that might be.

All this while he had kept his eyes steadfastly on his powerful advocate; and his ears were as watchful and attentive to
the impressions which the Duke's discourse made upon his
father.

The result of this debate was not only a toleration of music,
but also consent for a master to be employed in Halle. At his
departure from Weissenfels, the Duke filled his pockets with
money and told him with a smile that if he minded his studies, no encouragements should be wanting.

Richard Clark

The Legend of Whitchurch

On leaving Germany the young Handel spent three years in Italy.
Here he acquired a mastery of the most advanced Italian style. Later he
became Kapellmeister to the Elector of Hanover, but in 1712 went to
England, where he spent the second half of his life, visiting Germany
and Italy only occasionally for a few weeks at a time.

One of his first positions in England was that of chapelmaster to the
eccentric Duke of Chandos, which he held for three years. Here in
Whitchurch, near Cannons, he composed some of his finest works.

Richard Clark, almost a hundred years later, visited Cannons with
friends and succeeded in finding some old people who had heard stories
about Handel told by their parents and teachers. Blacksmith Powell's
sounds like a fairy tale; it is one. But in combination with the other
reminiscences, better founded, it gives a picture of the thirty-year-old
master. He was already conscious of his own talent and craftsmanship.

When Handel was at Cannons, the far-famed residence of the magnificent Duke of Chandos, near Edgware, he was one day overtaken, in his walks, by a heavy shower of rain. The great composer took shelter under a blacksmith's shop, by the roadside, where its laborious occupant was beating the iron on the anvil, and singing at his work. The varying sounds of the falling hammer on the metal mingled with the rude tones of the man's voice and entered into the very soul of the attentive listener. He carried home with him the feeling, the character, the inspiration of an idea admirable alike for the beauty and simplicity of its development, and gave us, for a "rich legacy," the notation of the few touching phrases which we have received under the name (bestowed upon them by himself) of *The Harmonious Blacksmith*; an effusion, the sweetness of which has drawn tears from many a gentle eye, and equally impressed with its melodious power the minds of the most refined musicians of Europe. . . .

A visit to the truly unique and beautiful little sanctuary of Whitchurch, formerly the chapel built for the ducal mansion, and now used for parish worship, is well worth a nine or ten miles' journey from town. It contains the organ upon which Handel played, during his occasional sojourns to Cannons, for four years; and a silver plate, inserted in the instrument, informs us that he availed himself of its aid while composing his majestic oratorio of *Samson*, one of the finest of his works. . . .

The following information was collected from various very aged persons in and about the Village of Edgware and Whitchurch who knew the blacksmith and his family, and who state that he was considered in the village a very good singer and a musical man, and that he lived at Edgware, and was moreover Parish Clerk at Whitchurch, where Handel was organist. . . .

✿   ✿   ✿

That the circumstances attached to the tune known by the name of the *Harmonious Blacksmith* took place before the year 1744 is obvious, because the Duke of Chandos died in that year and the establishment was broken up. It is therefore more than probable that Handel was not at Cannons after that time, as it appears that the same was sold by auction in 1747 in separate lots. Although this magnificent mansion cost upward of £250,000, yet, after deducting the expenses of the sale, it brought only £11,000. The beautiful marble staircase, each step in one piece 22 feet long, was purchased by the Earl of Chesterfield for his house in Mayfair. The fine marble columns were bought for the portico of Wanstead House, and the equestrian statue of George I is now the ornament of Leicester Square. The hinges of the doors were of silver or gold. . . .

The Duke had a group of the best vocal and instrumental musicians that could be procured, and was attended to church by eight old sergeants of the army, whom he took out of Chelsea College. The Duke was paymaster of the army to Queen Anne. These men walked their rounds at night, called the hours, and guarded the property; they all had neat apartments. Twelve of Handel's anthems were composed for the Duke and performed at Whitchurch and therefore called the *Chandos Anthems*. Thus it appears that Handel must have been much at Cannons; that he took shelter in Powell's shop is plain, and that Powell was singing at his work and beating time on his anvil as before stated; and that the editor has traced out and obtained the same anvil and hammer, the following evidence will prove:—The tone or sound of the anvil is now . . . precisely in the same key in which Handel set and arranged the *Harmonious Blacksmith;* and the anvil being struck with a hammer as herewith given, harmonizes in a very peculiar and singular manner, producing a beautiful ringing tone, such as the editor has never heard before or found in any other anvil, producing as it were a kind of har-

monics. He is informed that this proceeds from its peculiar
construction and the temper of the metal, which was not lost
on the great Handel.

*   *   *

His Grace the Duke of Chandos's domestic chapel is at his
seat at Cannons, Edgware. . . .

The church is dedicated to St. Lawrence and was built by
the Duke of Chandos (the tower excepted) and finished
about 1715. Handel composed his sacred oratorio of *Esther*,
which was first performed in this church, 29th of August,
1720; the words written by Colonel David Humphreys, an
American, who died at Canonbury, January 11, 1738, aged
forty. Dr. Randell of Cambridge, Beard and Savage were
among the vocal performers.

*   *   *

Handel . . . would frequently go in the afternoon to St.
Paul's Cathedral and there often met Mr. (afterward Dr.)
Greene, who was then an apprentice to Mr. Brind, the organist, by whom he was introduced to the gentlemen of the choir.
Handel was very fond of St. Paul's organ, then nearly a new
instrument, and built by his countryman Schmidt. Little en-
treaty was at this time sufficient to prevail on Handel to touch
the organ, and it was also with great reluctance he would quit
it. He has been known (after evening service) to play to an
audience as great as ever filled the choir. After his performance it was his practice to adjourn with the principal persons
of the choir to the Queen's Arms Tavern, in St. Paul's Churchyard, where was a great room with a harpsichord in it, and
oftentimes an evening was spent in music and musical conversation. At one of these meetings Handel played through
the whole of Matheson's *Lessons* (which that night only came
from the engravers) without the least hesitation, to the great
delight of those who were fortunate enough to be present;

for Handel was considered to be an exceedingly fine performer, especially on the organ.

Handel, finding that his own performance on the organ never failed to command the attention of his hearers, set himself to compose, or rather make up, concertos for that instrument. Of his first six organ concertos only the first and fourth are original compositions; both the second and third are taken from his sonatas; the fifth was a lesson for the harp, composed for the younger Powell, a fine performer on that instrument; and the sixth is a solo for the flute, as is apparent from the compass of it, and was made for the practice of a gentleman, one of Handel's friends. . . .

*   *   *

Handel being once in a country church asked the organist to let him play the people out, to which he very readily consented. Handel accordingly began to play, but in such a masterly manner as instantly to attract the attention of the whole congregation; who, instead of vacating their seats as usual, remained fixed to their seats in silent admiration and delight. The organist at length began to be impatient (perhaps dinner was ready) and advised him to relinquish the attempt, as he could not play them out.

Frederic Bonnet

The Water Music

The story of the *Water Music*, as recorded by history, is pure romance—we now know. It was related that King George I was very angry at Handel for years, but that when he heard the music in London—about 1715—he was so enchanted that he became reconciled with the composer.

This fairy tale was credited for centuries and much repeated. A document recently discovered in the Berlin Archives, a report by the Brandenburg envoy to the English Court, Frederic Bonnet, makes no mention of the moving story. This report was made the day after the performance took place (two years later than the legend says) and we know that the King was on good terms with the master during the preceding years.

In any case, the first performance of the *Water Music* in a boat on the Thames was a delightful event. It is here described by a witness.

SOME WEEKS ago the King expressed a wish to Baron von Kilmanseck to have a concert on the river, by subscription, like the masquerades this winter which the King attended assiduously on each occasion. The Baron addressed himself therefore to Heidegger, a Swiss by nationality, but the most intelligent agent the nobility could have for their pleasures. Heidegger answered that as much as he was eager to oblige His Majesty, he must reserve the subscription for the big enterprises, to wit, the Masquerades, each of which was worth from three hundred to four hundred guineas to him.

Baron Kilmanseck, seeing that His Majesty was vexed about these difficulties, resolved to give the concert on the river at his own expense, and so the concert took place the day before yesterday. The King entered his barge about eight o'clock with the Duchess of Bolton, the Countess of Godolphin, Madame de Kilmanseck, Madame Were and the Earl of Orkney, gentleman of the King's Bedchamber, who was on guard.

By the side of the Royal barge was that of the musicians to the number of fifty, who played all kinds of instruments, viz., trumpets, hunting horns, oboes, bassoons, German flutes, French flutes *á bec*, violins and basses, but without voices. This concert was composed expressly for the occasion by the famous Handel, native of Halle, and first composer of the King's music. It was so strongly approved by His Majesty that he commanded it to be repeated, once before and once after supper, although it took an hour for each performance.

The evening party was all that could be desired for the occasion. There were numberless barges, and especially boats filled with people eager to take part in it. In order to make it more complete Madame de Kilmanseck had made arrangements for a splendid supper at the pleasure house of the late Lord Ranelagh at Chelsea on the river, to where the King repaired an hour after midnight. He left there at three, and at half-past four in the morning His Majesty was back at St. James's. The concert cost Baron Kilmanseck £150 for the musicians alone, but neither the Prince nor the Princess took any part in the festivities.

Charles Burney

A Portrait of Handel Late in Life

Charles Burney (1726-1814) is one of the foremost English musicologists of the eighteenth century. His *General History of Music*—a four-volume work—combines literary merit with scholarship. Burney enjoyed the friendship of the most distinguished men of his time.

He himself calls his life of Handel, whom he observed from boyhood, only a sketch. But it is a highly reliable piece of writing. He knew Handel personally in different periods of his life, in good times and bad and according to modern musicologists, he made very few errors.

Handel, late in life, like the great poets Homer and Milton, was afflicted with blindness; which, however it might dispirit and embarrass him at other times, had no effect on his nerves or intellect in public, as he continued to play concertos and voluntaries between the parts of his oratorios to the last, with the same vigor of thought and touch for which he was ever so justly renowned. To see him, however, led to the organ after this calamity at upward of seventy years of age, and then conducted toward the audience to make his accustomed obeisance, was a sight so truly afflicting and deplorable to persons of sensibility as greatly diminished their pleasure in hearing him perform.

During the oratorio season, I have been told that he practiced almost incessantly; and, indeed, that must have been the case, or his memory uncommonly retentive; for after his blindness he played several of his *old* organ concertos, which must have been previously impressed on his memory by practice. At last, however, he rather chose to trust to his inventive powers than those of reminiscence; for, giving the band only the skeleton or ritornelles of each movement, he played all the solo parts *extempore, ad libitum,* while the other instruments left him, they waiting for the signal of a trill before they played such fragments of symphony as they found in their books.

Indeed, he not only continued to perform in public after he was afflicted with blindness, but to compose in private; for I have been assured that the duet and chorus in *Judas Macchabaeus* of "Zion now his head shall raise, Tune your harps to songs of praise" were dictated to Mr. Smith by Handel after the total privation of sight. This composition, so late in life and under such depressing circumstances, confirms an opinion of Dr. Johnson "that it seldom happens to men of powerful intellects and original genius to be robbed of mental vigor by age; it is only the feeble-minded and *fool-born* part of the creation who fall into that species of imbecility which gives occasion to say that they are superannuated: for these, when they retire late in life from the world on which they have lived by retailing the sense of others, are instantly reduced to indigence of mind."

* * *

The last oratorio at which he attended and performed was on the 6th of April, and he expired on Friday the 13th, 1759, and not on Saturday the 14th, as was at first erroneously engraved on his monument and recorded in his Life: I have indisputable authority for the contrary, as Dr. Warren, who attended Handel in his last sickness, not only remembers his dying before midnight on the 13th but that he was sensible of his approaching dissolution; and having been always impressed with a profound reverence for the doctrines and duties of the Christian religion, that he had most seriously and devoutly wished for several days before his death that he might breathe his last on Good Friday, "in hopes," he said, "of meeting his Good God, his sweet Lord and Savior, on the day of his resurrection," meaning the third day or the Easter Sunday following.

The figure of Handel was large and he was somewhat corpulent and unwieldy in his motions; but his countenance, which I remember as perfectly as that of any man I saw but yesterday, was full of fire and dignity, and such as impressed ideas of superiority and genius. He was impetuous, rough and peremptory in his manners and conversation, but totally devoid of ill-nature or malevolence; indeed, there was an original humor and pleasantry in his most lively sallies of anger or impatience, which, with his broken English, were extremely risible. His natural propensity to wit and humor and happy manner of relating common occurrences in an uncommon way enabled him to throw persons and things into very ridiculous attitudes. Had he been as great a master of the English language as Swift, his bons mots would have been as frequent and somewhat of the same kind.

Handel, with many virtues, was addicted to no vice that was injurious to society. Nature, indeed, required a great supply of sustenance to support so huge a mass, and he was rather epicurean in the choice of it; but this seems to have been the only appetite he allowed himself to gratify.

The late Mr. Brown, leader of His Majesty's band, used to tell me several stories of Handel's love of good cheer, liquid and solid, as well as of his impatience. Of the former he gave an instance which was accidentally discovered at his own house in Brook Street, where Brown, in the oratorio season, among other principal performers, was at dinner. During the repast Handel often cried out—"Oh—I have de taught"; when the company, unwilling that, out of civility to them, the public should be robbed of anything so valuable as his musical ideas, begged he would retire and write them down; with which request, however, he so frequently complied that at last one of the most suspicious had the ill-bred curiosity to peep through the keyhole into the adjoining room; where he perceived that *dese taughts* were only bestowed on a fresh hamper of Burgundy, which, as was afterward discovered, he had received as a present from his friend, the late Lord Radnor, while his company was regaled with more generous and spirited port.

Another anecdote which I had from Brown was the following: When the late Reverend Mr. Felton found that his first organ concertos were well received, he opened a subscription for a second set and begged of Brown to solicit Mr. Handel's permission to insert his name in the list. Brown, who had been in great favor with Handel the winter before, when he led his oratorios, remembering how civilly he had been attended by him to the door and how carefully cautioned, after being heated by a crowded room and hard labor, at the rehearsals in Brook Street, not to stir without a chair, had no doubt of his success: but, upon mentioning to him Felton's request as delicately as possible, one morning when he was shaving, by telling him that he was a clergyman, who being about to publish some concertos by subscription was extremely ambitious of the honor of his name and acceptance of a book, merely to grace his list without involving him in any kind of expense: Handel, putting the barber's hand aside, got up in a fury and, with his face still in a lather, cries out with great vehemence: "Tamm your seluf and go to der teiffel—a barson make concerto! why he no make sarmon?" etc. In short, Brown seeing him in such a rage with razors in his reach, got out of the room

as fast as he could lest he should have used them in a more
barbarous way than would be safe. Indeed, he had a thorough
contempt for all our composers at this time, from Dr. Green
down to Harry Burgess; and performers on the organ too; for
after being long an inhabitant of this country he used to say,
"When I came hither first I found, among the English, many
good players and no composers; but now they are all composers and no players."

       ❀   ❀   ❀

When Gluck came first into England, in 1745, he was
neither so great a composer nor so high in reputation as he
afterward mounted; and I remember when Mrs. Cibber in
my hearing asked Handel what sort of composer he was, his
answer, prefaced by an oath, was—"he knows no more of
contrapunto as mein cook Waltz."

But though he was so rough in his language and in the habit
of swearing, a vice then much more in fashion than at present,
he was truly pious during the last years of his life and constantly attended public prayers, twice a day, winter and summer, both in London and Tunbridge.

       ❀   ❀   ❀

Handel wore an enormous white wig, and when things went
well at the oratorio, it had a certain nod or vibration which
manifested his pleasure and satisfaction. Without it, nice ob-
servers were certain that he was out of humor.

At the close of an air, the voice with which he used to cry
out "Chorus!" was extremely formidable indeed; and at the
rehearsals of his oratorios at Carleton House, if the Prince
and Princess of Wales were not exact in coming into the
Music Room, he used to be very violent; yet such was the
reverence with which his Royal Highness treated him that,
admitting Handel to have had cause of complaint, he has
been heard to say, "Indeed, it is cruel to have kept these poor

people (meaning the performers) so long from their scholars and other concerns." But if the maids of honor or any other female attendants talked during the performance, I fear that our modern Timotheus not only swore but called names; yet at such times the Princess of Wales, with her accustomed mildness and benignity, used to say, "Hush! Hush! Handel's in a passion."

Handel was in the habit of talking to himself so loud that it was easy for persons not very near him to hear the subject of his soliloquies. He had by much persuasion received under his roof and protection a boy who had been represented not only as having an uncommon disposition for music, but for sobriety and diligence. This boy, however, turned out ill and ran away, no one, for a considerable time, knew whither. During this period Handel, walking in the park as he thought alone, was heard to commune with himself in the following manner:—"Der teiffel! de fater vas desheeved;—de mutter vas desheeved;—but I vas not desheeved;—he is ein t—d schauntrel—and coot for nutting."

Handel's general look was somewhat heavy and sour, but when he *did* smile it was like the sun bursting out of a black cloud. There was a sudden flash of intelligence, wit and good humor beaming in his countenance which I hardly ever saw in any other.

Sir John Hawkins

Handel the Master

Sir John Hawkins (1719-1789), the friend and executor of Dr. Johnson, was by profession a justice of the peace. All his life he was intensively occupied with literature and music. We have already spoken of his five-volume *History of Music,* published in 1776, which has remained a standard work.

He was personally acquainted with all the prominent figures in the England of his day. He portrays Handel at the height of his career; we see the triumphantly successful master whose reign culminated with the *Messiah*.

THE COURSE of his life was regular and uniform. For some years after his arrival in England his time was divided between study and practice, that is to say, in composing for the opera, and in conducting concerts at the Duke of Rutland's, the Earl of Burlington's and the houses of others of the nobility who were patrons of music, and his friends. There were also frequent concerts for the Royal Family at the Queen's library in the Green Park, in which the Princess Royal, the Duke of Rutland, Lord Cowper, and other persons of distinction performed; of these Handel had the direction. As these connections dissolved, he gradually retreated into a state of privacy and retirement, and showed no solicitude to form new ones. His dwelling was on the south side of Brooke Street, near Hanover Square, in a house now in the occupation of Sir James Wright, four doors from Bond Street and two from the passage to the stableyard. His stated income was six hundred pounds a year, arising from pensions; that is to say, one of two hundred pounds granted him by Queen Anne, another of two hundred pounds granted by George I, and another of the same amount for teaching the Princesses. The rest was precarious; for some time it depended upon his engagements with the directors of the Academy, and afterward upon the profits arising from the musical performances carried on by him on his own account. However, he had at all times the prudence to regulate his expense by his income. . . . When he found himself in a state of affluence and the produce of his oratorios amounted to more than two thousand pounds a season, he continued his wonted course of living, which was equally distant from the extremes of parsimony and profusion. In the latter part of his life he forbore yielding to a temptation which few in such circumstances as he was then in would

in these times be able to resist, that of keeping a carriage.
Indeed, when his sight failed him, he was necessitated occasionally to hire a chariot and horses, especially in his visits to
the City for the purpose of investing his money, which he
regularly disposed of at the end of the Lent season, under the
direction of Mr. Gael Morris, a broker of the first eminence,
whom he used to meet and confer with at Garraway's or
Batson's coffeehouse.

His social affections were not very strong; and to this it
may be imputed that he spent his whole life in a state of
celibacy; that he had no female attachment of another kind
may be ascribed to a better reason. His intimate friends were
but few; those that seemed to possess most of his confidence
were Goupy, the painter, and one Hunter, a scarlet-dyer at
Old Ford, near Bow, who pretended a taste for music, and at
a great expense had copies made for him of all the music of
Handel that he could procure. He had others in the City, but
he seemed to think that the honor of his acquaintance was a
reward sufficient for the kindness they expressed for him.

A temper and conduct like this was in every view of it favorable to his pursuits; no impertinent visits, no idle engagements to card parties or other expedients to kill time were
suffered to interrupt the course of his studies. His invention
was forever teeming with new ideas, and his impatience to
be delivered of them kept him closely employed. He had a
favorite Rucker harpsichord, the keys whereof, by incessant
practice, were hollowed like the bowl of a spoon. He wrote
very fast, but with a degree of impatience proportioned to the
eagerness that possesses men of genius of seeing their concep-
tions reduced into form.

As to his performance on the organ, the powers of speech
are so limited that it is almost a vain attempt to describe it
otherwise than by its effects. A fine and delicate touch, a
volant finger, and a ready delivery of passages the most difficult, are the praise of inferior artists; they were not noticed in

Handel, whose excellencies were of a far superior kind; and his amazing command of the instrument, the fullness of his harmony, the grandeur and dignity of his style, the copiousness of his imagination, and the fertility of his invention were qualities that absorbed every inferior attainment. When he gave a concerto, his method in general was to introduce it with a voluntary movement on the *diapasons* which stole on the ear in a slow and solemn progression, the harmony close wrought, and as full as possibly could be expressed, the passages concatenated with stupendous art, the whole at the same time being perfectly intelligible and carrying the appearance of great simplicity. This kind of prelude was succeeded by the concerto itself, which he executed with a degree of spirit and firmness that no one ever pretended to equal.

Such in general was the manner of his performance. But who shall describe its effects on his enraptured auditory? Silence, the truest applause, succeeded the instant that he addressed himself to the instrument, and that so profound that it checked respiration and seemed to control the functions of nature, while the magic of his touch kept the attention of his hearers awake only to those enchanting sounds to which it gave utterance.

JEAN PHILIPPE RAMEAU

> Born: Dijon, France
> October 23, 1683
> Died: Paris, France
> September 12, 1764

JEAN PHILIPPE RAMEAU was a lonely, unfathomable man, very reticent and very secretive. At fifty he began to write for the theater. We do not know how he lived before; he never told his friends or even his wife.

A hundred years of archive research has turned up the fact that by the age of seven he was already an accomplished clavecinist and when he was hardly older he could handle the organ and violin in masterly fashion. We know also that in 1701 he went to Italy for a short time. He was extremely poor.

He was nearly forty when he finally settled in Paris where he became organist at Sainte-Croix-de-la-Bretonnerie, and it was not long before he had gained the reputation of being the best organist in France. His first efforts at opera failed, although even these initial works were certainly superior to the products of Lully and his school. In 1737 he presented his masterpiece *Castor and Pollux*— the beginning of his brilliant career. For the next thirty years he held sway as monarch of French opera, and in his old age he was ennobled by the King.

Rameau created a new form of opera and was thus a musical revolutionary, much like Wagner in the nineteenth century. Being a revolutionary, Rameau was the subject of violent and impassioned controversy all his long life.

Hughes Maret

A Go-Getter

Hughes Maret (1726-1786) was a famous physician and a member of the Academy of Dijon. Rameau was made a member of this famous institution three years before his death.

Maret had known the composer and collected facts and anecdotes about him from all available sources. There is no doubt that the anecdote here recounted is perfectly in tune with the master's character as it has been described to us.

In 1702 Rameau became organist at the cathedral in Clermont en Auvergne. The contract with the canons of the cathedral was to run for six years; but Rameau decided he did not want to live up to the agreement. He was then twenty-two years old but already driven by the unscrupulous egoism which seems to have been his most prominent trait.

IF THE noble ambition to make his appearance in a wider sphere moved Rameau to reclaim his liberty, the superiority of his talents rendered the Chapter insensible to his pleas. Rameau was therefore obliged to have recourse to an extraordinary device—blameworthy indeed, but fully as effective as he hoped it would be. . . . On Saturday of the week following Corpus Christi Day, at morning exposition and benediction of the host, he climbed up to the organ, put his hand on the fingerboard and played the first and second verses. Thereupon he retired, closing the doors with a bang. It was assumed that the organ blower was absent and the incident made no impression. But at evening benediction it was not possible to misconstrue his conduct; he made it quite clear that he was determined to show his displeasure by displeasing others. With all the most disagreeable stops he combined every possible dissonance. He was given the usual signals to stop playing, in vain; they were finally forced to send a choirboy up to him. As soon as the child appeared Rameau left the organ and went out of the church. He had put so much art into his jumble of registers, into his most piercing dissonances, that the connoisseurs swore Rameau alone was capable of playing so unpleasantly.

The Chapter reproached him; but he responded that he would never play otherwise than this if they persisted in refusing him his liberty. It was felt that he could not be prevailed upon to give up the position he had taken. They yielded; the contract was terminated; and in the days following he evidenced his satisfaction and his gratitude by performing admirably on the organ. He surpassed himself on Thursday of the week after the return of the procession; this was the day he played for the last time. He put into his playing so much sweetness, delicacy and power, so much brilliance and harmony, that he succeeded in inspiring his listeners with whatsoever emotion he chose. Which rendered all the keener their regret at the loss they must now sustain.

Emile Dacier

The Bitter Struggle

Rameau was fifty when he finally succeeded in getting his opera *Hippolyte et Aricie* performed at the Academy of Music of Paris. It made more of a stir than had anything since the days of the great Lully. Rameau had introduced new forms, especially a varied treatment of the orchestra. He became the most daring renewer of European opera before Wagner—and he was equally hated and persecuted.

Dardanus, performed in November 1739, was the focal point of his career. Despite its great success, the opposition of the Lullists—those who clung to the old forms—forced Rameau to withdraw from battle. Not until he was seventy did he gain his ultimate triumph—the acclaim of the entire nation.

Here are some of the newspaper reports and comments just before and after the first performance of *Dardanus*. The respective headquarters of the two parties were the Café Procope and the Café du Palais Royal.

> On the 10th of November
> people begin talking about
> the new opera

Yesterday evening there was a tremendous crowd at the first general rehearsal of the opera *Dardanus*, which is said to be a marvelous work.

> The 14th of November

On Thursday the new opera *Dardanus* is to be performed; the music is by Rameau and the words by La Bruère. No one knows if it will have much success, since the impression it made at the rehearsals was not a decided one.

> The 18th of November

There is talk pro and con about the new opera *Dardanus* to be given tomorrow. Rameau's adherents praise it to the skies; others say that the music is very dark and gloomy and that the poem, though well written, is full of extravagant situations. Rameau complains that he has neither voices nor performers at the Opéra—aside from the celebrated Jéliotte— to render the great roles of his work as they should be rendered; it is observed that in truth the Opéra seriously suffers for lack of a school and it will be no surprise to see the Opéra close its doors one day due to the dearth of good singers.

Tomorrow the Opéra will offer the first performance of *Dardanus,* a tragedy in five acts with words by M. de la Bruère and music by the celebrated Rameau. A week ago all the boxes, first and second, were reserved. There have been several rehearsals which enough people were permitted to attend so that an opinion has already been formed. All who have heard the work seem to be unanimous in their judgment that it contains passages of beauty, especially a charming part in the second act, but that in general the music is too laborious, too difficult of execution and will not be received with unqualified favor except by the most extreme *"Ramoneurs"*. . . . .

At the Café de Dupuy there has been talk of a federation of more than a thousand *Ramoneurs* who have resolved to keep *Dardanus* going until Easter, not to miss a single performance; and it is reported that there is a countercabal which wants to ruin the piece. Rumor has it that more than six weeks ago the boxes were all reserved for two weeks.

So much is certain, Rameau will have a wonderful house and latecomers will find the box office closed.

The 19th of November

There will be people sitting in their seats at the opera today before noon, and many who could not obtain boxes, which were all reserved, will have to send their *valets de chambre* at nine o'clock in the morning to hold their seats.

The next day

Yesterday all Paris—or all of what we call genteel Paris— contented itself with getting to the Opéra and getting seated. The house was filled to bursting and there were more people turned away than admitted. Well, the work was performed and very nicely. In general it may be said that it contains much impressive and moving harmony, but the opera is so overburdened with music that the musicians of the orchestra did not have a chance to sneeze once in the whole three hours. For the rest, people are making much favorable comment and it will be a success, as much for the poem as for the music.

Although the libretto was written with genius and much imagination, it would be excellent material for one of the most delicious parodies ever made of an opera. Parodic inspiration simply leaps out at you joyously; it could be very easily served up to entertain a convivial supper party.

The 20th of November

Apparently the opera *Dardanus* did no better yesterday than it did the first time, rather the contrary. The sincere "Ramoneurs" admit that this work does not come up to their expectations and that there is nothing in it to compare with the beautiful ballet passages of *Zaide*. They fall back upon disapproving the performance, which is in fact gravely deficient in the tenor parts. A great many wagers are being laid as to how many performances will be given of *Dardanus* —whose libretto is being even worse reviled than the music. It was remarked that yesterday the receipts were less than 4.150 L., whereas quite often a second performance is more successful than the first. Nevertheless they say that the *Ramoneurs* intend to bend all their efforts to support *Dardanus* by going to every performance.

The 22nd of November

The "Ramoneurs" are in despair to see how the opera *Dardanus*, so loudly cried up by them before it opened, is losing with the public. At the Café of the Palais Royal the poet M. Le Roy seems to be reveling triumphantly in the declamations against the opera and its two authors.

The 25th of November

Yesterday there was a bigger attendance at the Opéra than on Sunday, which the Rameau enthusiasts take as a good sign; they are willing to wager that *Dardanus* will have more than forty consecutive performances. According to many people, beauties are being discovered in the music that at first escaped the ear.

The 28th of November

The opera *Dardanus* is suffering the fate predicted for it by the connoisseurs after the first performance. On Thursday receipts were only 1.000 L. and this in the best season from the court of Fontainebleau to Versailles. They are asking to have de Royer's opera back again (*Zaide*) on Thursdays, and the music of *Dardanus* may well fear the comparison.

The same day

The *Ramoneurs* are exulting in yesterday's triumph when the Opéra took in 3.700 L. It is observed that there are hardly any ladies who are not contributing to the success of Rameau's operas. There is a new engraving of Rameau in the taste and form of the first one ridiculing him for using only poets whom he can mulct of all the profits.

The *Mercure* of December,
however, puts things in their
proper light.

On November 19th the Académie Royale de Musique gave the first performance of *Dardanus,* a tragedy, with words by M. de la Bruère and music by M. Rameau. This opera

continues to draw many spectators, despite the opposition
it has encountered ever since its first presentation.

Charles Collé

Le Plus Insociable de Son Temps

Charles Collé (1709-1783) was a playwright and chansonnier. One
of his plays, *La Vérité dans le Vin,* made a great hit. For some years he
kept a diary which excellently pictures his time; it is too bitter, however, too ironic, too narrow-minded to be relied upon fully.

After Rameau's death, Collé wrote some lines about him in his
Journal. It is an acid portrait he draws of the great composer—but it
certainly contains some truth: Rameau *was* harsh and quarrelsome.

We do not know why Rameau refused to let his daughter marry, but
we know for certain that he deeply loved his family. Some of his biographers suspect him of an almost unnatural jealousy. Four months after
Rameau's death the girl married.

He was a hard man, very difficult to get along with, as narrow
and mulish as he was unjust. In his works he never looked
at anything directly but himself, not at the goal toward which
the opera should lead. He wanted to make music, and to
obtain his effect he put everything in the form of ballets,
dances and violin tunes. . . .

Everyone who worked with him was forced to throttle his
subjects, to disguise his poetry, to disfigure it in order to
provide Rameau with his *divertissements.* That was all he
wanted. He treated authors so offensively that no man of
spirit could bear to work with him a second time; only Cahuzac stuck to him; he made him into a sort of *valet de chambre*
librettist; Cahuzac's mean soul bowed to anything Rameau
demanded. Bernard's patience and supple mind gave him
too the strength to compose with Rameau three times; but

I believe if you were to ask him what he suffered he would have some tales to tell—provided he wished to speak frankly and honestly.

Rameau was even more cruel with his family; he declared to his daughter that he did not want to marry her off and that she should marry after his death. He was sordidly avaricious and he did not want to part with anything. After seeing *Dupuis et Desronais,* he said to M. de Monticourt: "I am Dupuis, that's me, only I will never let my daughter move and melt me and she shall never marry while I live"; these are his own words. What is more, he was the rudest mortal, the coarsest, the most unsocial of his time. . . .

Friedrich Melchior Grimm

Another Hostile Obituary

Grimm (1723-1807) was born in Germany but lived the greater part of his life in Paris as an enthusiastic amateur and renowned *littérateur.* The revolution drove him out of Paris and he went to Russia; there he obtained a post under Catherine II.

Grimm is not a reliable witness either; at the time of Rameau's death he was on bad terms with him. Certainly Rameau was stingy, for he came to Paris as poor as a churchmouse, and when he died he left about 200,000 livres—an enormous fortune. But it is also true that he gave his children an excellent education and tried to do the same for his nephew, Jean-François.

RAMEAU was of a harsh and savage nature; he was a stranger to all humane sentiment. I was present one day when he declared that he could not imagine why anyone should desire that M. le duc de Bourgogne display the qualities worthy of the throne. "What good will it do me?" he asked naively. "I shan't be any greater if he reigns." "But your children?" He could not understand at all that a man may well be interested in his children beyond the term of his own life. His ruling passion was avarice. He was insensible to reputation, to distinctions, to glory; he wanted money and he died rich. He was as remarkable for his appearance as he was celebrated for his works. Much taller than M. de Voltaire, he was just as wan and just as withered. . . .

Michel-Paul-Guide Chabanon

Eulogy

Michel-Paul-Guide Chabanon (1730-1792) was one of Rameau's very few friends. He was a writer of distinction, especially in the field of music. In 1780 he was made a member of the Académie Française—the highest honor for a citizen of France.

After Rameau's death Chabanon was chosen to speak his eulogy at the Académie. His tribute stands in sharp contrast to the extremely unflattering portraits drawn by Rameau's enemies and gives us a more just appraisal of the great man. Here is the conclusion of the eulogy.

WE CAN hardly believe that the curiosity of the public would be satisfied if we said nothing of M. Rameau's personal traits—especially the curiosity of the generations to follow ours, should I be fortunate enough to reach them with this record. Details of little interest to our contemporaries may well gain interest for their descendants. . . .

M. Rameau was very tall, thin and spare; he looked more like a phantom than a man. We are in complete ignorance of the events of his life over a period of nearly fifty years; it is obvious that he disclosed little of himself, spoke little of himself, either to his friends or in the bosom of his family. This is remarkable in a man so celebrated; it indicates a kind of self-indifference rare among those whom nature has set apart with high endowment. M. Rameau spent the greater part of the day strolling about alone, seeing no one and seeking no one. Seeing him thus, I long believed that he was plunged in learned meditation; but one day he assured me that he was not thinking of anything whatever, that he was always pleased when I addressed him and drew him out of this empty, idle reverie. Thereafter I availed myself of this permission, but I never addressed him without getting the impression, in the first moment, that he was returning from the depths of some profound ecstasy; several times I had to mention my name before he recognized me, although we had talked together only a few days previously.

He loved glory, there is no doubt of that, since he acquired so much of it; (this conclusion does not seem rash to me) but I am convinced that he concerned himself little with his own fame. Sometimes it even seemed to vex him; he would hide himself at the theater, take refuge from the gazing eyes of the public who pointed him out to one another and applauded. This was no display of false modesty; of that he was incapable and he was a stranger to any sort of affectation.

A year ago, after the first performance of *Castor* at Fontainebleau, I caught sight of him walking about in a lonely, very poorly lighted room; when I started running toward him to embrace him he took abruptly to his heels and did not come back until he had heard my name. Excusing the bizarre reception he had given me, he said "that he was fleeing compliments because they embarrassed him and he did not know what to answer." On this same occasion at Fontainebleau he told me more on the subject of several innovations they had tried to make him add to his opera: "My friend, I have more taste now than I used to have, but I have no more genius left at all."

His taste was not in the least exclusive; this he states himself in the Preface to his *Code de Musique*. Therein he condemns the national taste which tends only to narrow the limits of art; music is in effect the language of the entire world, different climates only change its dialects. . . .

He never prostituted his art and he could not do so; sufficient unto himself, he lived only with and for his genius and neglected even the society of men. The wise and tranquil independence he enjoyed was in no sense the fruit of reflection; it was part of his nature. He was born philosophical, just as the oak is born sturdy.

If he saw the great of this world it was only when they had need of him, and then he behaved with them as he did with ordinary men. He had his mind only on the business in hand and paid no attention to the high personages with whom he dealt. One day he was rehearsing an opera to be performed at court; the *maître de ballet* had for a long time been vainly remonstrating with Rameau that two minuets were too long. The composer seemed not to hear him. The dancer finally hit upon what he regarded as a sure means of lending authority to his advice and censure: attributing them to a personage of high place. "So-and-so finds your minuets too long, M. Rameau!" "Monsieur!" retorted M. Rameau, "if he hadn't been told to find them too long, he would have found them too short."

Such was the celebrated artist to whom we dedicate this eulogy. He died on August 23rd of this year 1764. He was married in 1726 to Marie-Louise Mangot, who survives him; he leaves three children of this marriage: Claude Rameau his son, Ecuyer Valet de Chambre of the King; a daughter in a convent and another daughter living with her mother.

CHRISTOPH WILLIBALD von GLUCK

Born: Weidenwang, Germany
July 4, 1714
Died: Vienna, Austria
November 15, 1787

CHRISTOPH WILLIBALD von GLUCK reformed the opera. The music he created performed the proper function of operatic music: it reinforced the sentiment of the poetry without interrupting the action or weakening it by superfluous ornament. To paraphrase his own words in his dedication to his opera *Alceste*: the relation of music to poetry is much the same as that of harmonious coloring and well-distributed light and shade to accurate drawing, animating the figures without altering their outlines.

He spent the first half of his life in Vienna and Italy; in these years he was a clever composer of charming operas in the Italian style, a musician of no particular distinction. He went to London and there his works proved to be a flat failure—but the mortifying visit had a salutary effect. It turned him to a serious study of the causes of his failure and to a change in his whole style of composition.

The years that followed, spent mostly in Vienna, saw the beginning of his really important operas, among them are *La Clemenza di Tito, Il Re Pastore, Orfeo ed Euridice,* and *Alceste*. They were all brilliant successes, despite the hostile criticism they provoked. In his old age Gluck spent some time in Paris, where *Orpheus* and *Alceste* met with equally impassioned acceptance and rejection.

Gluck is one of the very few great revolutionaries of opera who lived to see the ultimate triumph of his labors. He died rich and famous.

Karl Ditters von Dittersdorf

A Journey with Gluck

We have no first-hand accounts that give us any substantial information about Gluck's youth or his start as a composer. We find our first reliable recollections of Gluck in the biography of the composer Karl Ditters von Dittersdorf, who accompanied Gluck on one of his Italian trips. This was in 1761, when Gluck was forty-seven years old. He had already achieved some success with operas in the traditional *opera seria* style; there were admirers who already called him *divino*. But he had not yet found himself artistically.

Dittersdorf (1739-1799) was noted as both violinist and composer. The amusing description he gives us of the trip to Bologna is not profoundly revelatory, but we do get a picture of Gluck, already the sovereign master of his art, as a man who knows how to enjoy life. Dittersdorf was engaged as a violinist at the court opera in Vienna, where Gluck was conductor. Count Durazzo was the Kaiser's appointee in charge of the opera.

Two YEARS had elapsed since Gluck had been appointed Kapellmeister, with a salary of two thousand gulden. He had taken a fancy to me, when I was with the Prince. I now endeavored to keep myself in his good graces, and I succeeded so well, that he loved me as his own son.

✻   ✻   ✻

One day, Gluck informed me that he was bound for Bologna, having contracted to write an opera there. Would I like to travel to Italy with him, of course on an understanding that I paid one-half of the traveling expenses, and my own board? If so, he was quite prepared to get the consent of Count Durazzo.

"There is nothing I should like better," I answered, in a state of high enthusiasm, which such a man as Gluck, who knew of my passion for art, and was well acquainted with my whole history, ought to have appreciated. "But," I added sorrowfully, "I have no means."

"Oh, indeed!" answered Gluck, turning aside coldly. "Then I suppose the plan must fall through."

That very same evening, I happened to be dining with Herr von Preiss, the Hofagent of the time, and I told him of Gluck's offer.

"Nonsense!" he said. "Strike while the iron is hot, and take Gluck at his word."

"All very well," said I, shrugging my shoulders. "But where is the money to come from? Gluck is willing to take me with him, but I am to pay half the expenses."

"Pah!" answered the honest fellow — peace be to his ashes!—"I will see if it cannot be managed. Here are a hundred ducats for you! You need not pay me until you are better off. Dine with me tomorrow! I will invite Herr von Allstern, and over a good bottle of Gränzinger [the best Austrian wine] we will try and induce him to advance you the same amount. Besides this, in case of emergencies, you shall have my draft for six hundred gulden, so that altogether you will be upward of one thousand five hundred gulden to the good. That will be enough for you. We shall not press for payment. See Gluck as soon as possible tomorrow morning, square everything, and then come back and dine with me!"

With tears of joy, I thanked my noble benefactor. Next day I went straight off to Gluck. The news put him in the highest spirits; he ordered his carriage, and we drove off to Count Durazzo, who not only gave me my *exeat* and presented me with fifty ducats toward my traveling expenses, but promised me, in addition, a half-yearly advance from the funds of the theater. We prepared to start in a fortnight's time.

      ❀   ❀   ❀

Our journey was postponed for a few days, on account of a Signora Marini, who had been engaged as *prima donna* for two whole years at the theater at Prague, and now wished to return with her mother to Venice, her native place. Gluck had known her three years before in Italy, and was good enough to put off the journey for another five days on her account, stipulating, however, that she must consent to travel day and night, without stopping. To this she assented, and we drove away from Vienna in two carriages, with post horses.

Gluck made me paymaster, and I was to keep the accounts. Signora Marini asked me to do the same thing for her, presenting me with a well-filled purse, which she undertook to replenish when it was empty.

She was a very beautiful and interesting girl of about twenty-four years of age, quick, full of fun, and very amusing. Besides this, her behavior was dignified and becoming. At our very first dinner in Neustadt, she proposed that we men should change places at every station, as far as Venice, so that she might enjoy the conversation of both. Sometimes Gluck was to ride in her carriage, sometimes I. Her mother, a bright, cheery lady of some fifty years of age, as outspoken as her daughter, always drove in our carriage, having Gluck for her companion at one time, at another myself—so it was very pleasant for all of us. Gluck was polite, and wished to make himself agreeable; but I tried to spoil his game when my turn came, and our little jealousies helped to make the journey more piquant.

      ❀   ❀   ❀

We started for Bologna on Easter Eve. The opening of the grand new opera house, built entirely of freestone, was fixed for Whit Monday. The old theater had been burned to the ground a year before, and the new building was raised by the subscriptions of the wealthiest and foremost people of the city. The manager, Count Bevilaqua, an associate of the company, had selected Metastasio's *Il Trionfo di Clelia* as the opening piece, and Gluck was engaged to write the music for it.

❖   ❖   ❖

Count Bevilaqua, a courteous man, received us very kindly. Gluck introduced me to him as his pupil, for we had agreed that I was not to give myself out as a soloist till we had heard all the best violinists.

Gluck told the Count of his wish to hear the opera singers, so he forthwith arranged for a concert, to be given by thirty of the best artists, on the following afternoon, at his house, we three being the only persons present. I was enchanted with Girelli, Mansoli, and Tibaldi, but what took me most of all was an air in which Aquilar accompanied his wife on the oboe. Luchini and Spagnoletti each played a violin concerto. Gluck whispered to me:

"You have nothing to fear from these two magicians!"

I thought as he did, but I said:

"I think they are both very good, only everyone has a different method."

Gluck only began to compose now, but as he had already got well ahead with his work in Vienna, the first act was ready for the copyist in ten days' time. He worked of a morning and evening, never of an afternoon. After dinner we used to pay visits, and then we went to the coffeehouse, where we generally stayed until suppertime.

❖   ❖   ❖

On the afternoon of the day before the great *fête,* Gluck and I went to the church to hear Mazzoni's first set of *Vespers.* Chorus and band consisted of over a hundred. Though it was a fine, majestic work, I thought it too lively and secular for the church. Barring the masterly fugues, it was more like an *opera seria* than sacred music. Between the psalms, Spagnoletti played a concerto by Tartini, which I had practiced some years before. The church was crowded with connoisseurs and amateurs. You could see, from the faces of the audience, that he had made his impression.

"You may safely count on the applause of your audience tomorrow," said Gluck to me, "for your music, like your playing, is much more modern."

It had already got about that a German *virtuoso* was going to play a solo on the violin at High Mass next day. As we left the church, we overheard two gentlemen talking together.

"Tomorrow morning we are to hear a German *virtuoso,*" said one; to which the other answered:

"I am afraid he will make a fool of himself, now we have heard that excellent Spagnoletti."

But the next day, when I played a concerto of my own composition, the gentleman turned out to be a false prophet, for Gluck, Herr Bevilaqua, and Signor Mansoli congratulated me on my complete conquest of the audience. Gluck told me that he had elbowed his way to our two critics of yesterday, so as to hear their opinion. One of them exclaimed:

"*Per Dio!* that lad plays like an angel!"

And the other had chimed in:

"How is it possible that a German tortoise should arrive at such perfection?"

Whereupon he had taken the liberty to say to the second:

"By your leave, sir, I too am a German tortoise, and in spite of that, I have the honor of writing the new opera for the opening of the theater which has just been restored."

At this, one of them quite caved in, declaring that he was

entirely cured of his early prejudice against the German nation.

Charles Burney

A Visit to Gluck

We have already met the great English musicologist Charles Burney, who appeared in connection with Handel. In 1772 Burney took a trip through Germany and the Netherlands to visit the leading composers of his time and gather material for his writings on the history of music. The fruit of this journey was two volumes of observation and description.

In Vienna, then the musical capital of Europe, Burney visited the composers Gluck, Hasse, Wagenseil, Salieri, Haydn, Ditters von Dittersdorf, and Vanhall. By this time Gluck was an important figure at the Viennese Court and owned a big, luxurious house. He had behind him his first triumphs with *Orfeo ed Euridice, Paride ed Elena.*

Gluck's niece Marianne, of whom Burney tells us, was the daughter of his sister. Gluck and his wife, who were childless, adopted her when she was ten years old, and took her into their home; she died very young.

WEDNESDAY, SEPTEMBER 2ND. . . . At five o'clock Lord Stormont's coach carried Madame Thun, his Lordship, and myself, to the house of the Chevalier Gluck, in the Fauxbourg St. Mark. He is very well housed there; has a pretty garden, and a great number of neat and elegantly furnished rooms. He has no children; Madame Gluck, and his niece, who lives with him, came to receive us at the door, as well as the veteran composer himself. He is much pitted with the smallpox, and very coarse in figure and look, but was soon got into good humor; and he talked, sang, and played, Madame Thun observed, more than ever she knew him at any one time.

He began, upon a very bad harpsichord, by accompanying his niece, who is but thirteen years old, in two of the capital scenes of his own famous opera of *Alceste*. She has a powerful and well-toned voice, and sang with infinite taste, feeling, expression, and even execution. After these two scenes from *Alceste*, she sang several others, by different composers, and in different styles, particularly by Traetta.

I was assured that Mlle. Gluck had learned to sing but two years, which considering the perfection of her performance, really astonished me. She began singing under her uncle, but he, in a precipitate fit of despair, had given her up; when Signor Millico, arriving at Vienna about the same time, and discovering that she had an improvable voice and a docile disposition, begged that he might be allowed to teach her for a few months only, in order to try whether it would not be worth her while still to persevere in her musical studies, notwithstanding the late decision against her; which he suspected had its rise from the impatience and impetuosity of the uncle, more than the want of genius in the niece. Her performance now is an equal proof of the sagacity and penetration of Signor Millico, in making this discovery, and of the excellent method with which he conveys his instructions; for this young lady has so well caught his taste and expression, and made them so much her own, that they have none of the coldness of imitation, but seem wholly derived from her own feelings; and it is a style of singing, perhaps, still more irresistibly graceful and enchanting in a female, than even in Signor Millico himself.

Mlle. Gluck is thin, seems of a delicate constitution, and, as she sings so much in earnest, I should fear for her health if she were to make singing a profession; but she is not intended for a public performer.

When she had done, her uncle was prevailed upon to sing himself; and, with as little voice as possible, he contrived to entertain, and even delight, the company in a very high degree; for, with the richness of accompaniment, the energy and vehemence of his manner in the *Allegros,* and his judicious expression in the slow movements, he so well compensated for the want of voice that it was a defect which was soon entirely forgotten.

He was so good-humored as to perform almost his whole opera of *Alceste;* many admirable things in a still later opera of his, called *Paride ed Elena;* and in a French opera, from Racine's *Iphigénie,* which he has just composed. This last, though he had not as yet committed a note of it to paper, was so well digested in his head, and his retention is so wonderful, that he sang it nearly from the beginning to the end, with as much readiness as if he had had a fair score before him.

His invention is, I believe, unequaled by any other composer who now lives, or has ever existed, particularly in dramatic painting and theatrical effects. He studies a poem a long time before he thinks of setting it. He considers well the relation which each part bears to the whole; the general cast of each character, and aspires more at satisfying the mind than flattering the ear. This is not only being a friend to poetry, but a poet himself; and if he had language sufficient, of any other kind than that of sound, in which to express his ideas, I am certain he would be a great poet: as it is, music, in his hands, is a most copious, nervous, elegant, and expressive language. It seldom happens that a single air of his operas can be taken out of its niche, and sung singly, with much effect; the whole is a chain, of which a detached single link is but of small importance.

If it be possible for the partisans of *old French music* to hear any other than that of Lulli and Rameau, with pleasure, it must be M. Gluck's *Iphigénie,* in which he has so far accommodated to the national taste, style, and language, as frequently to imitate and adopt them. The chief obstacles to his fame, perhaps, among his contracted judges, but which will be most acceptable to others, is that there is frequently *melody,* and always *measure,* in his music, though set to *French words,* and for a *serious French opera.*

I reminded M. Gluck of his air, *Rosserena il Mesto Ciglio,* which was in such great favor in England so long ago as the year 1745; and prevailed upon him, not only to sing that, but several others of his first and most favorite airs. He told me that he owed entirely to England the study of nature in his dramatic compositions; he went thither at a very disadvantageous period; Handel was then so high in fame, that no one would willingly listen to any other than to his compositions. The rebellion broke out; all foreigners were regarded as dangerous to the state; the opera house was shut up, by order of the Lord Chamberlain, and it was with great difficulty and address that Lord Middlesex obtained permission to open it again, with a temporary and political performance, *La Caduta de Giganti.* This *Gluck* worked upon with fear and trembling, not only on account of the few friends he had in England, but from an apprehension of riot and popular fury, at the opening of the theater, in which none but foreigners and Papists were employed.

He then studied the English taste; remarked particularly what the audience seemed most to feel; and finding that plainness and simplicity had the greatest effect upon them, he has, ever since that time, endeavored to write for the voice, more in the natural tones of the human affections and passions, than to flatter the lovers of deep science or difficult execution; and it may be remarked, that most of his airs in *Orfeo* are as plain and simple as English ballads; and the additions that were made to it when first performed in England, by Messrs. Bach and Guglielmi, were of so different a texture, though excellent in another way, that they destroyed the *unity* of style and characteristic simplicity, for which, when performed at Vienna, this production was so much admired.

Olivier de Corancez

A Clearly Defined Position

In his maturity Gluck knew that he had revolutionized the opera of Europe. When *Iphigénie en Aulide* was performed for the first time, in Paris, on April 19, 1774, his position in operatic history was established for all time. Adverse criticism of his work pleased rather than offended him, and he had ready answers for all the critics.

Olivier de Corancez (1743-1810) was a French librettist known particularly for the book he had written for Jean Jacques Rousseau's opera *Daphnis et Chloé;* his interview with Gluck is most revealing; it clearly distinguishes his artistic conception from that of other masters like Mozart or Haydn. Gluck's is a sharp, deliberate mind concentrated exclusively upon the ways and means of the theater; for him "music for its own sake" does not exist.

ONE DAY the passage *"Peuvent-ils ordonner qu'un père"* from *Iphigénie* was being sung at my house. I perceived in the line *"je n'obéirai point à cet ordre inhumain"* there was a long note to *je* the first time it occurred, and a short note when it was repeated. I observed to M. Gluck that this long note had been unpleasant to me in the melody and I was the more astonished at his employing it the first time, seeing that he had dispensed with it afterward, he himself apparently not making much of it.

"This long note," he said, "which has displeased you so much at your own house—did it equally displease you in the theater?" I answered "No." "Well," he added, "I should be contented with that reply, and as you will not always have me near you, I beg you to look at the matter in the same way whenever such a case occurs again. When I have succeeded in the theater I have done what I set myself to do; it can matter little to me, and I assure you it affects me very little, to create a pleasant effect in a drawing room or at a concert. If you have often noticed that good concert music has no effect in a theater, it is surely in the nature of things that good theatrical music should frequently be unsuccessful in a concert room. Your question resembles that of a man who, being in the high gallery of the dome of the Invalides, should cry out to the painter below, 'Sir, what was your intention here—a nose, an arm?—it looks like neither.' The painter would, with more reason, say to him, 'Sir, come down here and judge for yourself.'

"I ought to add, however, that I had very good reasons not only for setting a long note to *je* the first time Agamemnon pronounces it, but also for suppressing it each time it is repeated. Remember that the prince is between the two most potent of all forces—nature and religion; nature finally gains the victory, but before articulating the terrible word of disobedience to the gods he must hesitate—my long note marks this hesitation; but once this word has been spoken, let him repeat it as often as he may, there will no longer be hesitation; the long note would in that case be only an error in prosody." I also complained to M. Gluck that in this same opera, *Iphigénie en Aulide,* the chorus of soldiers who advance so many times to demand loudly that the victim be given up to them, not only has nothing striking in itself, in point of melody, but that it is repeated each time, note for note, although variety seems so necessary.

"These soldiers," he replied, "have quitted all they hold most dear, their country, their wives, their children—in the sole hope of pillaging Troy. The calm surprises them in the middle of their progress and keeps them bound in the port of Aulis. A contrary wind would be less harmful, since then they could at least return home." "Suppose," he added, "that some great province is in famine. The citizens gather together in crowds and seek the chief of the province, who appears on the balcony: 'My children, what do you wish?' All reply at once, 'Bread!' 'My friends, we are . . .' 'Bread! Bread!' To every-

thing he says they will answer—'Bread!' Not only will they
utter nothing but this laconic word, but they will utter it
always in the same tone, because the great passions have only
one accent. Here the soldiers demand their victim; all the
circumstances count for nothing in their eyes: they see only
Troy or else a return to their own country; so they ought only
to employ the same words and always the same accent. I
might perhaps have written something more beautiful from a
musical point of view, and varied it so as to please your ears;
but in that case I should have only been a musician and should
have been untrue to nature, which I must never abandon. Do
not imagine, however, that in that case you would have had
the additional pleasure of hearing a fine piece of music; I
assure you to the contrary; for a beauty out of place has not
only the disadvantage of missing a great part of its effect, but
it is really pernicious, because it distracts the spectator, who
is no longer in the necessary disposition for following the dramatic action with any interest."

My absolute ignorance of the art of music did not repel
M. Gluck: I did not fear to question him, especially when it
was a case of criticizing some apparent faults. His replies had
always an air of simplicity and truth which only made my
esteem for his person increase day by day.

I begged him afterward to explain to me why the number in
Iphigénie en Aulide, describing the anger of Achilles, sent a
shiver through me, and transported me, so to speak, into the
situation of the hero himself; while if I sang it myself, so far
from finding anything terrible or menacing in it, I only saw
in it a melody pleasing to the ear.

"You must recognize before all," he said, "that music is a
very limited art, especially in that part of it which is called
melody. You would seek in vain, in the combination of notes
which compose the air, a character proper to certain passions:
it does not exist. The composer has the resource of harmony,
but that is frequently insufficient. In the piece you speak of,

all my magic consists in the nature of the air which precedes it, and in the choice of the instruments which accompany it. For some time previously you have heard nothing but the tender regrets of Iphigénie and her adieus to Achilles; the flutes and the mournful tones of the horns play the greatest part there. It is no wonder that when your ears, after being thus lulled to rest, are suddenly struck with the sharp tone of all the military instruments together, an extraordinary effect is produced on you—an effect, indeed, which it was my aim to produce, but which yet depends principally upon a purely physical sensation."

Claude Joseph Dorat

The Gluckists and the Piccinists

The most notorious struggle in musical history was the war between the Gluckists and the Piccinists. It embroiled everyone in Paris—with the exception of Gluck and Piccini.

Niccolo Piccini (1728-1800), an Italian composer, never felt the slightest desire to stir up a conflict between his admirers and those of Gluck. He was a timid, modest person who was dragged into the struggle by others. It was a battle between the "dramatic" opera of Gluck and the "musical" opera of Piccini. With the failure of Piccini's opera *Roland* and the tremendous success of Gluck's *Iphigénie en Tauride* (in 1779), the scandal quickly came to an end.

We print here the letter of an Irishman to the poet Claude Joseph Dorat (1734-1780). His account of the harangue he was subjected to at the first performance of *Roland* gives us a glimpse of the raging party fury.

BECAUSE of the great crowd I had come to the opera very early, and I took up the position that best permitted me to enjoy the spectacle. Every moment I beheld new faces

eagerly thrusting themselves forward, some full of good
cheer, others full of disquietude. Tall as I am, an onlooker
might have imagined I was commanding the movements of
all these little vessels that eddied around me. Alone in the
midst of the multitude, however, I let my thoughts circle
about in my head and paid no heed to the noisy confusion
that now began to reecho all around me. I was still fairly
much at my ease when I caught sight of a little man who
came in greatly heated and excited, drawing after him the
tide. He was round of figure, with a shrill voice, a twitching
eye and a rabid appearance; he rolled from place to place,
from one din to the next. I saw him trundle into my vicinity,
drawing after him his adherents.

I do not know by what accident he suddenly found himself standing quite alone, despite the stifling press of human-
ity in his neighborhood. At that moment silence fell and he
prepared to speak. . . .

"Really, gentlemen!" he began, "I believe all will go well.
What do you say to the simpleton who is obliged to ponder
on the function of song in music! Singing! Melody for French
ears! It is too insulting—here justice must be done." He spoke
further, and I am willing to wager that he did not know the
meaning of the expressions he employed. He spoke of
the melopoë, of the anapest, of the *Jungfrauenchor,* of the
rounding off of arias, of the richness of motifs. He stamped,
he spat, he sneezed, he blew his nose, and everyone said
he was perfectly right.

"This little Italian," he continued, "wants to combat Gluck
—Gluck who has received from nature, thanks be to God,
the power to give expression to the passions—he wants to
fight Gluck, who binds his melodies together, who graduates
his effects, who fills the orchestra with all the undulations of
harmony—Gluck, a genius such as never before has walked
the earth—in a word, a man who bewitches me—*me!*"

This senseless chatter—forcefully delivered, however—

soon became tedious to me; I bent my head to look at the man, and I perceived how he deported himself, how he panted, grew agitated, how the sweat beaded his brow, although everyone, out of pure esteem for his eloquence, was very careful not to irritate him.

I betook myself to my seat but as I did so could not restrain a compassionate smile; this smile stung him to the quick and robbed him of the few wits he still possessed.

From that moment on I noticed that he drew himself erect, gnashed his teeth with impatience, that he tried to address me, then again restrained himself, then rose anew to see me and be seen. I remained motionless as a stone. He was finally conquered by stupidity or curiosity; he broke the silence, seizing me by the arm:

"My dear sir—a Gluckist, I believe?"

"Who is addressing me?" I responded.

"I, sir, I am asking you," he replied, "whether you are a Gluckist or a Piccinist?"

"Neither the one nor the other!"

"But you have to be *something*, don't you?"

"How so, my dear sir? Is one nothing if one is not a Gluckist or a Piccinist?"

"To speak the truth, my good sir, I cannot conceive what else one may be!"

"Is it thus you judge?"

"Now to other things—where do you come from?"

"From China."

"So I think, for I have observed that in China people form opinions; here one expresses oneself without the prior exercise of judgment."

"Really?"

"In other words, my dear sir, you do not admire the Chevalier Gluck?"

"At any rate I do not admire him so hotly as you do; I respect him far too much for that. In my opinion one requires

time to appraise others properly; I have therefore reflected
upon Gluck as I was compelled to reflect upon him."

"And the fruit of your reflection?"

"The fruit, my good sir? That Gluck is a musician of the
first rank, perhaps the only one capable of producing sublime
effects; that he is strong, passionate, pleasing; that he is as
warm as he is forceful and impressive, that he rends the soul
with a shriek of pain; that even in his instrumental accompaniment he is exalted; that he inspirits the automatons of
your choirs with the breath of his genius—in a word, that
he is a man created to effect a revolution in music. But that
now and then he waxes a bit noisy and neglects a little the
magic of melody."

"Excellent!—Yes, there you have it! You are a Piccinist, as
I divined."

"Why do you conclude that I incline toward Piccini? I
do not know a note of his."

"No matter! You have found a fault in Gluck—it is clear
that you are his sworn enemy."

"I am neither his enemy nor his friend."

"No, you are in favor of song, you said so, you betrayed
yourself; you cannot retreat now. Very well, my dear sir—
you will now be so kind as to choose your party! Do you
intend to hiss *Roland?*"

"No, sir."

"Are you going to applaud it?"

"No, sir!"

"What? You will neither hiss nor applaud?"

"Correct."

"Have you no soul in your body? What will you do then?"

"I will listen!"

"Gentlemen!"—and with these words he turned to his
public—"Gentlemen, you realize that this man is threatening
us with his neutrality—it will be necessary to summon the
Guard!"

And in fact tempers were beginning to grow warm when the curtain fortunately rose. A current bore me away from my interlocutor—but I kept my word: I listened; indeed, I was not able to arrive at a well-founded judgment until I had attended all of twenty performances.

Michael Kelly

He Has Not His Equal

Michael Kelly (1762-1826) was an Irish singer and composer. When still a lad he was engaged as tenor at the Vienna opera. He became a particularly close friend of Mozart's—as we shall see later.

When Kelly first met Gluck the great master was seventy-four and at the height of his European fame. Emperor Joseph II of Austria, wishing to show respect for his distinguished guests—visiting princes— commanded the performance of two of Gluck's operas.

A NUMBER of foreign Princes, among whom were the Duc de Deux Ponts, the Elector of Bavaria, etc., with great retinues, came to visit the Emperor, who, upon this occasion, signified his wish to have two grand serious operas, both the composition of Chevalier Gluck—*Iphigénie en Tauride* and *Alceste*— produced under the direction of the composer; and gave orders that no expense should be spared to give them every effect.

Gluck was then living at Vienna, where he had retired, crowned with professional honors, and a splendid fortune, courted and caressed by all ranks, and in his seventy-fourth year.

Iphigénie was the first opera to be produced, and Gluck was to make his choice of the performers in it. Madame Bernasconi was one of the first serious singers of the day; to her was appropriated the part of Iphigénie. The celebrated tenor, Ademberger, performed the part of Orestes, finely. To me was allotted the character of Pylades, which created no small envy among those performers who thought themselves better entitled to the part than myself and perhaps they were right; however, I had it, and also the high gratification of being instructed in the part by the composer himself.

One morning, after I had been singing with him, he said, "Follow me upstairs, sir, and I will introduce you to one whom, all my life, I have made my study, and endeavored to imitate." I followed him into his bedroom, and, opposite the head of the bed, saw a full-length picture of Handel, in a rich frame. "There, sir," said he, "is the portrait of the inspired master of our art; when I open my eyes in the morning, I look upon him with reverential awe, and acknowledge him as such, and the highest praise is due to your country for having distinguished and cherished his gigantic genius."

Iphigénie was soon put into rehearsal, and a *corps de ballet* engaged for the incidental dances belonging to the piece. The ballet master was De Camp, the uncle of that excellent actress and accomplished and deserving woman, Mrs. Charles Kemble. Gluck superintended the rehearsals, with his powdered wig and gold-headed cane; the orchestra and choruses were augmented, and all the parts were well filled.

The second opera was *Alceste,* which was got up with magnificence and splendor worthy an imperial court.

For describing the strongest passions in music, and providing grand dramatic effect, in my opinion, no man ever equaled Gluck—he was a great painter of music; perhaps the expression is far-fetched, and may not be allowable, but I speak from my own feelings, and the sensation his descriptive music always produced on me. For example, I never could hear without tears the dream of Orestes, in *Iphigénie;* when in sleep, he prays the gods to give a ray of peace to the parricide Orestes. What can be more expressive of deep and dark despair?—And the fine chorus of the demons who surround his couch, with the ghost of his mother, produced in me a feeling of horror, mixed with delight.

Johann Friedrich Reichardt

Old Age

Johann Friedrich Reichardt (1752-1814) was a German composer, critic and writer on musical subjects; he was appointed Kapellmeister and court composer to Frederick the Great in 1776 and served until his dismissal in 1794. He is an important precursor of Schubert as a song composer.

Reichardt paints us a picture of Gluck as a very great man at the end of his life. It is 1783 and Gluck is still more illustrious, still richer, but now retired from the clamorous world to his castle Berchtolsdorf near Vienna. He is ill, very ill, and his wife is in a panic over everything and anything that may do him the slightest harm.

Four years later he suffered another apoplectic fit and died—after a gay luncheon given to two friends from Paris, one of those luncheons he so enjoyed.

I ARRIVED by coach and found a tall, majestic old man elegantly attired in gray with rich silver embroidery. He advanced to meet me, surrounded by his servants, and received me, a poor Kapellmeister in traveling dress, with more ceremony than I should have wished. We soon sat down to table and were very well served, but our hero, who had already suffered a first attack and was strictly watched by Madame Gluck, did less honor to the meal than he would have desired. The conversation was none the less animated for that; it was guided by an agreeable and intelligent lady of the house and by an abbé in residence to whom Gluck entrusted the care of his correspondence and his accounts.

For the great man, extremely attentive to market prices, neglected no opportunity to enrich himself. First there was much talk about Klopstock and the Margrave de Bade, at whose house Gluck had made the acquaintance of the author of the *Messiah*. I myself had known Klopstock for a long time, and during my travels in Italy with Lavater I had stopped at the home of the Margrave. The conversation had by now grown lively and I obtained the master's promise that after dinner he would let me hear the music he had composed to the *Hermannschlacht* and other odes of Klopstock but had not yet committed to paper. Madame Gluck protested energetically but in vain; when we had finished our coffee and hastily taken our little walk, Gluck sat down at the piano and with a few sustaining chords, in a hoarse, feeble voice, with a thick tongue, he sang me several pieces that filled me with enthusiasm. I was permitted to copy down, at his dictation, one of these compositions. In the various songs of the *Hermannschlacht* Gluck several times imitated the sound of the horns and the shouts of the combatants behind their shields; once he interrupted himself to tell me that he was looking for a new instrument for this work.

It is difficult to give an idea of what these songs were like, as the composer interpreted them. They rather resembled a prolonged declamation without any melody. What a pity that Gluck did not decide to write them down! . . . Had I not been hindered by my obligation to meet my beloved fiancée, with what delight I would have accepted Gluck's invitation and stayed with him for a time to copy down these compositions he was carrying in his head, works he was prevented from realizing by age, by sickness, above all by the anxiety of his Viennese entourage.

On the wall was hanging the beautiful portrait of Duplessis wherein we see the great man looking up to heaven, his face inspired. No sooner had I expressed a wish to possess a reproduction of this painting than Gluck promised it to me, and several months later I received a copy of the picture in Berlin, along with an extremely kind letter.

In the evening and the next morning we were alone in his study and the conversation turned on Paris. Gluck had a thorough knowledge of Paris and the Parisians. He spoke of them with undisguised irony and in that tone he described to me how he had made use of their obstinacy and snobbishness to force them to accept his innovations and his grand manner.

I had to promise him that I would go to hear his operas in Paris, where he said the tradition of style he had imposed still survived.

In the heat of conversation Gluck had promised to accompany me next day to Vienna and there to attend the déjeuner which Director Schroeder and the good Krause from Stockholm had arranged for him as an intimate and meaningful little celebration. The prospect apparently filled the vigilant mistress of the house with terror, and since Gluck did not seem to have quite recovered as yet from the exciting day he had spent with me—there had been one outing after the other, walks and drives—the project was dropped; I parted from him with the terrible conviction that I should never again see this wonderful man.

FRANZ JOSEPH HAYDN

Born: Rohrau, Austria
March 31, 1732
Died: Vienna, Austria
May 31, 1809

FRANZ JOSEPH HAYDN came of a peasant family. His father was a wagoner and parish sexton; his mother, a simple woman of homely interests. But they were both musical and in the evening his father liked to play the harp while his wife sang. A very able choirmaster, Johann Mathias Frankh, started giving young Franz violin and harpsichord lessons when he was six years old.

Like so many of his fellow musicians, Haydn experienced years of wretched poverty. There were times when he had to sleep in the streets of Vienna. Finally one of his masses attracted some attention; he received a number of commissions and his career began.

For a short time he was music director for Count Morzin; then Prince Paul Anton Esterházy took him to his residence in Eisenstadt, Hungary. For twenty-five years he held this post, directing daily concerts for the Prince. He wrote whole libraries of instrumental music for his orchestra and chamber ensembles.

Haydn lived the second half of his life in quiet, orderly, diligent composition in his house in Vienna, separate and

apart from his disputatious wife. Occasionally he went
to England to conduct performances of his new works.
His success in England was triumphant. Everybody talked
about Haydn and at length he was also recognized in
Germany as the greatest composer of his time.

His greatest masterpieces, *The Creation* (for orchestra
and chorus) and *The Seasons,* were written in his old age.

Joseph Carpani

What Haydn Told of His Boyhood

We have learned nothing about Haydn's childhood beyond what he
himself related to his friends from time to time. Those who knew him in
boyhood never wrote a line of reminiscence.

Giuseppe Antonio Carpani (1752-1825), an Italian musicologist,
lived in Vienna the last twenty-five years of his life. He saw Haydn as
often as he possibly could and questioned him about his musical career.
What the composer told him he wrote down verbatim. There can be
no doubt that Haydn, as a man of true integrity and modesty, told only
truth.

We print here Carpani's pieces in Stendhal's shortened version.

THE FATHER OF HAYDN united to his trade of cartwright the
office of parish sexton. He had a fine tenor voice, was fond
of his organ, and of music in general. On one of those journeys which the artisans of Germany often undertake, being
at Frankfort-on-the-Main, he learned to play a little on the
harp; and on holidays, after church, he used to take up his
instrument, and his wife sang. The birth of Joseph did not
alter the habits of this peaceful family. The little domestic
concert recurred every week, and the child, standing before
his parents with two pieces of wood in his hands, one of

which served him as a violin and the other as a bow, continuously accompanied his mother's voice. Haydn, loaded
with years and with glory, has often in my presence recalled
the simple airs which she sang; so deep an impression had
these first melodies made on a soul that was all music! A
cousin of the cartwright, whose name was Frank, a schoolmaster at Hainburg, came to Rohrau one Sunday and assisted the trio. He remarked that the child, then scarcely six
years old, beat time with astonishing exactitude and precision. This Frank was well acquainted with music and proposed to his relatives to take little Joseph to his house and
teach him. They accepted the offer with joy, hoping to succeed more easily in getting Joseph into holy orders if he
understood music.

He set out accordingly for Hainburg. He had been there
only a few weeks when he discovered in his cousin's house
two tambourines. By dint of trial and perseverance he succeeded in making on this instrument, which has only two
notes, a kind of tune, which attracted the attention of all
who came to the schoolhouse.

Nature had bestowed upon Haydn a sonorous and delicate
voice. In Italy at this time such an advantage might have
been fatal to the young peasant: Marchesi might have gained
a rival worthy of him, but Europe would have lost her sym-
phonist. Frank, who gave his young cousin—to use Haydn's
own expression—more cuffs than gingerbread, soon trained
the young tambourinist not only to play the violin and other
instruments but also to understand Latin and to sing at the
parish desk in a style that spread his reputation throughout
the canton.

Chance brought to Frank's house Reuter, chapelmaster of
St. Stephan's, the cathedral church of Vienna. He was in
search of voices for his children's choir. The schoolmaster
soon recommended his little relative to him; he came and
Reuter gave him a canon to sing at sight.

The precision, the purity of tone, the spirit with which the child executed it surprised him; but he was more especially charmed with the beauty of his voice. He only remarked that he did not trill, and asked him the reason with a smile. The child replied smartly, "How should you expect me to trill when my cousin does not know how himself?" "Come here," says Reuter, "I will teach you." He took him between his knees, showed him how to bring two notes together rapidly, hold his breath and agitate his palate. The child immediately made a good "shake." Reuter, enchanted with the success of his scholar, took a plate of fine cherries which Frank had brought for his illustrious colleague, and emptied them all into the child's pocket. His delight may readily be conceived. Haydn has often mentioned this incident to me and added, laughing, that whenever he happened to trill he still thought he saw those beautiful cherries.

It will be readily imagined that Reuter did not return to Vienna alone; he took the young "shaker" along with him. The boy was then about eight years old. We find no unmerited advancement given to the workman's son, nothing effected by the patronage of any rich man. It was because the people of Germany are fond of music that the father of Haydn taught it to his son; that his cousin Frank instructed him further; and that, at length, he was chosen by the *maître de chapelle* of the first church of the empire. These were natural consequences of the habits of the country relative to the art that we admire.

Haydn has told me that dating from this period he does not recollect having passed a single day without practicing sixteen hours, sometimes eighteen. It should be observed that he was always his own master, and that at St. Stephan's the children of the choir were obliged to practice only two hours. We conversed together respecting the cause of this astonishing application. He told me that from the tenderest age music had given him remarkable pleasure. There was no time when he would not have preferred to listen to any instrument whatsoever than to run about with his little companions. If he was playing with them in the square near St. Stephan's and heard the organ he would immediately leave them and go into the church.

Anonymous

Kapellmeister in Esterház

In 1761 Haydn accepted an offer of Prince Paul Anton Esterházy to go to Eisenstadt, Hungary, and later to the sumptuous new palace, Esterház. Here he spent the greater part of his life, all of thirty years. The Esterházys were among the most powerful and wealthiest princes in the country and, since they were passionate friends of music, much important work was accomplished in these great houses.

Haydn's second employer was Nikolaus "the Magnificent" (who reigned from 1762 to 1790). He loved and deeply admired the composer. It was the latter's function to conduct the castle orchestra and direct operatic productions in the charming castle theater. A great staff had to be engaged to fulfill the Prince's dream of a cultural center.

The following descriptions of the palace and the festivities given there in honor of the Empress Maria Theresa were written by contemporaries.

THE CASTLE is in Italian style, without visible roof, surrounded by a beautifully proportioned stone gallery. Most valuable are two rooms used by the Prince. One of them contains ten Japanese panels in black lacquer adorned with golden flowers and landscapes, each of which cost more than a thousand florins. The chairs and divans are covered with golden fabric. There are also some extremely valuable cabinets and a bronze clock which plays the flute. In the second room, richly adorned with golden ornaments, is another gilded clock with a canary on top that moves and whistles pleasant tunes when the clock strikes, as well as an armchair that plays a flute solo when you sit on it. The chandeliers are made from artistically wrought rock crystal. In the library there are 7,500 books, all exquisite editions, to which new volumes are being added daily. It also contains numerous manuscripts and many excellent old and new engravings by the best masters. The picture gallery is liberally supplied with first-class original paintings by famous Italian and Dutch masters, which fill the eye of the connoisseur with delight and admiration.

In an alley of wild chestnut trees stands the magnificent opera house. The boxes at the sides open into charming rooms, furnished most luxuriously with fireplaces, divans, mirrors, and clocks. The theater easily holds four hundred people. Every day, at 6:00 P.M., there is a performance of an Italian *opera seria* or *buffa,* or of German comedy, which is always attended by the Prince. Words cannot describe how both eye and ear are here delighted. When the music begins, its touching delicacy, the strength and force of the instruments penetrate the soul, since the great composer, Herr Haydn, is himself conducting. But the audience is also overwhelmed by the admirable lighting and the deceptively perfect stage settings. At first we see the clouds on which the gods are seated sink slowly to earth. Then the gods rise upward and instantly vanish, and then again everything is transformed into a delightful garden, an enchanted wood or, it may be, a glorious hall.

Opposite the opera house is a marionette theater, built like a grotto. All the walls, niches, and apertures are covered with variegated stones, shells, and snails that afford a very curious and striking sight when they are illuminated. The theater is rather large and the decorations are extremely artistic. The puppets are beautifully formed and magnificently dressed; they play not only farces and comedies, but also *opera seria.* The performances in both theaters are open to everyone.

Behind the castle is the park. Everyone entering it stands

still in amazement and admiration at the majestic sight, for it fills the soul with rapture. The park was built after the Prince's own designs, and is without doubt the most gorgeous of its kind in the whole kingdom. Art and nature are here combined in an extremely noble and magnificent way. In every corner there is something to attract the eye—statutes, temples, grottoes, water works; everywhere are the glory of majesty, gentle smiles of nature, joy, and delight!

At the gates stand the princely guard consisting of one hundred and fifty grenadiers, very handsome and finely trained men, mostly six feet tall. Their uniform is a dark-blue coat with red flaps and lapels, white tie, white vest and trousers, and a black bearskin cap with yellow visor.

*   *   *

On her arrival the Empress and her retinue were escorted in fifteen of the Prince's magnificent carriages through the park, the wonders of which Maria Theresa could not sufficiently admire, although she was used to a beautiful park in the French style at her own residence of Schoenbrunn. In the evening Haydn's burletta *L'infedeltà delusa* was performed, which so impressed the imperial guest that she was overheard to say: "If I want to enjoy a good opera, I go to Esterház" (a remark that before long was repeated all over Vienna). The performance was followed by a masked ball in the luxurious halls of the castle. Then the Empress was taken to the Chinese pavilion, whose mirror-covered walls reflected countless lampions and chandeliers flooding the room with light. On a platform sat the princely orchestra in gala uniform and played under Haydn's direction his new symphony *Maria Theresa* (No. 48 of the Collected Edition) together with other music. The Empress then retired to her magnificent suite, while her retinue continued to enjoy the masked ball until dawn. The next day a great banquet took place in the *sala terrena,* during which the virtuosos of the orchestra demonstrated their skill.

In the afternoon the Empress attended a performance of
Haydn's opera *Philemon und Baucis* in the marionette theater
and she was so fascinated by it that four years later she had
the complete outfit sent to Vienna for some special festivities.
After the *souper* the imperial guests watched huge fireworks
planned by the pyrotechnist Rabel, their variety and brilliance surpassing all expectations. Afterward the Prince took
the monarch to an immense open space, which was hung with
multicolored lights forming artistic designs. Suddenly about
a thousand peasants appeared in their beautiful Hungarian or
Croatian costumes and performed national dances to the en-
trancing tunes of their own folk music. The next morning the
Empress left, after distributing costly presents. Haydn received a valuable golden snuffbox filled with ducats. He was
proud to have impressed Her Majesty not merely as a musician, for during her stay he succeeded in killing with one
shot three grouse which were graciously accepted for the
Empress' table.

Georg August Griesinger

Haydn in London

Georg August Griesinger, a Saxon diplomat, who died in 1828, knew
Haydn intimately for ten years and wrote the first memoirs about him.
He was especially interested in Haydn's popular triumphs and asked
him again and again about his years in London. Haydn visited England
twice: from 1791-1792 and 1794-1795. His popularity and success in
London were phenomenal; he returned home with enough money for
the rest of his life.

Once I asked him jokingly if it was true that he had written
the *Andante* with the roll of the kettledrum to wake up the
Englishmen in his audience who had fallen asleep. I received

the answer "No, but I was anxious to surprise the public with something new and make a brilliant debut. I did not want to be outdone by Pleyel, my pupil; he was with an orchestra in London just at that time (the year 1792) and his concerts began a week before mine. Even the first *Allegro* of my symphony was received with innumerable Bravos, but the enthusiasm reached its high point at the *Andante* with the kettledrum. *Ancora! Ancora!* rang from every throat, and Pleyel himself complimented me on my idea."

Nepire, an English music dealer, had twelve children; he was about to be arrested for debt. Haydn arranged a full hundred Scottish songs for him in the modern manner, with contrabass and violin accompaniment, sometimes with the addition of a ritornello. These songs had such a good sale that Nepire was rescued from his financial embarrassment and instead of the fifty guineas he had paid Haydn for the first series, he was later able to offer him double for a second. Subsequently (and this work continued into the year 1803) he arranged old Scotch songs of this kind for the music publisher George Thomson in Edinburgh, two hundred and thirty in all, at one guinea a piece, some also at two guineas.

Haydn would very much have liked some of his work to be heard at the great concerts arranged every year by the King in London. Only Handelian compositions appeared on these programs. Haydn was given some hope, but shortly after came an order that nothing was to be performed at these concerts that had not been written thirty years before. On his second stay in London, however, Haydn prevailed. One of his symphonies was included in the program and was splendidly performed by the royal orchestra. Hereupon the King requested Haydn to play a Handelian psalm on the organ. Haydn, who had studied Handel's work with diligence, acquitted himself of this task to the general satisfaction.

He had the honor to perform a few times for the Queen, who presented him with a German oratorio of Handel's entitled

The Redeemer on the Cross, the only one he had written in that language. One evening Haydn played a long while for the Queen on the pianoforte. The King, who always spoke German, remarked that he knew Haydn was also a good singer and he would like to hear a few German songs from him. Haydn pointed to a joint of his little finger and said, "Your Majesty, my voice is only that big now." The King laughed and then Haydn sang his song *"I Am the Most in Love."*

The King and Queen wanted to entice him to stay in England. "This summer I shall give you an apartment at Windsor," said the Queen, and then added mischievously, with an oblique glance at the King, "we shall make music sometimes *tête à tête."* "Oh, I'm not jealous of Haydn," rejoined the King. "He's a good honest German." "To maintain that reputation," answered Haydn, "is my greatest pride." Urged repeatedly to stay in England, Haydn asserted that he was bound by gratitude to the house of his Prince and that he could not part forever from his native country or from his wife. The King offered to bring her over. "She does not voyage even across the Danube, let alone across the sea," replied Haydn. He remained inflexible; he believed it was for this reason that he never had a present from the King. The only one of the Royal Family who came to his benefit concert was the Duchess of York, and she sent him fifty guineas. He was received by her most graciously a few times, for she knew that her father, the King of Prussia, thought a great deal of Haydn. He conducted twenty-six compositions for the Prince of Wales; the orchestra often had to wait several hours until the Prince had risen from the table. Haydn received nothing whatever for his pains. On the advice of his friends, therefore, he sent a bill for a hundred guineas from Germany at the time Parliament was paying off the King's debts. This sum he received without delay.

His demand was taken amiss; people shouted avarice.

Apparently Haydn was expected to bestow gratis upon the English heir to the throne the time and labor he so well knew how to husband. Surely his submission of the claim was less an offense to dainty sensibilities than was the fact that he had been forced to ask for what was rightfully his due.

Dr. Burney was the first to propose to Haydn that he take a doctor's degree at Oxford. The ceremony was performed in a cathedral with many solemnities. The doctors come forward in a procession and ask the candidates whether they wish to be admitted, and the like. Haydn answered as his friend Salomon prompted him. The choice was explained to the gathering from a platform. The speaker enlarged upon Haydn's merits; he cited his works, and to the question, Was Haydn to be admitted? came a general shout of assent. The doctors dressed up in a neck ruff and a short cloak; thus garbed they showed themselves for three days. "If only my Viennese acquaintances could have seen me in this regalia!" His musical friends waved to him from the orchestra. The day after the election Haydn conducted the music. As soon as he appeared everybody shouted "Bravo Haydn!" "I thank you!" he replied in English, holding the hem of his cloak up in the air. This drew forth loud and delighted applause. Handel had spent thirty years in England, but the honor of an Oxford doctor's degree had never fallen to him. Several times Englishmen walked up to Haydn, looked him over from head to foot, and left him with the exclamation, "You are a great man!"

Albert Christoph Dies

Of Haydn's Character and Habits

Dies was a German painter (1755-1832) who lived in Vienna for many years. He called on the old and ailing Haydn at least thirty times and set down the contents of his conversations in his *Biographische Nachrichten von Joseph Haydn,* published in 1810. Haydn did not object to the inquisitiveness of his friends; he enjoyed looking back on the struggles of his childhood and youth.

I HAVE ALREADY STATED in my introduction that I can give no characterization of Haydn because I do not pretend that in the course of five years I so far fathomed his character as to be able to paint a clear picture. I did not want to do Haydn any injustice and therefore went to work cautiously, observed, examined. Nonetheless I dare not assert that I was in every instance able to distinguish properly between a character trait and a habit. Where I am in doubt I prefer to cast out my observation wholly. Hence the small number of these.

Haydn was something under middle height; the lower half of his figure was too short for the upper. This is frequently to be observed with small people of both sexes, but in Haydn it was very noticeable because he kept to the antiquated style of trousers reaching only to the hips, not up to the breast. His features were rather regular, his glance speaking, fiery and yet temperate, kindly, inviting. When he was in a serious mood his features, along with his glance, expressed dignity; otherwise he readily assumed a smiling mien in conversation. I never heard him laugh out loud. Haydn had a moderately strong build; his muscles were spare. His hawk nose (he suffered much from a nasal polyps which doubtless actually enlarged this organ) as well as the rest of his face was deeply marked with smallpox. The nose itself was pockmarked, so that the nostrils each had a different shape.

Haydn considered himself ugly and mentioned to me a prince and his wife who could not stand his appearance "because," he said, "I was too ugly for them." But this supposed ugliness lay not at all in the cut of his features but solely in the skin, eaten away with pockmarks and of a brown tint.

For the sake of cleanliness Haydn wore, even in his youth, a wig with a braid and a few side curls. Fashion had no influence on the shape of his wig; until his death he remained faithful to the same style and wore the wig only two inches above his eyebrows, so that his forehead looked disproportionately low.

Orderliness seemed as native to him as industry. Tidiness and cleanliness were conspicuous in his person and in his whole household. He never, for instance, received visits before he was fully dressed. If surprised by a friend, he sought to gain at least enough time to put on his wig again.

His love of order prompted Haydn to arrange a careful schedule of work and business hours; he was displeased when necessity forced him to a deviation. It would be far from true, however, to say he was a man who lived by the clock. At the end I will set forth his daily schedule; from this the reader will be able to observe how the hours were divided and assigned. He was a sensible manager of money. I several times heard him accused of avarice by people who did not know him very well. I had opportunity enough to inquire into this charge and found it false. The miser has no feeling for the want of others and does not help even his nearest relatives. When Hadyn needed money he was most energetic about earning it; but as soon as it had been acquired and was in his hands, he felt the disposition to share it. He would often call his household together with the words, "Children! Here is money," and give to each, according to his service, five, ten, fifteen or twenty florins.

If Haydn had been parsimonious he would never have been able to make the sacrifice he did for the sake of a certain delicacy of feeling. Once Swieten asked him to get one of his oratorios copied out for him, whatever the cost. The transcription was completed; Swieten asked the copyist what the fee was and received the reply sixty-two or sixty-three florins. Good, said Swieten, and fixed the day of payment. The man went on the day appointed and received, because Swieten had noted down the fee incorrectly, only six florins and a few kreuzer for his tremendous labor. When Haydn learned of this he did not want any discussion but made good the loss himself.

There was in his character much cheerfulness, sport and mischief, the more popular and also the more subtle, but always the most highly original, musical wit. People have often called it humor and have traced back to it, with justice, his predilection for musical teasing.

He was a man of gratitude; as soon as he could he secretly repaid kindnesses done him in his youthful years—but did not forget, meanwhile, his numerous relatives.

Honor and fame were the two driving forces that dominated him; yet no instance is known to me when they degenerated to a greed for renown. His natural modesty prevented this.

He never disparaged other musicians.

In younger years he was said to have been highly susceptible to love. Of this I would have said nothing, but I noticed that into old age he remained most courteous to women and even kissed their hands.

His division of the hours and the order that resulted may strike some of my readers as machinelike; but if you consider the many works that flowed from Haydn's pen you will admit that he simply used his time wisely. He had observed his body and knew what he could expect of it; idle he could not be; change gratified him; order had come to be second nature to him; and so his daily schedule took shape.

In the warmer season Haydn got up at half-past six and shaved himself at once; this task he left to no other hand until he was in his seventy-third year. Then he dressed completely. If a pupil was present while he was dressing, he had to play the lesson assigned on the piano. The mistakes were noted, principles thereon expounded, and a new assignment then given for the next lesson.

At eight o'clock Haydn took his breakfast. Right after that he sat down at the piano and improvised until he found ideas that served his intent; these he immediately committed to paper. Thus were born the first drafts of his compositions.

At half-past eleven he received visits or took a walk and paid visits himself.

The hour from two to three was set aside for dinner.

After dinner he always undertook some little domestic chore or else he went into his library and took a book to read.

At four o'clock he went back to his musical labors. He took the drafts sketched out in the morning and orchestrated them. To this work he devoted three or four hours.

At eight o'clock in the evening he usually went out but came home at nine and either set to work on his scores again or took a book and read until ten o'clock. The time around ten was reserved for the evening meal. Haydn had made it a rule to consume nothing in the evening but bread and wine; this rule he violated only now and then when he was invited somewhere for supper.

He loved gay talk at the table; in general he liked cheerful conversation.

At half-past eleven he went to bed; in his age even later.

Winter time, as a rule, made no difference to his daily schedule except that he rose half an hour later in the morning; everything else remained as in the summer.

In advanced age, especially in the last five or six years of his life, bodily weakness and illness ruined the schedule described above. The active man could at last no longer work;

in this period he had also accustomed himself to a half-hour's afternoon rest.

Stendhal

Haydn's Last Days

In 1814 one of the most famous French writers, Marie Henri Beyle, under the pseudonym Stendhal (1783-1842), published his *Lettres écrites de Vienne en Autriche, sur le celèbre compositeur J. Haydn par L. A. C. Bombet.*

These have little to do with Stendhal himself; the greatest portion are stolen from Carpani's *Le Haydine* (1812). Beyle paid no attention to the accusations of plagiarism hurled at him; he had his book translated into English in 1817, and an American edition appeared in 1839.

THESE IDEAS always occupy my mind when I approach the peaceful dwelling where Haydn reposes. You knock at the door; it is opened to you with a cheerful smile by a worthy little old woman, his housekeeper; you ascend a short flight of wooden stairs, and find in the second chamber of a very simple apartment, a tranquil old man, sitting at a desk, absorbed in the melancholy sentiment that life is escaping from him, and so complete a nonentity with respect to everything besides, that he stands in need of visitors to recall to him what he has once been. When he sees anyone enter, a pleasing smile appears upon his lips, a tear moistens his eyes, his countenance recovers its animation, his voice becomes clear, he recognizes his guest, and talks to him of his early years, of which he has a much better recollection than of his later ones: you think that the artist still exists; but soon he relapses before your eyes into his habitual state of lethargy and sadness.

The Haydn, all fire, so exuberant and original, who, seated

at his pianoforte, created musical wonders and in a few moments warmed and transported every heart with delicious sensations, has disappeared from the world. The butterfly of which Plato speaks has spread its bright wings to heaven, and has left here below only the gross larva. . . .

I go from time to time to visit these cherished remains of a great man, to stir these ashes, still warm with the fire of Apollo; and if I succeed in discovering some spark not yet entirely extinct, I go away with a mind filled with emotion and melancholy. This, then, is all that remains of one of the greatest geniuses that ever lived!

*   *   *

The musical career of Haydn terminates with the *Four Seasons*. The labor of this work exhausted his declining strength. "I have done," said he to me a short time after finishing this oratorio, "my head is no longer what it was. Formerly ideas came to me unsought; I am now obliged to seek for them, and for this I feel I am not formed."

He wrote, after this, a few quartets, but could never finish that numbered eighty-four, though he was employed upon it, almost without interruption, for three years. In the latter part of his life he employed himself in putting basses to ancient Scottish airs, for each of which he received two guineas from a London bookseller. He arranged nearly three hundred of these, but in 1805, by order of his physician, he discontinued this occupation. Life was slipping away from him; and he was seized with vertigo whenever he sat down at the pianoforte.

From this time he never left his garden at Gumpendorff. He sent to his friends, when he was desirous of reminding them of him, a visiting card of his own composition. The words of it are

"My strength is gone, I am old and feeble" (*Hin ist all mein Kraft. Alt und schwach bin ich*). The music which accom-

panies them, stopping in the middle of the period, without
arriving at the cadence, well expresses the languishing state
of the author. . . .

At present this great man, or rather what remains of him
here, is occupied by two ideas only: the fear of falling ill and
the fear of wanting money. He is continually sipping a few
drops of Tokay, and receives, with the greatest pleasure, presents of game, which serve to diminish the expense of his little
table.

The visits of his friends rouse him a little, and he sometimes
follows an idea pretty well. For instance: In 1805 the Paris
papers announced that he was dead, and as he was honorary
member of the Institute, that illustrious body, which has
nothing of the German sluggishness about it, caused a mass to
be celebrated in his honor. The idea of this much amused
Haydn. He remarked, "If these gentlemen had given me notice, I would have gone myself to beat time to the fine mass of
Mozart's which they had performed for me." But notwithstanding his pleasantry, in his heart he was very grateful to
them.

A short time afterward Mozart's widow and son gave a concert at the little théâtre de la Wieden, to celebrate Haydn's
birthday. A cantata was performed which the young Mozart
had composed in honor of the immortal rival of his father. We
must know the native goodness of German hearts if we are to
form any idea of the effect of this concert. I would engage that
during the three hours it lasted not a single pleasantry of any
kind passed in the room.

That day reminded the public of Vienna of the loss they
had already sustained, as well as of that which they were
about to suffer.

It was agreed to perform the *Creation* with the Italian
words of Carpani, and one hundred and sixty musicians assembled at the palace of Prince Lobkowitz.

They were aided by three fine voices, Madame Frischer, of

Berlin, and Messrs. Weitmuller and Radichi. There were more
than fifteen hundred persons in the room. The poor old man,
notwithstanding his weakness, was desirous of seeing, once
more, that public for which he had so long labored. He was
carried into the room in an easy chair. The Princess Esterházy
and his friend Madame de Kurzbeck went to meet him. The
flourishes of the orchestra and still more the agitation of the
spectators announced his arrival. He was seated in the center
of three rows of seats reserved for his friends and the most
illustrious of Vienna. Salieri, who directed the orchestra,
came to receive Haydn's orders before beginning. They embraced; Salieri left him, flew to his place, and the orchestra
commenced amidst the general emotion. It may easily be
judged whether this religious music would appear sublime to
an audience whose hearts were affected by the sight of a great
man about to depart from life. Surrounded by the great, by
his friends, by the artists of his profession, and by charming
women, with all eyes fixed upon him, Haydn bid a glorious
adieu to the world and to life.

The Chevalier Capellini, a physician of the first rank, observed that Haydn's legs were not sufficiently covered.
Scarcely had he given an intimation to those who stood around
him when the most beautiful shawls left their charming wear-
ers to assist in warming the beloved old man.

So much glory and affection caused Haydn to shed tears
more than once, and he felt very faint at the end of the
first part. His chair was brought. At the moment of leaving the
room he ordered the chairmen to stop; he thanked the public
first, by an inclination of the head; then, turning to the orchestra, with a feeling truly German, he raised his hands to heaven
and, with eyes filled with tears, pronounced his benediction
on the old companions of his labors.

WOLFGANG AMADEUS MOZART

Born: Salzburg, Austria
January 27, 1756
Died: Vienna, Austria
December 5, 1791

WOLFGANG AMADEUS MOZART is one of the most astounding child prodigies in musical history. At the age of four Amadeus began pianoforte lessons under his father, who was wholly responsible for the boy's education in music. He and his sister Marianne led the lives of true child prodigies, roaming from country to country, but it was Amadeus who, even in early boyhood, enjoyed the reputation of a very promising composer.

His later life was anchored to Salzburg and Vienna, but he continued to travel throughout Europe, especially Italy, France and Germany. The première of his first great opera, *Idomeneo*, took place in Munich during the Carnival on January 29, 1781.

At twenty-six he married Constanze Weber. He was extremely poor and as he could find few pupils, his chief source of income came from concert performances.

On May 1, 1786 his *Nozze de Figaro* (*Marriage of Figaro*) was performed with almost unprecedented success; one year later came the triumph of *Don Giovanni* in Prague. The Emperor was now induced to appoint him Kammercompositor at a salary of eight hundred gulden a a year. But his financial condition continued distressing. Life brought him glory, rising fame, but never the slightest financial security. His last opera was *Die Zauberfloete*.

Mozart is one of the two or three Olympic gods of music. He combines genius with the most thorough technical musical culture. The exquisite perfection of his work is such that one often feels it cannot be the product of mere mortal inspiration.

Johann Andreas Schachtner

Four Years Old and a Genius

In Wolfgang's fourth year his father, just for fun, began teaching him minuets and other pieces on the clavier. Very soon the boy was able to play them accurately. In his fifth year he composed little pieces, which his father then wrote down.

Most of the facts of Mozart's childhood are contained in a letter from Johann Andreas Schachtner, court trumpeter at Salzburg (died 1795).

Schachtner was not only a skilled musician but a man of considerable literary distinction. He was an intimate in Leopold Mozart's home, and little Wolfgang was much attached to him. The following letter was written to Mozart's sister; it is dated April 24, 1792.

YOUR VERY WELCOME LETTER reached me, not at Salzburg, but at Hammerau, where I was visiting my son, who is coadjutor in the office of Oberwestamtmann there.

You may judge from my habitual desire to oblige every one, more especially those of the Mozart family, how much distressed I was at the delay in discharging your commission. To the point therefore!

Your first question is: "What were the favorite amusements of my late lamented brother in his childhood, apart from his passion for his music?" To this question no reply can be made, for as soon as he began to give himself up to music, his mind

was as good as dead to all other concerns, and even his childish games and toys had to be accompanied by music. When
we, that is, he and I, carried his toys from one room into another, the one of us who went empty-handed had always to
sing a march and play the fiddle. But before he began to study
music he was so keenly alive to any childish fun that contained
a spice of mischief, that even his meals would be forgotten
for it. He was so excessively fond of me—I, as you know, being
devoted to him—that he used to ask me over and over again
whether I loved him; and when in joke I sometimes said "No,"
great tears would come into his eyes, so tender and affection-
ate was his dear little heart.

Second question: "How did he behave to great people when
they admired his talent and proficiency in music?" In truth
he betrayed very little pride or veneration for rank, for,
though he could best have shown both by playing before great
people who understood little or nothing of music, he would
never play unless there were musical connoisseurs among his
audience, or unless he could be deceived into thinking that
there were.

Third question: "What was his favorite study?" Answer: In
this he submitted to the guidance of others. It was much the
same to him what he had to learn; he only wanted to learn,
and left the choice of a field for his labors to his beloved father.
It seemed as if he understood that he could not in all the
world find a guide and instructor like his ever memorable
father.

Whatever he had to learn he applied himself to so earnestly,
that he laid aside everything else, even his music. For instance, when he was learning arithmetic—tables, stools, walls,
and even the floor were chalked over with figures.

Fourth question: "What particular qualities, maxims, rules
of life, singularities, good or evil propensities had he?" Answer: He was full of fire; his inclinations were easily swayed:
I believe that had he been without the advantage of the good

education which he received, he might have become a profligate scoundrel—he was so ready to yield to every attraction which offered.

Let me add some trustworthy and astonishing facts relating to his fourth and fifth years, for the accuracy of which I can vouch.

Once I went with your father after the Thursday service to your house, where we found Wolfgangerl ["little Wolfgang"], then four years old, busy with his pen.

Father: What are you doing?

Wolfg.: Writing a concerto for the clavier; it will soon be done.

Father: Let me see it.

Wolfg.: It's not finished yet.

Father: Never mind; let me see it. It must be something very fine.

Your father took it from him and showed me a daub of notes, for the most part written over ink blots. (The little fellow dipped his pen every time down to the very bottom of the ink bottle, so that as soon as it reached the paper, down fell a blot; but that did not disturb him in the least, he rubbed the palm of his hand over it, wiped it off, and went on with his writing.) We laughed at first at this apparent nonsense, but then your father began to note the theme, the notes, the composition; his contemplation of the page became more earnest, and at last tears of wonder and delight fell from his eyes.

"Look, Herr Schachtner," said he, "how correct and how orderly it is; only it could never be of any use, for it is so extraordinarily difficult that no one in the world could play it." Then Wolfgangerl struck in: "That is why it is a concerto; it must be practiced till it is perfect; look! this is how it goes."

He began to play, but could bring out only enough to show us what he meant by it. He had at that time a firm conviction that playing concertos and working miracles were the same thing.

Once more, honored Madame! You will doubtless remember that I have a very good violin which Wolfgangerl used in old times to call "Butterfiddle," on account of its soft, full tone. One day, soon after you came back from Vienna (early in 1763), he played on it, and could not praise my violin enough; a day or two after, I came to see him again, and found him amusing himself with his own little violin. He said directly: "What is your butterfiddle doing?" and went on playing according to his fancy; then he thought a little and said: "Herr Schachtner, your violin is half a quarter of a tone lower than mine, that is, if it is tuned as it was when I played on it last."

I laughed at this, but your father, who knew the wonderful ear and memory of the child, begged me to fetch the violin, and see if he was right. I did, and right he was, sure enough!

Some time before this, immediately after your return from Vienna, Wolfgang having brought home with him a little violin which some one in Vienna had given him, there came in one day our excellent violinist the late Herr Wentzel, who was a dabbler in composition.

He brought six trios with him, composed during the absence of your father, whose opinion on them he came to ask. We played these trios, your father taking the bass part, Wentzl playing first violin, and I second.

Wolfgangerl begged to be allowed to play second violin, but your father reproved him for so silly a request, since he had never had any instruction on the violin, and your father thought he was not in the least capable of playing.

Wolfgang said, "One need not have learned, in order to play second violin," whereupon his father told him to go away at once, and not interrupt us any further.

Wolfgang began to cry bitterly, and slunk away with his little violin. I interceded for him to be allowed to play with me, and at last his father said: "Play with Herr Schachtner then, but not so as to be heard, or you must go away at once." So it was settled, and Wolfgang played with me. I soon remarked with astonishment that I was quite superfluous; I put my violin quietly down, and looked at your father, down whose cheeks tears of wonder and delight were running; and so he played all the six trios. When we had finished, Wolfgang grew so bold from our applause that he declared he could play first violin. We let him try for the sake of the joke, and almost died of laughter to hear him play, with incorrect and uncertain execution, certainly, but never sticking fast altogether.

In conclusion, you ask concerning the delicacy and refinement of his ear:

Until he was almost ten years old, he had an insurmountable horror of the horn when it was sounded alone, without other instruments; merely holding a horn toward him terrified him as much as if it had been a loaded pistol. His father wished to overcome this childish alarm, and ordered me once, in spite of his entreaties, to blow toward him; but, oh! that I had not been induced to do it. Wolfgang no sooner heard the clanging sound than he turned pale, and would have fallen into convulsions, had I not instantly desisted.

This is, I think, all I can say in answer to your questions. Forgive my scrawl, I am too much cast down to do better.

Friedrich Melchior Grimm

True Miracles Are Rare

When they were still very small, Leopold Mozart took his two children, Wolfgang and Nannerl, on concert tours. They were tremendously successful, first in Vienna, at the court of the Empress Maria Theresa, then in Paris and London. In Paris they gave their first concert with the assistance of friend Grimm. The following letter is dated December 1, 1763. During this visit to Paris the young Mozart's first published compositions appeared, four sonatas.

TRUE MIRACLES are rare, but how wonderful it is when we have the opportunity to see one. A Salzburg Kapellmeister by the name of Mozart has just come here with two of the prettiest children in the world. His daughter, aged eleven, plays piano in the most brilliant fashion, performs the longest and most difficult pieces with astounding precision. Her brother, who will be seven next February, is such an extraordinary phenomenon that you can hardly believe what you see with your own eyes and hear with your own ears. It is easy for the child to play the hardest pieces with perfect accuracy, although his hands are scarcely big enough to take a sixth. You watch him, incredulous, while he improvises for the space of an hour, yielding himself to the inspiration of his genius and a wealth of delightful ideas; what is more, he orders these ideas, playing them in tasteful succession without confusion. The most consummate Kapellmeister cannot possibly have so deep a knowledge of harmony and modulation as this child, and he knows how to do unusual things that are nevertheless always right things. He is so dexterous on the keyboard that you can cover the keys with a napkin and he will go on playing on the napkin with the same velocity and accuracy. It is nothing for him to decipher whatever you put before him; he writes and composes with marvelous ease, does not find it necessary to go to the piano and look for his chords. I wrote out a minuet for him by hand and asked him to put a bass to it. The child seized a pen and without going to the piano he wrote the bass to my minuet. You can well imagine that without the slightest effort he can transpose and play any aria set before him in whatever key requested. But what I now describe, a thing I saw, is not less inconceivable. A lady asked him recently whether, without looking at it, he could accompany an Italian Kavatine that she knew by heart. She began to sing. The child tried a bass that was not entirely correct, for it is impossible to accompany with complete accuracy a song one does not know. But as soon as the song was ended he begged the lady to start over again from the beginning, and now he played not only the whole vocal part with his right hand but simultaneously added the bass with his left, showing not the least hesitation. Then he requested her ten times in succession to begin again and at each repetition he changed the character of his accompaniment. He would have had her repeat it twenty times if they had not begged him to stop. I absolutely predict that this child will turn my head if I listen to him much more. He makes it clear to me how hard it is to keep yourself from madness when you see miracles. I am no longer astonished that St. Paul lost his wits after his wondrous vision. Mozart's children have aroused the admiration of all who have seen them. The Emperor and Empress have over-whelmed them with kindness and they have met with a simi-lar reception at the courts in Munich and Mannheim. A pity that so little is understood of music in this country! The father plans to go from here to England and then to take his children to north Germany.

Johann Georg Leopold Mozart

A Very Earnest Letter to His Son

Wolfgang's father (1719-1787) was an excellent violinist and musi-cian. In 1762 he became court composer and Kapellmeister of the Prince-Bishop's orchestra in Salzburg. He possessed all the qualifica-tions for educating his gifted child. He was an upright man, devoted to the duties of his profession.

The twenty-two-year-old Mozart traveled with his mother to Paris, hoping for the same success he had met with as a child. But of course a young man, no matter what his genius, has not the appeal of a child prodigy. He composed much, but did not win the position he merited.

His father's letter gives an extraordinary picture of the impatient, un-stable, irritable character of the young man. This is the great Wolfgang before he had really come into his own.

My son! You are hot-tempered and impulsive in all your ways! Since your childhood and boyhood your whole character has changed. As a child and a boy you were serious rather than childish and when you sat at the clavier or were otherwise intent on music, no one dared to make the slightest jest. Why, even your expression was so solemn that, observing the early efflorescence of your talent and your ever grave and thoughtful little face, many discerning people of different countries sadly doubted whether your life would be a long one. But now, as far as I can see, you are much too ready to retort in a bantering tone to the first challenge—and that, of course, is the first step toward undue familiarity, which anyone who wants to preserve his self-respect will try to avoid in this world. A goodhearted fellow is inclined, it is true, to express himself freely and naturally; nonetheless it is a mistake to do so. And it is just your good heart which prevents you from detecting any shortcomings in a person who showers praises on you, has a great opinion of you and flatters you to the skies, and who makes you give him all your confidence and affection; whereas as a boy you were so extraordinarily modest that you used to weep when people praised you overmuch. The greatest art of all is to know oneself and then, my dear son, to do as I do, that is, to endeavor to get to know others through and through. This, as you know, has always been my study; and certainly it is a fine, useful and indeed most necessary one. As for your giving lessons in Paris, you need not bother your head about it. In the first place, no one is going to dismiss his master at once and engage you. In the second place, no one would dare to ask you, and you yourself would certainly not take on anyone except possibly some lady who is already a good player and wants to take lessons in interpretation, which would be easy work for good pay. For instance, would you not have gladly undertaken to give Countess von Luetzow and Countess Londron two or three lessons a week at a fee of two or three louis d'or a month, the more so as such ladies also put themselves to much trouble to collect subscribers for the engraving of your compositions? In Paris everything is done by these great ladies, many of whom are devoted lovers of the clavier and in some cases excellent performers. These are the people who can help you. As for composition, why, you could make money and gain a great reputation by publishing works for the clavier, string quartets and so forth, symphonies and possibly a collection of melodious French arias with clavier accompaniment like the one you sent me, and finally operas. Well, what objection have you to raise now? But you want everything to be done at once, before people have even seen you or heard any of your works. Read my long list of the acquaintances we had in Paris at that time. All, or at least most of them, are the leading people in that city and they will all be both delighted and interested to see you again. Even if only six of them take you up (and indeed one single one of the most influential of them would be enough), you would be able to do whatever you pleased.

Michael Kelly

Mozart Famous and Triumphant

Michael Kelly is the Irish singer whom we have already met with Gluck. As a lad in Vienna he was for a time on particularly close terms with Mozart, visiting him almost daily. It is to his *Reminiscences* that we owe one of the best contemporary pen portraits of the master. It shows us an extremely delicate spirit; we see here all the softness, irritability and sensibility of the great artist.

Kelly also describes the first performance of *Nozze de Figaro* (*The Marriage of Figaro*). Emperor Joseph II favored the work because he was sick of German opera, and he regarded Mozart's work as essentially Italian.

I WENT one evening to a concert of the celebrated Kozeluch's, a great composer for the pianoforte, as well as a fine performer on that instrument. I saw there the composers Vanhall and Baron Dittersdorf, and, what was to me one of the greatest gratifications of my musical life, was there introduced to that prodigy of genius—Mozart. He favored the company by performing fantasias and *capriccios* on the pianoforte. His feeling, the rapidity of his fingers, the great execution and strength of his left hand, particularly, and the apparent inspiration of his modulations, astounded me. After this splendid performance we sat down to supper, and I had the pleasure to be placed at table between him and his wife, Madame Constance Weber, a German lady of whom he was passionately fond, and by whom he had three children. He conversed with me a good deal about Thomas Linley, the first Mrs. Sheridan's brother, with whom he was intimate at Florence, and spoke of him with great affection. He said that Linley was a true genius, and he felt that, had he lived, he would have been one of the greatest ornaments of the musical world. After supper the young scions of our host had a dance, and Mozart joined them. Madame Mozart told me, that great as his genius was, he was an enthusiast in dancing, and often said that his taste lay in that art, rather than in music.

He was a remarkably small man, very thin and pale, with a profusion of fine fair hair, of which he was rather vain. He gave me a cordial invitation to his house, of which I availed myself, and passed a great part of my time there. He always received me with kindness and hospitality. He was remarkably fond of punch, of which beverage I have seen him take copious draughts. He was also fond of billiards, and had an excellent billiard table in his house. Many and many a game have I played with him, but always came off second best. He gave Sunday concerts, which I always attended. He was kindhearted, and always ready to oblige, but so very particular when he played that, if the slightest noise were made, he

~~instantly left off.~~ He one day made me sit down to the piano, and gave credit to my first master, who had taught me to place my hand well on the instrument. . . . He conferred on me what I considered a high compliment. I had composed a little melody to a canzonetta of Metastasio which was a great favorite wherever I sang it. It was very simple, but had the good fortune to please Mozart. He took it and composed variations upon it, which were truly beautiful; and had the further kindness and condescension to play them wherever he had an opportunity. Thinking that the air thus rendered remarkable might be acceptable to some of my musical readers, I have subjoined it.

Encouraged by his flattering approbation, I attempted several little airs, which I showed him, and which he kindly approved of, so much indeed, that I determined to devote myself to the study of counterpoint and consulted with him, by whom I ought to be instructed. He said, "My good lad, you ask my advice, and I will give it you candidly; had you studied composition when you were at Naples and when your mind was not devoted to other pursuits, you would perhaps have done wisely; but now that your profession of the stage must, and ought, to occupy all your attention, it would be an unwise measure to enter into a dry study. You may take my word for it, nature has made you a melodist, and you would only disturb and perplex yourself. Reflect, 'a little knowledge is a dangerous thing'; should there be errors in what you write, you will find hundreds of musicians, in all parts of the world, capable of correcting them, therefore do not disturb your natural gift."

"Melody is the essence of music," continued he; "I compare a good melodist to a fine racer, and counterpointists to hack post horses, therefore be advised, let well alone, and remember the old Italian proverb—'*Chi sa più, meno sa*'—'Who knows most, knows least.'" The opinion of this great man made on me a lasting impression.

*   *   *

There were three operas now on the tapis, one by Regini, another by Salieri (the *Grotto of Trophonius*), and one by Mozart, by special command of the Emperor. Mozart chose to have Beaumarchais' French comedy, *Le Mariage de Figaro*, made into an Italian opera, which was done with great ability by Da Ponte. These three pieces were nearly ready for representation at the same time, and each composer claimed the right of producing his opera as the first. The contest raised much discord, and parties were formed. The characters of the three men were all very different. Mozart was as touchy as gunpowder, and swore he would put the score of his opera into the fire if it was not produced first; his claim was backed by a strong party: on the other hand, Regini was working like a mole in the dark to get precedence.

The third candidate was *maestro di cappella* to the court, a clever, shrewd man, possessed of what Bacon called crooked wisdom, and his claims were backed by three of the principal performers, who formed a cabal not easily put down. Every one of the opera company took part in the contest. I alone was a stickler for Mozart, and naturally enough, for he had a claim on my warmest wishes, from my adoration of his powerful genius, and the debt of gratitude I owed him, for many personal favors.

The mighty contest was put an end to by His Majesty issuing a mandate for Mozart's *Nozze di Figaro*, to be instantly put into rehearsal; and none more than Michael O'Kelly enjoyed the little great man's triumph over his rivals.

Of all the performers in this opera at that time but one survives—myself. It was allowed that never was opera stronger cast. I have seen it performed at different periods in other countries, and well too, but no more to compare with its original performance than light is to darkness. All the original performers had the advantage of the instruction of the composer, who transfused into their minds his inspired meaning. I never shall forget his little animated countenance, when

lighted up with the glowing rays of genius; it is as impossible
to describe it, as it would be to paint sunbeams.

I called on him one evening; he said to me, "I have just finished a little duet for my opera, you shall hear it." He sat down
to the piano, and we sang it. I was delighted with it, and the
musical world will give me credit for being so, when I mention
the duet, sung by Count Almaviva and Susan, *"Crudel perche
finora farmi languire cosi."* A more delicious *morceau* never
was penned by man, and it has often been a source of pleasure
to me, to have been the first who heard it, and to have sung it
with its greatly gifted composer. I remember at the first rehearsal of the full band, Mozart was on the stage with his
crimson pelisse and gold-laced cocked hat, giving the time of
the music to the orchestra. Figaro's song, *"Non più andrai
farfallone amoroso,"* Bennuci gave with the greatest animation and power of voice.

I was standing close to Mozart who, sotto voce, was repeating, Bravo! Bravo! Bennuci! and when Bennuci came to the
fine passage, *"Cherubino, alla vittoria, alla gloria militar,"*
which he gave out with stentorian lungs, the effect was electricity itself, for the whole of the performers on the stage, and
those in the orchestra, as if actuated by one feeling of delight,
vociferated, "Bravo! Bravo! *Maestro! Viva, viva grande* Mozart!" Those in the orchestra I thought would never have
ceased applauding, by beating the bows of their violins
against the music desks. The little man acknowledged, by repeated obeisances, his thanks for the enthusiastic applause
bestowed upon him.

The same meed of approbation was given to the finale at the
end of the first act; that piece of music alone, in my humble
opinion, if he had never composed anything else good, would
have stamped him as the greatest master of his art. In the
sestetto, in the second act (which was Mozart's favorite piece
of the whole opera) I had a very conspicuous part, as the
Stuttering Judge. All through the piece I was to stutter; but

in the *sestetto,* Mozart requested I would not, for if I did, I should spoil his music. I told him that although it might appear very presumptuous in a lad like me to differ with him on this point, I did, and was sure the way in which I intended to introduce the stuttering would not interfere with the other parts, but produce an effect; besides, it certainly was not in nature that I should stutter all through the part, and when I came to the *sestetto* speak plain; and after that piece of music was over, return to stuttering; and, I added (apologizing at the same time, for my apparent want of deference and respect in placing my opinion in opposition to that of the great Mozart), that unless I was allowed to perform the part as I wished, I would not perform it at all.

Mozart at last consented that I should have my own way, but doubted the success of the experiment. Crowded houses proved that nothing ever on the stage produced a more powerful effect; the audience were convulsed with laughter, in which Mozart himself joined. The Emperor repeatedly cried out Bravo! and the piece was loudly applauded and encored. When the opera was over, Mozart came on the stage to me, and shaking me by both hands, said, "Bravo, young man, I feel obliged to you; and acknowledge you to have been in the right, and myself in the wrong." There was certainly a risk run, but I felt within myself I could give the effect I wished, and the event proved that I was not mistaken.

I have seen the opera in London, and elsewhere, and never saw the Judge portrayed as a stutterer, and the scene was often totally omitted. I played it as a stupid old man, though at the time I was a beardless stripling. At the end of the opera, I thought the audience would never have done applauding and calling for Mozart; almost every piece was encored, which prolonged it nearly to the length of two operas, and induced the Emperor to issue an order on the second representation that no piece of music should be encored. Never was anything more complete than the triumph of Mozart and his *Nozze di*

Figaro, to which numerous overflowing audiences bore witness.

Adolph Heinrich von Schlichtegroll

That Extraordinary Mixture Called Mozart

The obituary written by Schlichtegroll (1764-1822), writer, philologist and librarian, was the first comprehensive biography of Mozart. This little statement is our most important source of facts about Mozart's life; it is reliable because every detail was given to the writer by Mozart's sister, Marianne. It was translated into French by the great novelist Stendhal under the pen name Bombat; shortly afterward the English edition was published.

Mozart never reached his natural growth. During his whole life, his health was delicate. He was thin and pale, and though the form of his face was unusual, there was nothing striking in his physiognomy but its extreme variableness. The expression of his countenance changed every moment, but indicated nothing more than the pleasure or pain which he experienced at the instant. He was remarkable for a habit which is usually the attendant of stupidity. His body was perpetually in motion; he was either playing with his hands, or beating the ground with his foot. There was nothing extraordinary in his other habits, except his extreme fondness for the game of billiards. He had a table in his house, on which he played every day by himself, when he had no one to play with. His hands were so habituated to the piano that he was rather clumsy in everything else. At table he never carved, or if he attempted to do so, it was with much awkwardness and difficulty. His wife usually undertook that office.

The same man, who, from his earliest age, had shown the

greatest expansion of mind in what related to his art, in other respects remained a child. He never knew how properly to conduct himself. The management of domestic affairs, the proper use of money, the judicious selection of his pleasures, and temperance in the enjoyment of them, were never virtues to his taste. The gratification of the moment was always uppermost with him. His mind was so absorbed by a crowd of ideas, which rendered him incapable of all serious reflection, that, during his whole life, he stood in need of a guardian to take care of his temporal affairs. His father was well aware of his weakness in this respect, and it was on this account that he persuaded his wife to follow him to Paris, in 1777, his engagements not allowing him to leave Salzburg himself.

But this man, so absent, so devoted to trifling amusements, appeared a being of a superior order as soon as he sat down to a pianoforte. His mind then took wing, and his whole attention was directed to the sole object for which nature designed him, the harmony of sounds. The most numerous orchestra did not prevent him from observing the slightest false note, and he immediately pointed out, with surprising precision, by what instrument the fault had been committed, and the note which should have been played.

When Mozart went to Berlin, he arrived late in the evening. Scarcely had he alighted, when he asked the waiter of the inn whether there was any opera that evening. "Yes, the *Entfuehrung aus dem Serail.*" "That is charming!" He immediately set out for the theater, and placed himself at the entrance of the pit, that he might listen without being observed. But sometimes he was so pleased with the execution of certain passages, and at others so dissatisfied with the manner or the time in which they were performed, or with the embellishments added by the actors, that, continually expressing either his pleasure or disapprobation, he insensibly got up to the bar of the orchestra. The manager had taken the liberty of making some alterations in one of the airs.

When they came to it, Mozart, unable to restrain himself any longer, called out, almost aloud, to the orchestra, in what way it ought to be played. Everybody turned to look at the man in a gray coat who was making all that noise. Some people recognized Mozart, and, in an instant, the musicians and actors were informed that he was in the theater. Some of them, and among the number a very good woman singer, were so agitated at the intelligence, that they refused to come again upon the stage. The manager informed Mozart of the embarrasment he was in. He immediately went behind the scenes, and succeeded, by the compliments which he paid to the actors, in prevailing upon them to go on with the piece.

Music was his constant employment and his most gratifying recreation. Never, even in his earliest childhood, was persuasion required to get him to go to his piano. On the contrary, it was necessary to take care that he did not injure his health by his application. He was particularly fond of playing in the night. If he sat down to the instrument at nine o'clock in the evening, he never left it before midnight, and even then it was necessary to force him away from it, for he would have continued to modulate, and play voluntaries, the whole night. In his general habits he was the gentlest of men, but the least noise during the performance of music offended him violently. He was far above that affected or misplaced modesty which prevents many performers from playing till they have been repeatedly entreated. The nobility of Vienna often reproached him with playing, with equal interest, before any persons that took pleasure in hearing him.

An amateur, in a town through which Mozart passed on one of his journeys, assembled a large party of his friends to give them an opportunity of hearing this celebrated musician. Mozart came, agreeably to his engagement, said very little, and sat down to the pianoforte. Thinking that none but connoisseurs were present, he began a slow movement, the harmony of which was sweet, but extremely simple, intending by it to prepare his auditors for the sentiment which he designed to introduce afterward. The company thought all this very commonplace. The style soon became more lively; they thought it pretty enough. It became severe, and solemn, of a striking, elevated and more difficult harmony. Some of the ladies began to think it quite tiresome, and to whisper a few criticisms to one another; soon half the party were talking. The master of the house was upon thorns, and Mozart himself at least perceived how little his audience was affected by the music. He did not abandon the principal idea with which he commenced, but he developed it with all the fire of which he was capable; still he was not attended to. Without leaving off playing, he began to remonstrate rather sharply with his audience, but as he fortunately expressed himself in Italian, scarcely anybody understood him. They became, however, more quiet. When his anger was a little abated, he could not forbear laughing at his impetuosity himself. He gave a more common turn to his ideas, and concluded by playing a well-known air, of which he gave ten or twelve charming variations. The whole room was delighted, and very few of the company were at all aware of what had passed. Mozart, however, soon took leave, inviting the master of the house, and a few connoisseurs, to spend the evening with him at his inn. He invited them to supper, and upon their intimating a wish to hear him play, he sat down to the instrument, where, to their great pleasure, he played until after midnight.

An old harpischord tuner came to put some strings to his traveling pianoforte. "Well, my good old fellow," said Mozart to him, "what do I owe you? I leave tomorrow." The poor man, regarding him as a sort of deity, replied, stammering and confounded, "Imperial Majesty . . . M. de *Maître de Chapelle* of his Imperial Majesty! . . . I cannot. . . . It is true that I have waited upon you several times . . . . You shall give me a crown." "A crown," replied Mozart, "a worthy fellow like you ought not to be put out of his way for a crown;" and he gave him some ducats. The honest man, as he withdrew, continued to repeat, with low bows, "Ah! Imperial Majesty!"

Of his operas, Mozart esteemed most highly the *Idomeneus* and *Don Juan*. He was not fond of talking of his own works; or, if he mentioned them, it was in a few words. Of *Don Juan* he said, one day, "This opera was not composed for the public of Vienna, it is better suited to Prague; but to say the truth, I wrote it only for myself, and my friends."

The time which he most willingly employed in composition was the morning, from six or seven o'clock till ten, when he got up. After this, he did no more for the rest of the day, unless he had to finish a piece that was wanted. He always worked very irregularly. When an idea struck him, he was not to be drawn from it. If he was taken from the pianoforte, he continued to compose in the midst of his friends, and passed whole nights with his pen in his hand. At other times, he had such a disinclination to work that he could not complete a piece till the moment of its performance. It once happened that he put off some music which he had engaged to furnish for a court concert so long that he had not time to write out the part which he was to perform himself. The Emperor Joseph, who was peeping about everywhere, happening to cast his eyes on the sheet which Mozart seemed to be playing from, was surprised to see nothing but empty lines, and said to him: "Where's your part?" "Here," replied Mozart, putting his hand to his forehead.

The same thing nearly occurred with respect to the overture of *Don Juan*. It is generally esteemed the best of his overtures; yet it was only composed the night previous to the first representation, after the general rehearsal had taken place. About eleven o'clock in the evening, when he retired to his apartment, he desired his wife to make him some punch, and to stay with him, in order to keep him awake. She accord-

ingly began to tell him fairy tales, and odd stories, which
made him laugh till the tears came. The punch, however,
made him so drowsy that he could only go on while his wife
was talking, and dropped asleep as soon as she ceased. The
efforts which he made to keep himself awake, the continual
alternation of sleep and watching, so fatigued him, that his
wife persuaded him to take some rest, promising to awake
him in an hour's time. He slept so profoundly that she suffered him to repose for two hours. At five o'clock in the
morning she awoke him. He had appointed the music copyists
to come at seven, and by the time they arrived the overture
was finished. They had scarcely time to write out the copies
necessary for the orchestra, and the musicians were obliged
to play it without a rehearsal. Some persons pretend that
they can discover in this overture the passages where Mozart
dropped asleep, and those where he suddenly awoke again.

Franz Němetschek

The Last Days of Mozart

Franz Němetschek was a high-school teacher in Prague. He knew
Mozart personally, and after his death he went from one member of the
Mozart family to the other, inquiring and making notes. The data given
him by the widow turned out to be more exact and detailed than friends
of the composer had expected.

His book *Leben des k.k. Kapellmeisters Wolfgang Gottlieb Mozart,
nach Originalquellen beschrieben,* was published in Prague in 1798.

The great monarch of whose death Němetschek speaks is Joseph II,
who died in 1790.

BUT HIS END too was approaching. He was not long to survive
the great monarch. The year 1791, tragically filled with great
men's deaths, was destined to snatch away also the pride

of music. But before he died Mozart had drawn prodigally
upon the treasures of his spirit and lavished them upon posterity. The year is as memorable for the creation of his most
wonderful works as it is painful for his unexpected death.
In that year, it may be said as he approached the consummation of his life, he conceived the music for the *Zauberfloete,* for the tragic opera *La Clemenza di Tito,* and for the
noble *Requiem,* which he could not even finish. There is
no doubt that these three works alone would have assured
him a place among the great composers of his age, would
have assured him immortality. Hearing them, our longing
for the lost genius deepens; upon the sensitive listener, even
in the midst of his enjoyment, the thought urges itself irresistibly: "How much more the man could still have
achieved, what harmonies he could still have created!"

He put the *Magic Flute* to music for the well-known
Schikaneder, an old acquaintance of his. The music for *La
Clemenza di Tito* was ordered by the Bohemian patricians
for the coronation of Kaiser Leopold. This latter work he
began in the post chaise from Vienna and completed in the
short space of eighteen days in Prague.

The story of his last composition, the *Requiem* above-
mentioned, is as mysterious as it is unusual.

Shortly before the coronation of Kaiser Leopold, before
Mozart had even received the order to go to Prague, a letter
without signature was delivered to him by an unknown messenger. It contained, among various flattering expressions,
an inquiry as to whether Mozart was willing to undertake
the composition of a Requiem, what his price would be, and
when he would be able to deliver it. Mozart, who never took
a step without the knowledge of his wife, told her about the
strange commission and at the same time expressed a desire
to try what he could do in that line, especially since the more
exalted style of church music suited his genius. She advised
him to accept the order. He therefore wrote back to his un-

known patron that he would write the Requiem for such and such a fee; the exact date of completion, he said, he could not specify, but he would like to know where he was to deliver the work when it was finished. In a short time the same messenger reappeared, bringing not only the stipulated sum but a promise that, since he had set so low a price, he would receive a substantial additional payment when he had dispatched the completed work. He was to write as the spirit moved him but was not to make any effort to find out who his client was, since such effort would assuredly be fruitless.

Meanwhile Mozart had received the honorific and profitable commission to write the opera *Titus* for the coronation of Kaiser Leopold in Prague. To go to Prague, to write for his beloved Bohemians—here was an offer too tempting for him to refuse.

Just as he was getting into the post chaise with his wife, the messenger appeared again and stood there like a specter. He plucked at the lady's skirt and asked "What about the Requiem now?"

Mozart apologized, explained how necessary the trip was, excused himself on the ground that he had been unable to inform the unknown gentleman in advance. He promised that the Requiem would be the first thing he touched on his return; it just depended on whether his unknown client wanted to wait that long. The messenger was entirely satisfied.

Even in Prague Mozart was ailing and taking potions the whole time. His color was pale, his face sad, though in the society of his friends his natural cheerfulness still came out in frequent bursts of gaiety. When he had to leave the circle of his friends he became so melancholy that he shed tears. A presentiment of his approaching end seems to have brought on this melancholy, for even at this time he bore within him the seed of the disease which soon carried him off.

On his return to Vienna he at once commenced his Requiem and worked on it intensively, with lively interest; but his illness worsened visibly and disposed him to the most dismal melancholy. His wife watched him sorrowfully. One day she rode out with him to the Prater to divert and cheer him up a bit. They were sitting there alone together and Mozart started talking about death. He said he was writing the Requiem for himself. Tears stood in his eyes. . . "I feel myself too much," he said, "I can't last long now. They must have given me poison! I can't get rid of that idea."

The words fell heavy as lead on the heart of his wife; she hardly had the strength to comfort him and prove to him the groundlessness of his gloomy notions. Since she believed he was coming down with some sickness and that the requiem was too exhausting for his sensitive nerves, she called the doctor and took away the score.

His condition did in fact improve somewhat and he was able to write a little cantata which had been ordered by a society for some celebration. Its first performance and the acclaim it received gave his spirit a new impetus. He became rather more cheerful and repeatedly asked to go on with his Requiem and finish it. His wife now found no objection to giving him back his score.

This hopeful interlude was short, however; in a few days he relapsed into his melancholy, grew more and more languid and feeble, until he finally sank back helpless on his sickbed, never to rise again.

On the day of his death he had the score brought to his bed. "Didn't I prophesy I was writing this Requiem for myself?" So he spoke and looked through the whole thing attentively once more with wet eyes. It was the last anguished look of parting from his beloved art. . . .

Immediately after his death the messenger was announced again. He asked for the Requiem in its uncompleted form and received it. The widow never saw him again and never heard a thing about the Requiem or the client. The reader can well imagine that every effort was made to trace the mysterious messenger, but all in vain.

During his illness Mozart remained fully conscious until the very end; he died calmly but most unwillingly. This is entirely understandable when we consider that he had just been appointed Kapellmeister of St. Stephan's with all the emoluments that traditionally went with the position. Now for the first time he had the cheerful prospect of being able to live a tranquil life, with adequate income, no longer forced to struggle for a livelihood. At almost the same time he received important orders and contracts from Hungary and Amsterdam for periodical deliveries of certain compositions.

Strange, sad combination of circumstances! Harbingers of a happier fate, the while his present financial situation remained miserable; the sight of an inconsolable wife, the thought of two minor children—these were not likely to sweeten the bitterness of death for an admired artist, who had never been a stoic, in the thirty-fifth year of his life. "Why just now," he complained often during his illness, "why must I go now, when I could have begun to live without worry? Why do I have to leave my art now when I'm not the slave of fashion or speculators any more, when I could have followed my perceptions and my visions, when I could have written freely and independently as my heart prompted me! Why must I leave my family now, my poor children, just at the moment when I would have been able to provide better for their well being!"

His death followed in the night of December 5, 1791. The doctors were not agreed on the diagnosis of his illness. It may be said that countless tears flowed for Mozart, not only in Vienna, perhaps even more in Prague, where he was loved and admired. Every connoisseur, every friend of music regarded his loss as an irreparable one.

Joseph Deiner

The Death

Joseph Deiner was Hausmeister at the restaurant "Zur Silbernen Schlange" ("The Silver Serpent"), where Mozart went frequently. Deiner's simple, moving story of Mozart at the end of his life is a masterpiece of reporting.

It was a cold, unpleasant November day in 1791 when Mozart walked into the Silver Serpent tavern, in Vienna, where he went quite often. This *Bierhaus* was located in the Kaerntnerstrasse, then Number 1112, now Number 1074. Authors, singers and musicians used to gather there. . . . On the day in question Mozart found several new guests in the first *Extrazimmer,* so he immediately passed into the next room, a smaller one, which had only three tables. This little room had trees painted on the walls . . . .

Mozart dropped wearily into a chair, propped his right arm on the table and let his head sink into his hand. He sat this way for rather a long time, then he ordered the waiter to bring him some wine, although he usually drank beer. When the barkeeper had set the wine before him, Mozart remained sitting there motionless, without even tasting the drink.

Then Joseph Deiner, the caretaker, came in through a door leading to the little courtyard. He was a man well known to Mozart, who always treated him with confiding familiarity. When Deiner caught sight of the composer he stopped and looked at him attentively for a long time. Mozart was unusually pale, his powdered blond hair was disheveled and the little braid carelessly done. He suddenly looked up and saw the Hausmeister.

"Well, Joseph, how are things?" he asked.

"I ought to ask *you* that," answered Deiner. "You look sick and miserable, *maestro!* I heard you were in Prague and the air of Bohemia didn't do you any good . . . . Anyone can see that looking at you. You're drinking wine now, that's a good idea; I suppose you drank a lot of beer in Bohemia and spoiled your stomach. It's nothing serious, maestro!"

"My stomach is better than you think," said Mozart. "I've learned to swallow all sorts of things!"

A sigh accompanied these words.

"That's fine," Deiner replied. "All sickness starts in the stomach—that's what my General Laudon said when we stood before Belgrade and the Archduke Franz was sick for a few days too. But I don't think this is a good day to tell you about Turkish music—which you've laughed at often enough!"

"No," answered Mozart, "I have a feeling the music will be all played out soon. There's a chill come over me, and I can't understand it. Here, Deiner, drink up my wine and take this [he gave Deiner a coin]. Come to the house tomorrow morning. Winter's starting and we need wood. My wife will go with you to buy it; I'm even having a fire made up today."

He called the waiter now, pressed a silver coin into his hand and left the tavern. Hausmeister Deiner sat down to Mozart's wine in the first "extra room" and said to himself: "Such a young man thinking about dying! Well, there's plenty of time for that yet, I suppose. . . . But I mustn't forget about the wood, November is good and cold. . . ."

A crowd of Italian singers came into the Silver Serpent. Deiner hated these singers because they always tormented his beloved *maestro,* wouldn't leave him alone, so he too left the place.

The next morning at seven o'clock Deiner betook himself to No. 970 Rauhensteingasse. . . . When he knocked at the door of Mozart's apartment on the first floor, the maid opened the door; she knew him and let him in. She told him that she had had to call the doctor during the night, the Herr Kapellmeister was very sick. Nevertheless Deiner was called in by Mozart's wife. Mozart was lying in a bed with white covers which stood in a corner of the room. When he heard Deiner talking he opened his eyes and said barely audibly: "There's nothing doing today, Joseph, just doctors and druggists today!"

Joseph Deiner left the house. He remembered that the year before he had been at Mozart's discussing firewood. That time he had found Mozart with his wife in his study, which had two windows facing the Rauhensteingasse and one facing the Himmelpfortgasse. Mozart and his wife were dancing around the room in fine form. When Deiner asked if Mozart was teaching his wife to dance, he laughed and said, "We're only warming ourselves up, we're freezing and we can't buy any wood." Deiner ran right out and brought them some of his own wood. Mozart took it and promised to pay well for it when he had money.

On the 28th of November the doctors held a consultation about Mozart's condition. The then renowned Dr. Closset and Dr. Sallaba, chief physician of the general hospital, were present.

❊   ❊   ❊

Since Mozart's illness was growing more serious every minute, his wife once again called Dr. Sallaba on December 5, 1791. He came and shortly thereafter also Kapellmeister Suessmayer, to whom Sallaba confided privately that Mozart could not survive the night. Dr. Sallaba this time also prescribed a medicine for Mozart's wife, who felt sick too. After another glance at Mozart he took his leave.

Suessmayer remained at the side of the dying composer. At twelve o'clock at night Mozart sat up in bed, his eyes fixed; then he leaned over with his head against the wall and seemed to fall asleep again. At four o'clock in the morning he was dead.

At five o'clock in the morning there came a violent knocking at the door of the Silver Serpent. Deiner opened. Mozart's maid, Elise, was standing there sobbing. The Hausmeister asked what she wanted. "Mr. Deiner," said the maid, "you're to come over and dress the master." "For a walk?" "No, he's dead; he died an hour ago—but come quick!"

Deiner found Mozart's wife weeping and so weak she could not stand on her feet. He did for Mozart what one usually does for the dead. Next day Mozart was laid on his bier in a shroud of black cloth, which was customary at the time; this practice continued until the year 1818. His body was carried into the study and placed near his piano.

The church service was held on December 6th at three o'clock in the afternoon at St. Stephan's, not inside the church but at the north side, in the Kreuzkapelle. . . . A third-class interment took place, for which eight gulden thirty-six kreuzer was paid. The hearse cost an additional three gulden.

The night of his death was dark and stormy, and even at the church service it began to howl and bluster outside. Rain and snow fell together, as if nature were angry at the great composer's contemporaries so few of whom had come to attend his burial rites. Only a few friends and three women accompanied the body. Mozart's wife was not present. These few mourners stood with their umbrellas around the bier, which was then carried through the Grand Schulerstrasse to the cemetery. Since the storm was getting worse and worse, even these few friends decided to turn back at the Stubentor (one of the city gates), and they went into the Silver Serpent. Hausmeister Deiner had also been at the service in the chapel. He then went to Mozart's wife and asked her whether she didn't intend to put a cross on his grave. "Yes, yes," she answered, "he'll get one. . . ."

LUDWIG van BEETHOVEN

Born: Bonn-on-Rhine, Germany
December 16, 1770
Died: Vienna, Austria
March 26, 1827

LUDWIG VAN BEETHOVEN had a sordid childhood
in the little town of Bonn on the Rhine. He had a drunkard
for a father, a man who maltreated his son and squandered
his own small earnings on drink. He forced the boy to
practice long hours, even at night, so that he should attain
to fame and wealth at the earliest possible date.

In 1787 Beethoven went to Vienna and asked Mozart
to listen to him play. As soon as Beethoven began to improvise, Mozart recognized that he had a genius before
him. "He will make a noise in the world some day," he
remarked.

Five years later Beethoven returned to Vienna, this time
for good. He supported himself by playing the viola in a
theater orchestra. During this period he became acquainted with a number of the influential aristocracy; important
among these was Prince Karl Lichnowsky, who immediately recognized Beethoven's gifts and invited him to live
in his palace. The composer enjoyed this patronage all his
life.

He now forged ahead brilliantly—but as a pianist, not
a composer. A long, hard struggle lay between him and
recognition as a great composer.

The second productive period in Beethoven's life, when he was at the height of his creative powers, was marked by slowly increasing deafness. Between 1803 and 1804 he wrote his Piano Concerto in C Minor, his Kreutzer Sonata, his Waldstein and *Appassionata* Piano Sonatas, and the *Eroica* Symphony. His third epoch, beginning in 1817, yielded three gargantuan creations: the Missa Solemnis, the Ninth Symphony and the Piano Sonata Opus 106.

But his health was failing; he became almost totally deaf and suffered more and more acutely from a liver disorder. Even mentally he was unwell. In 1826 he contracted influenza, which developed into pneumonia, and he could fight no more.

Karl Czerny

A Young Boy Describes the Master

Karl Czerny (1791-1857), the eminent pianist and pedagogue, was almost the sole authority on pianoforte instruction in Germany, Austria and France during the first half of the nineteenth century. His piano studies are of lasting value.

As an old man he wrote his *Autobiography*—a book of simple but reliable facts.

The man who brought Czerny as a boy to Beethoven was Wenzel Krumpholtz, a violinist with the Vienna opera orchestra.

I was about ten years old when Krumpholz took me to Beethoven. With what joy and trembling I looked forward to the day when I was to see the great man! I have a lively recollection of it still. My father, Krumpholz, and I set out one winter day from the Leopoldstadt (where we were then living), for the street called Tiefe Graben. We mounted five or

six stories high to Beethoven's apartment, and were announced by a rather dirty-looking servant. In a very desolate
room, with papers and articles of dress strewn in all directions, bare walls, a few chests, hardly a chair except the rick-
ety one standing by the Walker piano (then the best make),
there was a party of six or eight people, among whom were
the two brothers Wranitzky, Süssmayer, Schuppanzigh, and
one of Beethoven's brothers.

Beethoven was dressed in a jacket and trousers of long,
dark goat's hair, which at once reminded me of the description of Robinson Crusoe I had just been reading. He had a
shock of jet-black hair (cut à la Titus) standing upright. A
beard of several days' growth made his naturally dark face
still blacker. I noticed also, with a child's quick observation,
that he had cotton wool, which seemed to have been dipped
in some yellow fluid, in both ears.

He did not appear at all deaf; I was at once required to
play, and as I was afraid to begin with one of his compositions,
I chose Mozart's grand C Major Concerto (the one beginning
with chords). Beethoven soon gave signs of attentive interest,
drew nearer to me, and played the orchestral melody with the
left hand in the passages where I had only the accompaniment. His hands were covered with hair, and the fingers very
broad, especially at the tips. The satisfaction he showed gave
me courage to play the Sonata *Pathétique,* which had just
come out, and then *Adelaide,* which my father sang in an excellent tenor voice. When I had finished, Beethoven turned to
my father and said, "The boy has talent; I will take him as a
pupil. Send him to me about once a week. But first of all get
him Emanuel Bach's manual on the true art of pianoforte
playing, and let him bring it with him next time." The friends
present congratulated my father on this favorable verdict,
Krumpholz was in ecstasies, and my father immediately went
in search of Bach's work.

Beethoven devoted the first few lessons to scales in all the

keys, and showed me (what at that time most players were
ignorant of) the only good position of the hands and fingers,
and especially the use of the thumb; rules whose full purport
I only understood in after years. Then he took me through the
exercises in Bach's book, making me pay particular attention
to the *legato,* of which he was so unrivaled a master, but
which at that time—the Mozart period, when the short
staccato touch was in fashion—all other pianists thought impossible. Beethoven told me afterward that he had often
heard Mozart, whose style, from his use of the clavecin—the
pianoforte being in his time in its infancy—was not at all
adapted to the newer instrument. I have known several
persons who had received instruction from Mozart, and their
playing corroborated this statement.

My father would not allow me to walk through the city
alone, and always took me himself to Beethoven's, but by so
doing he missed many of his own lessons; and as it also often
happened that Beethoven was composing and begged to be
excused, my instruction was discontinued after a time, and I
was again left to work by myself.

Bettina von Arnim

A Letter to Goethe

Bettina von Arnim (1785-1859), Goethe's famous young friend and
editress of his *Correspondence With a Child,* went to Vienna in 1810;
Beethoven was then thirty-nine years old.

The letter she wrote about him to Goethe is one of the finest bits of
writing we have on that great composer and on the general nature of
music. It was written on May 28, 1810.

I may confess to you that I believe in a divine charm as an
element of spiritual nature, and this Beethoven exercises in

his art: all that he can tell you of its working shows it to be
pure magic; every passage is a part of a lofty organisation;
and Beethoven thus feels himself the founder of a new sensuous basis in spiritual life. You will understand what I mean,
and what the truth is. Who could replace such a mind? Human affairs go on like clockwork around him, he alone freely
produces the uncreated and the unconceived: what has the
world to do with such a one, who is at his sacred work from
before sunrise till long past sunset, who is totally unmindful
of material wants, whom the floods of inspiration carry far
beyond the shores of dull daily life? He said himself, "When I
open my eyes, I can only sigh, for what I see is contrary to my
creed; and I must despise the world for not perceiving that
music is a higher revelation than any wisdom or philosophy.
It is the wine that inspires new creations, and I am the
Bacchus, who presses out this wine for men, and makes them
spiritually drunk; when they are sober they bring to shore all
kinds of things which they have caught. I have no friend, and
must live alone; but I know that in my art, God is nearer to
me than to others. I approach Him without fear, I have always
known him. Neither am I anxious about my music, which no
adverse fate can overtake, and which will free him who under-
stands it from the misery which afflicts others."

Beethoven told me all this the first time I saw him; a feeling
of reverence took possession of me when he expressed himself
so kindly and freely to one so insignificant; I was also astonished, for I had been told that he was very unsociable, and
would talk to no one. His acquaintances were afraid to take
me to him, and I had to seek him out alone. He has three
houses, in which he hides himself by turns—one in the country, one in the city, and the third at the Bastion, where I discovered him on the third story. I entered unannounced, and
found him at the piano. I mentioned my name, and he was
very kind, and asked if I would like to hear a song he had just
composed. Then he sang *Kennst du das Land* in a sharp in-

cisive tone, filling the hearer with the melancholy of the sentiment. "It is beautiful, is it not?—wonderfully beautiful, I will
sing it again," he said enthusiastically. He was pleased with
my lively approbation. "Most people are moved by a good
thing, but those are not artistic natures; artists are fiery, they
do not weep," he said. Then he sang another of the songs he
had composed within the last few days, *Trocknet nicht
Thränen der ewigen Liebe* ("Dry not tears of eternal love").

He accompanied me home, and on the way talked keenly
about art, but as he stood still in the street declaiming, it
required some courage to listen; he talked very rapidly and
passionately, and I am sure it was a wonder I did not forget
the way. The large party at our house were greatly surprised
to see him come in to dinner with me. After dinner he sat down
to the instrument unasked, and played long and marvelously,
spurred on both by his pride and his genius; under such
circumstances his mind brings forth the inconceivable, and
his fingers accomplish the impossible. Since then, he has come
here every day, or I go to him. For his sake I neglect parties,
galleries, theaters, and even St. Stephan's. Beethoven said,
"Ah, what would you see there? I will fetch you, and toward
evening we will go along the walks of Schönbrunn." Yesterday
I went with him into a glorious garden, full of flowers, all the
hothouses were open, and the perfume was stupefying. Standing in the full glare of the burning sun, Beethoven said,
"Goethe's poems have great power over me, not only by their
matter, but by their rhythm; I am moved to composition by
their language, and by the lofty spirit of harmony pervading
them. Melodies radiate from the forms of inspiration, I pursue them, and passionately bring them back; I see them dis-
appear in the varied mass of emotions, then I seize them in
renewed ardor, and cannot let them go; hurriedly and with
delight I develop them in all their modulations, and in the end
I triumph in the production of a musical thought—a symphony; yes, music is the medium between the spiritual and

sensuous life. I might say with Goethe, if he would understand me, melody is the sensuous life of poetry. Is not the intellectual meaning of a poem represented in sensuous feeling by
melody—is not the sensuous element in the song of Mignon
realized through the melody? and does not such emotion call
forth new creations? Then the mind expands into a boundless universality where everything unites to foster the feelings excited by simple musical thought, which would otherwise perish unnoticed: it is harmony which speaks in my
symphonies, the fusion of many forms into a compact whole.
We feel that there is something eternal and incomprehensible
in everything spiritual; and although I always have a sense of
success in my works, I feel a constant hunger, which seems for
a time appeased by composition but invariably returns. Speak
to Goethe of me; tell him he must hear my symphonies, and
he will agree with me that music is the only spiritual entrance
to a higher world of knowledge, comprehending but not comprehended by mankind.

"A sense of rhythm is necessary to the comprehension of the
nature of music, which has presages of the highest knowledge; its sensuous representations are the embodiment of
intellectual revelations. Although the soul lives on music as
bodies do on air, it is another thing to comprehend it; but the
more the soul draws its sensual nourishment from it, the closer
will be their union. But few attain to this, for as thousands
marry for love, without love ever revealing itself to them,
although they all profess it, so thousands are conversant with
music, yet do not know its secret. A lofty moral sense lies at
the basis of music as of every art; every true invention is
another step in moral progress. It is the unique principle of
art that it can submit to its own inscrutable laws, and curb
and guide the spirit of these laws, so that it may pour out its
own revelations; to find redemption and relief in the latter is
the impulse toward the divine, the element which rules the
fury of uncurbed forces, and so gives imagination its fullest

scope. Thus art always represents the divine, and man's relation to it is religion; what we achieve through art is God's gift of an aim for human endeavor to strive for."

Ludwig Spohr

Beethoven as Conductor

Ludwig Spohr (1784-1859), German composer, was appointed conductor of the orchestra at the Theater an der Wien, Vienna, in 1812 and resigned in 1815. During these three years he met Beethoven very often—as he tells us in his *Autobiography*—but never came to understand his music. He wrote with particular harshness of the master's last works.

IN THIS NEW FORM, *Fidelio* had a great success, and during a long series of performances drew large audiences. On the first night the composer was repeatedly called for, and now again became the object of universal attention. His friends made use of this favorable opportunity to arrange a concert at the great Redoutensaal for the performance of his latest composition. All available string, wind, and vocal forces were invited to cooperate, and not one of the great artists in Vienna was absent. I, of course, joined with my band, and for the first time I saw Beethoven conducting. Although I had heard a great deal about it, I was very much astonished by what I saw; Beethoven had become accustomed to indicating the marks of expression by all kinds of peculiar movements. Whenever a *sforzando* occurred, he would vehemently open both arms, which had before been crossed on his chest. For a *piano*, he would bend down, and the softer it was to be, the lower he would stoop; for a *crescendo*, he would draw himself up more and more, till at the arrival of the *forte*, he gave a leap into the air; he would frequently scream out to increase the *forte*, without being aware of so doing.

Seyfried, to whom I expressed my astonishment at this strange behavior, related a serio-comic accident which occurred at Beethoven's last concert at the Theater an der Wien (1808).

Beethoven was playing a new pianoforte concerto of his own, but at the beginning of the first *tutti*, forgetting that he was the soloist, he jumped up and began to conduct in his usual style. At the first *sforzando* he flung out his arms so violently as to extinguish both the lights on the piano desk; the audience laughed, and he was so put out by the disturbance, that he made the orchestra leave off and recommence. Seyfried, fearing lest the mishap should again occur when the same passage was repeated, sent for two choirboys to stand by Beethoven and hold the candles; one of them unsuspectingly drew near to look over the pianoforte part; when the fatal *sforzando* arrived, he received such a smart slap in the face from Beethoven's right hand, that he dropped his light in terror; the other boy, more cautious than his companion, had been anxiously following Beethoven's every movement, and by suddenly stooping, escaped the blow. If the audience had laughed heartily before, they now burst into a truly Bacchanalian roar. This threw Beethoven into such a rage that he broke half a dozen strings at the first chords of the solo. All efforts to restore quiet and attention were for the time being fruitless. The first *allegro* of the concerto was therefore quite lost. After this incident, Beethoven would never give another piano performance.

But the concert arranged by his friends achieved a brilliant success. Beethoven's new compositions met with unusual favor, especially the Symphony in A Major (the 7th), the wonderful second movement being encored; this also made a deep impression on me.

The performance was most masterly, in spite of Beethoven's uncertain and often absurd manner of conducting. It was quite clear that the poor deaf master could no longer hear the *piani* of his music: this was particularly striking in the second part of the first *allegro* of the symphony, in which two successive pauses are definitely indicated. Beethoven had probably forgotten them, for he recommenced beating before the orchestra had reached the second pause: he was therefore unconsciously ten or twelve bars in advance, when the orchestra went on again. The passage was *pianissimo* and after his usual style of indicating *pp*, Beethoven had disappeared under the desk. With the following *crescendo* he was again visible, and gradually rose higher and higher, till, when according to his reckoning the *forte* should begin, he gave a spring; the *forte* failing to appear, he looked round horrified, stared in amazement at the orchestra, who continued playing *pianissimo*, and only recovered himself when the long-expected *forte* at length arrived and became audible to him.

Karl Gottlieb Freudenberg

Hermitage in the Helenenthal

Karl Gottlieb Freudenberg (1797-1869) was an organist in Breslau, Silesia. In 1826, as a young man, he set out with almost empty pockets for Vienna, traveling mostly by foot. He wanted to see Beethoven. Later he described the visit in a book published after his death, in 1869, under the title, *Aus dem Leben eines Organisten* ("*From the Life of an Organist*").

BEETHOVEN had comfortably established himself in the St. Helenenthal, that quiet, romantic, enchanting region, traversed by lonely wood and mountain paths, where, far from man and nearer to God, you can commune with your inmost

soul, undisturbed by the tumult of the world. I was approaching Beethoven's house with rapid steps about two o'clock in
the afternoon of a hot July day. Beethoven, who had observed
me from the balcony, retreated when I drew near, anticipating, perhaps, a visit from one of the numerous traveling tribes
of so-called musical geniuses who pester him during the summer, like flies tormenting a noble steed. At first sight of my
strange student's costume and disheveled appearance, the
old housekeeper would not admit me. On my saying, "I wish
to see Beethoven," she replied quite angrily, with her arms
akimbo, "What, a tramp like you wanting to speak to my good
master Beethoven? Everybody could come in at that rate!
Barons, counts, and even princes are often refused admittance. They send a complimentary message, and that's all!"
"But dear, sweet mistress, I am a poor musician, I have walked
all the way from Breslau in Silesia, and I shall have no rest
day or night till I have seen my idol. I am like old Simeon,
who longed to see the child Christ before he died, and exclaimed, when his desire was fulfilled, 'Lord, now lettest thou
thy servant depart in peace, for mine eyes have seen thy salva-
tion.' " "Well, sir, I suppose you're not so bad as you look, I
can respect you; such a long journey on foot, it must have
been twenty or thirty miles!" "No, dear little mother, nearly
a hundred!" "Good heavens, Jesus Maria, it would be too hard-
hearted of my master to send you away without letting you
see him!"

She quickly trotted off to announce me, and returned with
a sheet of parchment and a pencil. On my asking what these
were for, she said, "But you know Beethoven is quite deaf, his
visitors must write down all they have to say." I had not been
aware that Beethoven was so deaf as this. How should I introduce myself? I wrote, "Freudenberg, music teacher, from
Breslau, desires to make the acquaintance of the great and
gifted Beethoven." Presently a thickset figure of middle height
appeared, and with friendly gestures and kind looks drew me

into his room, where I was given a seat on the sofa, and had an hour's pleasant talk over a cup of black coffee.

It will be readily understood, although my words may fail to express it, that this hour was to me one of the utmost sanctity, deepest artistic devotion, and sincerest happiness. The subject of our conversation was, of course, musical art and its votaries. I expected Beethoven to despise Rossini, who was at that time so idolized; but, on the contrary, he admitted that Rossini was a man of talent, a very melodious composer, that his music was adapted to the frivolous, sensuous spirit of the time, and that such was his productiveness that he composed an opera in a few weeks where a German took as many years. There was, he said, a great deal of good in Spontini; he was a splendid master of theatrical effects and musical war cries. Spohr indulged very freely in dissonances, and his chromatic melody interfered with the pleasing character of his music. Beethoven has great reverence for Sebastian Bach, who, from his endless, inexhaustible wealth of combinations and harmonies, should be called Meer, not Bach ["sea," not "brook"]. Bach was the beau ideal of organists. "In my youth," said Beethoven, "I used to play the organ a great deal, but my nerves could not stand the power of that gigantic instrument; an organist who is master of his instrument I place foremost among *virtuosi.*" Beethoven spoke a great deal against the Viennese organists; the appointments, he said, were made by favor, or according to old-established usages. The man who had served longest received such an office, and so the most wretched players got promotion. He complained of the organs with defective pedals, and concluded by censuring the great and rich, who do nothing for goodness and art because they understand them not at all.

To my inquiries about many of his works—why, for instance, *Fidelio* did not receive universal approbation—he replied, "We Germans have no sufficiently cultivated singers for the part of Leonora; they are too cold and feelingless. The

Italians sing and act with their whole souls." Beethoven made a great many pertinent remarks about church music; church music should be performed by voices alone, except for a *gloria* or a piece of that kind. For this reason he preferred Palestrina, but it would be folly to imitate his form without possessing his spirit and religious feeling; besides, it would be impossible for the singers of the present day to sing his long-sustained notes with purity. He gave no opinion about Allegri's celebrated *Miserere*, not having heard it; many have been enraptured by it, many also have remained cold. He regarded those composers as models who unite nature with art.

He did not accede to my repeated request that he play something on the piano; he said he was too weak and poorly to be able to satisfy me, although I had assured him that I only cared about his ideas, not his manipulative dexterity. I saw by his countenance and his absent-minded manner that he was living in his own sublime tone world, and he gave me to understand by pantomime that I must not rob him any longer of his precious time. Otherwise he was kind and gentle; once, however, he looked exceedingly wrathful, when I spoke of his last symphonies as strange. He said, by his looks, "What does a blockhead like you know about my works, and what do the rest of the faultfinding wiseacres know about them? You haven't the energy, the wing of the eagle bold enough to follow me." . . . The great Beethoven, in person rather small, with a wild, distracted appearance, and gray, shaggy hair, now stood up defiantly aloof, dismissing me with the words, "Remember me to my old acquaintance, Joseph Schnabel."

Franz Grillparzer

Estranged From All the Customs of the World

Franz Grillparzer (1791-1872), the great German dramatist and poet, is regarded as the National poet of Austria. For some time he was even ranked with Goethe and Schiller. His *Recollections of Beethoven* offers a good sample of his prose style—lucid, penetrating, and suggestive. It was he who made the famous speech at Beethoven's grave.

Beethoven died before he could write the music for the poet's libretto.

A YEAR or two later I lived with my parents during the summer in the village of Heiligenstadt, near Vienna. Our rooms looked toward the garden; Beethoven had rented the room looking on the street. Both apartments were joined by a common passage which led to the staircase. My brother and I did not think much of the wonderful man as he rushed muttering past us. Although he had become stronger, he went about very carelessly and even shabbily dressed. But my mother—a passionate lover of music—was overcome with joy, and when she heard him playing the piano went out and stood in the passage—not, indeed, at his door, but in the middle near our door—and listened with the deepest attention. This may have happened a few times when once Beethoven's door suddenly opened and he stepped out, caught sight of my mother, hurried back, and then immediately, hat on head, rushed down the stairs and out of doors. From this moment he never touched his piano. To no purpose did my mother assure him (through his servant, as all other opportunity was cut off from her) that not only would no one listen to him any more, but that our door on the passage would remain closed, and that all her household, instead of using the common staircase, would go out by a roundabout way through the garden. Beethoven remained inflexible and left his piano untouched until winter came and we returned to town.

During one of the following summers I often visited my grandmother, who had a country house in the neighborhood of Döbling. Beethoven also lived in Döbling at that time. Opposite my grandmother's windows stood the tumble-down house of a peasant named Flehberger, notorious for his sloven-liness. This Flehberger possessed, besides his ugly house, a daughter Lisa, very pretty indeed, but by report rather frivo-lous. Beethoven seemed to take a great interest in the girl. I can see him still as he came up the Hirschgasse, a white hand-kerchief in his right hand trailing along the ground, and then standing at the Flehbergers' yard gate, inside which the frivo-lous fair one, on a hay cart, giggled whilst she maneuvered with a pitchfork. I never saw Beethoven speak to her, but he used to stand there silently and look in until at last the girl, whose taste inclined more to peasant boys, drove him into a rage either by a teasing remark or by obstinately ignoring his presence. Then he would rush away suddenly with a quick right-about-face—but the next time would stop and stand at the yard gate again. His interest even went so far that when the girl's father was put in jail on account of a vulgar brawl, Beethoven personally applied for his release before the as-sembled parish. On this occasion, however, he treated the worthy magistrate so roughly, in his usual fashion, that he was very nearly obliged to keep his imprisoned protégé unwilling company. Later I saw him often in the street, and a few times in the coffeehouse, where he conversed a good deal with a poet, one Ludwig Stoll, long since dead and (except in Lavali's *Collection of Small Singers*) forgotten.

People said they were planning an opera together, but it was incomprehensible how Beethoven could expect anything usable, anything more than silly fancies—though perhaps well

versified—from this empty babbler. In the meantime I myself
had made my bow to the public. *The Ancestress, Sappho,* and
Medea had appeared, when an invitation suddenly came from
Moritz Dietrichstein, the manager of the two town theaters,
for me to write a libretto for Beethoven, as the latter had applied to him to know if he could get me to do it. This invitation put me in no small predicament. On the one hand, I
doubted that if I wrote a libretto, in itself a difficult enough
task, Beethoven would be in condition to compose an opera.
For at this time he had become quite deaf and his last composition, in spite of its great worth, had taken on a character of
hardness which contradicted the arrangement of the voices.
On the other hand, the thought of serving as the instrument by
which a great man should produce a work at least highly interesting, outweighed all other considerations and I consented.
I chose the fable of Melusina, picked out, so far as possible,
the elements I proposed to use, and endeavored to adapt
myself as much as I could to the character of Beethoven's
latest tendencies by the use of predominating choruses, powerful finales, and an almost melodramatic third act.

I at first omitted to confer with the composer on the matter
because I wished to keep the freedom of my point of view;
later on details could be altered and the book given him to
compose or not. Indeed, with regard to this last, I did not put
any constraint on him when I sent him the book by the same
channel—Count Dietrichstein—through which the invitation
had come. I was determined that he should not be influenced
or embarrassed by any sort of personal consideration. A few
days later Schindler, Beethoven's business manager, the same
man who later wrote his biography, came to see me. He invited me to visit his master, who was unwell at the time. I
dressed and went at once to Beethoven, who lived at that time
in the suburbs. I found him lying in untidy night attire on a
rumpled bed with a book in his hand. At the head of the bed
was a small door; as I saw later, it led into the pantry, which

Beethoven looked after himself to a certain extent. For later on, when a servant came out with butter and eggs, he could not prevent himself, even in the middle of eager conversation, from casting a searching glance at the amount that was being carried out. What a pathetic picture of his disorderly domestic life! As we entered, Beethoven rose from the bed, stretched out his hand to me, welcomed me effusively and began at once to speak of the opera. "Your work lives," he said, pointing to his heart. "In a few days I shall have recovered and then I shall at once begin to compose. Only I don't know how to begin with the hunting chorus, which forms the introduction. Weber used four horns; I should take eight, and where will that lead to?"

Although I saw the necessity of this reasoning as well as he, I explained to him that the hunting chorus could be left out entirely without spoiling the whole work, with which concession he seemed well contented, and neither then nor later did he make any other exception to the text or ask for any other alteration. Then he wanted to insist on making some sort of contract with me. The proceeds of the opera should be equally divided between us and so forth. I accordingly made it clear to him that I had not thought of a salary or anything of the kind for my work. He wished that there should be at least an understanding between us, but I would make no contract with him and made it clear that he could do what he liked with the book. After much discussion, and much more writing when Beethoven could not hear, I got off by promising to visit him at Hetzendorf when he should be settled there. I hoped he had given up the business side of his idea. But after a few days my publisher, Wallishauser, came to me and said that Beethoven insisted on a contract being drawn up. If I could not make up my mind to this, I was to make over my rights in the book to Wallishauser. He could then settle the matter with Beethoven, who was quite agreeable to this arrangement. I was glad to leave the thing thus: I let Wallishauser pay me a moderate sum, gave him all my author's rights and thought no more about it. If he really made a contract I do not know; but I think he must have done so, otherwise Wallishauser would not have failed to din into my head, after his custom, the money he had risked.

I only call attention to all this in order to disprove what Beethoven is supposed to have said to Herr Rellstab, viz.: "He wanted everything different from what I wanted." He was at that time so set on composing the opera that he had already thought out the details of production which could only be entered into when it was completely finished. In the course of the summer I visited Beethoven, on his invitation, at Hetzendorf, along with Herr Schindler. I do not know whether Schindler told me on the way or whether someone had said before that Beethoven had been prevented by the pressure of work previously undertaken from starting the composition of the opera. On that account I avoided talking about it. We went for a walk and entertained ourselves as well as was possible under such circumstances, half-speaking, half-writing as we went. It touches me still to remember how Beethoven, as we sat at table, went into the next room and brought out five bottles of wine. One he set before Schindler's plate, one before his own, and three he stood in a row before me, apparently to make clear to me in his simple, good-natured way that I should be master of the feast. When I went back to town—without Schindler, who remained in Hetzendorf—Beethoven insisted on accompanying me. He sat down with me in the open carriage and insisted on driving with me out of the immediate neighborhood and as far as the gates of the town, where he got out and, after a hearty handshake, set out alone on the long journey home. As he got out of the carriage I saw a paper lying on the seat. I thought he had forgotten it and beckoned him to come back. He only shook his head and with a loud laugh, as at a capital trick, ran off still faster in the opposite direction. I unrolled the paper and

found that it contained the exact sum I had fixed on with my
driver. His mode of life had so estranged him from all the
customs and usages of the world that it never occurred to
him what an offense such a proceeding would have been
under different circumstances. I, however, took his action as
it was meant and laughingly paid the coachman with the
money thus given.

Dr. L

Shadows of the Approaching End

In the *Deutsche Musikzeitung* for 1862 there appeared an article entitled "Beethoven at Gneixendorf." The author signed himself Dr. L.
The master is at the estate of his brother Johann, an apothecary of Linz
in Upper-Austria. The time of the visit is autumn 1826. His work is
done.

The particulars given by Dr. L. show the rapid decline of Beethoven's
bodily and mental powers. His burdens seem too heavy for him; there
is little trace of his old self.

CONVINCED that the smallest details are of importance which
serve to increase our knowledge of this incomparable composer, I applied, some time ago, to my early friend, K——, an
apothecary in Langenlois, asking him to tell me all he knew
about Beethoven's sojourn at Gneixendorf, in lower Austria,
a country seat belonging to Johann van Beethoven. Both he
and the present owner of the estate acceded most willingly to
my request. I give in the slight, fragmentary form in which I
received it, all that could be gathered by these trustworthy
inquirers.

One day Johann van Beethoven, accompanied by his
brother, Ludwig, and several other people, went from Gneix-

endorf to Langenfeld to visit the surgeon, Karrer, who was a friend of the family. He was not at home, having been summoned to a patient; but Frau Karrer, feeling highly flattered by a visit from the squire, entertained the party with all the hospitality in her power. The composer was sitting modestly and silently on the bench by the stove; and the mistress, mistaking him for a servant, filled an earthenware jug with wine, and handed it to him, saying kindly, "Here is a draught for you, too."

When the surgeon returned late in the evening, he at once guessed from the description who it was who had sat at the stove, and exclaimed, "My dear wife, what have you done! The greatest composer of the age has been in our house today, and you treated him in that disrespectful way!"

Johann van Beethoven happening to have some business with the syndic Sterz, at Langenlois, Ludwig accompanied him thither. During the somewhat lengthy interview, Ludwig stood at the office door, motionless and uninterested. Sterz bowed very respectfully when he left, and then said to his clerk Fux—a music enthusiast and especially Beethoven's admirer—"Who do you think the man was standing at the door?" Fux replied, "As you were so polite to him, sir, I can only suppose that he is a person of some importance; otherwise, I should have taken him for an imbecile." Fux was not a little horrified when his master told him the name of the man he had thought a fool.

This must be attributed, adds my informant, to the indifferent, apathetic bearing which Beethoven's deafness caused him to assume, for his expression of countenance was anything but one of imbecility, especially the wonderfully striking and almost wild flash of his eyes. To this I can bear personal testimony, since I, too, was fortunate enough to come face to face with this extraordinary man, even to attract his attention, although in no very agreeable manner. Being a youth, fresh from the country, I had not acquired the nimbleness and dexterity necessary for threading one's way through the crowded thoroughfare of the metropolis. So one day I ran against a man, who transfixed me with a penetrating glance, and walked on. I shall never forget that eye, into whose shining depths I had gazed. But is it surprising that, trying to reconcile the slovenly dress and sunburned face of the stranger with his look of intelligence and superiority, I came to the conclusion that I had fallen in with one of those shrewd sharpers who frequent large towns? With this idea in my mind, I used to look at him, whenever we met, with curiosity and, I regret to say, with anything but respect. He observed this, for he once darted at me from his small bright eyes a look half of astonishment and half of contempt, and then took no further notice. After I had been told by a friend who he was, I bowed to the ground every time I saw him, but he ignored my politeness as he had my rudeness.

*   *   *

Michael Krenn, who died a year ago, was one of the servants of the Gneixendorf establishment while Beethoven was staying there; and Michael, one of Krenn's three sons who are still living, was in service there at the same time. He gives the following account:

Michael Krenn was engaged by the mistress of the house to wait upon Beethoven. At first, however, the cook used to make his bed every day. One morning she could not help laughing at Beethoven as he sat at his table, waving his hands, beating time with his feet, and singing or humming. Beethoven, happening to turn around and see her, without more ado sent her out of the room. Michael was going to run away with her, but Beethoven detained him, gave him sixpence, and told him not to be afraid, that in future he must make the bed and keep the room tidy.

Michael was obliged to come up early, but generally had to knock a long time before the door was opened. Beethoven used to rise at half-past five, and sit down to write, beating time with feet and hands, and singing or humming. At first Michael used to slip away when he felt inclined to laugh, but he gradually grew quite accustomed to these proceedings. Breakfast was at 7:30; after which Beethoven always hurried out into the fields, where he would go along, waving his hands, screaming, walking by turns rapidly and slowly, then suddenly stand still, and write in a kind of pocketbook. One day, on returning home, he found he had dropped this. "Michael," he said, "run and fetch my book; I must have it at any cost, you are sure to find it." At half-past twelve, Beethoven returned to dinner, then stayed in his room till about three o'clock, when he again went out till sunset, after which he never left the house. Supper was at half-past seven; then he went to his room, and wrote till ten, when he went to bed. Beethoven occasionally played the piano, which did not stand in his room, but in the drawing room. Beethoven's parlor and bedroom, which no one but Michael entered, was the corner apartment, looking over the garden and courtyard; it is now a billiard room.

While Beethoven was out walking in the morning, Michael had to put the room in order. He often found money on the floor. When he gave it to Beethoven, he asked him where he had found it, and when Michael pointed out the spot where the money was, made him a present of it. This happened three or four times, then Michael ceased to find any money. He always had to sit with Beethoven in the evening, and answer in writing any questions that were put to him. Beethoven often asked him what had been said about him at dinner or supper. One day the lady of the house sent Michael to Stein, with five florins, to buy some wine and fish. Michael carelessly lost the money on the way, and returned at half-past twelve in dismay. His mistress asked where the fish was, and when he told her of the loss of the money, she immediately discharged him. Directly Beethoven came in to dinner, he asked where Michael was, and the lady told him what had occurred. Beethoven was fearfully angry, gave her five florins, and vehemently insisted that Michael should return at once. Beethoven never appeared at dinner again, but had it brought to him in his room, where he also took his breakfast. According to Michael, Beethoven, even before this scene, scarcely ever spoke to his sister-in-law, and very rarely to his brother. He also relates that Beethoven wished to take him with him to Vienna.

The present proprietor recently received, from two old peasants, a confirmation of Michael Krenn's statement as to Beethoven's strange behavior in the meadows at Gneixendorf.

They first thought he was mad, and avoided him; but they gradually grew accustomed to him, and, as soon as they learned that he was the squire's brother, always gave him a courteous salute, which, as he was always buried in thought, he seldom or never returned.

One of these peasants, then a young man, had a little adventure with Beethoven. He was driving a pair of young oxen, unaccustomed to the yoke, from Ziegelofen to the castle, when he met Beethoven screaming and violently gesticulating. The man called out, "Quieter, please"; but Beethoven took no heed. The oxen were frightened, and ran up a steep bank. The driver with difficulty stopped them, turned them round, and led them back to the road. Another time Beethoven was returning from Ziegelofen, singing and waving his hands; again the man called out, but in vain, and with their tails in the air the oxen rushed toward the castle, where someone stopped them. When the driver at length came up, he asked, "Who is that man who frightened my oxen?" When he was told that he was the squire's brother, he replied, "He is a pretty sort of brother!"

Anselm Hüttenbrenner

The Last Moments

Anselm Hüttenbrenner, composer (1794-1868), a friend of Beethoven, hurried to Vienna from his native town, Graz, upon learning of the master's fatal illness.

More than thirty years later he described his death in a letter to United States Consul Alexander W. Thayer, dated August 20, 1860. Thayer is famous for his *Life of Beethoven* and other contributions to Beethoven literature.

When I entered Beethoven's bedroom on March 26, 1827, about three o'clock in the afternoon, I found there Herr Hofrath Breuning and his son, Frau van Beethoven (wife of Johann van Beethoven, landowner and apothecary at Linz), and my friend Joseph Teltscher, a portrait painter.

Professor Schindler was, I believe, also present. After a while these gentlemen left, with little hope of finding the composer alive when they returned. During Beethoven's last moments, no one was in the room except Frau Johann van Beethoven and myself. He had been lying unconscious, and struggling with death from three till past five o'clock, when there came a loud peal of thunder, accompanied by a flash of lightning, which vividly illuminated the room. (Snow was on the ground.) After this unexpected phenomenon, which made a deep impression upon me, Beethoven opened his eyes, raised his right hand, and gazed fixedly upward for some seconds, with clenched fist, and a solemn threatening expression, as if he would say, "I defy you, you adverse powers! Depart! God is with me." Or his appearance may be described as that of a brave general, crying out to his fainting troops, "Courage, soldiers! Forward! Trust in me! Victory is ours!"

His hand dropped, and his eyes were half-closed. My right hand supported his head, my left lay on his breast. He gave no sign of life. The spirit of the great master had passed from this false world to the kingdom of truth. I closed his half-shut eyes, and kissed his brow, mouth, hands, and eyes. At my request Frau van Beethoven cut a lock of his hair, and gave it me as a sacred memorial of Beethoven's dying hour.

FRANZ SCHUBERT

Born: Vienna, Austria
January 31, 1797
Died: Vienna, Austria
November 19, 1828

FRANZ SCHUBERT was the son of a poor and simple schoolmaster in the Liechtental suburb of Vienna, Austria. His mother was one Elisabeth Vietz, an orphan who was a domestic servant before her marriage. Franz was the twelfth of their fourteen children.

All his life Schubert was poor. From his earliest years he displayed a passion for music; he practiced his first exercises on a worn-out old piano at home, without any teacher to guide him. At eleven he became a choirboy at the Chapel Royal and a student at the Imperial Seminary. The physical hardships he suffered during this period were appalling; he had no money, his food was scant and of the poorest quality. Nevertheless he soon began composing sonatas, masses, songs—even symphonies—and by the age of eighteen he had already written his *Erlkoenig* and *Heidenroeslein,* destined to become world famous.

He started teaching school, like his father, but after a short time he left his post to live by his music. Without the help of his many friends he would certainly have starved; he simply could not handle the practical realities of life. In his short span of years he composed over six hundred songs, much chamber music—such as his famous A Minor and D Minor quartets—piano sonatas, symphonies—the *Unfinished* alone would entitle him to a place among the world's foremost makers of music.

Ferdinand Schubert

Recollections of My Brother

The composer's father was a poor schoolteacher in the Viennese
suburb of Liechtental. Fourteen children were born of his first marriage,
but only five survived to maturity.

Ferdinand (1794-1859) was Franz Schubert's favorite brother; it
was in his arms that the composer died at thirty-one years of age.

Throughout their lives they exchanged letters, which are an important
source of information for Schubert biographers.

His FATHER, Franz Schubert, was the son of a peasant from
Neudorf in Moravia; he studied in Vienna and in 1784 went
to the Leopoldstadt as school assistant to his brother. His
schoolmaster's talent, supported by an honest and noble
character, secured him in 1786 the post of schoolmaster in the
parish of "the Fourteen Holy Friends in Need" at Liechtental.
Married to Elisabeth Vietz, he begot fourteen children, of
whom however only five remained alive: Ignaz, Ferdinand,
Karl, our Franz and Theresia. Married a second time, he begot five more children, of whom four still survive.

In Franz his father perceived great talent for music from
early childhood. Dear, good Franz now received lessons in
pianoforte playing from his brother Ignaz. Later he was
taught violin and pianoforte playing, as well as singing, by
the choirmaster Michael Holzer, who several times asserted
with tears in his eyes that he had never yet had such a pupil.
"For," said he, "whenever I wished to impart something new
to him, he always knew it already. I often looked at him in
silent wonder."

Schubert was then some ten years old, and in his eleventh
year he was a first soprano in the Liechtental church. Even
at that age he delivered everything with the most appropriate

expression; in those days he also played a violin solo in the organ loft of the church and composed small songs, string quartets and pianoforte pieces.

His rapid progress in music astonished his father, who was intent on affording him the opportunity of further education, and entering him at the Imperial Seminary for that purpose.

In October 1808, our Schubert was thus presented to the Imperial Seminary directorate and had to sing for his trial. The boy wore a light blue, whitish coat, so that the other people, including the many other children who were also to be admitted to the Seminary, made fun of him among themselves with such remarks as "That is doubtless a miller's son; he won't fail," etc. However, the schoolmaster's son made a sensation, in spite of his white frock coat; the Court Musical Directors Salieri and Eybler and the singing master Korner were much impressed by his singing as well as by his certainty in sight reading the trial songs submitted to him. He was accordingly admitted. He parted most sorrowfully with his father, mother, brothers and sisters; but the gold braid on his uniform seemed to make him calm and confident again.

At the Imperial Seminary he now had the opportunity of being present at certain musical performances. The great zeal he showed at the domestic music making, where in the absence of the music master Ruzicka he conducted the symphonies and overtures, as well as his compositions (such as *Hagar's Lament,* the *Corpse Fantasy,* a fantasy for pianoforte duet, string quartets, etc.), induced the first Court Musical Director Salieri to give him lessons in composition. Here again Schubert showed extraordinary gifts, to his master's astonishment, so that the latter, asked how Schubert was faring, replied: "That one knows everything; he composes operas, songs, quartets, symphonies, what you will."

For his father and his elder brothers it was an uncommon pleasure to play quartets with him. They did this mostly in the holiday months. The youngest of them all was the most sensitive. Whenever a mistake was made, no matter how small, he would look the guilty one in the face, either seriously or sometimes with a smile; if Papa, who played the cello, was in the wrong, he would say nothing at first, but if the mistake was repeated, he would say quite shyly and smilingly: "Sir, there must be a mistake somewhere!" and our good father would gladly be taught by him. In these quartets Franz always played the viola, his brother Ignaz second violin, Ferdinand (whom Franz favored most among his brothers) first, and Papa the violoncello.

To induce Schubert to compose for his brothers was an easy matter. Thus he wrote thirty minuets for Ignaz, together with trios, in a very easy style for the pianoforte; for Ferdinand a quintet overture, a violin concerto, a congratulatory cantata, and so on. In 1820 he wrote for the same brother six antiphons for Palm Sunday, in not more than thirty minutes (the manuscript of which, written in black chalk, still exists). For his Father's name day, he composed a trio for male voices with guitar accompaniment, the words for this having been written by himself as well. Altogether his rapidity in writing down his compositions was amazing. Schubert's very first pianoforte composition (1810) was a Fantasy for four hands in which more than twelve different movements occur, and indeed each with a character of its own: it consists of thirty-two very closely written pages. This was followed by two smaller ones. A peculiarity is that each of these Fantasies closes in a key different from that in which it began.

Soon the little master tried his hand at string quartets too; some twelve or fifteen gradually made their appearance.

Songs he composed with particular pleasure, even as a boy. His first seems to have been *Hagar's Lament*. How this little minstrel, young as he still was, knew how to set the musical accompaniment to poems of such great minds is incomprehensible.

When at last he left the Seminary owing to his extraordinary attachment to music, and later on was three times summoned by conscription to enlist as a soldier, he finally decided to serve as an assistant schoolmaster.

And indeed he did considerable service for three years at his father's school, where he kept strict order. During that time he was again active in the choir of the Liechtental Church every Sunday and holiday, and it was doubtless this which induced him to compose a grand Mass (1814), which made not a little sensation at Liechtental and was also performed ten days later at St. Augustine's Church in Vienna.

It was a touching sight to see young Schubert, who was the most youthful of all the musicians participating, conducting his composition. How seriously he did it, and with what care, so that the old gentlemen said, "Had he been Court Musical Director for the last thirty years, he could not do better." But it will be long before any music is again performed with such enthusiasm as this first Mass of his was. For his first teacher was choirmaster, his brother Ferdinand was organist, an excellent friend and his favorite singer the soprano, and the rest of musicians consisted of none but friends of his youth or people among whom he had grown up. In his heart's joy his father at that time presented him with a five-octave pianoforte.

Anton Holzapfel

In School

Anton Holzapfel (1792-1868) was a friend of Franz even in grammar school; theirs was a friendship that remained unspoiled throughout the composer's life. Holzapfel became a municipal councilor in Vienna.

At eleven Schubert began attending the Imperial Seminary and had to wear a gold-bordered uniform. He also became chorister and played violin in the school orchestra.

When I came into closer touch with Schubert he was in the 4th grammar form, a short, sturdy boy with a friendly round face, and strongly marked features. He was not a particular favorite of the clerical professors, yet he was no particular trouble to them by excessive liveliness. He proved that he possessed one of those quiet deep minds which made superficial pedagogues misjudge his silent nature as a sign of little talent. He was even then far in advance of his years mentally, as was proved by a poem written at that period which I kept for a long time but have since lost, and which was written in the style of Klopstock's *Odes*, hardly comprehended by us pupils, but which had for its theme God's omnipotence in the Universe. . . . Schubert had, as long as he was at the seminary, the tiresome task of looking after the music as well as the instruments of the orchestra, to see that they were properly strung, attend to the tallow-candle illuminations, give out the parts and place them on the musicstands, besides playing the violin.

Joseph Freiherr von Spaun

Shy, Awkward, Shabbily Dressed

When Schubert was a pupil at the Imperial Seminary of Vienna, he met Josef von Spaun (1788-1865). Schubert was his junior by nine years. They became great friends and Franz was indebted to him for presents and many acts of kindness.

From the beginning Spaun proved to be one of Schubert's truest and most disinterested friends. Even when they were separated by long distances and by years, Spaun continued to give evidence of his sincere

esteem for the musician. The two friends kept up an animated correspondence. Schubert dedicated to him his Sonata Opus 78 and several
songs.

SCHUBERT told me at that time that he had already composed
a great deal, a sonata, a fantasy, a little opera, and was now
going to write a mass. His difficulty was that he had no note-
paper and no money to buy it, so that he had to line ordinary
paper and often could not get hold of even that sort. I secretly supplied him with big sheets of paper, which he consumed
in unbelievable quantities. He composed extraordinarily fast
and regularly took time from his studies for the purpose, so
that his schoolwork certainly suffered. His father, otherwise
a very kind man, discovered why he was falling behind in
school and made a stormy scene, again forbidding him to
spend his time on music. But the young artist's wings were too
strong now, his ascent could no longer be restrained.

He often played me sonatas and other compositions of his,
all of them even then original and melodious. He had finished
whole masses, operas, even symphonies, but these he gradually destroyed and said they were only exercises. . . .

But around this time people were beginning to take notice
of his talent. The old court organist Ruziczka was commissioned to give Schubert lessons in ground bass. After the
second lesson the worthy old man, much moved, said to me
in Schubert's presence, "I cannot teach him anything, he has
learned it from the dear Lord!"

The barriers were down. His father recognized the boy's
great talent and let him go ahead and do as he liked. Now
came a series of songs and his first sonatas; he did a few
quartets at this time too. One day he sang a few little songs
of Klopstock to me and I was delighted with them. He looked
me candidly in the eyes and asked, "Do you really think I'll
ever be something?" I embraced him and said, "You're already something, something important, and time will make

you something much more important!" Then he said quite
meekly, "In my secret heart I hope so too, that I can make
something of myself—but who can do anything after Beethoven?"

During vacation time I offered to take him to the opera
sometimes. He had never heard opera music. So as to be able
to go often, my means being small, we had to set up our
headquarters on the fifth floor. The first opera he heard was
the *Schweizerfamilie* by Weigl. He was enraptured; both
Milder and Vogl aroused his unqualified admiration. Later
he heard Cherubini's *Medea, Johann of Paris, Aschenbroedl*
of Isouard, the *Magic Flute,* and so on. He always left the
theater absolutely beside himself with delight at what he had
heard, but Gluck's *Iphigénie en Tauride* affected him most of
all. This wonderful work transported him; he asserted that
there simply could not be anything more beautiful in this
world. The voice of Milder pierced his heart, he said, and if
everything else in the opera had not been so beautiful he
would have declared the aria of Iphigénie in the second act
with the women's chorus to be the most wonderful thing he
had ever heard. He regretted not knowing Vogl, he wanted
to fall at his feet for his achievement as Orestes. When we
left the theater we met the poet Koerner, with whom I was
very good friends. I introduced to him my little composer,
of whom he already knew something from me. Koerner was
glad to meet him and encouraged him to live for the art that
would bring him happiness. Koerner was as enthusiastic as
we were over *Iphigénie*—which, to the shame of the Viennese
be it spoken, played to an almost empty house. He invited
us to have supper with him at the Blumenstoeckl in the Ball-
gassel. While we were sitting there, still wallowing in the
memory of what we had just heard, a university professor at
the next table started making fun of our enthusiasm. He
stated that Milder had crowed like a cock, that she had no
idea how to sing, being incapable of either a run or a trill,

that it was an outrage for her to be presented as a great singer, and that Orestes had feet like an elephant. Our displeasure at these impudent utterances knew no bounds. Koerner and Schubert jumped up in a rage, the latter upsetting his full glass of beer simultaneously. It came to an exchange of heated words; the opponent being obstinate, these might well have led to deeds of violence had not a few pacifying voices, coming to our support, allayed the storm.

❋   ❋   ❋

One afternoon I went with Mayrhofer to see Schubert, who was at that time with his father in the Himmelpfortgrund. We found Schubert all afire, reading the *Erlkoenig* out loud. He walked up and down several times with the book, then suddenly sat down, and in the shortest time conceivable the magnificent ballad was on paper. We ran over with it to the seminary, since Schubert had no pianoforte, and there, that very evening, the *Erlkoenig* was sung to enchanted hearers. The old organist Ruziczka then sat down and played through all the parts himself, without the vocal; he played it with a deep interest and was much moved by the composition. A few of us were disposed to find fault with a certain dissonance that recurred several times, but Ruziczka sounded it again on the piano and showed us how necessary it was, how it corresponded to the text, made us see that it was actually beautiful and resolved itself perfectly.

Schubert, who always had to sing his songs himself, began to speak often of his desire to find a singer; his old longing to meet Hofopernsaenger Vogl now grew more intense. Our little circle resolved that Vogl must be won for the Schubert *Lieder*. The task was a difficult one; Vogl was highly inaccessible. Schober . . . had a few connections with the theater and these somewhat facilitated his approach to Vogl. He told the latter in glowing terms of Schubert's wonderful compositions and asked him to try them out. Vogl replied that he had music creeping out of his ears, that he was fed up with music, that he was more interested in avoiding music altogether than in becoming acquainted with any more of it. He said he had heard of a hundred and one young geniuses and had always been disappointed, and so it would doubtless be with Schubert. He wanted to hear no more of the matter, they were to leave him in peace. We were all painfully affected by this refusal, all except Schubert, who said he had expected just that answer and found it quite understandable.

Meanwhile Vogl was being beleaguered by Schober and others of Schubert's supporters, and finally he promised to come to Schober one evening and see what was in it, as he said.

He arrived at Schober's, very grave and punctual at the appointed hour, and when poor insignificant-looking little Schubert made a somewhat awkward bow and in his embarrassment stammered a few disconnected words about the honor of the acquaintance, the singer sneered a bit contemptuously. Our hearts misgave us; matters were beginning badly. "Well, what have you got?" Vogl asked finally. "Accompany me." With that he picked up the sheet lying nearest to hand, Mayrhofer's poem *Augenlied*, a pretty song, very melodious but not important.

Vogl hummed more than he sang, then said somewhat coldly, "Not bad." Now followed *Memnon, Ganymed* and other songs; he was accompanied but sang these also with only half a voice. He became more and more friendly as he sang, but he left without promising to come again. On his way out he slapped Schubert on the shoulder and said to him, "There's something in you, but you're too little of an actor, too little of a charlatan, you waste your wonderful ideas without making the most of them." To others he expressed himself far more favorably about Schubert; the songs had impressed him deeply. He returned to our circle uninvited, asked Schubert to come to him, rehearsed songs with him;

and when he realized the overwhelming impression his rendi-
tions made on us—on Schubert himself and the whole circle
of hearers—he grew more and more enthusiastic about the
songs. In the end he became Schubert's most ardent votary,
and instead of following his former intention of giving up
music, he turned to it newly inspired.

The delights that now fell to our portion are indescribable.
Blessed hours when we listened to what rejoiced us, shook
us, inspired us, often moved us to tears. Vogl had taken a
personal liking to the young artist and frequently helped him
out; Schubert accompanied him several times to Styer, to
Linz, to St. Florian, to Gmunden, to Gastein. Everywhere
they went the magnificent songs made the same profound
impression. The present generation has not been granted the
enjoyment of such pleasures. . . .

Gradually Schubert's reputation spread. Matthaeus Col-
lin, a relative of mine, then tutor to the Duke of Reichstadt,
had often heard Schubert at my house; he asked me to bring
the composer, along with Vogl, to his home, where he would
have various artist friends to meet Schubert. On this occasion
there were present the Patriarch Pyrker, Count Moriz Dietrichstein, Hofrat Mosel, Hofrat Hammer, Karoline Pichler
and many others; all were absolutely enraptured with the
songs. Hofrat Mosel, himself a distinguished musician, repeatedly declared that he had never heard anything like it.
One of the harpist songs, *An die Tueren will ich schleichen*
("I will creep to the doors"), he pronounced a masterpiece.

So widened the circle of those who recognized Schubert's
extraordinary talents and paid his songs their tribute—but he
was still without higher patronage and his situation was
really oppressive. There was not a publisher who would have
ventured to pay even a small sum for his wonderful creations. For years he remained the victim of money worries;
the man so rich in melody could not afford a piano. But
his troubles did not in the least lessen his diligence; he had

to write, it was his life. And he was always cheerful. For many years he was my guest, the guest of an old friend, at sociable, gay suppers, which mostly went on past midnight; he liked coming and was good company. If it was late he did not go home but made himself comfortable on a very modest couch in my room, where he always slept soundly, often with his perennial eyeglasses on. In the morning he would sit down in his shirt and trousers and write the most beautiful things, mostly songs, and once in a while he surprised us dance lovers with the loveliest German dances and *ecossaises,* then much in fashion. Gaby could play these delightful dances with such fire that he quite electrified the dancers. Schubert himself never danced.

❀   ❀   ❀

For a time he was in a darker mood and seemed somehow ailing. When I asked him what was the trouble he said only, "You will soon hear and understand." Then one day he said to me, "Come to Schober's today, I'll sing you a cycle of terrifying songs. I'm very curious what you'll say to it. I've never before been so affected by songs as by these." He sang through the whole *Winterreise* for us in an agitated voice. We were quite confounded at the dismal mood of these songs. Schober said he liked only one of them, *Der Lindenbaum.* Schubert answered simply, "I like these songs more than all the others, and you will like them too some day." And he was right; we were soon ardent admirers of the melancholy cycle, which Vogl sang in masterly fashion. There are probably no more beautiful German songs in existence, and they were his own swan song. From then on he was not well, ailing but never so noticeably as to cause anxiety. Many believed, and still believe, that Schubert was a tough, insensible fellow whom nothing could touch; those who knew him better realized how deeply his creations affected him and with what intensive labor he gave them birth. Nobody who has once seen him at work composing in the morning, radiant, eyes glowing, even his speech different, like that of a somnambulist—can ever forget it. . . .

Anselm Hüttenbrenner

Schubert's Only Love

In 1814 the seventeen-year-old Schubert composed his first Mass. It was sung on Sunday, October 16th, at the Liechtental. The famous composer Salieri boasted after the performance that Schubert was his pupil.

A fourteen-year-old girl, Theresa Grob, sang the soprano part. Young Schubert was deeply in love with her. He wrote continuously for her, many songs and hymns. His hopeless material circumstances seem to have been responsible for their failure to marry. She was forced by her mother to marry a master baker.

Anselm Hüttenbrenner (1794-1868), musician, composer, friend of Beethoven and of Schubert, heard the story of this love from Schubert himself.

DURING a country walk which I took with Schubert in 1821 I asked him if he had ever been in love. Because he showed himself to be so cold and unresponsive toward the fair sex, I had formed the opinion that he disliked women. "Oh, no," he replied. "I loved one with all my heart, and she loved me in return. She was somewhat younger than I, and she sang the soprano solos magnificently and with deep feeling in a Mass I composed. She was not beautiful, and her face was marked with smallpox, but she was good—good to the heart. For three years I hoped to marry her, but I could find no situation, which caused both of us great sorrow. She then married another man, because her parents wished it. I still love her, and since then no other can please me so well or better. The fact is, she was not destined for me."

Franz and Fritz von Hartmann

Schubertiads

It is not possible to talk of Schubert without mentioning the "Schubert-iads." The young composer was unknown to the larger public but had around him a circle of friends who recognized his genius. They gathered in his honor several times a week, at the apartment of one or another member. They played games, danced, and made speeches, but Schubert's compositions were the staple of entertainment. Schubert himself played and sang; a further attraction was the famous singer Vogl who attended regularly. Some of the closest friends would go to an inn after the Schubertiads. Occasionally the wine flowed a bit too freely.

There is no better way to give a picture of the Schubertiads than with some lines from the diaries of the two young brothers Hartmann. Although the names of the different participants mean nothing to us today, their number and variety give us the flavor of these gay evenings.

19. November 1826: With Fritz to the "Anchor," where there was a large gathering, including Schwind, who presented me with a small nosegay, Schubert and Bauernfeld. Spaun joined us later, too. At 11.30 we parted.

*   *   *

15. December 1826: I went to Spaun's, where there was a big, big Schubertiad. The Arneth, Witteczek, Kurzrock and Pompe couples, the mother-in-law of the Court and State Chancellery probationer Witteczek; Dr. Watteroth's widow, Betty Wanderer, and the painter Kupelwieser with his wife, Grillparzer, Schober, Schwind, Mayrhofer and his landlord Huber, tall Huber, Derffel, Baurenfeld, Gahy (who played gloriously *à quatre mains* with Schubert) and Vogl, who sang almost thirty splendid songs. Baron Schlechta and other Court probationers and secretaries were also there. I was almost moved to tears, being in a particularly excited state

of mind today, by the trio of the 5th of March, which always reminds me of my dear, good mother. When the music was done, there was grand feeding and then dancing. But I was not at all in a courting mood. I danced twice with Betty and once with each of the Witteczek, Kurzrock and Pompe ladies. At 12.30 we saw Betty home and went to the "Anchor," where we still found Schober, Schubert, Schwind, Derffel and Baurenfeld. Merry. Then home. To bed at 1 o'clock.

*   *   *

30. December 1826: We go to the "Anchor," where Schober, Schwind, Schubert, Bauernfeld and Derffel are. Spaun comes later, and Derffel and Bauernfeld leave. The talk is of chivalric novels, tall stories of the Seminary, etc. As we step out of the "Anchor," everything is deeply snowed under. We itch for a game of snowballs, which we engage in immediately. Spaun is on my side, Fritz and Schober on Schwind's. Schober always hits me hard and without fail, and I him or Schwind in particular. Spaun gloriously protects himself against the shots with his open umbrella. Schubert and Haas take no part in the fight. Home, where the house steward was rude because we rang loudly.

*   *   *

10. February 1827: At 7 o'clock I went with Franz to Schober's, pursuant to a long-standing invitation, which Josef von Spaun had repeated when he came to fetch us this forenoon. At Schober's I met among others Spaun, Gahy, Enderes, Schubert, Schwind and his brother, Bauernfeld; the ladies, little known to me, included Netty Hoenig, Fraeulein Puffer, Leopoldine Blahetka (the famous pianoforte player), Fraeulein Gruenwedel, etc. Most of the ladies were beautiful, which made a very pretty picture. For all that I did not enjoy myself very much at first, as I had the ill luck to dance the first cotillon with the only ugly girl among those present, a

misfortune I had perforce to endure. Her name was Fraeulein
Rinna. At the second cotillon I was more fortunate: I danced
with Fraeulein Blahetka. The music was splendid, for it consisted of nothing but waltzes by Schubert, played partly by
the composer himself and partly by Gahy. We remained at
Schober's until after 2 o'clock in the morning.

*   *   *

4. March 1827: We went to Schober's, where we met Spaun,
Schwind, Bauernfeld and Kriehuber with his wife and sister-
in-law ("the Flower of the Land"), because Schubert, who is
Schober's lodger, had invited us to hear some new compositions of his. Everybody was assembled, but friend Schubert
did not come. At last Schwind undertook to sing several of
Schubert's earlier songs, which enchanted us. At half-past
nine we all went to the "Castle of Eisenstadt," where Schubert
too arrived soon after us and won all hearts by his amiable
simplicity, although he had deceived our hopes by his artist's
negligence.

*   *   *

21. April 1827: At 7 o'clock we went to Spaun's with Maurus
Mayrhofer, Enk and Haas. There was a Schubertiad and an
enormous attendance, including uncle Franz in addition to
the members of the party on the 15th of December of last
year, and he was so delighted with it that he assured us he
had never heard anything so magnificent. We had *Bounds of
Mankind, Sunset Glow, The Wayfarer and the Moon, In the
Open, Who Dares, Dithyramb, Romance* from *Ivanhoe, Romance* from *Montrose* by Walter Scott, *Fragment from Aes-
chylus,* etc. Wonderful! We drank brotherhood with Otten-
walt, and so did Enk! At 12 o'clock we left there, and a large
party went to Bogner's Café, where, however, for that very
reason it was no longer particularly jolly, and the glorious
impressions of the Schubertiad were somewhat effaced.

*   *   *

Franz von Schober

Schubert's Death

Franz von Schober (1798-1883) was a wealthy man, who was also a poet. Schubert was still slaving at the school when Schober sought him out and helped, at least for a time, to put him in a position more suitable to his genius. Schober, who had a life without serious hardship, survived Schubert by fifty-five years.

Schober, together with Ferdinand, wrote the story of Schubert's death.

AT THE BEGINNING of September, Franz left Schober's house and went to his brother Ferdinand, who, after leaving the suburb of St. Ulrich, had settled in a new street attached to the Wieden suburb. The house which the brothers occupied had unfortunately been quite recently built, and Franz had moved into that quarter by advice of the Court physician, Dr. von Rinna, thinking that from such a starting point he could get away with less trouble and loss of time than would have been possible from the heart of the city; we hoped also, by air and exercise, to get some alleviation of his sufferings caused by constant giddiness and rush of blood to the head. The lodgings he had vacated at Schober's were for the future retained on his account.

At this time Schubert began to sicken, and physicians were called in. For a while he seemed to be getting better. At the beginning of October, accompanied by Ferdinand and two friends, he made a short excursion to Unter-Waltersdorf, and from thence to Eisenstadt, where he lingered for some time, pilgrim-like, at the grave of Joseph Haydn. During this five days' journey he was very moderate in the way of eating and drinking, but for all that his good spirits and cheerfulness never failed him.

On returning to Vienna, however, his illness became more alarming. One evening, at the end of October, he was dining at an hotel, and had hardly swallowed the first morsel of fish, when he suddenly threw down the knife and fork on his plate, declaring the food was absolutely odious to him, and tasted like poison. From that moment Franz took little else but medicine. He tried to cheer himself by fresh air and exercise, and occasionally took walks in the neighborhood. Early on the morning of November 3rd, he walked from the Neu-Wieden to Hernals, to attend a performance of a *Latin Requiem* composed by Ferdinand. This was the last music he ever heard. After divine service he again walked for three hours; but on his return home, complained greatly of fatigue.

He seems, however, soon afterward to have partially recovered, and to have entertained no apprehension of any serious illness, for on November 4th he called with Lanz, a pianoforte teacher still living at Vienna, on the court organist Sechter, for the purpose of discussing with the latter the subject of some studies in fugue writing, for which he desired Sechter's assistance. They agreed to go through the exercises by Marpurg's together, so far as that work might serve their purpose, and fixed on the time and number of hours which Schubert proposed to devote to the purpose. The project, Sechter says, was never realized, for Schubert's steadily increasing illness soon confined him entirely to his sickbed. The history of our composer's life was thus robbed of one of the strangest spectacles—that of Herr Sechter and Franz Schubert aborbed in a joint musical labor.

On November 11th Schubert's increasing weakness compelled him to keep to his bed. He felt, he said, no actual pain, but sleeplessness and depression reduced the once strong and healthy man to a state of great misery.

At first Dr. Rinna treated him, and Schubert wrote a letter about him (the last he ever did write) to Schober, a personal friend of the physician. Unfortunately Dr. Rinna himself fell ill, and a doctor by the name of Behring undertook his duty as a deputy, and sent daily bulletins of Schubert's health to his friend Schober.

During his illness, which lasted only nine days, Schubert was very particular about taking his medicines at the time prescribed, and for this purpose kept a watch hanging on a chair close by his bedside. During the first few days he tried to get up and spend a couple of hours in correcting the proof-sheets of the second part of his *Winterreise*. On the 16th the doctors had a consultation; they thought that the symptoms showed the likelihood of an imminent attack of nervous fever, but still all hopes of recovery were not abandoned. Several of his friends (Spaun, Bauernfeld, Lachner, J. Hüettenbrenner) visited him; others were kept back from fear of infection. On the evening of the 17th he raved more continuously, having hitherto suffered only at times and slightly from mental wanderings.

The evening before his death, he addressed his brother with the words: "Ferdinand! put your ear close to my mouth," and added in a mysterious tone, "Brother, what are they doing with me?" His brother answered, "They are taking great care of you, and doing all they can to make you well again; the doctor assures us you will soon be well again, only you must be patient, and keep to your bed a while yet." The whole day long he wanted to get up, and labored under the constant delusion that he was in some strange room. Two hours later the doctor appeared, and spoke to him in the same way as Ferdinand had done. But Schubert looked earnestly at him, clutched at the wall with his poor weak hand, and said slowly and in earnest tones: "Here, here is my end."

On the same day, probably at some early hour in the morning, the elder Schubert had written to his son Ferdinand as follows:

Dear son Ferdinand, The days of trouble and heaviness are lowering heavily upon us. The dangerous illness of our beloved Franz weighs heavily on our souls. All that we can do in this sad time is to seek comfort from our Heavenly Father, and bear every sorrow appointed us by a wise Providence with firm submission to His holy will. The result will convince us of the wisdom and goodness of God. Be of couarge, then, and put your trust in Him. He will strengthen you that you sink not under this sorrow; His blessing will still keep a happy future in store for you. Take every possible precaution that our dear Franz have administered to him at once the Holy Sacraments given to the dying, and I live in the cheerful hope that the Almighty will strengthen and preserve him.

Your father, afflicted and yet strengthened by trust in God,

FRANZ

On the afternoon of the same day, the father announced to the public the news of his son's death in the following obituary notice:

Yesterday afternoon, at three o'clock on Wednesday, my beloved son Franz Schubert, artist and composer, died after a short illness, and having received the Holy Sacraments of the Church. He died at the age of thirty-two. We beg to announce to our dear friends and neighbors that the body of the deceased will we taken on the 21st of this month, at half-past two in the afternoon, from house No. 694 in the new street on the Neuen-Wieden, to be buried near the bishop's stall in the parish church of St. Josef in Margarethen, where the holy rites will be administered.

FRANZ SCHUBERT
Schoolteacher in the Rossau

Vienna, November 20, 1828.

Dressed in the ordinary garb of a hermit of the time, a wreath of laurel twisted round the temples, and his face still unchanged by death, Schubert, more like a sleeping than a dead man, rested on his bier, which, in the course of the first day after his death, had been decked by the passing crowds of visitors with wreaths and garlands.

HECTOR BERLIOZ

Born: La Côte-Saint-André, France
December 11, 1803
Died: Paris, France
March 8, 1869

HECTOR BERLIOZ really initiated the development of the romantic orchestra, and with it the modern orchestra. In Berlioz the spiritual that we find in Beethoven is transformed into the programmatic; his is a purely personal expression.

Berlioz had red hair which well suited with his unruly temperament, his tumultuous spirit, his restlessness which moved him constantly from place to place, his tenseness that forbade him to relax, to contemplate, to wait for an inspiration to take form, or for an attachment to take root. During his student years he fell madly in love with Henrietta Smithson, an English actress rather older than he; he pursued her relentlessly, besieged her with threats of suicide, until she finally weakened and married him. It was at this time that he created his *Symphonie Fantastique*—a new departure in orchestra music. His *Romeo et Juliette, Benvenuto Cellini* and *Damnation de Faust* developed this new style. He became famous in Russia, Germany, England, but France rejected him.

He traveled from country to country, conducting his own works, in an effort to make a little money. In a sense this mobile existence was appropriate to the nature of his compositions: never facile, unsusceptible to outside influence, ever inclined to choose the storm instead of the calm, movement instead of peace. He was consistently unlucky in his relations with women—unhappy with his second wife as with his first; he was hated by many other musicians whom he had for years attacked in his writings as a music critic. He became lonelier and lonelier and died, after a long, painful illness, a bitter and disappointed man.

Ernest Legouvé

A Young Romantic

Hector Berlioz, born in a small town of southeastern France, was a contemporary of the poets, artists and thinkers who devoted their genius to the Romantic School—Lamartine, Alfred de Musset, Balzac, Delacroix, Chateaubriand.

He was perhaps the most eccentric and egocentric composer of all time—but he was also the most misunderstood, especially in his own country. Throughout his life he was isolated, even persecuted. He never had a sufficient income; his two marriages were extremely unhappy.

Ernest Legouvé (1807-1903) was a very popular French dramatist. He was a sincere friend of Berlioz. He describes the young revolutionary's appearance and manner—Berlioz never hesitated to express anything he felt. He fell deeply in love with the young English actress Harriet Smithson, who later became his first wife.

THE FIRST TIME I heard the name of Berlioz was in Rome at the French Musical Academy in the year 1832. He had just left the latter institution and was spoken of as an artist of talent, as a clever and intelligent man, but strange and taking pride in being strange. People were inclined to look upon him as a poseur. Madame Vernet and her daughter defended him against that charge and were loud in his praise. Women have a quicker perception than we have with regard to superior men. One day Mlle. Louise Vernet sang to me an air composed

for her by Berlioz during his stay among the mountains of
Subiaco. It was entitled *La Captive.* The poetry and sadness
of it moved me deeply, and from that moment I felt a kind of
mysterious bond of sympathy with that unknown man. I asked
Mlle Vernet to give me a letter of introduction and on my
return to Paris I took immediate steps to find him, but failed.
No one seemed to know anything about him. I had almost
given up the thing when one morning at an Italian hairdresser's of the name of Decandia on the Place de la Bourse I
hear one of the assistants say to the chief, "This stick belongs
to M. Berlioz." "M. Berlioz!" I exclaim, turning to the hairdresser, "you know Mr. Berlioz?" "He is one of my best cus-
tomers; I expect him here today." "Well, give him this letter,
please." It was Mlle Vernet's letter.

That same evening I went to hear the *Freischutz,* and the
house being crowded, I could only find standing room in the
second gallery (upper boxes). All at once in the middle of
the opening bars of Gaspard's song, one of my neighbors rises
from his seat and bending toward the orchestra shouts in a
voice of thunder, "You don't want two flutes there, you brutes,
you want two piccolos! Two piccolos, do you hear! Oh, the
brutes!" Having said which, he simply sits down again, scowl-
ing indignantly. Amidst the general tumult, provoked by this
outburst I turn round and behold a young man trembling
with passion, his hands clenched, his eyes flashing, and a head
of hair—such a head of hair! It looked like an immense umbrella of hair, projecting like a movable awning over a beak of
a bird of prey. It was both comical and diabolical at the same
time. Next morning there is a ring at my door, I happen to
open it myself and the moment I catch sight of my visitor I
exclaim,

"Monsieur, were you not at the Opera last night?"

"Yes, monsieur."

"In the second gallery?"

"Yes, monsieur."

"It was you who shouted, 'You want two piccolos!' "

"Of course I did. I have no patience with a set of brutes who do not know the difference between—"

"Then you are M. Berlioz."

"I am M. Berlioz, my dear Legouvé." Thereupon we fell into each other's arms as if we had known each other all our lives.

In fact, in a short time we were fast friends, for everything contributed to our intimacy. We were of the same age, and we had, moreover, a passionate love for art in common. Berlioz worshipped Shakespeare as I did, I worshipped Mozart as he did. When Berlioz was not composing music he was reading poetry; when I was not writing verse I was playing. The last and strongest bond of all was that I had, out of sheer enthusiasm, translated *Romeo and Juliet* and that he was madly in love with the celebrated artist, Miss Smithson, who played Juliet. His love passion virtually set our friendship ablaze. First of all he scarcely knew a sentence of English, and Miss Smithson was even more ignorant of our language than he was of hers; a fact which made their conversation rather awkward, not to say comical. Secondly, she was more or less afraid of her savage admirer. Lastly, Berlioz' father strenuously opposed all idea of marriage. All this was enough and more than enough to create the demand for a confidant-in-ordinary. But as it was a function entailing a great deal of application and which might well have sufficed for two people, he gave me a coadjutor in the shape of a supplementary confessor, namely my friend Eugene Sue, for whom he had a great admiration.

Our consultations were of a strange character indeed, and an accident which had happened to Miss Smithson (she had sprained her ankle while getting out of a cab) gave rise one day to a very characteristic conversation. On that morning Berlioz had sent me a note in a small, cramped handwriting. It ran:

"I wish to see you most urgently. Send word to Sue. Oh, my friends, the agony of it."

Thereupon I send a note to Sue:

"A wild hurricane is blowing. Berlioz has summoned us to appear. Tonight, at supper, at my place at midnight."

At the time appointed, Berlioz makes his appearance, his eyes beclouded with tears, his hair dropping over his forehead like a weeping willow, and uttering sighs which he seemed to draw from his feet.

"Well, what is the matter?" we asked.

"Oh my friends, life has become impossible for me."

"Is your father as relentless as ever?"

"My father," shouts Berlioz at the top of his voice and trembling with rage, "my father says 'Yes.' He wrote to me to that effect this morning."

"Well then, it seems to us . . ."

"Wait, wait, do not interrupt me. The receipt of this letter drives me frantic with joy. I rush to her place, I enter her room, almost out of my senses and dissolved in tears. I exclaim, 'My father consents, my father consents!' And would you know her answer? Well, she said very calmly, 'Not yet, Hector; not yet. My foot hurts me too much.' What do you say to that?"

"What we say is this, that the poor girl was no doubt in great pain."

"In great pain?" he replied. "Is there such a thing as great pain with people who are in ecstasies? Look at me—well, if someone had plunged a knife into my breast at the moment she told me she loved me I should not have felt it. She on the other hand . . . she could . . . and did . . . and dared . . ." Then suddenly interrupting himself: "How could she have dared? . . . I am simply wondering that she was not afraid of my strangling her!" The sentence was uttered with such simplicity and conviction that Eugene Sue and I burst out laughing. Berlioz stared at us absolutely stupefied. He

was under the impression of having said the most commonplace thing possible and we had the greatest difficulty in
bringing home to him that there was not the slightest connection of ideas between a woman who complains of being in
pain with a swollen ankle and a woman who is being stran-
gled; and that Miss Smithson would have been utterly surprised at her admirer's clutching her by the throat in the
manner Othello does. The poor fellow listened to us without
grasping a word of what we said; he hung his head and the
tears ran down his cheeks. Then he said at last, "I don't care
what you say, she does not care for me, she does not care for
me."

"She does not love you in the same way you love her," replied Sue, "that's evident enough, and moreover, very fortunate, for two people who loved as you do would lead a very
strange life together." Berlioz could not help smiling. Then I
chimed in, "My dear friend, you are thinking of the Portia of
Shakespeare who strikes herself in the thigh to induce Brutus
to give her his confidence. But Miss Smithson does not play
the Portias; she plays the Ophelias, the Desdemonas and the
Juliets, that is, weak, loving, tenderhearted and timid creatures, women who are essentially womanly, and I feel certain
that her character is like the parts she plays."

"That's true," he said.

"That her soul is as delicately attuned as those of the characters she represents."

"Yes, that's true, delicate is the only word for it."

"And if you had wished to remain worthy of her or rather
of yourself, instead of flinging this joy in her face, you would
have applied it like a balm to her wound. Your divine Shakespeare would not have failed to do so if he had had to write
that scene."

"You are right, you are right," exclaimed the poor fellow
when I had finished speaking. "I am a brutal lout, I am a
savage. I do not deserve to be loved by such a heart. If you

only knew what a fund of affection there is stored in that heart. Oh, how I will implore her pardon tomorrow. But after all, my dear friends, see how well advised I was to consult you. I came here in despair, exasperated, and now I feel happy, confident and wishing to laugh aloud."

And all at once, with the simplicity, with the quickly changing emotion of a child, he began to enlarge upon the joy of his coming marriage. . . .

Ferdinand Hiller

The Personality of Berlioz

Ferdinand Hiller (1811-1885) was one of the best-known musicians in Germany during his lifetime—composer, teacher, pianist, conductor. He wrote over two hundred operas, oratorios, psalms, chamber music. He was also an able journalist and wrote, among other books, reminiscences of his friends Mendelssohn and Berlioz.

As a very young man he lived in Paris for seven years; here he came in close contact with Rossini, Chopin, Cherubini, Meyerbeer, Liszt, Berlioz.

His portrait of Berlioz is excellent because it reveals the double-faced personality of the romantic master. It also passes on to us what Berlioz told him of his childhood and parents.

HECTOR BERLIOZ was a man of full rich color who never belied his own nature; but that nature was compounded of the most varied—sometimes actually antithetic—traits and propensities. Energetic to the point of heroism, self-willed, aggressive, yet pliant, obliging, even weak—deliberate, patient, persevering, yet prone to yield utterly to momentary impressions—good-natured, amiable, kindly, grateful—and again bitter, caustic, indeed vindictive. He had a goodly measure of contempt for the world and for life, and with it a boundless ambition; success intoxicated him—yet he gave most violent

expression to his contempt for the public. He gave himself and
his full powers to the important tasks confronting him;
he shunned no labor, however tedious, however mindless, if
he must perform such labor to attain his goal—yet he could
waste his time like a boy, squander his hours on a mad caprice.
One passion dominated him more than was proper: he loved
to contemplate continuously his own intense feelings and
sensations, his own thoughts and actions. He was one of those
people who find it necessary always to be interesting in their
own eyes, who must attach some exalted significance to the
most trivial thing they do, feel, suffer, to everything, good or
bad, that happens to them. Yet he did not give the impression
of vanity; this is the more remarkable since he talked about
himself a great deal, almost exclusively. . . .

Most people would like to talk incessantly about themselves
if others would tolerate it—La Rochefoucauld is of opinion
that a man would rather say something bad about himself
than nothing at all; but I do not think I have ever encountered
this predilection in so extreme a form as with Berlioz, except
among actors. Fortunately his personality was so attractive,
so singular, his speech so lively, so picturesque, his thinking
so incisive and individual—now clear, clean logic, now humorous hyperbole, witty, biting, acid—his enthusiasm was so
fiery, his antipathy so unmistakable—that it was a pleasure to
indulge him. . . .

Berlioz was in the full sense of the word a gentleman. He
had perhaps a few passionate weaknesses for which to reproach himself—but his personal dignity held him aloof. . . .
He was a stranger to any sort of intrigue; he would rather have
worked havoc for himself and others with his highhandedness
than have achieved an end by devious means. His artistic self-
consciousness was very strong. If in later years he was sometimes less frank as a critic than his nature dictated, he yielded
to the pressure of circumstance only to give praise; neither
jealousy nor self-interest ever induced him to disparage works

or people whose worth he was obliged to recognize in his heart of hearts. At times his irritation made him unnecessarily harsh in his censure of what he did not like—his was in fact an excessively nervous nature, steeped in passion.

I do not believe anyone could meet Berlioz without being struck with surprise at the utter originality and singularity of his features. His high brow, sharply cut over the deep-set eyes, his strongly aquiline hawk nose, the narrow, finely chiseled lips, the rather short chin, all crowned by an extraordinary abundance of light-brown curls whose fantastic waywardness yielded not even to the constraining iron of the hairdresser—once you had seen that head you could not forget it. And then the uncommon mobility of his face: the glance, one moment flashing, actually burning, and the next moment dull, lusterless, almost dying—the expression of his mouth, alternating between energy and withering contempt, between friendly smiling and scornful laughter! His figure was of middle size—slender but not elegant—his bearing extremely careless. His speaking voice was rather weak but of course reflected the constant shifting of his emotions and his moods. His singing voice too was agreeable and had his excitement been less intense he could have brought out the full meaning and beauty of many of his own vocal compositions. But the overflowing emotion interfered with the listener's understanding of the music; if the performing artist wishes to move others, he must not be too deeply moved himself.

A few months after I had arrived in Paris in the fall of 1828 I made Berlioz' acquaintance. The previous summer he had attracted attention with a concert program including several of his compositions—and shortly thereafter the Institut de France awarded him second prize. Eight years older than I, he had come to know the meaning of the struggle for existence; compared with me at least, he was a man matured by sad experience, although his youthful nature still displayed the southern vivacity that never entirely left him. I felt myself

very strongly attracted by this abundant heart. What I had
to offer in return was of a musical character. Only a short time
before he had become acquainted with Beethoven in his
symphonies; these had been revealed to Parisian music lovers
by Habeneck in the so-called Concerts of the Conservatory.
Berlioz' enthusiasm knew no bounds. We went into raptures
together, and I was privileged to introduce him to the sonatas of the master and enjoy his delight in them. Our meetings became more and more frequent; day by day he won yet
more of my sympathy by what he told me of his youth in his
parents' house and the years of his apprenticeship.

Although he had been born in a small town, la Côte-Saint-
André, his education had preserved that tranquil and solitary
character generally possible only in the country. Hector's
father, a highly esteemed physician of broad education, was
his only son's only teacher. The instruction Hector received
must certainly have been thorough and superior; but since it
had to fit in with the demands of an important medical practice, it must also have been most irregular. The boy was left
much to his own resources and perhaps he was able to indulge
his predilection for solitary daydreaming in the open air more
than was good for him. The study of Latin in particular was
earnestly pursued and the father's unusually strong preference for Virgil's works was gradually passed on to the son. I do
not believe Berlioz ever became so deeply conversant with
any other poetry as he was with the Aeneid. It must have been
a moving thing for his friends to see him turn back, at the end
of his career, to this first love and write the verse and music for
his opera *The Trojans*.

Of his mother Berlioz spoke with love—love mixed with a
compassionate regret caused by what he termed her preju-
dices with regard to religion and art. Having decided to become a musician, he was made to suffer severely for his decision. But he remembered his two sisters most tenderly, especially the younger, to whom he was bound by a warm

sympathy. All in all his youth may be said to have been a happy time. He received intellectual stimulation but was not overfatigued; he lived a life free of care in the midst of beautiful natural surroundings; he was sheltered by love and was able to give himself in freedom to his innocent enjoyments. In these boyhood years he was quite untouched by that doubt of everything and everyone that so heavily shadowed his later life. He lived in purity, faith and naiveté, far removed from the torments and anxieties of school, safe from the disagreeable encounters that school life often brings with it; the days slipped by, and his pursuit of musical endeavors in particular gave him blessed hours. Here too his serious-minded father was his first teacher a few insignificant musicians later helped out. The boy readily learned to sing at sight and quickly attained some instrumental dexterity as well. But what were the instruments on which he was obliged to gratify his passion for music? The flageolet, the flute, and the guitar!

Richard Wagner

With Admiration, Without Sympathy

When *Roméo et Juliette* made its appearance in 1839, Berlioz was thirty-six years old; he was regarded by a chosen few as a genius whose superiority rendered him inaccessible to the vulgar.

Richard Wagner was ten years younger than Berlioz. In his posthumous autobiography (in the chapter on his sojourn in Paris) he admits that Berlioz' work made an intensely vivid and altogether unexpected impression on him.

But the personal relations between the two great men never became really cordial. The contrast between their temperaments and artistic views was too sharp, the gap too wide.

I WAS anxious to become more intimately acquainted with Berlioz. I had been introduced to him some time previously at Schlesinger's office, where we used to meet occasionally. I had presented him with a copy of my "Die zwei Grenadiere"

("Two Grenadiers") but could never learn any more from
him concerning what he really thought of it than the fact that
as he could only strum a little on the guitar, he was unable to
play the music of my composition to himself on the piano.
During the previous winter I had often heard his grand instrumental pieces played under his own direction, and had
been most favorably impressed by them. During that winter
(1839-40) he conducted three performances of his new symphony, *Roméo et Juliette*, at one of which I was present.

All this, to be sure, was quite a new world to me, and I was
desirous of gaining some unprejudiced knowledge of it. At
first the grandeur and masterly execution of the orchestral
part almost overwhelmed me. It was beyond anything I could
have conceived. The fantastic daring, the sharp precision
with which the boldest combinations—almost tangible in their
clearness—impressed me, drove back my own ideas of the
poetry of music with brutal violence into the very depths of
my soul. I was simply all ears for things of which till then I
had never dreamed and which I felt I must try to realize. True,
I found a great deal that was empty and shallow in his
Roméo et Juliette, a work that lost much by its length and
form of combination; and this was the more painful to me
seeing that, on the other hand, I felt overpowered by many
really bewitching passages which quite overcame any objec-
tions on my part.

During the same winter Berlioz produced his *Sinfonie Fantastique* and his *Harold (Harold en Italie)*. I was also much
impressed by these works; the musical genre pictures woven
into the first-named symphony were particularly pleasing,
while *Harold* delighted me in almost every respect.

It was, however, the latest work of this wonderful master,
his *Grande Symphonie Funèbre et Triomphale*, most skill-
fully composed for massed military bands during the summer
of 1840 for the anniversary of the obsequies of the July heroes,
and conducted by him under the column of the Place de la

Bastille, which at last did thoroughly convince me of the greatness and enterprise of this incomparable artist. But while admiring this genius, absolutely unique in his methods, I could never quite shake off a certain peculiar feeling of anxiety. His works left me with a sensation as of something strange, something with which I felt I should never be able to be familiar, and I was often puzzled at the mysterious fact that, though ravished by his compositions, I was at the same time repelled and even wearied by them. It was only much later that I succeeded in clearly grasping and solving this problem, which for years exercised such a painful spell over me.

It is a fact that at that time I felt almost like a little school-boy by the side of Berlioz. . . .

Sir Charles Hallé

Genius, Peculiarities and Limitations

The memoirs of Sir Charles Hallé shed illumination on the character and musical methods of his friend Berlioz. We see the romantic genius as he really was—in some ways an amateur. He had never learned the art of conducting or the art of composing; he knew only a few of Beethoven's sonatas; he was bored to death by Bach—and nevertheless he managed to become a great creative musician.

Berlioz himself tells the story of Habeneck's behavior at the first performance of the *Requiem* in his *Memoirs*. On the other hand, a number of his close friends who were present at the concert and sitting with Berlioz, assert that the incident never occurred. It is impossible to ascertain the truth.

Sir Charles Hallé (1819-1895) was a well-known pianist and conductor who became Principal of the Royal Manchester College and conductor of the Manchester Hallé Concerts. He was very active in bringing Berlioz' music to a wider public.

THE MOST important friendship I formed at that time (or it may have been at the end of 1837) was that with Hector

Berlioz—*le vaillant Hector,* as he was often called—whose powerful, dominating personality I was glad to recognize. How I made his acquaintance is now a mystery to me—it seems as if I had always known him—I also wonder often how it was he showed such interest in an artist of so little importance as I then was; he was so kind to me and, in fact, became my friend. Perhaps it was because we could both speak with the same enthusiasm of Beethoven, Gluck, Weber, even Spontini, and perhaps, not less because he felt that I had a genuine admiration for his own works. There never lived a musician who adored his art more than did Berlioz; he was, indeed, "enthusiasm personified." To hear him speak of, or rave about, a real chef d'œuvre, such as *Armida, Iphigénie* or the C Minor Symphony, the pitch of his voice rising higher and higher as he talked, was worth any performance of the same. And what a picture he was at the head of his orchestra, with his eagle face, his bushy hair, his air of command, and glowing with enthusiasm. He was the most perfect conductor that I ever set eyes upon, one who held absolute sway over his troops, and played upon them as a pianist upon the keyboard. But discussion of his genius and his work is superfluous at the present time; even his life is so thoroughly known that I need only relate of him what has come to my personal knowledge.

He also visited my humble lodgings quite often, and I must say that his visits to me were more frequent than mine to him; for even at that time Madame Berlioz, the once charming and poetic Ophelia, had become somewhat repellent, and it was impossible to imagine her acting or anybody falling in love with her. To her honor it must, however, be said that she sustained Berlioz in his hardest struggles, always ready to endure the greatest privations when it was a question of his saving money enough for the organization of a concert on a large scale, concerts which seldom yielded any profit. Berlioz was no executant upon any instrument (for being able to strum a few chords on the guitar does not count), and he was

painfully aware how much this was a hindrance to him and to
his knowledge of musical literature, which, indeed, was limited. I was often astonished to find that works familiar to
every pianist were unknown to him; not merely works written
for the piano, such as Beethoven's sonatas, of which he knew
but few, but also orchestral works, oratorios, etc., known to
the pianist through arrangements, but of which he had not
chanced to see a score. Perhaps many undoubted crudities in
his works would have been eliminated had he been able to
hear them before committing them to paper, for I had several
proofs that the eye alone was not sufficient to give him a clear
idea of the effect of his musical combinations. Thus at the
time when he scored *Invitation à la Valse* for the orchestra, he
made me play it to him, and when I had come to the point
where, after the digression into C Major, the theme is re-
sumed in the original key, D Flat, he interrupted me with the
words, "*Après tout, cela va*," confessing that from the perusal
of the piece he had thought that modulation too harsh and
almost impossible. On another occasion, much later, he arrived at my house and eagerly told me he had found a new
cadence to end a movement with. "The last chord," he said,
"is the chord of G Major, and I precede it by the one in B
Minor." When I told him there were hundreds of examples of
such an ending, he would not believe me, and was greatly
astonished when we searched for and found them.

In some of the most interesting moments of Berlioz's musical career in Paris I had the privilege of being with him. Thus
on December 5, 1837, I went with him to the Hôtel des Invalides to witness the first performance of his *Requiem*, and
was, therefore, an eyewitness of what took place on that occasion. Habeneck, after Berlioz the most accomplished *chef
d'orchestre* in Paris, conducted by rights, and Berlioz sat in a
chair near him. Habeneck, who conducted not only the Grand
Opera but also the Concerts of the Conservatory, had the
habit of now and then putting his conducting stick down and

listening complacently to the performance of his orchestra. It was, therefore, perhaps force of habit that made him discard the baton at the commencement of the *Tuba mirum,* this time not to listen, but leisurely to take a pinch of snuff! To my amazement I suddenly saw Berlioz standing in Habeneck's place and wielding the baton to the end of the movement. The moment had been a critical one; four groups of brass instruments, stationed at the four corners of the large orchestra, which with the chorus was placed under the dome in the center of the building, having to enter successively, and, without Berlioz' determination, disaster must have ensued, thanks to the unfortunate pinch of snuff. Habeneck, after the performance, thanked Berlioz effusively for his timely aid, and admitted that his own thoughtlessness might have caused a breakdown, but Berlioz remained persuaded that there had been no thoughtlessness, and that the breakdown was intended. I could not believe this, for the simple reason that when such a thing occurs it is always the conductor on whose shoulders the blame of the breakdown is laid, and most deservedly so; it is, therefore, most unlikely that he should himself try to provoke one. The effect of the *Requiem,* and especially of the *Tuba mirum,* was so overpowering that I have never dared to play it in England, where it has been my joy to conduct so many of Berlioz' works; the placing of four orchestras at the corners of the principal one is impossible in our concert rooms, and I consider it indispensable for the due effect of the movement and the carrying out of the composer's intention.

Of his perfect command over the orchestra Berlioz gave an extraordinary proof on the occasion of a grand concert given by him a few years later in the Cirque Franconi. There had been a very long rehearsal in the morning, at which I was present, as I had to play Beethoven's G Major Concerto, then very seldom performed. After some hours' hard work Berlioz dismissed the orchestra; I remained with him, and hardly had the last member of the band vanished when Berlioz struck his forehead, exclaiming, "I have forgotten the overture!" He stood speechless for a few minutes, then said with determination, "It *shall* go nevertheless." Now this overture was the one to *Le Carneval Romain,* to be performed that evening *for the first time,* and never rehearsed. Musicians who know the work, with its complicated rhythm and all its intricacies, will easily understand how bold the venture was, and will wonder that it could be successful. But to see Berlioz during that performance was a sight never to be forgotten. He watched over every single member of the huge band; his beat was so decisive, his indication of all the nuances so clear and so unmistakable, that the overture went smoothly and no unitiated person could guess at the absence of a rehearsal. This absolute command over the orchestra I had already admired during the preparations for the first production of his *Roméo et Juliette* in 1839, which took a long time, but resulted in a magnificent performance, stirring the public to enthusiasm. His own public I mean; totally distinct from the general one, which did not appreciate or understand his music. Berlioz had at all times a not inconsiderable number of devoted followers, who made up in zeal and admiration for their want of numbers, and to whom he was warmly and somewhat gratefully attached. The indifference shown by the crowd, and even by many musicians, toward his works he felt deeply, although he tried to make light of it, and any real success, however temporary, was eagerly welcomed, and brightened up his life for a while.

Camille Saint-Saëns

In Reality He Had a Kind Heart

The famous French composer Saint-Saëns (1835-1921) was a lifelong friend of Berlioz. Saint-Saëns probably knew him best of all. He discovered the real heart of the man in whom the world saw only hauteur, spitefulness, and evil.

BERLIOZ was unfortunate in having a self-torturing disposition. He sought the impossible, and would have it at any cost. One misconception, very current through his advocacy of it, was that the imagination of the composer should not reckon with material obstacles. He tried to pass over the fact that the musician is not like the painter, who disposes inert material on canvas as his fancy dictates, while the musician must make allowances for the endurance of the performers, and the extent, large or small, of their technique.

Public favor began to come to Berlioz in the last years of his life, and his oratorio, the *Infancy of Christ*, in its simplicity and suavity succeeded in triumphing over the gross prejudice which could see in Berlioz nothing but a lover of deafening noise, a promoter of vast circuses. He did not die, as has been said, owing to the injustice of men, but from gastritis, caused by his obstinacy in refusing to follow the advice of his physicians, a strictly hygienic regimen. I saw this clearly, without being able to remedy it, during an artistic tour on which I had the fortune to accompany him. "It is extraordinary," he said to me one morning, "I have no pain at all." He used to tell me of his various pains, his continual colics, and how strictly forbidden he was to take any stimulant, to exceed a certain regimen under penalty of the most tormenting suffering, which only went from bad to worse. Nevertheless he followed no regimen whatever, took whatever he wanted without thought for the morrow. On the evening of this very day we went to a large banquet. I sat near Berlioz and did all I could to keep him from coffee, champagne, and Havana cigars—all in vain; the next day the poor man was writhing in his usual torture.

Berlioz demanded, in his younger days, of orchestras far inferior to those of today, efforts that were truly superhuman. If there are some difficulties in all new and original music, impossible to avoid, there are others which can be spared the performers without detriment to the work. But Berlioz did not concern himself with these practical details. I have seen him conduct twenty, even thirty rehearsals for a single work, fairly tearing his hair, smashing batons and music stands without accomplishing the desired results. The poor orchestra players did what they could, but the task was beyond their powers. In short, our orchestras had to improve with years, in order that Berlioz' music should come to public hearing as it was conceived.

Two things seriously affected Berlioz' career—the enmity of the Grand Opera in setting aside his *Trojans* for Bellini's *Romeo*, which, after all, fell flat; the other, the coldness of the Société des Concerts as far as his music was concerned. We know the reasons since the publication of the history of the society by Deldevez. It was due to the influence of their orchestra leaders. This was a natural attitude for Deldevez, a profound, scholarly musician who had every qualification of an authority. It is probable that he only appreciated classical music, for it was that which he had studied thoroughly; very likely his antipathy to Berlioz was purely instinctive.

Beyond my full admiration, I had for Berlioz a deep affection, thanks to the kindhearted way in which he treated me, and of which I was justly proud, and thanks also to those hidden traits of character which I came upon, so contrary to the world's estimation of him, where he was thought to be inflated with pride, hateful and malicious. In reality he was kindhearted almost to weakness, grateful for the slightest sign of interest in him, and delightfully simple, so that his mordant wit and spicy epigrams stood out in higher relief, because there was in them no straining after effect, none of that effort which takes the bloom off so much that is good.

FELIX MENDELSSOHN-BARTHOLDY

Born: Hamburg, Germany
February 3, 1809
Died: Leipzig, Germany
November 4, 1847

FELIX MENDELSSOHN-BARTHOLDY was the son of the banker Abraham Mendelssohn and grandson of the revered philosopher Moses Mendelssohn, called "the German Socrates." The family had a big house on the Neue Promenade in Berlin. Felix' mother began giving him piano lessons when he was four.

By seventeen he was already a full-fledged composer. In that year he performed his *Midsummer Night's Dream* for the first time; it was his initial work of marked genius and it established him in the musical world as a composer. He first played it with his favorite sister, Fanny, as a duet for piano.

Ignaz Moscheles, the celebrated pianist, was his teacher and his friend. He induced the young Mendelssohn to go to London and make his name in the great world. His success was now assured. The young man was not only a great composer but an inspired pianist and organist and one of the most stimulating conductors of his day. He traveled through Germany, Austria, Italy, France, Switzerland, bringing to a vast audience his immortal *Songs Without Words, Hebrides* Overture, *Reformation* Symphony, and other brilliant works.

In 1835 he accepted the conductorship of the Gewandhaus orchestra in Leipzig. This was an event of high significance, not only for his own career but for the musical
life of the whole world. In Leipzig he also established the
Conservatory of Music.

He ruled as unchallenged monarch, beloved *virtuoso*,
and he was a happily married man. But his life was too full
and too active for his store of strength. The sudden death
of his sister Fanny fatally shocked his nervous system;
within a few months after her death he passed away.

Ludwig Rellstab

The Boy's Visit to Goethe

The opportunities Felix Mendelssohn enjoyed as a boy to meet and
see the great Goethe (1749-1832) in the poet's own home gave an impulse to his whole life. Goethe's presence strengthened and fostered
the child's natural love of perfection.

Their first meeting was arranged by Mendelssohn's teacher, the old
composer Carl Friedrich Zelter (1758-1832), a friend of Goethe's. Felix
was then only twelve years old but already displayed extraordinary
musical productivity. He had written two operas, six symphonies, a
quartet for piano and strings. And Goethe grew every day more
fascinated with the charming, handsome, gifted young artist. He spent
hours in his company. "Every afternoon," so the boy writes home,
"Goethe opens his Streicher piano and says 'I have not heard you at all
today, you must make a little noise for me.' Then he sits down next to
me, and when I have finished I beg for a kiss, or else I take one."

Our report here is taken from Ludwig Rellstab's (1799-1860) Autobiography, *Aus meinem Leben*.

IN THE EVENING, we assembled in Goethe's rooms for tea; for
he had invited a large party of his Weimar musical friends to
make them acquainted with the boy's extraordinary talents.

Presently Goethe made his appearance: he came from his study, and had a habit—at least I generally noticed it—of waiting till all the guests were assembled, before he showed himself. Till that moment his son and daughter-in-law did the duties of host in the most amiable way. A certain solemnity was visible among the guests, prior to the entrance of the great poet; and even those who stood on terms of intimacy with him experienced a feeling of veneration. His slow, serious walk; his impressive features, which expressed the strength rather than weakness of old age; the lofty forehead; the white, abundant hair; lastly, the deep voice, and slow way of speaking—all united to produce the effect. His "good evening" was addressed to all; but he walked up to Zelter first, and shook his hand cordially. Felix Mendelssohn looked up with sparkling eyes at the snow-white head of the poet. The latter, however, placed his hands kindly on the boy's head and said, "Now you shall play us something." Zelter nodded his assent.

The piano was opened, and lights arranged on the desk. Mendelssohn asked Zelter, to whom he displayed a thoroughly childish devotion and confidence, "What shall I play?"

"Well, what you can," the latter replied, in a peculiarly sharp voice; "whatever is not too difficult for you."

To me, who knew what the boy could do, and that no task was too difficult for him, this seemed an unjust depreciation of his faculties. It was at length arranged that he should play a fantasia; which he did to the wonder of all. But the young artist knew when to leave off; and thus the effect he produced was all the greater. A silence of surprise ensued when he raised his hands from the keys after a loud finale.

Zelter interrupted the silence in his humorous voice with a loud "Ha! you must have been dreaming of hobgoblins and dragons!" The playing, as it could not well otherwise, aroused the highest admiration of all present; and Goethe, especially, was full of the warmest delight. He encouraged the lad, in whose childish features joy, pride, and confusion were at once depicted, by taking his head between his hands, patting him kindly, and saying jestingly, "But you will not get off with that. You must play more pieces before we recognize your merits."

"But what shall I play?" Felix asked: "Herr Professor"—he was wont to address Zelter by this title, "what shall I play now?"

I cannot say that I have properly retained the pieces the young virtuoso now performed; for they were numerous. I will, however, mention the most interesting.

Goethe was a great admirer of Bach's fugues, which a musician of Berka, a little town about ten miles from Weimar, came to play to him repeatedly. Felix was therefore requested to play a fugue of the grand old master, Zelter selected it from his music book, and the boy played it without any hesitation and with perfect certainty.

Goethe's delight grew. . . . Among other things he requested him to play a minuet.

"Shall I play you the loveliest in the whole world?" he asked with sparkling eyes.

"Well, and which is that?"

He played the minuet from *Don Giovanni.*

Goethe stood by the instrument, listening, joy lighting up his features. He wished for the overture of the opera after the minuet; but this the player roundly declined, with the assertion that it could not be played as it was written and nobody dared make any alteration in it. He offered to play the overture to *Figaro,* however. He commenced it with a lightness of touch, a sureness and clearness I have never heard since. At the same time he gave the orchestral effects so magnificently that the result was extraordinary; and I can honestly state that it afforded me more gratification than ever an orchestral performance had. Goethe grew more and more cheerful and kind, and even played tricks with the talented lad.

"Come now," he said, "you have only played me pieces you know; now we will see whether you can play something you do not know. I will try you out."

Goethe went out, re-entered the room in a few moments, with a roll of music in his hand. "I have fetched something from my manuscript collection. Now we will test you. Do you think you can play this?"

He laid a page with clear but small notes on the desk. It was Mozart's handwriting. Whether Goethe told us so, or it was written on the paper, I forget, and only remember that Felix glowed with delight at the name; and an indescribable feeling came over us all, partly enthusiasm and joy, partly admiration and expectation. Goethe, the aged man, laying a manuscript of Mozart, who had been buried thirty years, before a lad so full of promise for the future, to play at sight—in truth it was a rare moment.

The young artist played with the most perfect certainty, not making the slightest mistake, though the manuscript was far from easy reading. The task was certainly not difficult, especially for Mendelssohn, as it was only an *adagio;* still there was difficulty in doing it as the lad did; for he played it as if he had been practicing it for years.

Goethe kept to his good-humored tone, while all the rest applauded. "That is nothing," he said, "others could read that too. Now I will give you something you will trip over; so take care."

With these words, he produced another paper, which he laid on the desk. This certainly looked very strange. It was difficult to say if these were notes or only a paper, ruled, and splashed with ink and blots. Felix Mendelssohn, in his surprise, laughed loudly. "How is that written? who can read it?" he said.

But suddenly he became serious; for while Goethe was saying, "Now, guess who wrote it?" Zelter, who had walked up to the piano, and looked over the boy's shoulder, exclaimed,

"Why, Beethoven wrote that! Anyone could see it a mile off.
He always writes with a broomstick, and passes his sleeve
over the notes before they are dry. I have plenty of his manuscripts. They are easy to recognize."

At the mention of the name, as I remarked, Mendelssohn
had suddenly grown serious—even more than serious. A shade
of awe was visible on his features. Goethe regarded him with
searching eyes, from which delight beamed. The boy kept his
eyes immovably fixed on the manuscript; and a look of glad
surprise flew over his features as he traced a brilliant thought
amid the chaos of confused, blurred notes.

But all this lasted only a few seconds; for Goethe wished to
make a severe trial, and give the performer no time for preparation. "You see," he exclaimed, "I told you you would stick.
Now try it: show us what you can do."

Felix began playing immediately. It was a simple melody;
if clearly written, a trifling, I may say no task, for even a
moderate performer. But to follow it through that scrambling
labyrinth required a quickness and certainty of eye such as
few are able to attain. I glanced with surprise at the leaf, and
tried to hum the tune; but many of the notes were perfectly
illegible, or had to be sought at the most unexpected corners,
as the boy often pointed out with a laugh.

He played it through once in this way, generally correctly,
but stopping at times, and correcting several mistakes with a
quick "No, so"; then he exclaimed, "Now I will play it to
you." And, this second time, not a note was missing. "This is
Beethoven, this passage," he said once turning to me, as if
he had come across something which sharply displayed the
master's peculiar style. "That is true Beethoven. I recognize
him in it at once."

Goethe concluded the trial with this piece. I need not add
that the young player again reaped the fullest praise, which
Goethe veiled in mocking jests, that he had got stuck here
and there, and had not been quite sure.

William Smyth Rockstro

Mendelssohn at the Height of His Career

Rockstro (1823-1895), an English musician and writer, was the author of *History of Music for Young Students, Life of Handel, Life of Mendelssohn,* and many textbooks on harmony and counterpoint.

He made the acquaintance of Mendelssohn in London, and when he later decided to go to Germany it was only in order to be able to study in Leipzig, where Mendelssohn was teaching at the Conservatory.

We chose the following excerpts from his book because they show Mendelssohn as a conductor of unusual power, as a pianist of unusual imagination, and as teacher of unusual responsibility.

In February 1844, Mendelssohn received from the Philharmonic Society in London an invitation to direct the last six concerts of the season. The engagement was a delightful one. Leaving his family quietly settled at Frankfort, he arrived in London for the eighth time on the 10th of May, once more became the guest of his old friend, Klingemann, and, on the 13th of the month, assumed command of the famous orchestra. The season was a brilliant one, and in addition to the interest it derived from his presence, was rendered memorable by the first appearance in London of Ernst, Joachim, and Piatti. The chief attractions of its varied program were the *Walpurgis-Nacht,* the *Midsummer Night's Dream,* the Overtures to *Leonora* (No. 1), *Egmont,* and the *Ruins of Athens,* Bach's Orchestral Suite in D Major, and Schubert's Overture to *Fierabras.* At the last concert of the season (June 24th) Mendelssohn astounded the orchestra by his powerful rendering of the Overture to *Egmont,* the *sforzandi* in the last movement of which had never before been correctly played by our English orchestras. It was at this concert, also, that he played, for the first time in England, Beethoven's Pianoforte Concerto in G Major. The effect produced by his interpretation of the five bars of unaccompanied solo with which this great work opens, will never be forgotten by those who were fortunate enough to hear it. The delicacy of the piano was perfect, yet every note penetrated to the remotest corner of the room.

At the rehearsal, on Saturday the 22nd, he enriched the first movement with a magnificent *extempore cadenza,* in which he worked up the varied subjects of the piece with the skill which never failed him when he gave rein to his exuberant fancy. On reaching the trill at its close he found the orchestra a little uncertain in taking up its point. In order to remove all fear of misunderstanding, he again extemporized a *cadenza* entirely different from the first, though not a whit less beautiful. The orchestra again missed its point so decidedly that he found it necessary to make a third trial. This last *cadenza* was by far the longest and most interesting of the three, and totally different, both in matter and in style, from its predecessors. It had, moreover, the effect of rendering the orchestral point so safe that no fear whatever was anticipated with regard to the Monday performance.

It will be readily understood that all present looked forward to this performance with intensest excitement; feeling certain that another new *cadenza* would be improvised at the concert. And it really was so. The same subjects were placed in so different a light, that their treatment bore not the slightest shade of resemblance to the Saturday performance, until the approach of the final trill, which was so arranged as to enable the orchestra to take up its point with the most perfect accuracy.

❋   ❋   ❋

Mendelssohn was anxious to return to Leipzig. On the 3rd of January 1846, he entered upon a course of active service at the Conservatory, assuming the sole command of two pianoforte classes, and one for composition, and in the management of both fulfilling the duties of a hard-working professor with no less enthusiasm than that which he had so long displayed in his character of conductor at the older institution.

We all met regularly, for instruction, on Wednesday and Saturday afternoons, each lesson lasting two hours. The first pianoforte piece selected for study was Hummel's Septet in D Minor: and we will remember the look of blank dismay depicted upon more than one excitable countenance, as each pupil in his turn after playing the first chord, and receiving an instantaneous reproof for its want of sonority, was invited to resign his seat in favor of an equally unfortunate successor. Mendelssohn's own manner of playing grand chords, both in *forte* and *piano* passages, was peculiarly impressive; and now, when a student had tried, and failed, he himself sat down to the instrument, and explained the causes of his dissatisfaction with such microscopic minuteness, and clearness of expression, that the lesson was simply priceless. He never gave a learner the chance of mistaking his meaning; and though the vehemence with which he sometimes expressed it made timid pupils desperately afraid of him, he was so perfectly just, so sternly impartial in awarding praise, on the one hand, and blame on the other, that consternation soon gave place to confidence, and confidence to boundless affection. Carelessness infuriated him. Irreverence for the composer he could never forgive. "*Es steht nicht da!*" ["It isn't written there!"] he almost shrieked one day to a pupil who had added a note to a certain chord. To another, who had scrambled through a difficult passage, he cried, with withering contempt, "*So spielen die Katzen!*" ["That's how cats play!"] But where he saw an earnest desire to do justice to the work in hand, he would give direction after direction, with a lucidity which we had never heard equaled. He never left a piece until

he was satisfied that the majority of the class understood it
thoroughly. Hummel's Septet formed the chief part of each
lesson, until the 25th of February. After that it was relieved,
occasionally, by one of Chopin's studies, or a fugue from the
Wohltemperierte Klavier. But it was not until the 21st of
March that it was finally set aside, to make room for Weber's
Concert-Stueck, the master's reading of which was superb.
He would make each pupil play a portion of this great work
in his own way, comment upon its delivery with the most
perfect frankness, and, if he thought the player deserved encouragement, would himself supply the orchestral passages
on a second pianoforte. But he never played straight through
the whole of the piece which formed the subject of the lesson.
On a few rare occasions—we can only remember two or three
—he invited the whole class to his house; and on one of these
happy days, he played an entire sonata—but not that which
the members of the class were studying. And the reason of
this reticence was obvious. He wished his pupils to understand the principles by which he himself was guided in his
interpretation of the works of the great masters, and at the
same time to discourage servile imitation of his own rendering of any individual composition. In fact, with regard to
special forms of expression, one of his most frequently re-
iterated maxims was, "If you want to play with true feeling,
you must listen to good singers. You will learn far more from
them than from any players you are likely to meet with."

Upon questions of simple technique he rarely touched,
except—as in the case of our first precious lesson upon the
chord of D Minor—with regard to the rendering of certain
special passages. But the members of his pianoforte classes
were expected to study these matters, on other days of the
week, under Herr Plaidy, or Wenzel, professors of high
repute, who had made the training of the fingers and wrist
their specialty. It would be impossible to overestimate the
value of this arrangement, which provided for the acquire-

ment of a pure touch, and facile execution, on the one hand, while, on the other, it left Mendelssohn free to direct the undivided attention of his pupils to the higher branches of art. An analogous plan was adopted with regard to the class in composition. The members of this simultaneously studied the technicalities of harmony under Herr F. Richter; those of counterpoint and fugue under Herr Hauptmann, the cantor of the Thomas-Schule, and the most learned contrapuntist in Europe; and those of form and instrumentation under Herr Niels W. Gade.

Mendelssohn himself took all these subjects into consideration, by turns, though only in their higher aspect. For counterpoint, he employed a large blackboard, with eight red staves drawn across it. On one of these staves he would write a *Canto fermo;* always using the soprano clef for the soprano part. Then, offering the chalk to one of his pupils, he would bid him write a counterpoint above or below the given subject. This done, he would invite the whole class to criticize the tyro's work; discussing its merits with the closest possible attention to every detail. Having corrected this, to his satisfaction, or, at least, made the best of it, he would pass on the chalk to someone else—generally to the student who had been most severe in his criticism—bidding him add a third part to the two already written. And this process he would carry on, until the whole of the eight staves was filled. The difficulty of adding a sixth, seventh or eighth part, to an exercise already complete in three, four, or five, and not always written with the freedom of an experienced contrapuntist, will be best understood by those who have most frequently attempted the process. It was often quite impossible to supply an additional part, or even an additional note; but Mendelssohn would never sanction the employment of a rest, as a means for escape from the gravest difficulty, until every available resource had been tried in vain.

One day, when it fell to our own lot to write the eighth part,

a certain bar presented so hopeless a deadlock that we confessed ourselves utterly vanquished. "Can't you find a note?"
asked Mendelssohn. "Not one that could be made to fit in,
without breaking a rule," said we. "I am very glad," said he in
English, and laughing heartily, "for I could not find one myself." It was, in fact, a case of perfect checkmate.

We never knew, beforehand, what form the lessons in this
class would assume. Sometimes he would give out the words
of a song, to be set to music, by each member of the class,
before its next meeting; or a few verses of a psalm, to be set
in the form of a motet. When summoned, towards the end
of May 1846, to direct the Lower Rhine Festival, at Aix-La-
Chapelle, the task he left for completion during his absence
was a quartet for stringed instruments. When any trial compositions of this kind pleased him, he had them played by
the orchestral class; and would even play the viola himself,
or ask Herr Gade to play it; striving, by every means of encouragement within his power, to promote a wholesome
spirit of emulation among his pupils. It was not often that this
kindly spirit met with an unworthy response; but the least appearance of ingratitude wounded him, cruelly. When the
quartets we have mentioned were sent to him for examination,
he found one of them headed *Charivari*. At the next meeting
of the class, he asked for an explanation of the title. "The time
was so short," stammered the composer, "that I found it impossible to write anything worthy of a better name. I called
it *Charivari*, to show that I knew it was rubbish." We could
see that Mendelssohn felt deeply hurt; but he kept his temper
nobly. "I am a very busy man," he said, "and am, just now,
overwhelmed with work. Do you think you were justified in
expecting me to waste my time upon a piece which you yourself knew to be rubbish? If you are not in earnest, I can have
nothing to say to you." Nevertheless, he analysed the quartet
with quite as much care as the rest, while the culprit stood
by, as white as a sheet.

Eduard Philipp Devrient

A Strange and Fascinating Character

Eduard Devrient (1801-1877) was an excellent baritone and musician, playwright and librettist. At the height of his career as an opera singer he suddenly lost his voice. He turned actor and stage director, again with great success.

Devrient met Felix for the first time in Berlin, when both were still boys. He participated in the literary evenings at the house of Felix' very wealthy parents, and in his wonderful voice he sang his young friend's first songs. This friendship never died. Devrient was one of the very few from whom the oversensitive composer would take adverse criticism.

Felix had now completed his twentieth year; his productive powers had already shown that his strength lay in picturesque composition; he was a great conductor, and his personal character was permanently fixed.

Of middle height, slender frame, and of uncommon muscular power, a capital gymnast, swimmer, walker, rider and dancer, the leading feature of his outward and inner nature was an extraordinary sensitiveness. Excitement stimulated him to the verge of frenzy, from which he was restored only by his sound, deathlike sleep. This restorative he had always at hand; he assured me that he had but to find himself alone and unoccupied in a room where there was a sofa, to go straightway to sleep. His brain had from childhood been taxed excessively, by the university course, study of modern languages, drawing and much else, and to these were added the study of music in its profoundest sense. The rapidity with which he mastered a score; his perfect understanding of the requirements of new compositions, the construction and complications of which were at once transparent to him; his marvelous memory, which placed under his hand the entire range of great works; these wondrous gifts filled me with frequent doubts as to whether his nervous power could possibly sustain him through the length of an ordinary life.

Moreover, he would take no repose. The habit of constant occupation, instilled by his mother, made rest intolerable to him. To spend any time in mere talk caused him to look frequently at his watch, by which he often gave offense; his impatience was only pacified when something was being done, such as music, reading, chess, etc. He was fond of having a leaf of paper and pen at hand when he was conversing, to sketch down whatever occurred to him.

His manners were most pleasing. His features, of the Oriental type, were handsome; a high, thoughtful forehead, much depressed at the temples; large, expressive dark eyes, with drooping lids, and a peculiar veiled glance through the lashes; this, however, sometimes flashed distrust or anger, sometimes happy dreaming and expectancy. His nose was arched and of delicate form, still more so the mouth, with its short upper and full under lip, which was slightly protruded and hid his teeth, when, with a slight lisp, he pronounced the hissing consonants. An extreme mobility about his mouth betrayed every emotion that passed within.

His bearing retained from boyhood the slight rocking of the head and upper part of the body, and shifting from foot to foot; his head was much thrown back, especially when playing; it was always easy to see whether he was pleased or otherwise when any new music was going on, by his nods and shakes of the head. In society his manners were even then felt to be distinguished. The shyness that he still retained left him entirely during his subsequent travels, but even now, when he wished to propitiate, he could be most fascinating, and his attentions to young ladies were not without effect. In his affections filial love still held the foremost place; the veneration with which he regarded his father had in it something religious and patriarchal; with his sisters the fondest intimacy prevailed; from his brother disparity of age still somewhat divided him. His elder sister, Fanny, stood musically most closely related to him; through her excellent nature, clear sense, and rich fund of sensibility (not perceptible to every one), many things were made clear to him. For his youngest sister, Rebecca, now in the bloom of her girlhood, he had an unbounded admiration, sensitive as he was to all that was fair and lovely.

Felix's nature fitted him particularly for friendship; he possessed even then a rich store of intimates, which increased as he advanced in life. To his friends he was frankly devoted, exquisitely tender; it was indeed felicity to be beloved by Felix. At the same time it must be confessed that his affection was exclusive to the utmost; he loved only in the measure that he was loved. This was the solitary dark speck in his sunny disposition. He was the spoiled child of fortune, unused to hardship or opposition; it remains a marvel that egotism did not prevail more than it did over his inborn nobleness and straightforwardness.

The atmosphere of love and appreciation in which he had been nurtured was a condition of life to him; to receive his music with coldness or aversion was to be his enemy, and he was capable of denying genuine merit in anyone who did so. A blunder in manners, or an expression that displeased him, could alienate him altogether; he could then be disagreeable, indeed quite intolerable. The capital musician, Bernhard Klein, he never could bear, and simply because—as he himself confessed to me—Klein, sitting beside Felix in a box at the opera when Felix was yet a boy and his feet, when he sat on a chair, did not reach the ground, impatiently muttered, "Cannot that boy keep his feet from dangling?" About such small things he could be unforgiving, for he could not accustom himself to hearing what displeased him, and he never had been compelled to conform cheerfully to the whims of anyone. I often took him to task about this, and suggested that, like the Venetian, he should keep a book of vengeance, in which to enter a debtor and creditor account for offenses. I could venture to speak thus jokingly to him, for he knew that I could never have believed him capable of retaliation, even for unkindness and spite.

But his irritability, his distrustfulness even toward his most intimate friends, were sometimes quite incredible. A casual remark, a stupid jest that he often accepted from me with perfect good temper, would sometimes suddenly cause him to drop his lids, look at me askance, and ask doubtfully, "What do you mean by that? Now I want to know what you wish me to understand by that?" and it was difficult to restore his good humor. These pecularities in Mendelssohn caused him, though much beloved, to be judged often unfavorably; but those who knew him intimately accepted these few faults, the natural product of his exceptional position, and prized none the less all that was excellent in him.

He was exquisitely kindhearted and benevolent, even toward dumb animals. I recollect him, when a boy of thirteen, ardently pleading for the life and liberty of a small fish which had been given to his brother Paul, who wished to have it fried for himself. Felix in anger said, "If you were anything of a boy, you would put it back in the water directly." Although the mother took the part of her nestling, the father decided the point with, "Paul, put the fish back in the water. You are no fisherman, and are not entitled to his life; for pleasure or for daintiness' sake we are not to take the life of any creature." Felix joyfully seized the little fellow's hand, ran with him to the pond, and threw in the struggling fish. I often thought of that fish when I later saw Felix take the part of those who were in trouble.

ROBERT SCHUMANN

Born: Zwickau, Germany
June 8, 1810
Died: Endenich, Germany
July 29, 1856

ROBERT SCHUMANN is one of the leading composers of the German "Romantics." He is the founder of the Romantic movement in German music.

He wrote first—opus 1 to 23—for the piano; these early works include the popular *Papillons,* the delightful and inimitable *Kinderscenen* and all the symphonic *études.* Later came his famous songs—*Frauenliebe und Leben*—and his symphonies and operas. In order to promote their new revolutionary ideas, he and his friends banded together into the "Davidsbuendler" society, because they, like David, had to fight the Philistines who were prostituting art. The group published a magazine of its own in Leipzig, *Neue Zeitschrift fuer Musik* ("New Journal of Music") which exerted tremendous influence.

Schumann married Clara Wieck, the daughter of his teacher. She was to become Europe's most celebrated pianist after Liszt, Moscheles, and Rubinstein. The marriage was an exceptionally happy one. The mystic collaboration between the two great musicians was famed in their lifetime and has become a legend.

Robert's health soon began to weaken. He was appointed Kapellmeister at Duesseldorf; shortly after they

had moved to that city, he suffered a severe attack of
nervous exhaustion. He was forced to give up all strenu-
ous work. In 1854, during a fit of mental depression, he
threw himself into the Rhine. He was rescued and taken
to an asylum near Bonn, where he died two years later.

Friedrich Wieck

Letter to Robert's Mother

Robert Schumann is the central figure of nineteenth-century musical
romanticism. He is also the most tragic figure among the musicians of
that century. Heredity accounts for the mental instability that increased
from year to year until he was dragged down to total insanity, severe
suffering and death.

The most influential of his teachers was Friedrich Wieck in Leipzig
(1785-1873); this man's knowledge of music and musical technique was
boundless. His little daughter Clara was the most famous child prodigy
in Europe.

Friedrich Wieck's letter, dated August 1830, is in answer to a desperate inquiry of Robert's mother, who was set against his musical ambi-
tions. Wieck is convinced of Robert's genius—but there is no doubt that
he has already seen signs of the youngster's mental confusion.

                                              Leipzig, August 1830
Honored Madame,

I hasten to answer your esteemed favor of the 7th inst.,
without further assuring you in advance of my warmest sympathy. But my answer can only be quite short, since I am
pressed by business of various kinds, and since I must talk
over the greater part of it with your son, if a satisfactory result is to be obtained. My suggestion would be that in the

first place (for many and far-reaching reasons of which I hope
to persuade your son) he should leave Heidelberg—the hot-
bed of his imagination—and should return to our cold, flat
Leipzig.

At present I merely say that with your son's talent and
imagination I pledge myself to turn him into one of the greatest pianists within three years. He shall play with more
warmth and genius than Moscheles and on a grander scale
than Hummel. The proof of this I offer you in my eleven-
year-old daughter, whom I am now beginning to present to
the world. As to composition, our Cantor Weinlig will no
doubt be sufficient for present needs. But:

1. Robert very mistakenly thinks "that the whole of piano
playing consists in pure technique"; what a one-sided conception! I almost infer from this, either that he has never
heard a pianist of genius at Heidelberg or else that he himself
has advanced no farther in playing. When he left Leipzig
he knew better what belongs to a good pianist, and my
eleven-year-old Clara will show him something different.
But it is true that for Robert the greatest difficulty lies in the
quiet, cold, well-considered, restrained conquest of technique, as the foundation of piano playing. I confess frankly
that when—in the lessons which I gave him—I succeeded,
after hard struggles and great contradictoriness on his part,
after unheard-of pranks played by his unbridled fancy upon
two creatures of pure reason like ourselves, in convincing him
of the importance of a pure, exact, smooth, clear, well-marked
and elegant touch, very often my advice bore little fruit for
the next lesson, and I had to begin again, with my usual affection for him, to expound the old theme, to show him once
more the distinctive qualities of the music which he had
studied with me, and earnestly to insist on my doctrines (remember that I cared only for Robert and for the highest in
art). And then he would excuse himself for the next week
or fortnight or even longer; he could not come for this or

that reason, and the excuses lasted—with a few exceptions—
until he went to a town and to surroundings which in truth
are not designed to restrain his unbridled fancy or quiet his
unsettled ideas. Has our dear Robert changed—become more
thoughtful, firmer, stronger, and may I say calmer and more
manly? This does not appear from his letters.

2. I will not undertake Robert (that is if he means to live
wholly for art in the future) unless for a year he has an hour
with me almost every day.

Why? For once I ask you to have unquestioning confidence
in me. But how can I do this now that I have a class in Dresden as well, and at Christmas am going to establish another
in Berlin, Vienna and probably also in Paris? What will
Robert's so-called Imagination-Man say to it if the lessons
(lessons in touch, with an unemotional theme) have to be
stolen from me and he is left to himself for from three to six
weeks, to go in the right direction? Honored lady, neither of
us can tell that; Robert himself knows best; he alone can say
if he really has any determination.

3. Without committing myself further at present, I declare
that the piano *virtuoso* (if he does not happen to be a very
famous composer whose name has been honored for years)
can earn his living only if he gives lessons—but then, very
easily and well. Good, intelligent teachers who have received
an all-around education are wanted everywhere, and it is
known that people pay 2-4 thaler an hour in Paris, Vienna,
St. Petersburg, Berlin etc., and 6-8 thaler in London. I am
educating my daughter to be a teacher first of all, though—
child as she is—she is already far superior to all other women
pianists in the world, for she can improvise freely—yet I do
not allow this to mislead me in any way. Robert would be
able to live very comfortably in such places, as a piano
teacher, since he has a small income of his own. For I should
be sorry to think that he will eat up his capital.

But I wish to know if Robert will decide at once to give

lessons here, since teaching needs years of training? Robert surely remembers what I demand from a good piano teacher? That is one question which I cannot answer; nor can I say whether Robert himself can answer it.

4. Can Robert determine to study dry, cold theory, and all that belongs to it, with Weinlig for two years? With instruction in the piano I always combine lessons in the practical study of simple chords by means of which I impart a beautiful and correct touch, etc.—in a word everything that is not and never will be found in any piano school.

Has Robert condescended to learn even this small amount of theory, although in any case my lessons are sufficiently interesting? I must say, No. Will Robert now decide like my Clara to give some hours every day to writing exercises in three-and-four-part composition? It is work which almost wholly silences the imagination—at least such a one as our Robert enjoys.

5. If Robert will not do all that I have said, then I ask: "What part will he play, and what outlet will his imagination find?"

From the frankness with which I have spoken of this, even if it has not been possible to treat it fully, you can easily see that I deserve to have his confidence if your son comes back to Leipzig, when he and Dr. Carus can discuss everything with me more fully and we can take counsel together.

Your son will excuse me for not having answered his letter to me. My business and the education of my daughter must excuse all such neglect on my part, as well as the haste in which I have written this letter.

Most honored friend, do not be anxious—compulsion is of little use in such matters: we must do our part as parents: God does the rest. If Robert has the courage and the strength to clear away my doubts when he is with me—and they might really be removed in six months (so that in the contrary case everything would still not be lost)—then let him go in peace and give him your blessing. In the meantime you will be awaiting his answer to these few lines, the writer of which respectfully signs himself

Your most devoted servant,

Fr. Wieck

F. Gustav Jansen

How the Young Schumann Looked

Young Robert Schumann studied in Leipzig, stayed there almost fourteen years. There he fought for his Clara—whom her father forbade to marry him—and there he founded his world-famous magazine *Neue Zeitschrift fuer Musik,* wherein he wrote passionate articles in favor of modern music. And there his first important works were performed in the Gewandhaus.

He invented a company of dauntless warriors for his magazine, the Davidsbuendler; it was the duty of these valiants to wield the pen against the routine music makers, whom he called "the Philistines." Of course most of the Davidsbuendler were Robert himself.

F. Gustav Jansen (1831-1910) was a young musician who knew Schumann personally; he later interviewed everyone who had lived and worked with Schumann during those fourteen Leipzig years.

SCHUMANN'S CONVERSATION had not the wit or eloquence to be found in his writings, nor was there anything in his outer appearance that could have been said to mark him as a "genius." He was of stately figure, powerfully built, his bearing was rather distinguished and aristocratic; his clothes were never striking, never gave evidence of an effort to impress. As H. Truhn describes him, "He had a big, roomy head, true Germanic, richly adorned with soft, dark blond hair, a full, beardless face, with lips so shaped and held that he always looked as if he were about to begin whistling very softly; his eyes were a beautiful blue but neither large nor expressive of energy or power; they always looked as if he had something he must fathom and listen to intently deep in his own soul. His posture was rigidly erect, but he walked with a soft, yielding step, as if the strong, broad-shouldered body had no bones at all. He was shortsighted and made much use of the lorgnette, but without a trace of coquetry— an observation hardly necessary, since his nature was diametrically opposed to everything studied or affected." In personal intercourse he was mostly laconic and displayed very little social adroitness; he lacked entirely the gift of talking much and saying little . . . .

Brendel tells a revealing story illustrative of his taciturnity: "Schumann had discovered an excellent wine, Markobrunner, in Gohlis, and he invited me to accompany him there for lunch. Side by side in the burning heat we wandered through the Rosenthal in silence, saying not a word; we arrived, and the Markobrunner did in fact prove to be the goal and consummation of the journey. There was not a word to be got out of him, and on the way back it was the same thing; we were absolutely silent the whole time. He made only one remark, and it afforded me a glimpse at the feelings that filled his heart. He spoke of the peculiar beauty of such a summer day, when all voices are silent, when nature is in complete repose. He was engulfed in this sensation of peace and simply remarked that the ancients had an apt expression for such a moment, Pan sleeps. We made two of these Markobrunner trips, and each time we achieved a perfect silence. In moments like these Schumann took notice of the external world only when it chanced to play in with his dreams. Human companionship was there for him at such times only to relieve him of the sense of loneliness . . ."

In 1846 Hanslick had the following characterization from the lips of R. Wagner: "Schumann is an extremely gifted musician but an impossible person. When I came here from

Paris I visited him, I told him about my Paris experiences, I talked about French musical affairs, then of German, I talked about literature and politics—but he remained practically mute for the length of an hour. You can't always talk *alone*. An impossible person!" Schumann's opinion of Wagner, which Hanslick also reports, is characteristic. Schumann stated that "Wagner—whom he seldom saw—was certainly a well-instructed and clever man, but he talked incessantly, and in the long run that becomes intolerable."

          ❊   ❊   ❊

After working all day, Schumann used to go to Poppe's "Kaffeebaum" in the late evening hours; this was the gathering place of a group of young people practicing the most diverse professions.

It would be a grave error to imagine that Schumann occupied a preponderant position in this circle or sat in judgment upon the living and the dead. Nothing of the sort. An atmosphere of unconstrained good cheer prevailed, as far from the spirit of clique snobbishness as it was from that of bacchanalian revelry. Schumann had his place in a hidden corner that he particularly liked. Says Brendel, "He used to sit sideways at the table so that he could lean his head on his hand; he would sit and from time to time stroke back his hair, which often fell over his forehead, with his eyes half-closed, withdrawn into himself, sunk in dreams. But then when something evoked an interesting exchange of ideas among his companions, he would liven up, even become talkative and animated; it may be said that you could actually see him awakening from his abstraction, emerging to the outer world—and you could see too how his eyes, usually turned backward, looking into himself, now turned toward the external world, displaying at one and the same time an acute intelligence and a fantastic splendor."

In this high-spirited and alert society Schumann was perfectly at ease, since he was not obliged to put the slightest
compulsion upon himself. Sitting in his regular seat at the
head end of the table, the inevitable cigar in his mouth, he
did not even have to call for a fresh glass of beer; he had it
so arranged that another glass was brought to him, without
his signaling, as soon as the innkeeper or waiter noticed
that he had drunk up. The moment the waiter set before him
the glass he intended for his last, he paid his bill—also in
silence and nearly always with a tip. On most evenings the
Kaffeebaum company was small and Schumann did not stay
past the customary *Buergerstunde* (the hour when respect-
able people went home). Now and then he would leave the
place precipitately as if in response to a military summons;
he would rush out without saying good night to anybody.
These were the times when he had music in his head and was
hurrying home to write it down.

✻   ✻   ✻

During the first years Schumann changed his lodgings
frequently, but then in 1836 he moved into a room pleasantly
situated and he did not move again until his marriage. This
room was in a house built around a court—the house was
called "the red college"—and it had a view of the so-called
lower park. Its window faced the woodiest and bushiest part
of the promenade that girdles old Leipzig. Next to his was
a larger room with two windows; this probably belonged to
his apartment, since there was never a sound to be heard in
it. It was so quiet and peaceful in these rooms that when the
trees rustled outside the window you could fancy yourself
translated to some lonely castle way out in the woods, one
of those castles that dawn and shimmer in the rosy morning
and evening glow of Eichendorff's wonderland romances.
Right outside the window were bushes, with only a footpath

running through; when the wind moved the branches they could almost touch the windowpane. Sitting there, it was impossible to believe you were in the middle of populous, industrial Leipzig . . . . At the window, which was set rather high above the floor, was a table on a so-called "step" or platform, with an inkstand and a hook for hanging up a watch. There was also the most delightful miniature leaning against the inkstand, the head of a girl with a thoughtful look; Schumann's watch, which he carried on a twist of hair, also hung there. I was not permitted to ask him who the girl in the picture was or whether she bore any relation to the hair watch chain. Although this little poet's room had only one window, it was broad and deep enough to hold a grand piano, and against the opposite wall, which had the door leading into the next room, a sofa, standing beside its companion table. To complete the description: the room was oblong; the thick walls formed a kind of niche at the window—opposite the door—and here Schumann used to work . . . .

Friedrich Niecks

Darkness Falls

Friedrich Niecks (1845-1924) was a German violinist, educator and writer. His last post—of various ones—was that of Professor of Music at Edinburgh University, which chair he filled for twenty-three years.

He himself tells us in his biography of Schumann that he saw Schumann only in Duesseldorf and never spoke with him because he was only a little boy at the time. He also saw the great man conducting. But father Niecks knew the master well and told his son and interested friends many things that he remembered about the great romantic.

AT THE TIME of Schumann's stay in Düsseldorf I was still a little boy; my personal recollections are therefore few and

unimportant. I remember very well my father pointing him
out to me as he was slowly walking by himself in the public
park (Hofgarten). And I see still the quiet face, the protruding
rounded lips (as if he were whistling, or pronouncing O), and
the absorbed, absent look. I must have often seen him conduct, but remember distinctly only one occasion—namely, a
rehearsal of a Mass at the St. Maximilian Church on a Saturday afternoon before some great church festival. The organ
loft, the disposition of the chorus and orchestra, the bearing
of the conductor, and the light that fell upon the group
through the large windows behind them, form a picture in-
delibly impressed upon my mind. This was one of the occasions on which Schumann became so entirely oblivious of
the work he was engaged on that he let his baton fall. With
regard to this point, I must, however, caution the reader.
For although I seem to remember the circumstance well
enough, I nevertheless cannot help feeling a little doubtful
about it. Memory often plays such curious tricks. It not only
combines different events, but also what we have experienced
with what we have been told. It is, however, an indubitable
fact that Schumann let his baton fall on several occasions.
My father told me often how one day, before the commencement of a rehearsal, he was standing at his desk and Schumann came up to him and showed him a baton with a string
attached to it, which later was wound around his wrist, and
said, with childlike simplicity and a satisfied and pleased
expression on his face and in his voice, "Look, now it can't
fall again!"

How Schumann's imagination was always busy is shown
by the following occurrence: At the first rehearsal of a new
work of his one of the trombone players left out some notes
intended by the composer, either because the passage was
not in his part, or because he had made a mistake in counting.
Schumann duly noted and pointed out the omission. After the
same movement had been played at the second rehearsal, the

composer turned to the trombone player in question, who this time had been as silent as on the previous occasion, and remarked: "It is all right now, and sounds very well."

Schumann's absent-mindedness led sometimes to curious encounters and scenes. Let me give you two examples. While a pupil of Leipzig Conservatory, Dr. Langhans with some fellow students, played a work of Schumann's at one of the evening entertainments of the institution. The composer, evidently pleased with the performance, sent word through Ferdinand Wenzel to the young violinist to come to him. Inexpressibly happy, the youth hastened to the revered master. Imagine his feelings when, on presenting himself to Schumann, the latter remained dumb. After waiting respectfully for a while, the disappointed hero worshiper ventured to say something; whereupon Schumann made an effort, and asked him: "What countryman are you?" (*Was sind Sie fur ein Landsmann?*) and then relapsed into silence. A more interesting case is the following one. From 1849 to 1854 there existed at Paris a concert society, a Société Sainte-Cécile, founded and conducted by Francois Jean-Baptiste Seghers. The advancement of art, not gain, was the object of all concerned in the undertaking. I have been told by a friend of mine who was one of the body that the executants gave their services *gratis.* M. Seghers and his enthusiastic supporters were especially anxious to make the Parisians acquainted with the best modern works. Among the various new compositions which were brought them for a first hearing in Paris was Schumann's Overture to *Manfred.* The performance, however, gave rise to disagreements between the conductor and some of the players, among whom the Teutonic element was strongly represented. The question was, What are the *tempi* intended by the composer? To settle the debated points, Carl Witting, who was then preparing to go to Germany, was commissioned to visit Düsseldorf, and in the name of the Société Sainte-Cécile lay the matter before the composer.

Herr Witting arrived at Düsseldorf, called on Schumann, was received by him, and explained to him the object of his visit. When he had ended, and was looking forward to an answer that would set at rest all doubt, Schumann, who was smoking a cigar, said, "Do you smoke?" "Yes," was Herr Witting's reply. But the composer had already become—or rather, had again become—oblivious of his visitor, for he neither offered him a cigar nor gave him an answer to his questions. After waiting for some time, Herr Witting made another effort to get the desired information, but with exactly the same result— the words "Do you smoke?" followed by silence. A third attempt elicited as little as the two previous ones; and Herr Witting took his leave of the composer just as wise as when he greeted him on entering.

✦   ✦   ✦

The relation between Schumann and his wife was beautiful. We know from his literary works, and, still better, from his letters, how he loved her, and how she inspired him. Those people who lived near them know equally well how she watched over him, placed herself between the outside world and him, and prevented, as far as possible, those rubs which tortured his sensitive mind. Schumann, on the other hand, owing to his self-absorption, may have caused her unwittingly and unconsciously much annoyance, and even inflicted upon her many a severe pang. Of the two anecdotes I shall now tell, the second shows how precious her husband's approval was to Madame Schumann. Dr. Langhans met the composer and his wife at an evening party at the house of the family Preusser of Leipzig. It is needless to say that there was music. Among the works performed was Schumann's quintet, in which Madame Schumann took the pianoforte part. In all this is, of course, nothing unusual; but the reader may perhaps think it sufficiently remarkable that the composer, to prevent his wife, a great pianist, from hurrying the *tempi*, beat time on her shoulders. The next anecdote describes a scene which took place several years later at Düsseldorf. Madame Schumann had played at one of the subscription concerts some unaccompanied solo pieces. Her husband sat not far from her, behind the piano. When she had finished there was a general rivalry among the audience and the musicians on the platform to give expression to their delight, which she, however, little heeded, for she saw her husband motionless and cold. "Have I not played well, Robert?" But there came no response, and she wept whilst the hall was ringing with ecstastic applause.

Wilhelm Josef von Wasielewski

Final Collapse

Von Wasielewski (1822-1896), a German composer of no importance, a conductor and a violinist, also wrote historical and critical books on music. Since he was on the closest terms with Robert Schumann from October 1850 to June 1852, in Duesseldorf, he had from the master's own lips all the details of his life and work that he passes on to us. Schumann also sent him written material for a biography.

Both Clara Schumann and Johannes Brahms, Schumann's favorite pupil, charged Von Wasielewski with a certain lack of taste and also with inaccuracy. His story of Schumann's death, however, adheres chiefly to the events which he himself witnessed. Schumann left Duesseldorf on the 4th of March 1854, accompanied by his physician, Dr. Hasenclever, and two keepers. There followed two years of misery at the asylum of Endenich, near Bonn.

EVEN in 1851, alarming symptoms of this terrible, slowly developing, and anxiously watched disease, appeared. He wrote of it, on June 11, 1851, "We are all tolerably well, except that I am the victim of occasional nervous attacks, which sometimes alarm me; especially a few days ago, when I fainted after hearing Radecke play the organ." These "nervous attacks" increased in 1852, and were accompanied by peculiar symptoms. Pre-eminent among them was that difficulty of enunciation from which he had always suffered, though never to such a degree. It was also noticeable, that, on hearing music, he always thought the time too fast; he longed to have it slower, and insisted upon it when he led. This was clearly because he was no longer able to follow a brisk movement. His demeanor was sad; and his reception of intimate friends, in spite of apparent cordiality, revealed great apathy. He took little interest in the male choral festival held at Düsseldorf on the first four days of August 1852, although he had been chosen one of the directors; and it was evident that he was exhausted, both mentally and physically, by the slight exertion of leading a few pieces.

On medical advice, he sought cold baths to alleviate his illness; and was sent by his physician to a watercure at Scheveningen, whence he returned at the end of September. His health did not, however, permit him to resume his official duties at once; wherefore, at his request, Julius Tausch assumed the direction of the first two winter concerts. At length he so far recovered that he was able for the last time in his life to devote himself, with ever-lessening powers, to his profession. He directed, as usual, all the subscription concerts, dating from the third, and composed a number of works in the year 1853.

The morbid symptoms so often recurring in 1852 not only reappeared in 1853, but new ones were added. This was the time of "table-tipping," which put Schumann into perfect ecstasies, and in every sense of the word, captivated him. Table-tipping agitated many prudent people at that time, going the rounds of the boudoirs and teaparties of nervous ladies, and the studios of otherwise earnest men; but their feelings were different from Schumann's nervous frenzy. While visiting Düsseldorf in May 1853, I one day entered his room, and found him on the sofa reading. To my inquiry as to the subject of his book, he replied in an excited tone, "Oh! don't you know anything about 'table-tipping'?" I laughingly answered, "Well!" Upon this, his eyes, generally half-shut and in-turned, opened wide, the pupils dilated convulsively, and with a peculiar, ghostlike look, he said, slowly and mournfully, "The tables know all." When I saw that he was in dead earnest, rather than irritate him I fell into his humor, and he soon grew calm. He then called his second daughter and began to experiment with her aid and a small table, which tapped out the beginning of Beethoven's C Minor Symphony. The whole scene struck me with terror; and I well remember that I expressed my distress to acquaintances at the time. He wrote of his experiments to Ferd. Hiller, April 25, 1853: "We *tipped the table* yesterday for the first time. Wonderful power! Just think! I asked for the first two measures of the C Minor Symphony! It delayed longer than usual with the answer: at last it began, but rather slowly at first. When I said, 'But the time is faster, dear table,' it hastened to beat the true time. When I asked if it could give the number which *I was thinking of*, it gave it correctly as *three.* We were all filled with wonder." And to the same, on April 29th, "We have repeated our experiments in magnetism; we seem surrounded with wonders."

There were also occasional auricular delusions, which caused him to hear an uninterrupted sound, and in his nervous excitement he really heard it, although there was nothing in the slightest degree approaching a sound. The violinist Ruppert Becker of Frankfort-on-the-Main, who then lived in Düsseldorf, told me that he was at a modest restaurant with Schumann one evening. Suddenly Schumann threw down the paper saying, "I can read no more; I hear an incessant A."

The close of 1853 brought two joyful events to Schumann—
the second especially delighting him. In October he met
Johannes Brahms, whom he himself had introduced to the
musical world as the "Messiah of art" by an enthusiastic
recognition of his merits in the columns of his journal. In
November he and his wife took a trip through Holland, which
was a triumphal procession. "We made a journey to the
Netherlands, which was, from beginning to end, guided by
good fairies. In every city we were welcomed with joy, ay,
with honor. To my great surprise, I find that my music is almost as well known in Holland as at home. Everywhere there
were fine performances of my symphonies, even the most
difficult—the second and third; and, in the Hague, my *Rose*
was given," he writes to Strackerjan.

On December 22nd, he returned to Düsseldorf from his
trip in Holland. The dreadful event was fast approaching
which was to tear him forever from art and the world. With
the exception of a short visit to Hanover, he lived quietly in
the bosom of his family during the months of January and
February 1854. Besides the edition of his *Collected Writings*
which he was preparing for the press, he was very busy with
a literary labor, which he called *The Garden of Poets*. The
idea, which was to collect all said of music by the poets from
most ancient times down to the present day, had occurred
to him in his youth; and he had made extracts from the writings of Shakespeare and Jean Paul for the purpose. He was
now searching the Bible and the Greek and Latin classics.
This was quite difficult, since he had entirely neglected the
dead languages while at school and in college. But he was
not destined to complete his task; for when it was but half-
done, the dangerous symptoms of the preceding year not only
returned, but increased to such a degree, that the morbid
mental darkness, from which he never recovered, soon gained
the upper hand.

The auricular delusions again appeared. He imagined that

he heard a tone, which pursued him incessantly, and from which harmonies, indeed, whole compositions, were gradually developed. Spirit voices were heard whispering in his ear, now gentle, now rude and reproachful. They robbed him of sleep for the last two weeks of his wretched existence. One night he rose suddenly, and called for a light, saying that Franz Schubert and Mendelssohn had sent a theme which he must write out at once, which he did, in spite of his wife's entreaties. During his illness, he composed five piano variations on this theme. This was his last work.

One of the ideas that occupied his mind was the belief that he "could never be cured at home," but must resign himself to the cure of some physician. On one occasion he sent for a carriage, arranged his papers and compositions, and prepared to depart. He was perfectly aware of his condition, and, when violently excited, would beg his family to help him. His wife made every effort to dissipate the fantoms and delusions which haunted his fevered imagination. Hardly had she succeeded when some new fancy would disturb his distracted brain. He declared again and again that he was a sinner who did not deserve to be loved. Thus the unhappy master's agony increased, until at last, after a fortnight of terrible struggle against his disease, he gave way, and his sufferings drove him to a desperate step.

On Monday, February 27, 1854, he received a noonday visit from his physician, Dr. Hasenclever, and his musical friend, Albert Dietrich. They sat and chatted together sociably. During the conversation, Schumann, without a word, left the room. They supposed he would return; but when some time passed, and he did not come, his wife went in search of him. He was nowhere to be found. His friends hastened out to look for him—in vain. He had left the house in his dressing gown, with bare head, gone to the bridge that spans the Rhine, and sought to end his misery by plunging into the stream. Some sailors jumped into a boat, rowed after him, and pulled him out. His life was saved, but to what purpose! Passersby recognized the wretched master, and he was carried home. The news was broken to his wife, who was not permitted to see him in his lamentable state. A second physician was called in, for a fearful paroxysm at once ensued, which finally ceased. He now required constant watching.

Clara Schumann

From Her Diaries

Schumann found in Clara a true wife; though she was ten years his junior, her love and her devotion gave him shelter. The only conflict in this harmonious relationship arose when Clara wanted to show herself in public. She kept diaries all her life. These and her letters provide us with important source material; from them we learn to understand much not only about the master but about the whole musical life of the nineteenth century.

Schumann's end could not have been better told than it has been told by Clara. She and Johannes Brahms were the last who received occasional permission to see him.

JOHANNES saw him, but both he and the doctor begged me not to see him, told me that it was my duty to my children not to subject myself to such a shock, etc., etc. In short, I returned without having seen him. But I could not long endure the pain, the longing to receive but one more look from him, to let him feel me near him—I had to go to him, and on Sunday the 27th I traveled back with Johannes. I saw *Him* between six and seven in the evening. He smiled, and put his arm round me with a great effort, for he can no longer control his limbs. I shall never forget it.

Not all the treasures in the world could equal this embrace. My Robert, it was thus that we had to see each other again, how painfully I had to trace out your beloved features! What a sorrowful sight it was!

Two and a half years ago you were torn from me without any farewell, though your heart must have been full, and now I lay silent at your feet hardly daring to breathe; only now and then I received a look, clouded as it were, but unspeakably gentle.

Everything about him was holy to me, even the air which he, my noble husband, breathed with me. He seemed to speak much with spirits, and would suffer no one to be near him for long, or he became restless, but it was almost impossible to understand him any longer. Only once I understood "My," "Clara" he would no doubt have added, for he looked at me affectionately; and then once again, "I know—" "You" probably.

On Monday the 28th, Johannes and I spent the whole day out there, going in and out of his room, but often only looking at Him through the little window in the wall. He suffered dreadfully, though the doctor would not admit it. His limbs twitched continuously and he often spoke vehemently. Ah! I could only pray God to release him, because I loved him so dearly.

For weeks he has taken nothing but wine and jelly—today, I gave it to him, and he took it with the happiest expression and in real haste, sucking the wine from my finger—ah! he knew that it was I.

On Tuesday the 29th, he was to be released from his suffering. At four o'clock in the afternoon he fell peacefully asleep. His last hours were quiet, and he passed away in his sleep without its being noticed, no one was with him at the moment. I did not see him till half an hour later. Joachim had come from Heidelberg in consequence of a telegram from us, and this had kept me in town longer than usual after dinner.

His head was beautiful, the forehead so transparent and slightly arched. I stood by the body of my passionately loved husband, and was calm. All my feelings were absorbed in thankfulness to God that he was at last set free, and as I kneeled by his bed I was filled with awe, it was as if his holy spirit was hovering over me. Ah! if only he had taken me with him! I saw him for the last time today—I laid some flowers on his head—my love he has taken with him.

On Wednesday, the 30th, Fräulein Reumont gave me Robert's things. . . . What pain to touch them!—my letters, which he had tied together with a pink ribbon, the pictures of me and the children, Johannes and Joachim, in which he had so often taken pleasure. He asked for mine at the very hour at which I made up my mind to hasten to him. All his papers were in perfect order. He had written out his accompaniment to Paganini's 24 *Études* very, very neatly.

The funeral was at seven o'clock on Thursday, the 31st. I was in the little chapel at the churchyard. I heard the funeral music. Now he was lowered into the grave. Yet I had a clear sense that it was not he, but his body only—his spirit was with me—I never prayed more fervently than at that hour. God give me strength to live without him.

Johannes and Joachim went before the coffin, which was carried as a mark of respect, by members of the *Concordia-gesellschaft,* who once serenaded him in Düsseldorf. The mayors went with them, and Hiller came from Cologne, but there were no other friends. I had not let it be known, because I did not wish a number of strangers to come. His dearest friends went in front, and I came (unnoticed) behind, and it was best thus; he would have liked it so. And thus, with this departure, all my happiness is over. A new life is beginning for me.

FREDERIC FRANÇOIS CHOPIN

Born: Zelazowa Wola, Poland
February 22, 1810
Died: Paris, France
October 17, 1849

FREDERIC FRANÇOIS CHOPIN was born of a Polish family. From early childhood he displayed a kind of exalted melancholy; he was irresistibly attracted to the mournful melodies of his nation's folk songs. His first concerts established him in the world's opinion as the greatest musical genius ever born.

He soon left Poland and settled in Paris, which was at that time the center of Europe's intellectual and artistic life; it was likewise the new home of exiled Polish society who had been forced to flee the Russian terror. Chopin very soon received the veneration to which his genius entitled him. His success enabled him to maintain the curiously aristocratic attitude that people fairly adored.

The most decisive episode of his life, his liaison with the celebrated George Sand, lasted from 1836 to 1847. As long as love endured, she showered him with the tenderest of care, particularly when his fatal illness (consumption) began to take hold.

After his break with George Sand he composed no more. His health declined rapidly and he knew his days were numbered. In his last home, on the Place Vendome in Paris, he was surrounded by tenderly loving friends until his death.

Felix Mendelssohn

Chopin at Twenty-Five

Young Chopin's arrival anywhere in Germany, Austria or France invariably excited the connoisseurs. When he came to Leipzig Friedrich Wieck, Schumann's teacher and Clara's father, set himself the task of disproving the general belief that no one in Germany was capable of playing Chopin's compositions. "We will see what Clara can do!" And in fact Clara played his works so brilliantly that Chopin showered her with praise.

Mendelssohn very quickly became a warm and sincere friend to the young genius, who was already seriously ill. Here is Mendelssohn's account in a letter dated October 6, 1835, addressed to his sister Fanny Hensel and his father.

. . . I CANNOT DENY, dear Fanny, that I have found lately that your criticisms are unjust to Chopin; perhaps when you heard him he was not in the mood for playing, which may often happen with him; but his playing has charmed me anew, and I am convinced that if you and Father had heard some of his better things, as I have heard them, you would agree with me. There is something radically original in his playing, and at the same time so very masterly that he may be called a truly perfect *virtuoso;* and since I love and delight in all forms of perfection, this has been a most agreeable day for me, although so different from the day before with you Hensels. It was a pleasure for me to be with a proper musician once more, not with these half-*virtuosi* and half-classicists who would like to unite in music *les honneurs de la vertu et les plaisirs du vice,* but with an artist who has his own perfectly defined style. Even if it is as far from mine as heaven from earth, I can get along with it splendidly—only not with these mediocrities. Sunday evening brought me a strange experience: I had to play him my oratorio with inquisitive Leipzigers pushing

in surreptitiously to get a look at Chopin; then between the
first and second parts he dashed off his new *Études* and a new
concerto for the astonished Leipzigers, whereupon I went on
with my *St. Paul*—as if an Iroquois and a Kaffir had met and
were conversing. He also has a very pretty new nocturne; I
remember a good deal of it to play by heart to Paul [Felix'
brother] for his pleasure. And so we were merry together, and
he promised in all seriousness to come back during the winter
on condition that I compose a new symphony and perform it
in his honor. We both took our oath upon it before three witnesses, and we shall see if we both keep our word. . . .

Franz Liszt

Chopin's Personality and Appearance

Chopin and Liszt met in Paris. Chopin marveled at Liszt, but was
always dubious of his sincerity. At first Liszt was enthusiastic over both
Chopin's work and his playing; later he showed jealousy.

On one occasion Chopin took offense at his ruthlessness; he could not
forgive Liszt, and they never met again.

In his relations and intercourse with others, he always
seemed occupied with what interested them; he was careful
not to lead them from the circle of their own personality, lest
they should intrude on his. If he gave up but little of his time
to others, at least of that which he did relinquish, he reserved
none for himself. No one ever asked him to give an account of
his dreams, his wishes, or his hopes. No one seemed to wish
to know what he sighed for, what he might have conquered, if
his white and tapering fingers could have linked the brazen
chords of life to the golden ones of his enchanted lyre! No one
had leisure to think of this in his presence. His conversation

was rarely upon subjects of any deep interest. He glided lightly over all, and as he gave but little of his time, it was easily filled with the details of the day. He was careful never to allow himself to wander into digressions of which he himself might become the subject. His individuality rarely excited the investigations of curiosity, or awakened vivid scrutiny. He pleased too much to excite much reflection. The ensemble of his person was harmonious, and called for no especial commentary. His blue eye was more spiritual than dreamy, his bland smile never writhed into bitterness. The transparent delicacy of his complexion pleased the eye, his fair hair was soft and silky, his nose slightly aquiline, his bearing so distinguished, and his manners stamped with so much high breeding, that involuntarily he was always treated *en prince*. His gestures were many and graceful; the tone of his voice was veiled, often stifled; his stature was low, and his limbs slight. He constantly reminded us of a Convolvulus balancing its heaven-colored cup upon an incredibly slight stem, the tissue of which is so like vapor that the slightest contact wounds and tears the misty corolla.

His manners in society possessed that serenity of mood which distinguishes those whom no ennui annoys, because they expect no interest. He was generally gay, his caustic spirit caught the ridiculous rapidly and far below the surface at which it usually strikes the eye. He displayed a rich vein of drollery in pantomime. He often amused himself by reproducing the musical formulas and peculiar tricks of certain *virtuosi,* in the most burlesque and comic improvisations, imitating their gestures, their movements, counterfeiting their faces with a talent which instantaneously depicted their whole personality. His own features would then become scarcely recognizable, he could force the strangest metamorphoses upon them, but while mimicking the ugly and grotesque, he never lost his own native grace. Grimace was never carried far enough to disfigure him; his gayety was so much the more piquant because he always restrained it within the limits of perfect good taste, holding at a careful distance all that could wound the most fastidious delicacy. He never made use of an inelegant word, even in moments of the most entire familiarity; an improper innuendo, a coarse jest would have been shocking to him.

❊   ❊   ❊

On some occasions, although very rarely, we saw him deeply agitated. We saw him grow so pale and wan, that his appearance was actually corpse-like. But even in moments of the most intense emotion, he remained concentrated within himself. A single instant for self-recovery always enabled him to veil the secret of his first impression. However full of spontaneity his bearing afterward might seem to be, it was the product of instantaneous reflection, of a will which governed the strange conflict of emotional and moral energy with conscious physical debility; a conflict whose strange contrasts were forever warring fiercely within. The dominion exercised over the natural violence of his character reminds us of the melancholy force of those beings who seek their strength in isolation and entire self-control, conscious of the uselessness of their lively indignation and vexation, and too jealous of the mysteries of their passions to betray them gratuitously.

He could pardon in the most noble manner. No rancor remained in his heart toward those who had wounded him, though such wounds penetrated deeply into his soul, and festered there in vague pain and internal suffering, so that long after the exciting cause had been effaced from his memory, he still experienced the secret torture. By dint of constant effort, in spite of his acute and tormenting sensibilities, he subjected his feelings to the rule rather of what ought to be, than of what is; thus he was grateful for services proceeding rather from good intentions than from a knowledge of what would have been agreeable to him. Nevertheless the wounds caused by such awkward miscomprehension are, of all others, the most difficult for nervous temperaments to bear. Condemned to repress their vexation, such natures are excited by degrees to a state of constantly gnawing irritability, which they can never attribute to the true cause. It would be a gross mistake to imagine that this irritation existed without provocation. But as a deviation from what appeared to him to be the most honorable course of conduct was a temptation which he was never called upon to resist, because in all probability it never presented itself to him; so he never, in the presence of more vigorous and therefore more brusque and positive individualities than his own, unveiled the shudder, if repulsion be too strong a term, caused by their contact or association.

The reserve which marked his intercourse with others extended to all subjects to which the fanaticism of opinion can attach. His own sentiments could only be judged by that which he did not do within the narrow limit of his activity. His patriotism was revealed in the course taken by his genius, in the choice of his friends, in the preferences given to his pupils, and in the frequent and important services which he rendered to his compatriots; but we cannot remember that he took any pleasure in the expression of this sentiment. If he sometimes entered upon the topic of political ideals, so violently attacked, so warmly defended, so frequently discussed in France, it was rather to point out what he deemed dangerous or erroneous in the opinions advanced by others than to win attention for his own. In constant association with some of the most brilliant political figures of the day, he knew how to limit his relations with them to a personal attachment entirely independent of political interests.

Democracy presented to his view an agglomeration of elements too heterogeneous, too restless, wielding too much savage power, to win his sympathies. . . . The increase of popular discussion of social and political questions was compared,

more than twenty years ago, to a new and bold incursion of
barbarians. Chopin was peculiarly and painfully struck with
the terror this comparison aroused. . . . He feared the de-
struction of art, its monuments, its refinements, its civiliza-
tion; in a word, he dreaded the loss of the elegant, cultivated,
if somewhat indolent ease described by Horace. Would the
graceful life, the high culture of the arts, really be safe in the
rude and devastating hands of the new barbarians?

George Sand

Terrors and Phantoms

Chopin first met George Sand, the famous writer (1804-1876), in
the winter of 1836; his ill-health led indirectly to the liaison. From her
affection maternelle of the early stages a *grande affaire* developed, culminating in their escape to Majorca in October 1838. For years they
lived together, first in Majorca, then in the monastery Valdemosa, in
Nohant, and finally in Paris.

In her *Histoire de Ma Vie* George Sand describes her life with Chopin.
We include some short selections: the first two show him in Valdemosa, the third in Nohant, the last in Paris.

As THE WINTER ADVANCED, sadness more and more paralysed
my efforts at gaiety and cheerfulness. The state of our invalid
grew always worse; the wind wailed in the ravines, the rain
beat against our windows, the voice of the thunder penetrated
our thick walls and mingled its mournful sounds with the
laughter and games of the children. The eagles and vultures,
emboldened by the fog, came to devour our poor sparrows,
even on the pomegranate tree which shaded my window. The
raging sea kept the ships in the harbors; we felt ourselves
prisoners, far from all enlightened help and from all effective

sympathy. Death seemed to hover over our heads to seize one of us, and alone we contended with him for his prey.

＊   ＊   ＊

The poor great artist was a detestable patient. What I had feared, but unfortunately not enough, happened. He became completely demoralised. Bearing pain courageously enough, he could not overcome the disquietude of his imagination. The monastery was for him full of terrors and phantoms, even when he was well. He did not say so, and I had to guess it. On returning from my nocturnal explorations in the ruins with my children, I found him at ten o'clock at night before his piano, his face pale, his eyes wild, and his hair almost standing on end. It was some moments before he could recognize us.

He then made an attempt to laugh, and played to us sublime things he had just composed, or rather, to be more accurate, terrible or heartrending ideas which had taken possession of him, as it were without his knowledge, in that hour of solitude, sadness, and terror.

It was there that he composed the most beautiful of those short pages he modestly entitled *Préludes*. They are masterpieces. Several present to the mind visions of deceased monks and the sounds of the funeral chants which beset his imagination; others are melancholy and sweet—they occurred to him in the hours of sunshine and of health, with the noise of the children's laughter under the window, the distant sound of guitars, the warbling of the birds among the humid foliage, and the sight of the pale little full-blown roses on the snow.

Others again are of a mournful sadness, and, while charming the ear, rend the heart. There is one of them which occurred to him on a dismal rainy evening; it produces a terrible mental depression. We had left him well that day, Maurice and I, and had gone to Palma to buy things we re-

quired for our encampment. The rain had come on, the tor-
rents had overflowed, we had traveled three leagues in six
hours to return in the midst of the inundation, in the dead of
night, without boots, abandoned by our driver, having passed
through unheard-of dangers. We made haste, anticipating the
anxiety of our invalid. It had been indeed great, but it had
become as it were congealed into a kind of calm despair, and
he played his wonderful *Prélude* weeping. On seeing us enter
he rose, uttering a great cry, then he said to us, with a wild
look and in a strange tone: "Ah! I knew well that you were
dead."

When he had come to himself again, and saw the state in
which we were, he was ill at the retrospective spectacle of
our dangers; but he confessed to me afterward that while
waiting for our return he had seen all this in a dream and that,
no longer distinguishing this dream from reality, he had
grown calm and been almost lulled to sleep while playing the
piano, believing that he was dead himself. He saw himself
drowned in a lake; heavy and ice-cold drops of water fell at
regular intervals upon his breast, and when I drew his attention to those drops of water which were actually falling at
regular intervals upon the roof, he denied having heard them.
He was even vexed at what I translated by the term imitative
harmony. He protested with all his might, and he was right,
against the puerility of these imitations for the ear. His genius
was full of mysterious harmonies of nature, translated by
sublime equivalents into his musical thought, and not by a
servile repetition of external sounds. His composition of this
evening was indeed full of the drops of rain which resounded
on the sonorous tiles of the monastery, but they were transformed in his imagination and his music into tears falling
from heaven on his heart.

*   *   *

His creation was spontaneous and miraculous. He found it without seeking it, without foreseeing it. It came on his piano suddenly, complete, sublime, or it sang in his head during a walk, and he was impatient to play it to himself. But then began the most heartrending labor I ever saw. It was a series of efforts, of irresolutions, and of frettings to seize again certain details of the theme he had heard; what he had conceived as a whole he analyzed too much when wishing to write it, and his regret at not finding it again, in his opinion, clearly defined, threw him into a kind of despair. He shut himself up in his room for whole days, weeping, walking, breaking his pens, repeating and altering a bar a hundred times, writing and effacing it as many times, and recommencing the next day with a meticulous and desperate perseverance. He spent six weeks over a single page to write it at last as he had noted it down at the very first.

I had for a long time been able to make him consent to trust to this first inspiration. But when he was no longer disposed to believe me, he reproached me gently with having spoiled him and with not being severe enough with him. I tried to amuse him, to take him out for walks. Sometimes, taking all my brood off in a country *char à bancs*, I dragged him away in spite of himself from this agony. I took him to the banks of the Creuse, and after being for two or three days lost amid sunshine and rain in frightful roads, we arrived, cheerful and famished, at some magnificently situated place where he seemed to revive. These fatigues knocked him up the first day, but he slept. The last day he was quite revived, quite rejuvenated on returning to Nohant, and he found the solution of his work without too much effort; but it was not always possible to prevail upon him to leave that piano which was much oftener his torment than his joy, and by degrees he showed temper when I disturbed him. I dared not insist. Chopin when angry was alarming, and as, with me, he always restrained himself, he seemed almost to choke and die.

*   *   *

He was a man of the world *par excellence*, not of the too formal and too numerous world, but of the intimate world, of the salons of twenty persons, of the hour when the crowd goes away and the habitués crowd round the artist to wrest from him by amiable importunity his purest inspiration. It was then only that he exhibited all his genius and all his talent. It was then also that after having plunged his audience into profound contemplation or into painful sadness, for his music sometimes discouraged one's soul terribly, especially when he improvised, he would suddenly, as if to take away the impression and remembrance of his sorrow from others and from himself, turn stealthily to a glass, arrange his hair and his cravat, and show himself suddenly transformed into a phlegmatic Englishman, into an impertinent old man, into a sentimental and ridiculous Englishwoman, into a sordid Jew. The types were always sad, however comical they might be, but perfectly conceived and so delicately rendered that one could not grow weary of admiring them.

All these sublime, charming, or bizarre accomplishments which he could summon from himself made him the soul of select society, and there was literally a contest for his company; his noble character, his disinterestedness, his self-respect, his proper pride, enemy of every tasteless vanity and of every insolent réclame, the security of intercourse with him, and the exquisite delicacy of his manners, made him a friend equally serious and agreeable.

To tear Chopin away from so many indulgences, to associate him with a simple, uniform, and constantly studious life, he who had been brought up on the knees of princesses, was to deprive him of that which made him live, of a fictitious life, it is true, for, like a painted woman, he laid aside in the evening, on returning to his home, his verve and his energy, to give the night to fever and sleeplessness; but of a life which would have been shorter and more animated than that of retirement and of intimacy restricted to the unchanging circle of a single family. In Paris he visited several salons every day, or he chose at least every evening a different one as a milieu. He had thus by turns twenty or thirty salons to intoxicate or to charm with his presence.

Alfred James Hipkins

How Chopin Played

Alfred James Hipkins (1826-1903) was an English pianist and authority on old-time musical instruments, particularly the harpsichord and clavichord. He kept diaries and notebooks, from which this personal record of Chopin and his playing is taken. Hipkins later became a Chopin pioneer, being the first to give Chopin recitals in England.

MY RECOLLECTIONS are limited to the year 1848 when Chopin came to London with Sir Charles Hallé, Alexander Billet, and others. He had been obliged to leave Paris on account of the revolution which deposed and exiled Louis Philippe. He had been in London earlier, in 1837, when symptoms of the disease to which he was to succumb had caused anxiety; then he was accompanied by the pianist and piano maker, Camille Pleyel. Almost the only record of this visit has been preserved in the Broadwood family; the late James Shudi Broadwood, at that time residing at 49 Bryanston Square, invited Pleyel to dinner with his friend Chopin, who tried to put on a quasi-anonymity by masquerading as "Monsieur Frits." Chopin had no need to adopt this harmless deception, for at that time his name was unknown in this country, unless it were to a few advanced musicians. However, his incognito was upset, when after dinner he was asked to try the piano. In the Broadwood circle his fame would seem to have gone before him; although the thought cannot be suppressed that Pleyel had quietly let out the secret. The recollection of the Broadwood piano and its responsiveness to his sensitive touch remained with Chopin, so that when he returned to London in the April of 1848, one of the first visits he paid was to Broadwood's warehouse in Great Pulteney Street.

That was the first time I saw him. He paid many subsequent visits, and it was on those occasions I heard him play. It was the first near experience I had of genius: I had seen Mendelssohn conduct *Elijah;* I had heard Thalberg in his remarkable and original displays of piano playing; but they were as prose to Chopin's poetry. As to Sterndale Bennett, he would have nothing to do with Chopin—at least in his public performances. When afterward I attempted to play some of Chopin's works, Bennett good-naturedly laughed at me.

On one occasion Chopin came with his pupil Miss Stirling and the late Frederick Beale of Cramer and Co. (the publishers) to play the new waltzes in A Flat and in C Sharp Minor, since so popular, which Beale had secured for publication. This was a great privilege for me; but of all he played when I heard him I best remember the *Andante spianato*.

To save Chopin fatigue, he was carried upstairs (he died the following year). Physical weakness was not, however, the cause of his tenderly subdued style of playing. This was his own, and inseparable from his conception of pianoforte touch; it was incapable of modification from any influence whatever. His *fortissimo* was the full pure tone without noise, a harsh inelastic note being painful to him. His nuances were modifications of that tone, decreasing to the faintest yet always distinct *pianissimo*. His singing *legatissimo* touch was marvelous. The wide, extended *arpeggios* in the bass were transfused by touch and pedal into their corresponding sustained chords, and swelled or diminished like waves in an ocean of sound. He kept his elbows close to his sides, and played only with finger touch, no weight from the arms. He used a simple, natural position of the hands as conditioned by scale and chord playing, adopting the easiest fingering, although it might be against the rules, that came to him. He changed fingers upon a key as often as an organ player.

Hallé, who heard Chopin in 1847, gave Dannreuther an account of how Chopin played the *forte* passages toward the end of the *Barcarolle pianissimo*, with all manner of refinements.

Very strong impressions remain on the memory; although fifty-one years have all but passed, I remember Chopin, his look, his manner and his incomparable playing, as vividly as if my meeting him had been last year. He was ill, but only showed it painfully in his weakened breathing power; he could not walk upstairs; my father-in-law, Mr. Black, and my wife's uncle, Mr. Murray, carried him. He came to Broadwood through the recommendation and courtesy of the Pleyel House in Paris; he brought one of the Pleyel pianos with him, but only used it once, at an evening at the Countess of Blessington's at Kensington Gore, directly after his arrival. He immediately took to the Broadwood pianos, and after that occasion used them exclusively in England and Scotland, until, in effect, his return to Paris in November of that year, 1848.

He was invited by the Duchess of Sutherland to a soirée at Stafford House, where he played before the Queen.

His matinées were not given in Willis's Rooms as stated by the *Times* critic, but in the houses of the Earl of Falmouth and Fanny Kemble. He gave public recitals in Glasgow and Edinburgh and played in one of the Gentlemen's Concerts at Manchester; also, and lastly, at the Polish Ball, Guildhall, London.

He was frequently at Broadwoods: of middle height, with a pleasant face, a mass of fair curly hair like an angel, and agreeable manners. But he was something of a dandy, very particular about the cut and color of his clothes.

He was painstaking in the choice of the pianos he was to play upon anywhere, as he was in his dress, his hair, his gloves, his French; you cannot imagine a more perfect technique than he possessed! But he abhorred banging a piano; his *forte* was relative, not absolute; it was based upon his exquisite *pianos and pianissimos*—always a waving line, *crescendo* and *diminuendo*. To play with great strength was German, as he told Mrs. Goddard in Paris, when she took her daughter Arabella Goddard, a child of seven or eight, to play to him. "Why," he said, "she plays like a German," and when they left the house, as Mrs. Goddard told me lately, Chopin's last words were, "Never let the child play loud."

Here, in 1848, his compositions were almost unknown. Every time I heard him play, the pieces were strange to me, and I had to rush across Regent Street to Wessel, his English publisher, to discover what I had been hearing. Fancy the interest of this to me, a young man, who for the first time came in contact with genius!

To return to pianos, he especially liked Broadwood's Boudoir cottage pianos of that date, two-stringed, but very sweet instruments, and he found pleasure in playing them. He played Bach's 48 all his life long. "I don't practice my own compositions," he said to von Lentz. "When I am about to give a concert, I close my doors for a time and play Bach."

Chopin never played his own compositions twice alike, but varied each according to the mood of the moment, a mood that charmed by its very waywardness; his playing resembling nothing so much as the tender delicate tints seen in mother-o'-pearls and it flowed apparently without the least effort. His touch was elusive, and his repression so new, that his art was little understood.

Anne Richmond Richie

A Child Listens

Mrs. Anne Richmond Richie was a daughter of the novelist William Makepeace Thackeray. As a child she was taken to visit Chopin by a staunch friend and pupil of his, Miss Jane Stirling. Chopin was alone and very ill during this second visit to London, in 1848.

THE CARRIAGE stopped at the door of a little house in a side street; the visitors reached a second floor, and rang a bell; and the door was instantly opened by a slight, delicate-looking man with long hair, bright eyes and a thin hooked nose, whose two hands the lady took in hers, and reproached him for coming to the door. The visitors entered the bare room, with nothing in it but an upright piano and a few small chairs and their host asked them if they would like to hear him play something he had just composed. They would dearly like it, but would it tire him; it would not be good for him?

He smiled again, shook back his long hair, and sat down immediately; and then the music began, and the room was filled with continuous sound, he looking over his shoulder now and then to see if we were liking it.

The lady sat absorbed and listening, and as I looked I saw tears in her eyes—great clear tears rolling down her cheeks. . . . When he stopped at last and looked round, the lady started up. "You mustn't play any more," she said; "no more, no more, it's too beautiful"—and she praised and thanked him in a motherly, pitying sort of way; and then hurriedly said we must go; but as we took leave she added almost in a whisper with a humble apologizing look—"I have brought you some of the jelly, and my sister sent some of the wine you fancied the other day; pray, pray try to take a little."

He again shook his head at her, seeming more vexed than grateful. "It is very wrong; you shouldn't bring me these things," he said in French. "I won't play to you if you do"—but she put him back softly; and hurriedly closed the door upon him and the offending basket. . . . She looked hard at me as we drove away. "Never forget that you have heard Chopin play," she said with emotion, "for soon no one will ever hear him play any more."

Moritz Karasowski

Death of Chopin

A friend of Chopin, Charles Gavard, wrote reminiscences of the last days of the composer. He placed the manuscript at the disposal of the Polish cellist Moritz Karasowski (1823-1892), who reproduced it word for word in the twelfth chapter of his Chopin biography, without alteration.

Frederick Niecks, the first reliable biographer of Chopin, saw the original of Gavard's manuscript and verified it.

FROM THAT DAY the disease made rapid strides. Chopin did not fear death, but seemed in a manner to long for it. The thought of quitting a life so full of sad remembrances was not altogether unwelcome. His moments of respite from pain became fewer and fewer. He spoke with perfect consciousness and calmness about his death and the disposal of his body. He expressed a wish to be buried in the churchyard of Père Lachaise beside Bellini, with whom, between 1832 and 1835, he had been very friendly.

He was so much worse by the beginning of October that he could not sit up. His relatives were informed of his condition, and Chopin's eldest sister, Madame Louise Jedrzejewicz, immediately hastened to him with her husband and daughter.

The meeting between brother and sister must be imagined rather than described. In 1844 Louise had nursed her beloved brother through a dangerous illness, and afterward spent a few weeks with him at Nohant. She felt now directly she saw him that he would only need her tender care a short time. Sometimes, when free from pain, he was still cheerful and hopeful. He even took a new house, No. 12 Place Vendôme, and gave minute directions about furnishing it.

At length the last hour approached. His sister and his faithful pupil, Gutmann, never left him for a moment. The Countess Delphine Potocka, who was at some distance from Paris, set off to return the instant she heard of the hopeless condition of the revered master, that she might receive his farewell. In the room adjoining the apartment where Chopin lay speechless, were some friends anxious to see him before he closed his eyes forever. It was a Sunday, the 15th of October, and the streets were quieter than usual. His sufferings were intense, yet he tried to smile at the friends around him; and when he saw the Countess Potocka, who was standing beside his sister weeping bitterly, he asked her softly to sing something. By a strong effort of self-control she mastered her emotion, and in a ringing voice of bell-like purity, sang Stradella's *Hymn to the Virgin,* so beautifully and so devoutly that the dying man—artist and lover of the beautiful to the very last— whispered with delight, "Oh, how beautiful! My God how beautiful! Again, again." As if endowed with supernatural strength the Countess sat down to the piano and sang a psalm by Marcello. Those standing at his bedside saw that he was growing weaker every second and sank noiselessly on their knees. The solemn stillness was broken only by Delphine Potocka's wonderful voice, which sounded like that of an angel summoning the great master to the realms of the blessed; all suppressed their sobs that they might not disturb the enjoyment of his last moments.

Evening was closing in; his sister knelt by his bedside,

weeping. The next morning Chopin felt a little better. He asked for extreme unction, and Alexander Jelowicki, a very pious and learned priest, who was held in high esteem by his countrymen, was sent for. The dying man confessed to him twice, and, in the presence of his friends, received the last sacrament. He then called them all one by one to his bedside and blessed and commended them to God. After that he quite lost the power of speech and seemed unconscious. But a few hours later he revived and desired the priest to pray with him. Resting his head on Gutmann's shoulder, Chopin, in a clear voice, repeated after the priest every word of the Litany. When the last agony commenced he said, "Who is near me?" Then he asked for some water, and when he had moistened his lips he inclined his head and kissed the hand of Gutmann, who was supporting him. After this last sign of gratitude and affection, he sighed once more as if released from a burden, and then closed his eyes forever. At this moment the bells of Paris struck three o'clock in the morning of October 17, 1849. A few minutes afterward the doors of the chamber were opened and the friends and acquaintances in the next room came to look once more on the beloved face of the dead.

FRANZ LISZT

Born: Raiding, Hungary
October 22, 1811
Died: Bayreuth, Germany
July 31, 1886

FRANZ LISZT was the world's greatest pianist. As a composer, he developed a new orchestral form: "program" music. He wrote oratorios, songs, piano concertos. Moreover, he was the most generous patron of music and the most inspired piano teacher in history. He was a great lover, a courtier and social lion, a star of the salon, an idolized *virtuoso* flitting between London and Moscow—whose work reflected all the richness of his life. His character, his experience and his work bear a clear relationship to one another in every period of his life.

He made his debut at the age of nine in Oedenburg, Hungary. He made such an impression that a group of Hungarian nobles endowed his family with an income of six hundred florins yearly to enable the boy to study in Vienna.

In December 1823 he came to Paris. He was at once hailed as a sensational child prodigy. He was lionized wherever he performed; women fluttered around him and worshipped. In 1834 he commenced a passionate love affair with the Countess d'Agoult, by whom he had three children.

In 1849 he settled in Weimar, where he lived for fifteen years as conductor of the Court Theater. He introduced many important new works to the public at the Weimar opera, among them Wagner's *Flying Dutchman, Tannhäuser* and *Lohengrin,* Schumann's *Genoveva,* Berlioz' *Benvenuto Cellini.* Later he lived for intervals in various other cities—Rome, Budapest, Bayreuth. Wherever he settled he held court, as monarch of the musical world.

Adam Liszt

Notes of a Tender Father

"Behold a young *virtuoso,* seemingly dropped from the clouds, who arouses the greatest astonishment. The performances of this boy border on the miraculous." So runs a Viennese account of the young Franz. Only a year or so later Paris went wild over the prodigy. His father, Adam Liszt, was an accountant in Eisenstadt, Hungary, to the same Prince Nicholas Esterházy who had Joseph Haydn as his Kapellmeister. Adam was musical himself, played nearly every instrument. He was so strongly impressed with all the signs of promise in his son that he devoted a diary just to him. Here is a page from it.

AFTER HIS VACCINATION, a period commenced in which the boy had to struggle alternately with nervous pains and fever, which more than once imperiled his life. On one occasion, in his second or third year, we thought him dead and ordered his coffin made. This agitated condition continued until his sixth year. In that year he heard me playing Ries' Concerto in C Sharp Minor. He leaned upon the piano and was all ears. Toward evening he returned from the garden and sang the theme. We made him repeat it but he did not know what he was singing. This was the first indication of his genius. He incessantly begged that he might commence piano playing. After three months' instruction, the fever returned and compelled us to discontinue it. His delight in learning did not lessen his pleasure in playing with children of his own age, although from this time forth he sought to live more for himself alone. He was not regular in his practice but was always tractable up to his ninth year. It was during this period that he played in public for the first time, in Oedenburg. He performed a Concerto in E Major by Ries and extemporized. The fever attacked him just before he seated himself at the piano, yet he was strengthened by the playing. He had long manifested a desire to play in public and exhibited much ease and courage.

Marie Countess d'Agoult

Fascination

It is perhaps no exaggeration to say that the Countess d'Agoult was the only woman for whom Liszt ever felt a really profound love. He had scores of liaisons, all fugitive affairs. In later years he loved the Princess Wittgenstein, but this attachment was only a kind of friendship in return for her blind devotion to him and to his art.

Liszt met the countess in Paris, when he was twenty-two, she twenty-eight. She was estranged from her husband, but had borne him three children. Liszt and the countess eloped together; they reached Geneva in August 1835. Three children were born to them—the second, Cosima, later became the wife of Wagner. Their liaison lasted eleven years.

There was not just one Liszt, there were always two, whom he never succeeded in harmonizing: the religious fanatic and the worldly charlatan.

PEOPLE were tormented by the desire for the ideal life, and sought in everything for a sign from heaven. Hardly free yet

from that formidable struggle in which all the assizes of the
world had been shaken to their foundations, men still shud-
dered under the expectation of the unknown, the extraordinary, the impossible . . . . All these warring impulses, these
abrupt changes in the experiences of men and of nations
delivered up the young to all the winds of doubt. An ardor,
a skeptical torment of the senses and of the intellect caused a
ferment in them, powerful but bitter, compact of sadness
and irony.

It was in these intellectual and moral circumstances, in
this atmosphere charged with electricity, that Franz and
Marie met. The love that swiftly flamed within them bore all
the marks of the milieu in which it was born. These two more
than others were bound to come under its influence, for they
were both endowed with the sensibilities of the poet and the
artist. Strong affinities of race and temperament brought
them together, but the extreme differences in their education
and their stations in life of necessity placed innumerable
difficulties in their path. A thousand obstacles arose between
them and endowed the passion that drove them toward each
other with a dolorous intensity which, in more balanced days
than those, love will never again know.

*   *   *

From the beginning our conversations were very serious, and,
by common accord, quite free from anything banal. Without
hesitation, without effort, by the natural inclination of our
souls, we embarked at once upon elevated subjects, which
alone had any interest for us. We talked of the destiny of
mankind, of its sadness and incertitude, of the soul and of
God. We exchanged grave thoughts on the present times, on
the future life, and on the promises of religion with regard
to that life. We said nothing that came too near the personal
or the intimate; but the very tone of our talks showed that

we were both exceedingly unhappy, and that, young as we were, we had been through more than one bitter experience. In these sous-entendus, these veiled confidences, these out-pourings that were at the same time very frank and very discreet, Franz spoke with a vivacity, an abundance, and an originality of impressions that awoke a whole world that had been slumbering in me; and when he left me I was sunk in reveries without end. Although his education had been very incomplete, he having been compelled to apply himself to his art from very infancy, he had so often come to grips with the hardships of life, he had seen the world under so many diverse aspects, from the dazzling celebrity of his public career to the privations of an existence precariously depen-dent on the mob and its caprices, today dandled, like the little Mozart, on the knees of queens and princesses, tomorrow condemned to isolation and cruel poverty, that he had come to realize better than I the inconsequence, the injustice, the folly, the cruel levity and tyranny of public opinion. More adventurous by nature and by the force of circumstances than I was, he had speculatively reached out further than I had into the sphere of good and evil. Though he was still, in imagination at least, an ardent Catholic, and the rumors of his taking holy orders were not without foundation, the in-quietude of his mind impelled him toward heresy. During the last few years he had assiduously listened to the preachings of the sects and schools that announced new revelations. He had frequented the meetings of the disciples of St. Simon; under the trees of La Chénaie he had drunk in greedily the teachings of the illustrious Croyant Lammenais, who had been condemned by Rome. In politics, as in religion, he hated mediocrity, and his opinions were audaciously advanced. He despised the bourgeois monarchy of Louis Philippe and the government of the juste milieu; he cried out with all his being for the reign of justice, that is to say, a republic as he con-ceived it. With the same effervescence he gave himself up to the new movements in letters and the arts that were then menacing the old traditions: Childe Harold, Manfred, Werther, Obermann, all the proud or desperate revolutionaries of romantic poetry, were the companions of his sleepless nights. With their aid he rose to a haughty disdain of conventions; like them, he quivered under the detested yoke of aristocracies that were founded on neither genius nor virtue; he cried out for an end to submission, an end to resignation, for a holy, implacable hate that should avenge all iniquities . . . . The voice of the young enchanter, his vibrant speech, opened out before me a whole infinity, now luminous, now somber, forever changing, into which my thoughts plunged and were lost. Nothing of coquetry or of gallantry was blended with our intimacy, as so often happens between fashionable persons of opposite sexes. Between us there was something at once very young and very serious, at once very profound and very naive.

*   *   *

From that day my relations with Franz took on a new aspect. Henceforth I saw him only rarely, and even then seldom tête-à-tête; and there were times when I did not know whether I really desired these meetings or feared them, so disturbing were they to me. Into our briefest conversations, which were often interrupted, something had crept that was no longer entirely us. If at bottom our talks remained the same as before, their tone had become something quite different. Franz brought to them a fantastic temper; I was ill at ease. Sometimes there would be long silences between us; at others, Franz would talk with feverish animation, affecting a mocking gaiety that made me uncomfortable. He who had once been so full of enthusiasm, so eloquent in his talk about the good and the beautiful, so ambitious to give elevation to his life, to dedicate it to great art, so religious in all his thoughts, never spoke of anything now except in tones of irony. He paraded his doubts, he seemed deliberately to merge all the things he respected and scorned and admired and sympathized with in an all-embracing indifference. He sang the praises of mundane wisdom and the easygoing life; he undertook the defense of freethinkers. Suddenly, without any apparent reason, he broke out with strange ideas of a kind I had never heard from him before: he lauded what he called my fine life, congratulated me on my brilliant position in the world, admired what he called my royal establishment, the opulence and elegance of everything around me. Was he serious? Was it merely by way of persiflage? His impassive air, his dull accents, made it impossible for me to decide. And strangely enough, his talent seemed to me as completely changed as his mind. When he improvised at the piano it was no longer, as of old, to evoke suave harmonies that opened up the heavens to me; it was to set vibrating discordant strident tones from those powerful fingers of his.

Josef Fischhoff

Liszt as Monarch of Piano Virtuosos

Josef Fischhoff (1804-1857) was a pianist and one of the most popular piano teachers in Vienna. He also published several literary works on music.

His description of Liszt's playing is taken from Fischhoff's private correspondence with Robert Schumann; it was published, shortly after it was written, in the *Neue Zeitschrift für Musik*.

Liszt appeared in Vienna in the spring of 1838. His success was glorious here as elsewhere; the public's enthusiasm was almost delirium.

THE IMPRESSION is too new and powerful, too unexpected to give place as yet to commentary, that is, to reflection. A phenomenon so entirely different from all other artists has never yet been seen. The general standard is here of no use; for it is not alone the giant power, which is indeed difficult, but not impossible to fathom, no, it is the peculiar spirituality, the immediate breath of genius . . . .

Imagine an extremely thin, narrow-shouldered man, with hair falling over his face and neck, an uncommonly intellectual, lively, pale, highly interesting countenance, an extremely animated manner, an eye capable of every expression, beaming in conversation, a benevolent glance, strongly accentuated speech, and you have Liszt, as he is in general; but when he seats himself at the instrument, he strokes his hair behind his ear, his glance is staring, his eyes hollow, the upper part of the body quieter, only the head moves, and the expression of the face changes, and mirrors every passing mood that seizes him, or that he wishes to call forth, wherein he always succeeds. This fantastic exterior is only the covering of an interior volcano, from which tones are hurled like flames and gigantic ruins, not caressing, but with the force of thunderbolts. One thinks neither of his hands, nor of the mechanism, the technique, or the instrument; he seizes our soul, carried away by an unknown impression, and raises it violently to his own height, making all Philistines giddy. When he can carry them no higher, he holds them aloft for a while, then suddenly the Titan is touched with compassion and sets his hearers unexpectedly, and therefore not seldom rudely, back on earth, leads them through green meadows, yet does not grant them the comfortable repose for which they long, but makes their hearts pound even harder by maliciously summoning serpents and other reptiles from the odorous shrubs.

The piano seems only the weak instrument of an inner tumult, and he stands so high above all technicality that an analysis is not to be thought of, even for the purpose of taking something of this greatness for one's own. He is therefore no model to imitate; only a gigantic spirit could follow him, one equal to his and seeking an independent path. In a word, one can form no idea of this playing, one must hear it. This has twice been granted me. On the day of his arrival he played, at Professor Fischhoff's, some *Etudes* of his own composition, then he read at sight Schumann's *Phantasie-Stueck,* but in so perfect a manner, and particularly the "end of the song," so touchingly, that I shall never forget it. After this he eagerly seized compositions that he had not yet found in Italy, such as Mendelssohn's Preludes and Fugues for the Organ which he played on the piano alone without pedals, but with swells and redoublings it was quite heavenly. Then some new *Etudes* by Chopin, which for the most part were unknown to him. Thursday he played in Gross' *atelier,* in presence of Clara Wieck, Czerny (his former teacher), and many others: he executed two fantasias (he called them *Etudes*), and the second especially, in G Flat, was played with immense effect; then a part of his fantasia on the *Puritans,* and finally a scherzo by Czerny from his older Sonata, Opus 7. In truth, he shook our inmost souls.

Richard Wagner

My First Meetings with Liszt

In his *Autobiography* Wagner tells us how he first met, in Paris, the man who later became his best friend and most eminent patron. He then describes the second meeting, years later, in Berlin, at the house of the famous singer Wilhelmine Schröder-Devrient.

In Berlin Liszt is a little over thirty. He is at the height of his career as piano *virtuoso.* The world, especially the feminine world, is intoxicated by his art, his charm, his beauty. He has played in Paris, London, Vienna, and we know that his tours have taken him also to Spain, Portugal, Germany, Turkey, Poland, Russia.

THIS SHORT VISIT to Berlin was memorable for my meeting with Franz Liszt, which afterward proved of great importance. It took place under singular circumstances, which placed both him and me in a situation of peculiar embarrassment, brought about in the most wanton fashion by Devrient's exasperating caprice.

I had already told my patroness the story of my earlier meeting with Liszt. During that fateful second winter of my stay in Paris, when I had at last been driven to be grateful for Schlesinger's hackwork, I one day received word from Laube, who always bore me in mind, that F. Liszt was coming to Paris. He had mentioned and recommended me to him when he was in Germany, and advised me to lose no time in looking him up, as he was "generous," and would certainly find means of helping me. As soon as I heard that he had really arrived, I presented myself at the hotel to see him. It was early in the morning. On my entrance I found several strange gentlemen waiting in the drawing room, where, after some time, we were joined by Liszt himself, pleasant and affable, and wearing his indoor coat. The conversation was carried on in French, and turned upon his experiences during his last professional journey in Hungary. As I was unable to take part, on account of the language, I listened for some time, feeling heartily bored, until at last he asked me pleasantly what he could do for me. He seemed unable to recall Laube's recommendation, and all the answer I could give was that I desired to make his acquaintance. To this he had evidently no objection, and informed me he would take care to have a ticket sent me for his great matinée, which was to take place shortly. My sole attempt to introduce an artistic theme of conversation was a question as to whether he knew Löwe's *Erlkoenig* as well as Schubert's. His reply in the negative frustrated this somewhat awkward attempt, and I ended my visit by giving him my address. Thither his secretary, Belloni, presently sent me, with a few polite words, a card of admission to a concert to be given entirely by the master himself in the Salle Erard. I duly wended my way to the overcrowded hall, and beheld the platform on which the grand piano stood, closely beleaguered by the cream of Parisian female society, and witnessed their enthusiastic ovations of this *virtuoso*, who was at that time the wonder of the world. Moreover, I heard several of his most brilliant pieces, such as Variations on *Robert le Diable*, but carried away with me no real impression beyond that of being stunned. This took place just at the time when I was abandoning a path which had been contrary to my truer nature, and had led me astray, and on which I now emphatically turned my back in silent bitterness. I was therefore in no fitting mood for a just appreciation of this prodigy, then shining in the blazing light of day, while I had turned my face to the night. I went to see Liszt no more.

As already mentioned, I had given Devrient a bare outline of this story, but she had noted it with particular attention, for I happened to have touched her weak point of professional jealousy. As Liszt had also been commanded by the King of Prussia to appear at the grand state concert at Berlin, it so happened that the first time they met Liszt questioned her with great interest about the success of *Rienzi*. She thereupon observed that the composer of that opera was an altogether unknown man, and proceeded with curious malice to taunt him with his apparent lack of penetration, as proved by the fact that the said composer, who now so keenly excited his interest, was the very same poor musician whom he had lately "turned away so contemptuously" in Paris. All this she told me with an air of triumph, which distressed me very much, and I at once set to work to correct the false impression conveyed by my former account. As we were still debating this point in her room, we were startled to hear, from the next, the famous bass part in the "Revenge" air from *Donna Anna*, rapidly executed in octaves on the

piano. "That's Liszt himself," she cried. Liszt then entered
the room to fetch her for the rehearsal. To my great embarrassment she introduced me to him with malicious delight
as the composer of *Rienzi*, the man whose acquaintance he
now wished to make after having previously shown him the
door in his glorious Paris. My solemn asseverations that my
patroness—no doubt only in fun—was deliberately distorting
my account of my former visit to him, apparently pacified
him so far as I was concerned, and, on the other hand, he had
no doubt already formed his own opinion of the impulsive
singer. He certainly regretted that he could not remember
my visit in Paris, but it nevertheless shocked and alarmed
him to learn that anyone should have had reason to complain
of such treatment at his hands. The hearty sincerity of Liszt's
simple words to me about this misunderstanding, as con-
trasted with the strangely passionate raillery of the incorri-
gible lady, made a most pleasing and captivating impression
upon me. The whole bearing of the man, and the way in
which he tried to ward off the pitiless scorn of her attacks,
was something new to me, and gave me a deep insight into his
character, so firm in its amiability and boundless good nature.
Finally, she teased him about the Doctor's degree which had
just been conferred on him by the University of Königsberg,
and pretended to mistake him for a chemist. At last he
stretched himself out flat on the floor, and implored her
mercy, declaring himself quite defenseless against the storm
of her invective. Then turning to me with a hearty assurance
that he would make it his business to hear *Rienzi*, and would
in any case endeavor to give me a better opinion of himself
than his evil star had hitherto permitted, we parted.

The almost naive simplicity and naturalness of his every
phrase and word, and particularly his emphatic manner, left
a most profound impression upon me. No one could fail to
be equally affected by these qualities, and I now realized for
the first time the almost magic power exerted by Liszt over

all who came in close contact with him, and saw how erroneous had been my former opinion as to its source.

Amy Fay

One of Many Pupils

    Amy Fay (1844-1928) was a well-known American pianist. She
studied in Berlin with Tausig, Deppe, and Kullak, and in Weimar with
the great Liszt.

    On April 30, 1873, she arrived at Weimar to study with the Abbé
(Liszt had by that time taken orders). The diaries give us many striking
facts about Liszt's methods and personality. He hated being known as
a *professeur du piano;* he taught without regard to monetary reward.
It was taken for granted that anyone who came to him already had an
excellent technical background.

    Amy Fay succumbed deliriously to the magnetism of the master.

Weimar, May 1, 1873

LAST NIGHT I arrived in Weimar, and this evening I have been
to the theater, which is very cheap here, and the first person
I saw, sitting in a box opposite, was Liszt, from whom, as you
know, I am bent on getting lessons, though it will be a difficult
thing I fear, as I am told that Weimar is overcrowded with
people who are on the same errand. I recognized Liszt from
his portrait, and it entertained and interested me very much
to observe him. He was making himself agreeable to three
ladies, one of whom was very pretty. He sat with his back
to the stage, not paying the least attention, apparently, to
the play, for he kept talking all the while himself, and yet no
point of it escaped him, as I could tell by his expression and
gestures.

    Liszt is the most interesting and striking looking man imaginable. Tall and slight, with deep set eyes, shaggy eye-brows, and long iron-gray hair, which he wears parted in the middle. His mouth turns up at the corners, which gives him a most crafty and Mephisthophelean expression when he smiles, and his whole appearance and manner have a sort of Jesuitical elegance and ease. His hands are very narrow, with long and slender fingers that look as if they had twice as many joints as other people's. They are so flexible and supple that it makes you nervous to look at them. Anything like the polish of his manner I never saw. When he got up to leave the box, for instance, after his adieus to the ladies, he laid his hand on his heart and made his final bow—not with af-fection, or in mere gallantry, but with a quiet courtliness which made you feel that no other way of bowing to a lady was right or proper. It was most characteristic.

But the most extraordinary thing about Liszt is his won-derful variety of expression and play of feature. One moment his face will look dreamy, shadowy, tragic. The next he will be insinuating, amiable, ironical, sardonic; but always the same captivating grace of manner. He is a perfect study. I cannot imagine how he must look when he is playing. He is all spirit, but half the time, at least, a mocking spirit, I should say. I have heard the most remarkable stories about him already. All Weimar adores him, and people say that women still go perfectly crazy over him. When he walks out he bows to everybody just like a king! The Grand Duke has presented him with a house beautifully situated on the park, and here he lives elegantly, free of expense, whenever he chooses to come to it.

Weimar, May 7, 1873

There isn't a piano to be had in Weimar for love or money, as there is no manufacturer, and the few there were to be disposed of were snatched up before I got here. So I have lost

an entire week in hunting one up, and was obliged to go
first to Erfurt and finally to Leipsig, before I could find one—
and even that was sent over as a favor after much coaxing
and persuasion. I felt so happy when I saw it in my room! As
if I had taken a city! However, I met Liszt two evenings ago
at a little tea party given by a friend and protégé of his to
as many of his scholars as have arrived, I being asked with
the rest. Liszt promised to come late. We only numbered
seven. There were three young men and four young ladies,
of whom three, including myself, were Americans. Five of
the number had studied with Liszt before, and the young men
are artists who have already appeared before the public.

To fill up the time till Liszt came, our hostess made us
play, one after the other, beginning with the latest arrival.
After we had each "exhibited," little tables were brought in
and supper served. We were in the midst of it, and having
a merry time, when the door suddenly opened and Liszt
appeared. We all rose to our feet, and he shook hands with
everybody without waiting to be introduced. Liszt looks as
if he had been through everything and has a face *seamed*
with experience. He is rather tall and narrow, and wears a
long abbé's coat reaching nearly down to his feet. He made
me think of an old-time magician more than anything, and I
felt that with a touch of his wand he could transform us all.
After he had finished his greetings, he passed into the next
room and sat down. The young men gathered round him and
offered him a cigar, which he accepted and began to smoke.
We others continued our nonsense where we were, and I
suppose Liszt overheard some of our brilliant conversation,
for he asked who we were, I think, and presently the lady
of the house came out after Miss W. and me, the two American strangers, to take us in and present us to him.

After the preliminary greetings we had some little talk.
He asked me if I had been to Sophie Menter's concert in Berlin the other day. I said yes. He remarked that Miss Menter

was a great favorite of his, and that the lady from whom I had brought a letter to him had done a good deal for her. I asked him if Sophie Menter was a pupil of his. He said no, he could not take the credit for her artistic success to himself. I heard afterward that he really had done ever so much for her, but he won't have it said that he teaches! After he had finished his cigar, Liszt got up and said, "America is now to have the floor," and requested Miss W. to play for him. This was a dreadful ordeal for us new arrivals, for we had not expected to be called upon. I began to quake inwardly, for I had been without a piano for nearly a week, and was not at all prepared to play for him, while Miss W. had been up since five o'clock in the morning, and had traveled all day. However, there was no getting off. A request from Liszt is a command, and Miss W. sat down, and acquitted herself as well as could have been expected under the circumstances. Liszt waved his hand and nodded his head from time to time, and seemed pleased, I thought. He then called upon Leitert, who played a composition of Liszt's own most beautifully. Liszt commended him and patted him on the back. As soon as Leitert had finished, I slipped off into the back room, hoping Liszt would forget all about me, but he followed me almost immediately, like a cat with a mouse, took both my hands in his, and said in the most winning way imaginable, "*Mademoiselle, vous jouerez quelque-chose, n'est-ce pas?*" I can't give you any idea of his *persuasiveness,* when he chooses. It is enough to decoy you into anything. It was such a desperate moment that I became reckless, and without even telling him that I was out of practice and not prepared to play, I sat down and plunged into the A Flat Major Ballade of Chopin, as if I were possessed. The piano had a splendid touch, luckily. Liszt kept calling out "Bravo" every minute or two, to encourage me, and somehow I got through. When I had finished, he clapped his hands and said, "Bravely played." He asked with whom I had studied, and made one or two little criticisms. I hoped he would shove me aside and play it himself, but he didn't.

Weimar, June 6, 1873

When I first came there were only five of us who studied with Liszt, but lately a good many others have been there. Day before yesterday there came a young lady who was a pupil of Henselt in St. Petersburg. She is immensely talented, only seventeen years old, and her name is Laura Kahrer. It is a very rare thing to see a pupil of Henselt, for it is very difficult to get lessons from him. He stands next to Liszt. This Laura Kahrer plays everything that ever was heard of, and she played a fugue of her own composition the other day that was really vigorous and good. I was quite astonished to hear how she had worked it up. She has made a grand concert tour in Russia. I never saw such a hand as she had. She could bend it backward till it looked like the palm of her hand turned inside out. She was an interesting little creature, with dark eyes and hair, and one could see by her Turkish necklace and numerous bangles that she had been making money. She played with the greatest aplomb, though her touch had a certain roughness about it to my ear. She did not carry me away, but I have not heard her play many pieces.

However, all playing sounds barren by the side of Liszt, for *his* is the living, breathing embodiment of poetry, passion, grace, wit, coquetry, daring, tenderness, and every other fascinating quality that you can think of! I'm ready to hang myself half the time when I've been to him. Oh, he is the most phenomenal being in every respect! All that you've heard of him would never give you an idea of him. In short, he represents the whole scale of human emotion. He is a many-sided prism, and reflects back the light in all colors, no matter how you look at him. His pupils *adore* him, as in fact everybody else does, but it is impossible to do otherwise with a person whose

genius flashes out of him all the time like that, and whose
character is so winning.

One day this week, when we were with Liszt, he was in
such high spirits that it was as if he had suddenly become
twenty years younger. A student from the Stuttgart conservatory played a Liszt concerto. His name is V., and he is dreadfully nervous. Liszt kept up a little running fire of satire all
the time he was playing, but in a good-natured way. I
shouldn't have minded it if it had been I. In fact, I think it
would have inspired me; but poor V. hardly knew whether
he was on his head or on his feet. It was too funny. Everything that Liszt says is so striking. For instance, in one place
where V. was playing the melody rather feebly, Liszt suddenly took his seat at the piano and said, "When *I* play, I
always play for the people in the gallery [by the gallery he
meant the cock loft, where the rabble always sit, and where
the places cost next to nothing], so that these people who pay
only five groschens for the seat also hear something." Then
he began, and I wish you could have heard him! The sound
didn't seem to be very *loud,* but it was penetrating and far-
reaching. When he had finished, he raised one hand in the air,
and you seemed to see all the people in the gallery drinking
in the sound. That is the way Liszt teaches you. He presents
an *idea* to you, and it takes fast hold of your mind and sticks
there. Music is such a real, visible thing to him, that he always
has a symbol, instantly, in the material world to express his
idea.

The Reverend Hugh R. Haweis

Liszt Plays for Me

The following incident must have taken place in 1880. Liszt was an old man, his greatest triumphs were over—as was his passion for the Princess Jeanne Elisabeth Carolyne Wittgenstein, with whom he had lived a great part of his life. Now he was living his epilogue.

The reference is probably not to *La Campanella*, which was written about 1838, but the *Angelus*, in the Third Book of the *Années de Pèlerinage*. The Reverend Hugh R. Haweis lived from 1838 to 1901. The extract printed here is from his *Memories of a Musical Life*.

WE HAD again reached the upper terrace of the Villa d'Este, where the Abbate's midday repast was being laid out by his valet. It was a charming situation for lunch, commanding that wide and magnificent prospect to which I have alluded; but the autumn was far advanced, there was a fresh breeze, and the table was ordered indoors. Meanwhile, Liszt laying his hand upon my arm, we passed through the library, opening into his bedroom, and thence to a little sitting room (the same which commanded that view of the Campagna). Here stood his grand Erard piano. "As we were talking of bells," he said, "I should like to show you an *Angelus* I have just written," and opening the piano, he sat down. This was the moment which I had so often and so vainly longed for.

When I left England, it seemed to me as impossible that I should ever hear Liszt play, as that I should ever see Mendelssohn, who has been in his grave for thirty-three years. How few of the present generation have had this privilege! At Bayreuth I had hoped, but no opportunity offered itself, and it is well known that Liszt can hardly ever be prevailed upon to open the piano in the presence of strangers. A fortunate pupil, Polig, who was then with him at the Villa d'Este, told me he rarely touched the piano, and that he himself had seldom heard him—"but," he added, with enthusiasm, "when the master touches the keys, it is always with the same incomparable effect, unlike anyone else, always perfect."

"You know," said Liszt, turning to me, "they ring the Angelus in Italy carelessly; the bells swing irregularly, and leave off, and the cadences are often broken up thus": and he began a little swaying passage in the treble—like bells tossing high up in the evening air: it ceased, but so softly that the half-bar of silence made itself felt, and the listening ear still carried the broken rhythm through the pause. The Abbate himself seemed to fall into a dream; his fingers fell again lightly on the keys, and the bells went on, leaving off in the middle of a phrase. Then rose from the bass the ring of the Angelus, or rather, it seemed like the vague emotion of one who, as he passes, hears in the ruins of some wayside cloister, the ghosts of old monks humming their drowsy melodies, as the sun goes down rapidly, and the purple shadows of Italy steal over the land, out of the orange west!

We sat motionless—the disciple on one side, I on the other. Liszt was almost as motionless: his fingers seemed quite independent, chance ministers of his soul. The dream was broken by a pause; then came back the little swaying passage, of bells, tossing high up in the evening air, the half-bar of silence, the broken rhythm—and the Angelus was rung.

RICHARD WAGNER

Born: Leipzig, Germany
May 22, 1813
Died: Venice, Italy
February 13, 1883

RICHARD WAGNER may not be admired as the dictator of nineteenth-century opera, but there is no denying that his influence has been immense and far-reaching. His life was one long war, and he fought it with really extraordinary vigor and persistence. He was many things—composer, conductor, librettist, pamphleteer.

When he was a child his father introduced him to the glittering world behind the footlights; from that time forth he remained passionately addicted to the theater. He composed his first music drama, *Die Feen*, when he was twenty; it showed nothing of the reformer's impulse, not even decided talent.

In 1836 he married Minna Planer—a pretty woman who did not understand him but patiently suffered poverty and insecurity, even her husband's open infidelities. In Riga and in Paris, amidst his many personal troubles, he wrote *Rienzi* and *The Flying Dutchman*. In 1843 he was given a post at the Royal Court of Saxony, but this did not last long. He joined forces with the revolutionaries of 1848, was outlawed from Dresden, and entered upon years of exile and bitter, exhausting poverty.

In Switzerland he met Mathilde Wesendonk, the wife

of Otto Wesendonk; they fell in love and she served as inspiration for *Tristan*. Years of struggle followed for Wagner, years in which he found recognition only in a very limited circle of friends. Fate finally took him back to Germany. Despite the hissing and whistling of his enemies, his operas gradually gained favor, were more and more frequently performed. He divorced his wife. He met Cosima Liszt, wife of the famous conductor von Buelow, and later married her. He met young King Ludwig who appointed him Royal Director of Music in Munich. On his fifty-ninth birthday, the cornerstone of the Festspielhaus was laid in Bayreuth.

His success was long delayed, but when it came it was tremendous. After Wagner opera could never be as it had been before he worked his magic.

Ferdinand Praeger

Richard the Boy

Ferdinand Praeger (1815-1891) was a pianist, a pupil of Hummel; later he became London correspondent for Robert Schumann's magazine *Neue Zeitschrift für Musik*. An ardent admirer of Wagner, he worked diligently—and not in vain—to bring Wagner over to England (in 1855) as guest conductor of the London Philharmonic concerts.

His book *Wagner As I Knew Him* (London 1885) quickly won fame, but was withdrawn from circulation by the publishers because of alleged inaccuracies. Its description of Wagner's youth is excellent; the sources for this part of the book are far more reliable than the author's own memories of the master in manhood.

THROUGHOUT his life Wagner was always remarkably prim and neatly dressed, caring much for his personal appearance.

. . . He was no sooner at school than he attracted to himself a few of the cleverest boys by his early developed gift of ready speech and sarcasm. *"Die Dummen haben mich immer gehasst"* ("the stupid have always hated me") was a favorite saying of his in afterlife. The study of the dead languages, his principal subject, was a delight to him. He had a facility for languages. It was one of his gifts. History and geography also attracted him. He was an omnivorous reader, and his precise knowledge on any subject was always a matter of surprise to the most intimate. It could never be said what he had read or what he had not read, and here perhaps is the place to note a remarkable feature in Wagner's disposition, viz., his modesty. If he required information on any subject, his manner of asking was childlike in its simplicity. He was patient in learning and in mastering the point. But it should be observed that nothing short of the most complete and satisfactory explanation would content him. And then the thinking power of the man would declare itself. The information he had newly acquired would be thoroughly assimilated and then given forth under a new light with a force truly remarkable.

In stature Wagner was below the middle size, and like most undersized men always held himself strictly erect. He had an unusually wiry, muscular frame, small feet, an aristocratic feature which did not extend to his hands. It was his head, however, that could not fail to strike even the least observant: here one had before him no ordinary mortal. The development of the frontal part, which a phrenologist would class at a glance as belonging beyond doubt to a mastermind, impressed everyone. His eyes had a piercing power, but were kindly withal, and were ready to smile at a witty remark. Richard Wagner lacked eyebrows, but nature, as if to make up for this deficiency, had bestowed on him a most abundant crop of bushy hair, which he kept carefully brushed back, thereby exposing the whole of his really Jupiter-like brow.

His mouth was very small. He had thin lips and small teeth, signs of a determined character. His nose was large and in afterlife somewhat disfigured by the early acquired habit of snuff taking. The back of his head was fully developed. According to phrenological rules, this indicated power and energy. The shape of his head was very similar to that of Luther's, with whom, indeed, he had more than one point of character in common. . . .

As a boy he was passionate and wilful. His violent temper and obstinate determination were not to be thwarted in anything he had set his mind to. Among boys such wilfulness causes frequent dissensions, and so it was with Wagner. He rarely, however, came to blows, for he had a shrewd wit and was winningly entreating in speech, adroit in bending the other boys to his whims.

Erysipelas sorely tried him during his school life. Every change in the weather troubled him. As regards the loss of his eyebrows, an affliction which he always regretted, Wagner attributed it to a violent attack of St. Anthony's fire, as the painful malady is also called. The attacks were preceded by depression of spirits and irritability of temper. Conscious of his growing peevishness, he would seek refuge in solitude. As soon as the attack was over, his bright animal spirits returned and the adventurous little fellow was hardly recognizable as the taciturn misanthrope of some days before.

Practical jokes were a favorite sport of his, but he indulged only in harmless pranks and only when chance turned up some absurd situation. I think it was impossible for Wagner to hurt anyone intentionally. He was always kind and would never start anything that might cause real pain.

His superabundance of animal spirits, well supported by an active body, often led him into harebrained escapades that threatened a fatal issue. But his intrepidity was tempered and governed by a strong self-reliance which always came to the rescue at the critical moment.

On one occasion the boys of the Kreuzschule were assembled in class for their daily session when an unexpected holiday was announced. This was a rare occurrence in continental schools. The boys, wild with excitement, rushed pell-mell from the building and manifested their delight in the usual tumultuous manner of schoolboys freed from bondage. Caps were tossed in the air; Wagner, seizing that of one of his companions, threw it with extraordinary force and it landed on the roof the schoolhouse. The feat was loudly applauded by the other scholars. One dissenting voice there was, that of the unlucky boy whose cap had been thus ruthlessly snatched. He burst into tears. Wagner could never bear to see anyone cry; with the prompt decision characteristic of him all his life, he resolved to climb up to the roof for the cap. He went back into the schoolhouse, rushed up the stairs to the cock loft, climbed out on the roof through a ventilator and gazed down on the applauding boys. He then set about crawling along the steep incline toward the cap. The boys stopped cheering as they watched and drew back in fright. Some ran to the *custodes*. A ladder was brought and carried upstairs to the loft, the boys crowding eagerly behind. Meanwhile Wagner had secured the cap and safely slid back into the dark loft, just in time to hear excited voices on the stairs. He hid in a corner behind some boxes, waited for them to set up the ladder and the *custodes* to climb up; thereupon he emerged from his hiding-place and in an innocent tone inquired what they were looking for—a bird, perhaps? *"Ja, ein Galgenvogel!"* ("Yes, a gallows bird!") was the angry answer of the infuriated "custodes"—nevertheless they were glad enough to see the boy safe and sound, he was a general favorite. On this occasion he did not go unrebuked by his masters; they threatened to punish him severely the next time he undertook such a foolhardy journey.

Wagner told me that while he was on the roof, which, like all the roofs of old German houses, was very steep, he went giddy and was seized with a dread of falling. Bathed in hot perspiration, he had cried aloud, *"Liebes Muetterchen!"* ("Dear Mommy!"), whereupon he was a new man. The words had acted on him like magic and helped him retrace his steps from a position that would have appalled a trained gymnast. Many years later Wagner's eldest brother, Albert, referring to Richard's participation in the uprising of the people of Saxony in 1849, which Albert himself strongly disapproved, told me the above story in illustration of Richard's extreme foolhardiness. The episode was confirmed by Wagner, who then told me of his terror on the roof.

It was not only in climbing that Richard excelled. He was known as the best tumbler and somersault-turner in his big Dresden school. He was in fact expert in every type of physical exercise; and since he never lost his high animal spirits, he went on with his boyish tricks until he was nearing three-score and ten. Not infrequently I made reference to the roof of the Kreuzschule, and when Wagner proposed some venturesome enterprise I would say, "You're on the roof again."

"But I'll get down safe again too," was the answer, accompanied by his pleasant boyish laugh.

Richard early began to exhibit his predilection for acrobatic feats. When he was only seven he frequently terrified his mother by sliding down the banisters with daring rapidity and by jumping downstairs. Since his stunts were always successful, his mother and the other children came to take for granted that he would not come to grief, and sometimes he was asked to demonstrate his skill for visitors. Doubtless this increased the boy's self-confidence—which never deserted him as long as he lived.

Friedrich Pecht

Miserable Interlude in Paris

Pecht (1814-1903) was a painter of historical pictures and portraits
who lived in Paris for a time.

Wagner had lost his position as opera conductor in Riga in March
1839; he fled his many creditors by night, taking along his wife Minna
Planer and his dog Robber. They crossed the Russian border, in constant danger of being shot down by the guards, and had an adventurous
journey from Libau to London. On September 17th, they arrived in
Paris.

There Wagner met with nothing but hardship. He was unknown to
the musical world. Pecht gives us an excellent account of his first confused days in the French capital—of his growing influence upon the
little group of German bohemians.

Heinrich Laube (1806-1884) was a much admired German writer,
the leader of the literary movement *Junges Deutschland*. In later years
he became a violent opponent of Wagner.

For the rest of his life Wagner could never forget the terrible misery
he had experienced in Paris.

As SOON as I met Laube in the Salon Carré he said, "I'm going
to introduce you to some compatriots, a younger brother of
our cousin and your friend Frau Friedrich Brockhaus, lately
Kapellmeister at Riga, but just arrived here with his wife.
You are both planning to seek your fortune here; *he* is trying
to get an opera performed." Before long a youthful pair advanced to Laube, and the strikingly distinguished-looking
man, well-favored and attractive into the bargain, was presented to me as Herr Richard Wagner. His features then
showed nothing of that sternness which forty years of battle
later stamped upon them; on the contrary, they had something soft, for all their marked intelligence and animation.

Manifestly distracted and occupied with quite other things than Rubens and Paolo Veronese, whose pictures I was discussing with all the enthusiasm of a warm admirer, Wagner pleased me very well, but he made no deep impression on me. He looked much too neat and nice. There was a certain shimmer of refinement about his whole appearance. It must be admitted, something *unapproachable* as well; we were less accustomed to this quality in German geniuses then than nowadays. . . .

Wagner's absent-mindedness at this first encounter was only too understandable; he had arrived in a foreign capital without resources, he was not even a real master of the language, and he was at his wits' end—which he no longer concealed from us as our acquaintance wore on. . . .

Good comrade that Laube always was, he soon introduced us to Heine. The occasion was a dinner together at Brocci's, a famous Italian restaurant in the Rue Lepelletier, opposite the Grand Opéra. Heine brought his wife, in those days entrancingly beautiful, merry and naive as a child; she was a feast for all eyes and even put Frau Wagner's beauty in the shade. Laube was just the man to jolt Heine from the blasé indifference of his first greeting; the graceful tact of Iduna Laube did the rest. She evoked a perfect deluge of witty repartee—which sounded very much as if he had prepared it carefully beforehand. Beneath this meteoric downpour Wagner also thawed out of his silence and displayed that curious resilience of his, that most rare faculty of detaching oneself completely from the cares and worries of daily life. He had the knack of telling a good story, the sharpest of eyes for comic relief, the keenest of ears for the accents of nature, the surest of taste for everything fine in the plastic arts. He had just made a hazardous voyage from Riga in a tiny sailing vessel and was driven off his course up the coast of Norway; we were soon deeply absorbed in the tale.

❊   ❊   ❊

We young Germans who knew him and cared for him, attracted alike by the inexhaustible riches of his intellect and the charm of his lovely wife, were all as poor as churchmice. The only comfort we could offer him was proof that he was not utterly forsaken, that there were people who believed in him and formed a little community of which he remained the undisputed center. You see, he was already creating immortal works, however underrated then—and we were all just plain scholars and were aware how he towered over us. . . . A hundred times he cursed the fate that doomed him to make arrangements of Donizetti's music for Schlesinger; he would dissect its sugared triviality with comic wrath but so perspicuously that even I, an utter layman, could understand him. . . . The wonderful resilience he displayed at our evening reunions, the way he managed, for all his misery, to rise above the vexations of the day, his inexhaustible wit in characterizing the great musicians one after the other, so that they became living, breathing individuals for us to see—all this still astonishes me; for neither I nor any of my friends at that age could have come anywhere near him, not one of us was equipped to deliver such terse and accurate judgments on any artist. When his seething brain had come to some kind of calm or repose, he was never prone to mere disparagement—the first resort of the young. Even his intimate knowledge of the music of all ages was wellnigh incredible in so young a man. He knew the earlier Italians, Palestrina, Pergolesi and others just as well as the older German school; from him I got my first understanding of Bach, and Gluck was his constant preoccupation. Haydn's nature painting, Mozart's genius, the unhappy influences of his position at Salzburg and Vienna; the idiosyncrasies of the French, of Lully, Boieldieu, Auber; Mendelssohn's elegant drawing-room music; and Beethoven, the monarch of them all: each of these he brought before us, singing snatches of their melodies with such vivacity, such flexibility and power, that they linger in my memory today

just as he rendered them. I recall that even then he insisted
that music is a language of which much, if not all, in course of
time grows antiquated, unpalatable or unintelligible. So that
a good deal of Mozart was already out of date—he would hum
the passages as he explained—I was appalled at this assertion
then. Even the continuous transformation of musical instruments, he contended, must inevitably lead to antiquation; and
instrumentation was going to be revolutionized, Beethoven
had been the first to put the orchestra on the right road. Then
he would sketch with wonderful precision the specific character of every instrument, describe the function for which it
was peculiarly adapted, the color and flavor of its tone, and
so on. I had no idea at that time that color and mood were distinguishing qualities of his talent; it was impossible to discover them in his harum-scarum playing. He educated us
also with regard to the absurdity of modern opera, against
which he was already preparing to do battle. Never have I
heard Rossini so aptly criticized, though Wagner always gave
his lavish gifts their due. Our young friend, quite unknown
to the world, spoke of all these famed musicians as his equals.
We should have found this attitude altogether presumptuous
in a budding painter; in him we found it altogether natural
and justified, it never struck us as self-conceit. Obviously because it was nothing of the kind.

Malwida von Meysenbug

Tannhäuser in Paris

In 1848 and 1849 Wagner took part in the Sachsen revolution and
was exiled from Germany. He settled in Switzerland. The greatest event
in his dark years of exile was the first performance of *Tannhäuser* in Paris
in 1861. This performance—one of his greatest hopes and bitterest disappointments—encountered such violent hostility that it was necessary

for him to withdraw the work after three evenings. Close on that public
failure came the private one of Minna's final break with him.

Malwida von Meysenbug (1816-1903), the tutor of Olga, daughter
of the famous revolutionary Alexander Herzen, was a woman of outstanding character and intelligence. Her friendship with Wagner survived all the vicissitudes of their lives. She describes it in her famous
book *Memoiren einer Idealistin,* 1876. Her account of the turbulent
première in Paris shows the master at his best: as a courageous, uncom-
promising fighter.

IN THE MEANTIME, the rehearsals of *Tannhäuser* were going
on, and Wagner asked me to come to the first complete orchestral rehearsal. There were only a few favored ones in the large
Opera House—Wagner's wife and I were the only women.
Thus for the first time I heard the music played by a complete
orchestra. I was affected as by something sublime and sacred
and touched as by some great truth. Everything went beautifully and after the glorious sextette, where the Minnesingers
greet Tannhäuser just back from the Venusberg, the orchestra stood up and cheered Wagner enthusiastically. It was one
o'clock in the morning before the rehearsal was over.

Wagner was very happy and excited, for all seemed to
promise such glorious things, and he invited me and his wife
to have supper in the Maison d'Or on the Boulevard des Ital-
iens. We sat in a small room by ourselves. This was a happy
hour. Wagner told us how he had explained the ideally beautiful part of Elizabeth to young Marie Sachs. He had chosen
her for the role on account of her magnificent voice, although
she was only a beginner. He had explained to her among
others the place where she had to answer Wolfram's question
with a silent gesture: "I thank you for your tender friendship,
but my path leads where no one can accompany me."

Shortly after this rehearsal, the prospects of great success
were dimmed. The killjoy hobgoblins which delight in frus-
trating an ideal moment in the lives of men were busy blowing
clouds of envy and ill-humor from all sides. Political scandal-

mongers were dissatisfied that Princess Metternich should
have been the one to introduce this work of art, so foreign to
the French temperament. The press was dissatisfied because
Wagner did not, like Meyerbeer and others, give its representatives fine dinners to bribe their tastes. The claque, usually engaged by every composer, foamed with rage because
they were banned by Wagner. In the orchestra, too, different
factions arose; the incapable director had suddenly become
hostile. We, the friends and followers, were deeply distressed
that Wagner had refused in the beginning to direct the opera
himself, as we all had so ardently wished him to do. And
lastly—this was the principal thing—the young Paris lions, the
men of the Jockey Club, were indignant that there was no
ballet of the usual type and at the usual time—that is, in the
second act.

It was a known fact that the ladies of the ballet had their
earnings increased by these gentlemen and that the latter
were accustomed to go to the opera after dining, not to hear
beautiful harmonies, but to see the most unnatural and most
terrible product of modern art, the ballet. After the performance, they became better acquainted with the dancing
nymphs behind the scenes.

What did these aristocratic rakes care about the performance of a chaste work of art which celebrated the victory of
sacred love over the frenzy of emotion? Not only did they
care nothing for it, they must hate and condemn it even before hearing it. . . . These men were the principal instiga-
tors of the intrigues which doomed the performance to failure. They had the baseness to buy small whistles beforehand,
with which they intended to air their opinion of art.

Thus the clouds gathered even more threateningly, and
with fear and trembling I went to the dress rehearsal. I also
took Olga because I wanted her to learn to love music in its
best and highest form. The dress rehearsal took place without
any outward disturbance. The large audience consisted

mostly of friends, among whom was the Princess Metternich—she was enthusiastic. It was a heavenly evening for me, for it was the fulfillment of what I had long wished for. Although I felt that there was much to be desired in the performance and that Wagner would not be satisfied, yet much of it was very beautiful—as for instance the role of Elizabeth, as sung by Sachs—and I now had an idea of the whole, which fully confirmed my anticipation. The magic worked on little Olga too, as I had hoped it would; she sat lost in awe and enthusiasm, not growing tired, although it was very late before the rehearsal was over. On coming out of the opera, I met Wagner, who was waiting for his wife. I saw by his face that he was not satisfied and I saw how little he expected a victory over the hostile forces working against him.

One more day of thrilling anticipation passed by and then came the day of the actual performance. I sat in a box with several women and Czermak. The overture and the first act went off without any disturbance, and, although the setting of the ghostly dance of the gods in the Venusberg fell far short of Wagner's idea and the three Graces appeared in pink ballet dresses, I nevertheless heaved a sigh of relief and hoped that our fears were ungrounded. However, at the change of the scene, during the ravishing poetic progression from the dreary Bacchanalia below to the peaceful morning stillness of the Thuringian valley, at the sounds of the flute and the Shepherd's song, a long-prepared attack suddenly broke out, and loud hissing and shouts interrupted the music. Naturally, Wagner's friends and those of the audience who wanted to hear it to the end before judging it, did not remain silent. As these were stronger in numbers, they were victorious and the performance continued; the singers remained undisturbed, doing their best.

Unfortunately it was not long before the noise began again. Likewise the protest against it, which retained the upper hand; thus the performance was finished, though because of these frightful interruptions it was impossible for anyone to get a correct impression of the whole.

Words cannot express my excitement and indignation and other admirers were likewise indignant. Czermak was so furious that it was difficult to restrain him from laying hands on some of the leaders of the opposition. These gentlemen did not hesitate, but sat in full view, holding in their gloved hands the little whistles which, on a given signal, sounded shrill notes.

The following day I went to the Wagners'. I found him perfectly composed, so much so that even the papers most violently opposed to him in the fight which had also broken out in the press, admitted that he had conducted himself in a most dignified manner during the storm of the evening performance. He wanted to withdraw the score and prevent a second performance, because he realized that there could be no real success with such an audience as that of the Paris Opera. We, his close friends, were opposed to this and were anxious for a repetition as we felt positive that it would be successful. In our great excitement we did not stop to consider that this was now an absolute impossibility.

The time for the second performance drew near. The hostile party had armed itself still more. So had the friendly party. The fight was much more bitter than the first time. I was in a box with Wagner's wife and the Hungarian woman who had introduced us. Next to us were Frenchmen who outdid themselves in whistling, hissing and shouting. I was completely beside myself with indignation and gave vent to my anger quite loudly. "So this is the audience that boasts of good taste and pretends to dictate to the world what is beautiful and excellent in art! A lot of street urchins who haven't even enough manners to let people of another opinion listen in peace and quiet." I went on speaking in this way so that Mrs. Wagner was frightened and whispered to me: "Heavens, you are bold, you will get yourself into trouble." However, I thought of nothing but my anger and my contempt for such an audience. Finally I faced my neighbors and said: "Gentlemen, at least remember that the wife of the composer is sitting here next to you." They were startled for a moment and quieted down. Then, however, they began afresh. Nevertheless, they did not succeed in bringing down the curtain and the performance was carried through to the end.

Wagner was now more inclined than ever to stop further scandal, but we others all voted for a third performance. It was to be given on a nonsubscription night and we hoped that his opponents would stay away and only those who wanted to hear it would attend. Wagner had decided not to go, so as to escape the unnecessary excitement. Nor did his wife attend the performance. I had taken a box so as to bring Olga and little Marie who lived with us. I hoped they would enjoy it undisturbed.

Unfortunately, however, this was not to be. The disturbers were there en masse to carry on their work, arriving for the very beginning, which was unusual for them. The singers were really heroic; they often had to stop for fifteen minutes or more, to let the storm which raged in the audience blow over. They stood quietly, looking into the audience, unshaken, and as soon as it became quiet, sang and went on to the end. Of course, the outburst spoiled all enjoyment of the fine individual achievements and beautiful scenic effects.

Little Olga was just as indignant as I. She admired Wagner greatly and was moved to the depths of her young soul by this music. It affected her in so wonderful a way that I felt anew the inner truth of it. Olga took part in the fight with true courage, leaning over the edge of the box to call with all her might, *"A la porte, à la porte!"* and pointing to the elegant hissing men. Two men in the adjoining box seemed charmed with her eagerness and said several times, *"Elle est charmante!"*

It was two o'clock in the morning when we joined friends in the foyer and went to the Wagners, who would, we were sure, wait for an account of the performance. We were not mistaken. They were sitting comfortably at supper, Wagner smoking a pipe. He received the news of the repeated and even more bitter fight with smiling complacency. He joked with Olga, telling her he had heard that she had hissed him. However, I felt by his trembling, when I shook hands with him, that the disagreeable occurrence had excited him. Even though such behavior was a reflection on the public that was guilty of it, there was another hope gone and the dreary path of life, which remained obstinately rugged, again lay desolate, weary and hopeless before him. It broke my heart the more, as all my attempts to help had proved fruitless.

Wagner now withdrew the score and thus put an end to the fight at the theater.

Eliza Wille

Refuge in Mariafeld

François Wille was a former newspaper editor in Hamburg. He and his wife lived in style on a small estate at Mariafeld, near Zurich, Switzerland. Frau Wille was very sympathetic to the penniless exile; she helped him whenever she could. It was to Mariafeld that he fled in March 1864, when his debts made it necessary for him to leave Vienna in a hurry.

Eliza Wille (1809-1893) was a mediocre poet and fiction writer. She was Mathilde Wesendonk's best friend and therefore her and Richard's confidante during their love affair. She saw the great man as he was, and he frankly confessed to her all his weaknesses, vices and dreams. She knew his craving for luxury, his pretentiousness, his thirst for fame that so oddly combined with his increasing estrangement from the world.

THE WEATHER was stormy and cold despite approaching spring; I was sorry that Wagner would have to stay at lonely Mariafeld without the genial company of the master of the house. Nor was his visit with me brightened up by any external event, or any that I could call important. I settled him in and arranged everything in accordance with our honored guest's wishes as expressed in the letter I have told you about. He wanted to work, he wanted to be left absolutely alone and to feel free and at his ease; I even gave him his own private servants. When it was noised abroad that the famous man was at Mariafeld a number of visitors came from Zurich, prompted by curiosity and interest. I turned them away; Wagner was in no mood to put up with that sort of annoyance. He wrote and received many letters. He asked me not to worry about him at all, to pay no attention to him, to let him eat alone in his room if this would not upset the household too much. It was a pleasure for me to let our friend have things his own way so far as possible. He did not want to go to Zurich; he was not satisfied with the way his work was progressing, but he went for long walks by himself. I can still see him pacing back and forth on our garden terrace in his brown velvet robe, with his black cap for headgear, like a patrician out of Albrecht Durer's pictures.

✻   ✻   ✻

I have never felt it just to record as an indisputable "yes" or "no" of character what the moment of intercourse with friends now gives and now takes away. The outbursts of tormented and deluded hopes, of exasperation, of raging fantasy brought on by Wagner's present depression of spirits are like the restless domination of the elements in nature—the wind must drive the clouds apart, then we are in the sun again!

✻   ✻   ✻

And there was sunshine on many a happy day when Wagner felt in the mood to spend a little time in my sitting room. Everyone who has ever known him knows how kind and warm he can be. The sons at their mother's side received the friendliest attention. He was well aware that the "good woman," as he called me, probably valued her boys above all the godlike splendor of antique Greek youth, even above the Nordic splendor of Siegfried! Wagner was a past master of teasing and storytelling. He had liked Vienna, he called it the only musical city of Germany.

But his good humor was soon gone. Letters came that put him out of sorts. He withdrew to the solitude of his room, and when he met me alone he poured himself out in words that held little cheer for the future.

*   *   *

With every day it became clearer to me that something extraordinary must happen, some good fortune must drop from the blue; mere diligence and patience would not enable this artistic giant to tear free from the cliff to which hostile gods had chained him.

I had collected every imaginable sort of book and put them in Wagner's room: works on Napoleon, on Frederick the Great, even the works of German mystics, who meant much to Wagner, whereas he rejected Feuerbach and Strauss as bone-dry scholars.

Whatever I could I gave him eagerly, in all simplicity; but I could not cheer him up.

I still see him sitting in the chair near my window, I see him as he sat then, listening impatiently one evening while I spoke to him of the splendor of the future that surely lay before him. The sun had just gone down in glory, earth and heaven were radiant.

Wagner said: "Why are you talking about the future when

my manuscripts are lying locked up in the cupboard! Who is going to perform the work of art that I, only *I* can create with the help of happy demons—who is going to perform it so that all the world says yes, that's it, that's the way the Master saw his work and wanted it?"

He walked up and down the room excitedly. Stopping before me suddenly, he said, "I'm organized differently, I have sensitive nerves—I must have beauty, brilliance and light! The world owes me what I need! I can't live on a miserable organist's salary, like your Master Bach! Is it an unheard of presumption if I think I'm entitled to the bit of luxury I like? I who give pleasure to the world, to thousands!"

So speaking, he raised his head as if in defiance. Then he sat down in the chair at the window again and stared in front of him. What did he care about the magnificence of the view or the peace of nature?

Cosima Wagner

From the Diaries

Wagner's first wife, born Wilhelmine Planer, died in 1866 in Dresden. On August 25, 1870, Wagner married Cosima von Buelow, Lizt's younger daughter, who had been divorced from her husband.

From both her father and her mother, the highly gifted Countess Marie d'Agoult, Cosima inherited intelligence, indomitable energy, and marked executive ability. From the day of her marriage to Wagner she devoted herself solely to him and his work. After his death, she regarded it as her one mission in life to direct the Bayreuth festivals.

These few lines from her diaries reveal her exalted, almost religious adoration of Richard. His triumph was long delayed, but when it came it was tremendous; his friends worshipped him as a demigod.

Triebschen, Spring 1869

He said he knows only one thing: That since the world began no man of his age has ever loved a wife as he loves me.

❧   ❧   ❧

Triebschen, 21. August 1870

I wrote to Frau Wesendonk. I asked him whether he was
satisfied with the letter. He thought it was too much; he said
he had cast a poetic veil over the relationship so that its triviality might not be so obvious, but the poetic element had
faded away even for him and he did not like to be reminded
of it.

He said he had to laugh like a child when he read my signature: Cosima Wagner; he said it was like a dream for him. . . .

❧   ❧   ❧

Triebschen, 5. February 1871

I stay with him while he writes the last words [of *Siegfried*].
This is the event of today that filled me with bliss.

Sophie Rützow

In Bayreuth

Sophie Rützow was a German journalist, born in Bayreuth, Her grand-
father, the historian Friedrich Töpfer, was a Wagner disciple when the
master was still considered a madman by most people. He fought courageously for the fulfillment of Wagner's Bayreuth idea.

Sophie Rützow's father also was a true adherent of Wagner. She was
thus reared in a strong pro-Wagner atmosphere.

In 1943 she decided first to write her own recollections and then collect and write down the impressions of people who had worked and lived with the great old man in Bayreuth. She talked with old shop-keepers, innkeepers, officials, waiters, gardeners, as well as singers, musicians, theatrical people and critics.

Richard Wagner was still cheerful enough in the company of his friends and guests—or seemed cheerful, despite his mental depression; but those who knew him were aware of the heavy clouds that so often overshadowed Wahnfried. Ever and again the struggle recommenced, ever and again financial ex-igency threatened. He had to make exhausting concert tours to bring in funds; hostility hammered away at Bayreuth. Those who knew these things knew also the place of Wagner's deepest self-communion. . . . It was in the garden of Wahn-fried, one spot under the tall murmuring trees of the Hof-garten: the Wagner grave.

When they moved into Wahnfried the grave was already finished. A little door, which Wagner had asked as a favor from the King in 1873, led into the castle garden; near this door lay the grave. In June of the same year he wrote to Ludwig II: "It is a wonderfully comforting thing for us to know the exact spot, and to tend it daily—the spot where we shall one day find heavenly rest, in the ground and soil for which we have the generosity of your love to thank. . . ."

While it was being dug, Wagner came to see the grave every day. He frequently climbed down to the bottom of it and engaged in reflective conversations on death and dying with his workmen. During one such discussion the Bayreuth carpenter Strunz remarked, "But Master! a famous composer like you has not time to die! You still have to write many great works for the world!" Richard Wagner was silent for a while, shook his head and said, "Oh, I wish I were lying in there already!" . . .

Having this grave on his own property enabled him to

realize a long-cherished desire. He had always wanted to have his animals near him after death. Now he could bed them beside his own future resting place. Under the trees of Wahnfried sleep his dogs, and the words on the little stones are still legible today: "Here lies and watches Wagner's Russ," "Here lies Wahnfried's faithful guardian and friend, the good and beautiful Marke," and—"Our good Faf and Frisch."

Before going to bed Wagner often came and stood on the steps leading from the salon to the garden and looked over at the grave. And the first evening after they moved into Wahnfried it was the grave that they went to look at before anything else, he and Cosima. In her diary she captured the silent, solemn minutes of that contemplation: 'Moonlight. I walk out onto the balcony with Richard, we see the grave . . . .' "

* * *

Oftener than was agreeable to Richard Wagner and Cosima, trunks were carried out of the "House of the Last Happiness." Another long trip. The Bayreuthers had their immediate surmise: the Master was either going on a concert tour or he was going to look for singers. In this latter conjecture they were not seldom right.

. . . Those singers! Wagner raged and thundered against what he called operatic stereotype, against the puppet singers. "What good does it do me to write the most wonderful notes—when I can't find singers who know how to sing them?" he once cried in desperation, and at the commencement of his Bayreuth period he lamented to singing master Hey: "What use is the house to me if I can't put in the right singers!" But then, in the same breath, he went on—and this is typical of his talent for weaving artistic progress out of lacks and insufficiencies—"But if things in general go the way we hope at Bayreuth I am thinking of starting a training school

for operatic style and expression and instrumental music.
That might tie together the annual Festspiel performances
and bring us rising talents."

Between his repeated quests for singers and his longed-for
discoveries there intervened the serious building crisis of
1873. Not until this was over and the Festspielhaus well under
way could he think of convoking his prospective singers in
Bayreuth. "I shan't lack men, but I haven't much to show in
the way of women," he wrote to Emil Heckel in Mannheim.
But when the first little flock gathered at Bayreuth for audition and rehearsal in the summer of 1874, there were not only
Scaria, Betz, Hill, Unger, there were also a few women.
Materna of Vienna was among them. She sang for Wagner
and her singing was a decisive event. He knew at once that he
had found in her his Bruennhilde.

But the others—what a laborious task it was educating and
training and polishing them! One singer who fancied himself a
Mime was incapable of pronouncing the letter "s"; two women
singers recommended as Waldvogel and Erda had such poor
enunciation that their words were absolutely unintelligible;
Scaria, the proposed Hagen, had never tried to read the libretto of the *Ring* and had not the faintest idea what it was
about; Betz, the future Wotan, complained that his role was
demonic. "Do you regard demoniacality," Wagner finally
asked with malice, "as an artistic specialty?"

Ah yes, these singers with a record of popular successes,
these baritones and sopranos and basses and tenors, they had
to be handled with indulgence if the Master hoped to keep
them well-disposed for the extraordinary tasks awaiting them.
But he called himself "the schoolmaster" and with warrant.
He knew where and how to set about their education. In
January 1875, he sent those with whom he was agreed their
contract letters, along with an invitation to the summer rehearsals. Because he did not want these rehearsal weeks in
Bayreuth to be too great a sacrifice for them, he already

planned their participation in the profits earned by the Fest-spiele of 1877 and 1878.

All he summoned came. Bayreuth filled up with artists. In every corner of every house somebody was learning a role. The hotel rooms rang with the notes of the Nibelungen. . . . At the "Sun" lived the Valkyrie; in another Gasthof the Giants had made their abode, in a third the Gods. . . .

The singers foregathered every evening for a few hours at Wahnfried. Until rehearsals began at Bayreuth, most of them knew only fragments from the *Ring*. At the first rehearsals much seemed strange, incomprehensible, almost weird. Gradually their uneasiness turned into amazement, their amazement into veneration and enthusiasm. What had been unintelligible one day was plain and clear to them the next, spreading before them like a wonderfully woven fabric. Now for the first time Richard Wagner heard his works sung, by artists inspired with good will and understanding.

Lilli Lehmann, Marie Lehmann, her sister, and Minna Lammert had been selected for the Daughters of the Rhine. They knew their parts first and were thus the first to sing at Wahnfried. "My noblest memory, I would say," writes Lilli Lehmann in her memoirs, "was the moment when we saw the big tears rolling down Richard Wagner's cheeks during the trio from the *Rheingold* and heard Frau Cosima sobbing aloud." When Liszt arrived the Rheintoechter sang for him, too, the scene from the *Goetterdaemmerung*. He shook his head in laughing admiration. "You can't believe your ears! That passages like that should come off—!"

❊ ❊ ❊

All who saw Wagner in his role of "schoolmaster" to his singers declare his coaching was incomparable. Adolf Wall-noefer, who it will be remembered was at this time Nibe-

lungen assistant, witnessed Wagner's transports of demon-
stration. "When he was Mime he hunched himself together,
slid across the floor, sang in a croaking voice and had a deceit-
ful look," Wallnoefer still recalls. "When he was a God he
would draw himself up, stretching his little figure until he
actually seemed to grow before our eyes. He was very well
satisfied with the Rheintoechter, but Sieglinde was always
too spiritless for him. 'Have you two no idea of the volcanic
love that is consuming her?' he cried out passionately. And
to make clear to Sieglinde the wellnigh superhuman character of her love, he threw himself on Siegmund's breast with
such ardor that the big, powerful Albert Niemann tottered
for a moment."

Wagner took the greatest pains of all with Unger, the young
Siegfried. He wanted, as he once expressed it, to mold this
favorite creature of his entirely anew, to develop him so to
say "out of the egg." It was not easy to make Unger over into
a Bayreuth Siegfried. His form was fine and powerful, but his
rather rough voice lacked the marvelous freshness that Siegfried's voice should have. And he had trouble moving naturally; Hofballettmeister Fricke had a lot of work to do on him.
Small wonder that the young singer was occasionally rather
dejected. But seeing him thus, Wagner would take double
pains with him, interlarding his instruction with jokes so that
poor Unger's courage should not desert him. . . .

Without meaning to, Unger played Wagner a nasty trick
just before the Festspiele began. Unger had a beard, and
Wagner had often remarked "Unger would probably be better
without a beard." After the last Siegfried rehearsal the artists
and we Nibelungen assistants convened at Angermann's,
where Unger dropped certain mysterious hints concerning a
surprise he had in store for the Master. Sure enough—at the
final dress rehearsal he showed up—without his beard!

We were one and all horrified. Wagner clapped his hands
over his eyes and groaned in a dull, dead voice, "Unger with-

out a beard—impossible! You have no chin! And the King will
be there!"

High excitement prevailed. But it was true; Unger really
had no chin. He was so disappointed at the miscarriage of his
surprise that he burst into oaths and curses. This did him no
good whatever. The theater hairdresser was obliged to supply
him with a hasty beard of youthful character. Meanwhile
Richard Wagner was suffering a real heart attack from the
excitement, but even in the moments of his pain he was kind,
gasping, "It's not Unger's fault, he meant well!"

Remembering such things, we breathe again the atmosphere of struggle and anxiety that hung about those rehearsal
days. What disappointments, what vexations, what adversi-
ties beset poor Wagner! One day Scaria was gone; nothing
was heard of him again. Niemann walked out in the middle
of rehearsal and left town. Says Wallnoefer, "Strangely
enough, that highly gifted singer was the one artist who
always felt offended at something or other. 'Isn't anybody
leaving today?' we used to ask one another when we met at
Wahnfried—a long-standing joke that came at last to have a
kind of resignation in it."

"It is frightful what irritations, trivialities and annoyances
Wagner is exposed to," wrote the faithful Fricke in his Bayreuth diary at this time. "All sorts of outrages and mortifica-
tions and insults, in addition to the usual worries! It is admirable how he bears it, how he fights! Everlastingly young
and full of jokes—and with it all he is in continuous contact
with everyone, he doesn't lose sight of the smallest detail—it
is inexplicable how he can still compose, how he doesn't break
down. . . ."

Paul von Joukowsky

Everything Is Over

This letter to Malwida, Wagner's friend, was written from Bayreuth on February 22, 1883. Paul von Joukowsky was a Russian painter who came to Bayreuth in 1880. He is the creator of the first *Parsifal* stage designs.

He reports the master's death without any romantic embellishments. Wagner had leased the luxurious Vendramin Palace in Venice. Early in February he had an unusually severe attack of angina pectoris, and on the 13th he died in Cosima's arms.

THE MASTER'S DEATH was as glorious as his life. We were all waiting for him at the table, since he had sent us word to start eating. Meanwhile he had sent for the doctor because of his usual pains; then he had told Betty to call Frau Wagner. This was around two-thirty. At three the doctor came and we all felt easier; but toward four we began to worry because no one came out of the room. Suddenly George came and told us everything was over. He had died about three o'clock in the arms of his wife, without suffering, he just fell asleep with the most exalted, peaceful expression; I will never forget the look on his face.

GIUSEPPE VERDI

Born: Le Roncole, Italy
October 10, 1813
Died: Milan, Italy
January 27, 1901

GIUSEPPE VERDI started out as one of many talented
Italians who composed traditional opera music. In time
he educated and disciplined himself to the attainment of
true originality, grandeur, and beauty.

He was a poor boy. For years he studied in the little
town of Busseto simply because he did not have the money
to live in Milan. He married the daughter of his teacher
and protector, Barezzi, and by the time he managed to
move to Milan he already had two children. His first operas
were only moderately successful. While he was scoring his
comic piece *Finto Stanislao*, tragedy struck: within the
space of three weeks his wife and both children died.

He produced three or four operas a year, but *Rigoletto*
(1851) was the first fruit of his liberated genius. It was an
immense success. Thereafter he refused to be hurried. He
retired to his farm, Villa Sant 'Agata, with his beloved
friend Giuseppina, whom he later married. Now came one
masterpiece after the other, paving his road to fame: *Il
Trovatore, La Traviata, Simone Boccanegra, Un Ballo in
Maschera, Aida, Otello,* and finally, *Falstaff.*

After Giuseppina died, the old man longed only to follow her. He lived four more years, joyless and lonely, suffering deeply in his solitude.

Francis Toye

Childhood of Poverty

Francis Toye (born 1883) is an excellent, extremely reliable musicologist and a music critic for English newspapers.

When he decided to write a Verdi biography, he found the records
touching the master's early childhood altogether insufficient. He went
to Italy and stayed some time in Busseto, tracking down all the old men
and women who might possibly know something about the boy
Giuseppe, his father, his relatives, his school life. Toye was successful
in his search. These first-hand reports, combined with the fruits of scholarly investigation, produced the first authentic picture of those long-ago
days in a poor Italian village at the start of the nineteenth century.

Le Roncole is nothing but a hamlet, and the tiny inn where
Verdi was born and passed his infancy is little more than a
hovel on the side of the road. A modern millionaire might
think it not quite good enough for his prize cows. We know
that, to make both ends meet, Carlo Verdi sold coffee and
sugar and tobacco as well as wine, the circumstances of the
family differing in no wise from those of the peasants by
whom they were surrounded. In fact they were peasants,
and to the day of his death Verdi retained some characteristics, bad as well as good, of his class and upbringing.

The little Giuseppe was a serious child, the idol of his
mother, whom he adored. He seems to have been a queer
mixture of shyness and fierceness, and we are told that nothing brought him out of himself except music. Thus, when
quite a little boy, he used to stand in ecstasy at the exploits of

an old wandering violinist who came from time to time to play for the delectation of Carlo Verdi's patrons. Indeed, it is said that it was this strolling minstrel, struck by the boy's musical sensitiveness, who first advised the father to give his son a musical education.

When he was only seven years old, little Giuseppe Verdi gave a further striking proof of his musical sensibility. Like many Italian peasant boys to this day, he was employed on Sundays and feast days to sing in the choir of the church and to serve the priest as acolyte during Mass. On one of these occasions he heard the organ played for the first time and the novel sound seems almost to have paralyzed him. So absorbed was he in the delicious sensation that when the priest asked him for water three times in a row, he paid no attention. Whereupon the exasperated ecclesiastic, to rouse the boy from his trance, gave him such a push that he fell down the three steps leading to the altar and fainted away. It is characteristic of his determination even in those early years that, on his recovery, he did not cry or rage as most children would have done, but merely asked his father once again if he could study music.

The story of the music-enchanted acolyte must have made some stir in the community, for a short time afterward, when his father, yielding at last to the boy's desire for instruction in music, bought an old spinet for him, a neighboring workman volunteered to repair it for nothing; the pedals had gone (if they ever existed) and the hammers were without leather. Its condition, probably dilapidated enough anyhow, was further aggravated by an assault with a hammer made by the hot-tempered little boy, who had by chance lighted on the wholly satisfying chord of C Major and vented on the instrument his fury at not being able to find it again.

With a true Latin sense of craftsmanship, the repairer left a record inside the instrument of the extent of his labors. As an example of simple pride and as a record of a generous action the inscription is worth recording in all its original inexactitude:

> By me, Stefano Cavaletti, these key hammers were renewed and lined with leather, and I fitted pedals, which I gave as a present; as I also repaired gratuitously the said key hammers, seeing the excellent disposition the young Giuseppe Verdi shows to learn how to play this instrument—which suffices to give me complete satisfaction.

It is possible to attach too much importance to the stories of Giuseppe's musical precocity; the history of music is littered with such anecdotes among both professionals and amateurs who have, nevertheless, failed to achieve fame. It is easy, when a man has become great, to be wise after the event. As a matter of fact, Verdi's early compositions prove conclusively that he possessed none of the miraculous facility of a Mozart or a Mendelssohn. Like Wagner, he attained to musical power by the sweat of his brow. There can be no doubt, however, that this spinet played a leading part in the first scenes of his life's drama. It was the great friend of his childhood. Seated at the miserable instrument when tired of working in the fields or the inn, when bored with playing the inevitable game of bowls with the village children, he dreamed dreams that seemed inexplicable even to himself.

There is nothing Arcadian about the plain of Parma, in the winter cold and foggy, or wind-swept, in the summer sunbaked and unshaded. The roads during the hot weather are so dusty that today, when a motor car passes over them, there is a dense cloud as of steam escaping from the pistons of a locomotive. The trees (such as they are), the vines, the fields of corn within fifty yards of the road, are gray with a layer of dust. Emphatically Verdi's boyhood was no Theocritean idyl; it was essentially practical and poverty-stricken. Many years afterward the composer summed it up, with typical conciseness, to a friend: "My youth was hard." From Verdi, who hated talking about himself, the avowal indicates much. The best proof of what the spinet meant to him is that he kept it all his life. Can it not still be seen in the museum of Milan?

When Verdi's father bought the spinet, he arranged at the same time with the local organist, an old man called Bais-trocchi, to give the boy some musical instruction, perhaps in the elements of music, certainly in organ and spinet play-ing. Here, for the first time, we catch a glimpse of superior musical gifts, for after three years' study little Giuseppe re-placed his old master as organist of Le Roncole. The instru-ment at his disposal was primitive and the duties cannot have been exacting, but few boys of twelve would have been able to undertake them at all. The salary was proportionately modest—rather less than two pounds a year, increased by special fees for funerals, weddings, and the like to about four pounds. Apparently, also, the youthful organist was al-lowed to make a collection for himself once a year at the harvest festival. This represented little enough, but the in-habitants of Le Roncole probably did their best for the lad. We know that they were both proud and fond of him, for when, a little later, there was talk of his being replaced by a protégé of the Bishop, there was almost an insurrection among the villagers, who clamored loudly and successfully for the retention of their *maestrino*.

Giulio Ricordi

Verdi Told Me

Young Verdi arrived in Milan in 1832, and pitifully poor he was. He planned to enter the Conservatory as a student—but the directors would have none of him: he was over the usual age for admission. In later years he told his publisher Ricordi the story of his struggle to make his way in the face of all obstacles and hardships.

To Verdi, Signore Ricordi (1840-1912) was not only publisher, he was admirer and devoted friend as well. In the course of intimate conversation, Ricordi was fortunate enough to garner the following particulars from the composer's own lips which he jotted right down.

The Philharmonic Society was an association of distinguished amateurs. During the winter they gave a grand concert in the hall of the Philodramatic Theater.

ABOUT 1833 or 1834 there was at Milan a Philharmonic Society composed of good musical elements. It was directed by a *maestro* named Masini, who, although he was not distinguished by much knowledge, had at least patience and firmness of purpose, which are in truth the qualities necessary for a society of amateurs. At that time they were getting up the execution of an oratorio of Haydn, the *Creation;* my master, Lavigna, asked me if, in order to improve myself, I should like to take part in the rehearsals, which offer I accepted with pleasure.

No one paid the slightest attention to the short young man who was modestly seated in a dark corner. Three *maestri,* Perelli, Bonoldi, and Almasio, conducted the rehearsals; but lo! one fine day, by a remarkable coincidence, all three failed to appear. Those who were to take part lost patience, and Masini, who did not feel equal to sitting down at the pianoforte and accompanying from the score, turned to me to beg me to serve as accompanist, saying, little confident as he perhaps was in the skill of an unknown young artist, "It will be sufficient if you just put in the bass."

I was then just fresh from my studies, and certainly did not find myself embarrassed before an orchestral score. I agreed, and sat myself at the pianoforte to begin the rehearsal. I well remember the ironical smiles of some of the amateurs, and it seems that my youthful physiognomy, my spare figure and my modest dress were not of a nature to inspire great confidence.

However this may have been, we began the rehearsal, and little by little becoming warmed and excited, I did not confine myself to accompanying, but began to conduct with the right hand, playing with the left alone. When the rehearsal was over, I received on all sides compliments and congratulations, especially from Count Pompeo Belgiojoso and Count Renato Borromeo.

As a sequel to this incident, whether the three *maestri* of whom I have spoken were too busy to continue to take the engagement or whether for other reasons, it ended in my being entrusted with the entire direction of the concert; the public performance took place with such success that a second was given in the great hall of the Casino dei Nobili, in the presence of the Archduke and the Archduchess Raineri and of all the great society of that time.

A short time afterward, Count Renato Borromeo charged me with the composition of the music of a cantata for voice and orchestra, on the occasion, if I remember rightly, of the marriage of a member of his family. It is well to remark on this subject that from all this work I derived no pecuniary advantage, and that my assistance was entirely gratuitous.

Masini, who, it appears, had great confidence in the young artist, then proposed to me to write an opera for the Philodramatic Theater, which he directed, and forwarded to me a libretto, which subsequently, modified in part by Solera, became *Oberto di San Bonifacio.*

I accepted the offer gladly, and returned to Busseto, where I was engaged as organist. There I stayed for about three years. My opera completed, I once more undertook the journey to Milan, carrying my finished score with me, in perfect order, having taken the trouble to extract and copy all the voice parts myself.

But here began my difficulties: Masini was no longer director of the Philodramatic Theater; it was, therefore, no longer possible to give my opera. However, whether he really

had confidence in me or whether he wished in some way to
prove his gratitude (after the *Creation,* I had helped him on
several other occasions in preparing and in directing the execution of different pieces, among others *La Cenerentola,* and
always without recompense of any kind), he was not discouraged in the face of difficulties, and promised me that he would
do all he could to get my opera presented at La Scala, on
the occasion of the annual soirée which was given for the
benefit of the Pio Istituto. Count Borromeo and the advocate Pasetti promised Masini he could rely upon their support; but I must say, to keep strictly to the truth, that
this support produced no more than a few commonplace
words of recommendation. On the other hand, Masini gave
himself much trouble, and he was strongly backed up by the
violoncellist Merighi, who had faith in me. I had known him
in the orchestra of the Philodramatic Theater, of which he
was a member.

At last they succeeded in making all arrangements for the
spring of 1839, and in such a manner that I had the double
fortune of bringing out my work at the theater of La Scala
and of having as its interpreters four artists really remarkable:
Signora Strepponi, the tenor Moriani, the baritone Giorgio
Ronconi, and the bass Marini.

The parts were distributed and the vocal rehearsals had
scarcely begun, when Moriani fell seriously ill! Everything
was thus interrupted, and the production of my opera was
no longer to be thought of. I was quite disconcerted, and was
getting ready to return to Busseto, when one morning I saw
arrive at my door a member of the staff of La Scala, who
said to me in a gruff tone of voice:

"Are you the *maestro* from Parma who was going to give
an opera for the Pio Istituto? Come to the theater; the *impresario* is waiting for you."

"Really?" I cried.

"Yes, *signor.* I was ordered to go and find out the *maestro* from Parma who was going to give an opera. If it is you, come."

And I went.

The *impresario* of La Scala at that time was Bartolomeo Merelli. One night, behind the scenes, he had overheard a conversation between Signora Strepponi and Giorgio Ronconi, a conversation in the course of which Strepponi spoke very favorably of the music of *Oberto di San Bonifacio,* which Ronconi also found to his taste.

I presented myself then to Merelli, who without any preliminaries said that in consideration of the favorable opinion of my opera which he had heard expressed, he was of his own accord disposed to put it on the stage during the next season; but that if I closed with the offer, I should have to make some alterations in my score, the artists who would play in it not being the same as those who were to have sung it originally. It was a brilliant offer for me; young, unknown, I had found an *impresario* who dared to put on the stage a new work without asking of me an idemnity of any sort, an indemnity, moreover, which it would have been quite impossible for me to raise. Merelli, taking on his own shoulders all the necessary expenses, proposed to divide with me in equal parts the sum which I should get if, in case of success, I sold my score. Let no one suppose that this was a burdensome proposition; it was the work of a beginner that was in question; and, in fact, the result turned out succesful enough to induce the publisher Giovanni Ricordi to consent to acquire the ownership of my opera at the price of two thousand Austrian liri.

Oberto di San Bonifacio attained a success if not very considerable, at least sufficient to warrant a certain number of performances . . . .

Mariana Barbieri-Nini

Dictatorial Attitude

Mariana Barbieri-Nini (1818-1887) was one of the most interesting singers on the Italian stage. She was remarkably ugly and unattractive, but her theatrical talents were so overpowering that the public forgave her everything.

She was the first interpreter of Lady Macbeth in Verdi's opera *Macbeth.* This was one of his earlier works, first performed in Florence on March 14, 1847. In this opera his artistic conscience reaches maturity.

Verdi's attitude toward the interpreters of his work was always, throughout his life, that of a merciless tyrant. Nothing counted but his work. Unyielding will and indefatigable energy were perhaps his chief characteristics.

THE PIANOFORTE and orchestra rehearsals ran to over a hundred, for Verdi was never satisfied with the performance; he demanded that the artists give a better rendition. Partly because of his exaggerated expectations and partly because of his reserved and taciturn character, the musicians cherished no particular affection for him. The minute the *maestro* appeared for morning and evening rehearsal, all eyes in the rehearsal hall and on the stage turned to him—all eyes sought to read from his facial expression how matters stood. If he came in smiling it could be taken for granted that he wanted some extra rehearsal that day.

I remember that there were two culminating points in the opera: the sleepwalking scene and my duet with the baritone. It sounds almost incredible, but the fact is that the sleepwalking scene alone required three months' study. For three months I labored, morning and evening, to imitate someone talking in her sleep, someone—so the *maestro* told me—who speaks more or less without moving her lips, the rest of her face motionless, her eyes closed . . . . It was enough to drive

you crazy! . . . And the duet with the baritone beginning
"Fatal, mia donna, un murmure"—unbelievable as it may
sound—that duet was rehearsed one hundred and fifty times;
Verdi's aim, as he explained, was to achieve an effect of
speaking rather than singing. Well, it was finally over and
done with.

On the evening of the final rehearsal, with the house already full, Verdi took it into his head to insist that the artists
put on their costumes—and when he set his heart on something, argue who dared! We were all dressed and ready finally, the orchestra was in order, the stage properties in place—
whereupon Verdi signed to me and Varese, called us into the
wings and asked us to do him the favor of going into the
rehearsal hall with him and working over that accursed duet
once more.

"*Maestro*," I said in alarm, "we're all in costume already—
how can we do that?"

"Throw a cloak over your shoulders."

Varese, indignant at the strange and unreasonable demand,
could not refrain from saying in a loud voice, "But for God's
sake, we've rehearsed it a hundred and fifty times!"

"In half an hour you won't be saying that any more—because it will be a hundred and fifty-one times!"

There was nothing for it but to yield to the tyrant's will.
I still remember the furious look Varese threw at his back
walking after Verdi into the rehearsal hall, his hand on his
sword hilt as though he intended to strike down the master
as he must later strike down King Duncan. Nevertheless he
resigned himself at last and the hundred and fifty-first rehearsal took place while the public fumed impatiently, mill-
ing about the parterre. But let it not be said simply that the
duet evoked enthusiasm—that would be gross understate-
ment; what happened was something incredible, something
absolutely new, something never experienced before. Everywhere else that I have since sung in *Macbeth* and especially

in the evening during the season, I had to repeat that duet two, three, even four times. One evening we had to do it a fifth time!

I shall never forget the evening of the first performance, the way Verdi kept circling around me uneasily before the sleepwalking scene, which is one of the last in the opera. He did not say a word, but it was very clear that although the success of the performance was already tremendous, he would not regard it as absolute until after this scene. I made the sign of the cross over myself (a custom followed on the stage even today in difficult moments) and walked out . . . .

The newspapers of the time can testify as to whether or not I rendered faithfully the dramatic and musical ideas of the great master. I know only one thing: The roar of applause had hardly subsided, I had gone to my dressing room, trembling all over and incapable of uttering a word, when the door opened—I was already half-undressed—and I saw Verdi come in. He was gesturing with his hands and moving his lips as if he wanted to deliver a speech—but he did not succeed in producing a sound. I laughed and cried and likewise spoke not a word, but looking at the master I perceived that he too had red eyes.

We pressed each other's hands firmly and warmly, and then he dashed out. This scene of genuine emotion richly compensated me for so many months of unremitting labor and incessant agitation . . . .

Blanche Roosevelt

Rigidity and Equilibrium

Blanche Roosevelt (Tucker) (1853-1898) was an American singer, writer, and journalist, known for her books on the lives of Longfellow and Doré. She traveled much in France and Italy.

Blanche Roosevelt made the acquaintance of Verdi as early as 1875, in Paris, and she never lost track of him thereafter. She was one of his most fervent and consistent admirers. Whenever she met him she was once more struck by his appearance of an ordinary middle-class Italian, "taken altogether, a man one would never turn a second time to look at." Her characterization excellently summarizes many of his peculiar traits.

VERDI looked in youth as he does now, like a very good-natured peasant, or shopkeeper, or perhaps a commercial traveler. Beyond a certain pontifical dignity of manner, acquired from the conqueror's position and long habit of the ermine of success, Verdi is anything but a striking man. He has perfectly acquired his role of human superiority, which like the part played by kings and queens prior to the invention of dynamite, was in itself a model of perfect ease and grace.

On looking at Verdi, I defy any human being to think him a man either of genius or any uncommon talent. His face is pleasant but rather stolid, his smile develops a certain cunning, faithful replica of what you have previously remarked in the eyes: that gleam you often see on the face of a peasant bargaining on market days, or perhaps Shylock when he referred to his ducats and his daughter. I can very readily imagine the *maestro* Verdi selling his wares, calling in his farmers to expostulate with them; Verdi deciding on the price of corn or cabbage; but I cannot imagine Verdi the man I have studied and repeatedly seen—the genius writing the adorable *Parigi o cara* of *La Traviata,* or the touching, even more refined, measures of *Ah, inseparabile* in *Rigoletto.*

Verdi lives in such quiet at Sant'Agata that he is rarely disturbed. In fact, the only persons whom he ever allows to interrupt him are his farmers or tenants; and any day he would stop in the midst of the divinest phrase to see if one of his men had sharpened the second scythe; if another had mowed a meadow patch, or another had planted early seed for an early harvest. Verdi's nature is absolutely inexpansive, and without effusion; even from his earliest youth his character was the very diamond of honesty and uprightness, and we have seen that when he was living near the Porta Ticinese he not only looked worried, but was quite ill several days beforehand, fearing that on the hour when his rent money fell due he should be unable to meet the quarterly payment. The same foreshadowing persistency, and taking time by the forelock habit, have followed Verdi throughout life. He is the one composer who has nothing of the bohemian in his nature, and with the single exception of one dangerous illness which disabled him from meeting his contracts, we have never heard of his not having fulfilled to the smallest iota the most difficult and pressing of his engagements; an irreproachable model of virtue, and yet what is it that jars on our nature? There is no reason why a man of genius should not be upright; but alas! there is a great deal of precedent to the contrary, and we poor creatures of education and observation have inherited the old traditions with the old idea. We believe that Verdi would have been choked in that special atmosphere mentioned by Baudelaire as genius oxygen. Such moral recititude frightens us; habit causes us to doubt the hexameters of a godly man, but rarely questions those of a bohemian.

Verdi was as strict with others as he was strict with himself, and seems all through life to have had an ancient idea of justice in his mind: to quote Scripture, "an eye for an eye, and a tooth for a tooth."

With all his stern rigidity and moral equilibrium, the master has been not alone one of the most generous of men, but one of the most loyal friends and protectors. With the same austerity he has never let his right hand know what his left has done.

One instance we can mention—his kindness to his librettist Piave, who for many years was ill, and incapacitated from working, and would have been on the verge of starvation had Verdi not come in opportunely and extended a helping hand. He not only aided Piave very early in his illness, but during fifteen years gave the poet an annual allowance from his own earnings, not only enough to keep him above want, but to enable him to live in content and comfort.

Theatrical directors in Italy and elsewhere have complained a great deal about Verdi's hardness, and even this year there was a great scene among the box holders at La Scala because Verdi and the Ricordis together insisted that if the new opera of *Otello* were to be brought out at this theater, another of Verdi's operas should also be included in the grand Carnival repertory. The screw thus having been put on for the new work, the subscribers found themselves obliged to listen for the twelfth consecutive season to *Aida*. There is no reason why Verdi should not work in his own interest, and there is every reason why the Ricordis should work in theirs; but when we look at the matter closely the whole affair seems rather exacting. Verdi simply said, "If you don't give *Aida* you shall not give *Otello*," and that settled it. Perhaps he remembered when, in that same theater, his *Nabucco* came last on the big playbill, and in that same town his talents were not considered worthy of tuition in the great Milanese Conservatory. He may be excused if, knowing his powers, he occasionally makes a show of them.

Verdi is at present the possessor of very great wealth, and beyond his niece and grand niece and nephew, there is no one to inherit the vast estate of Sant'Agata, or his other extensive properties; we have been told of a still greater charity which he has in his mind, and one which will put to shame his generosity even to poor Piave. Beyond a suitable remembrance to his niece and her children, the whole of Verdi's estate, amounting to something like two or three millions of francs, perhaps more, is to be devoted to the building of a hospital at Busseto, in which asylum all sorts and conditions of indi-

gent or suffering creatures of all nations and classes may find
a permanent refuge. This is Verdi's one ambition, and the
pride of his life is in thinking that when he is gone the money
which he has earned by his own hands and talent will be the
means of doing some good in the world, and specially benefit
the poor. You will see that Verdi will give away millions, yet
he would not yield an inch when the box holders of La Scala
proposed, instead of *Aida*, to bring out the opera of perhaps
some poor and struggling composer. These are strange anom-
alies in a man's character which I, for my part, shall never
attempt to explain, and I do not know that any one is called
upon to explain. Verdi's talent may belong to the world, but
his private affairs certainly concern no one but himself.

Verdi's name is world-famed, yet he has few friends and
fewer acquaintances. No one knows Verdi. The extraordinary
secretiveness of his nature, so to speak, the vein of suspicion,
and a strange want of demonstrativeness, are his chief characteristics. Perhaps a remembrance of his early youth and early
vicissitudes have sealed his nature with the royal seal of im-
passibility. As I have said, Verdi has not many friends: he
can count them on his fingers. He has never made himself
common. I do not suppose there is a person living who can
recall any "good times" with Verdi; no human being ever
spoke of him as "such a good fellow," or referred to any bohemian revelry, midnight suppers, or, in fact, any letting
himself go of any sort. Verdi would never give himself to
any of the pettinesses so common among all musicians. He
is worshipped in Italy for the simple reason that he is a
myth or a god; but he is not a man whom the people know.
He has received titles, distinctions, and decorations without
number. He is a senator of Italy's united kingdom; his ribbons
and stars would be enough to set up any modest duchy in
hereditary honors for centuries to come; and yet when you
see Verdi, he is the plain, unassuming man who might be your
poorest neighbor in any land. Never from word or deed could

you imagine him a famous or great person in his own country. Perhaps he is great in his way; if simplicity be greatness, then Verdi is the model of all greatness. He never speaks of himself, and is absolutely unpretentious in manner and personality.

Antonio Ghislanzoni

The Villa of Sant'Agata

Ghislanzoni (1824-1893) was an Italian operatic baritone, a novelist, a music editor, and the librettist of *Aida*.

In 1848 Verdi purchased a farming estate just outside Busseto; he retired to this estate on every possible occasion and it was destined to play an important part in his life. Here he developed an engrossing interest in practical farming, and here he spent most of his later years with his beloved wife, Giuseppina.

THE VILLA of Sant' Agata is about two miles distant from Busseto, and is almost isolated in the midst of a vast plain. The church, which bears the name of the saint, and two or three villagers' houses form the surroundings of the luxurious and elegant dwelling of the master.

Nature has shed no charm on this neighborhood. The plain is monotonous, and covered only with those natural riches which, although the joy of the husbandman, offer no inspiration to the poet. In the midst of those long rows of poplars which fringe a ditch without water, the eye remains surprised, and almost saddened by the sight of two weeping willows leaning against a gate. These two enormous trees, which, perhaps, elsewhere might not produce so deep an impression, here strike the mind as an exotic vision. The person who had these trees planted must have had nothing in com-

mon, regarding the character and habits of life, with the
population of the vast plain which you have passed through.
The inhabitant of the house which you get a glimpse of at a
short distance must be an eccentric person—an artist, a poet,
a thinker, perhaps even a misanthrope. To reach the door
you must cross a bridge, the only means of communication
which connects the residence of the artist with that of other
living people. Those who know the inmate of this house, as
they draw near to it at eventide, can fancy they hear singing
among the branches of these melancholy trees, the funeral
hymn of *Trovatore,* or the last wail of a dying Violetta.

If this is the abode of a genius, you will naturally understand that it is the genius of grief, the genius of strong and
powerful passions. A thick belt of trees conceals the house
on the side of the highroad from the sight of the inquisitive,
whilst on the opposite side the bright and pleasant garden
descends to the banks of a small artificial lake. We may be
permitted, however, to suppose that in the course of years,
when the new plantations have grown up, gloom and sadness will completely overshadow this habitation.

Beyond the garden, crossed by a long avenue in which the
eye loses itself, spread the vast possessions of the master,
scattered with the houses of the country people, with small,
well-built farms. The farming shows that perfection which is
learned in foreign countries less favored by nature. All the
advanced agricultural science of England and France has
been utilized by the keen-sighted intelligence of Verdi for
the benefit of this locality. Whilst the willows of the garden,
the thick trees, the somber arbors, and the winding and melancholy lake display the passionate nature of the artist, the
agriculture and this fruitful country seem, on the contrary,
to reflect the well-regulated mind of the man, that practical
and absolute good sense which in Verdi is found united with
an exuberant fancy and a vivacious and irritable temperament.

This practical and absolute good sense shows itself even more clearly in the architecture of the house, in the choice of furniture, in everything which has to do with the comfort and inward order of the family. There is but one word, a *musical* word, which is capable of expressing this marvelous order, this happy alliance of art with the material necessities of life—it is the word *harmony*. The most exquisite taste and the most learned forethought have presided over its construction. Here everything is beautiful, everything is elegant and simple; but what is of much more importance, everything answers the requirements of health, convenience, and comfort.

The master generally composes in his bedroom—a room situated on the ground floor, spacious, airy and light, furnished with artistic profusion. The windows and the doors, also glazed, look out on the garden. There is a magnificent pianoforte, a bookcase, and an enormous piece of furniture of eccentric shape, which divides the room into two parts, and exhibits a delightful variety of statuettes, vases, and artistic fancies. Above the piano is the portrait in oils of the aged Barezzi, protector of Verdi, who professes for his venerable friend a kind of worship . . . . From this room, in the silence of the night, rise the exciting harmonies that spring from the creative brain. Here was written *Don Carlos,* and this colossal work, which rivals the greatest compositions of the French lyric stage, was completed in the space of six months.

In one of the upper rooms I was shown the first piano which replaced the meager spinet already described . . . . It was near this piano that I heard related piquant anecdotes with regard to the first dramatic compositions of the illustrious master, which contradict many of the current accounts . . . .

The *maestro* Verdi is at present fifty-five years of age. Tall in stature, active, vigorous, endowed with an iron constitution and with great energy of character, his vitality seems inexhaustible. Twenty years ago, when I saw him for the first time, his general appearance presented alarming symptoms. While at that time the thinness of his limbs, the pallor of his face, the hollowness of his cheeks, and the rings around his eyes, gave rise to sinister forebodings, at present nothing can be remarked in his general aspect but the health and strength of a man destined for a long career.

And, his mind and character seem to have undergone equally favorable modifications. No one could be more open to impressions, more cordial, or more expansive. What a difference between my taciturn messmate of the year 1846 and my vivacious and at times astonishingly gay host of the year 1868! I have known artists who, in their youth negligently prodigal of good humor and affability, later, under the varnish of glory and honors, became somber and almost unapproachable. One would say that Verdi, on the contrary, passing from triumph to triumph, left at each step of his way a part of that hard and rough bark which encased him in the years of his youth.

The villa of Sant' Agata is still the favorite dwelling place of the *maestro* Verdi. Here his prodigious activity of body and mind can find vent more freely than elsewhere. At five o'clock in the morning he walks through the park, visits the fields and the farms, amuses himself rowing on the lake in a little boat, which he manages like a skillful waterman. Not a moment of respite. As a rest from music, Verdi has recourse to poetry; to temper the strong emotions of the latter and the former he takes refuge in the history of philosophy. There is no side of human knowledge into which his restless mind, greedy for culture, does not throw itself with transport.

Arrigo Boito

The End

In the last week of January 1901, Verdi lay dying; all Italy waited anxiously for the bulletins. Telegrams of inquiry poured in from the King, from ministers and deputies, from admirers all over Europe. Crowds stood night and day outside his hotel in Milan. Arrigo Boito (1842-1918), Verdi's last librettist and his friend, recognized the inner significance of the drama being enacted. When the curtain fell he wrote only a few lines—but how magnificent they are in their expressiveness!

Boito, composer, poet and music critic, made his debut at La Scala in 1868 with his *Mefistofele*, which attracted the attention of the musical world. Eminent critics hailed him as a genius.

He wrote the libretti for Verdi's *Otello* and *Falstaff*.

THE *maestro* is dead. He carried away with him a great quantity of light and vital warmth. We had all basked in the sun of his Olympian old age. He died magnificently like a fighter redoubtable and mute. The silence of death fell on him a week before he died. With his head bent, his eyebrows set, he seemed to measure with half-shut eyes an unknown and formidable adversary, calculating in his mind the force that he could summon in opposition. Thus he put up a heroic resistance. The breathing of his great chest sustained him for four days and three nights; on the fourth night the sound of his breathing still filled the room; but what a struggle, poor *maestro!* How magnificently he fought up to the last moment! In the course of my life I have lost persons whom I idolized, when grief was stronger than resignation. But I have never experienced such a feeling of hate for death, such loathing for its mysterious, blind, stupid, triumphant, infamous power. For such a feeling to be aroused in me I had to await the end of this old man of ninety.

JOHANNES BRAHMS

Born: Hamburg, Germany
May 7, 1833
Died: Vienna, Austria
April 3, 1897

JOHANNES BRAHMS made an auspicious entry into the musical world when he was still young, but this did not save him from the musician's customary years of struggle. He earned his living by playing in dancehalls and teaching piano at the equivalent of twenty-five cents a lesson. He was discovered by the great Hungarian violinist Eduard Reményi, who brought him into contact with Joseph Joachim (later also a famous violinist) and, finally with Liszt.

But Brahms' career really began with his visit to Robert Schumann in Duesseldorf. When Schumann heard him he cried excitedly, "Clara must hear this!" And when she entered the room: "Listen, Clara dear, you will hear music such as you have never heard before!"

This was the big beginning for Brahms. The milestones of his career were Vienna, Hamburg, Zuerich, Heidelberg—but in 1878 he returned to Vienna and stayed there until his death. In Vienna he succeeded in winning recognition, with the strong backing of Eduard Hanslick, an eminent critic. The masterpieces that made him famous were his *German Requiem,* his Hungarian Dances, the *Liebeslieder,* the First Symphony.

Brahms is regarded as the leader of the group who renewed the classical-romantic forms of the past, who carried on in the spirit of Bach, Beethoven and Schumann—and were, therefore, hotly opposed to the program music of Liszt and Wagner. As a composer of songs Brahms ranks with Schumann, Wolf, and Musorgsky, although it may be justly said that some of his most inspired songs place him on a level with Schubert.

Eduard Marxsen

A Hard Beginning

The parents of Brahms, who lived in Hamburg, were poor, very poor. His father, Johann Jakob (1806-1872), was a mediocre bass violist who managed to earn the barest subsistence. His wife Johanna ran a small haberdashery. Her health was delicate, and worse still, she was seventeen years older than her husband. At seven the boy "Hannes" was sent to Otto Cossel for piano lessons. Cossel was an imaginative and conscientious teacher. After a bit he recognized the boy's important talent and took him to his own teacher, Eduard Marxsen, regarded as the best music teacher in Hamburg. Marxsen was reluctant to teach Brahms, but in the end let himself be persuaded.

Eduard Marxsen (1806-1887) was an excellent pianist and some of his compositions contain passages of genius.

JOHANN JAKOB was an ordinary sort of musician who played several string and wind instruments, dance and entertainment music. In the early fifties he was bass violist for several years with the Stadttheater orchestra. For the rest, he was an altogether upright character of limited mental powers and of great good nature. The mother too was an honest soul, totally uneducated but, as the phrase runs, possessed of more native intelligence than her husband.

Johannes was most tenderly attached to his parents, and as soon as he possibly could he turned his youthful energies to a diligent effort at supplementing the family's insufficient means. On occasion he took his father's place in the orchestra or played with him, sometimes he even played alone at dances or parties. Later on he made arrangements for the publisher Cranz, fantasies and potpourris which appeared under the name of Marks or Wuerth. He had an older sister, Elise, and a younger brother, Fritz—who later became a much sought after music teacher in Hamburg. With the additional pocket money he earned, the tender, dreamy young boy, eager to learn, bought himself books. . . .

There is the following to tell about his course of studies:

My pupil Cossel was an excellent teacher as far as technique was concerned; in this he was highly respected and very popular. In 1843 he brought the ten-year-old boy to me. Johannes was then attending the regular elementary school, which did not change until early confirmation. I was asked to examine the boy and find out if he had any musical potentialities. He played me a few *études* from the first book of Cramer with real competence. Cossel praised his industry and expressed the wish that I might instruct him if I saw talent. At this time I refused, however; I felt that the instruction he had been receiving was good and would probably suffice for a while longer. After a few months the father came to me and repeated the request in Cossel's name and his own, whereupon I yielded to the extent of promising that I would give the boy an hour a week on condition that Cossel should continue his lessons as usual. This was done, but hardly a year had passed before Cossel was once more beseeching me to take over all the instruction; the boy was making such progress that he no longer trusted himself to give him any criticism whatsoever. He had indeed made considerable progress but without revealing uncommon talent; his achievement was rather the fruit of diligence and zeal. From now on I was his only teacher and was glad of it for two reasons—first, because I had grown fond of the boy, and second because his parents were unable to make sacrifices for his further education. His playing went ahead splendidly and new talents kept cropping up. But later, when I started him on composition, I discovered a rare acuteness that fascinated me. However insignificant his first efforts at creative work, I could not but recognize in them a spirit that convinced me here was unusual and important talent of extraordinary depth and individuality. I therefore spared no pains to waken and develop these gifts, to cultivate one who might some day serve as high priest of the art of music, preaching in a new way nobility and truth and immortality, by the very deed.

Robert Schumann

New Paths

On September 30, 1853, Johannes, young, unknown and poor, paid his first visit to Robert Schumann at Duesseldorf. Schumann was at this time tormented by the warning symptoms of his comming derangement. These took the form of attacks of deep melancholy and fits of nervous irritation.

Brahms made an immense impression on him—"absolutely like a spell." He promptly translated enthusiasm into action. He got a publisher to put out some of Brahms' early compositions, but what was perhaps more effective, he wrote an article for the *Neue Zeitschrift fuer Musik* entitled "New Paths"; this article established Brahms' reputation in Germany. Never before had a musician come out with such a panegyric on a new talent. It vividly describes the man and the pianist.

YEARS HAVE PASSED BY—almost as many as I spent in editing
these pages in past days: namely, ten—so that I might well
have turned my attention to such a fertile source of reminiscences. I have often felt impelled to do so, in spite of my
own intense productive activity; many new and remarkable
talents appeared, a new force in music seemed to be foreshadowed, as many of the artists of recent days bear witness
by their high aspirations, even though their productions are
known only to a quite restricted circle. (Note: I have in mind
Joseph Joachim, Ernst Naumann, Ludwig Norman, Wolde-
mar Bargiel, Theodor Kirchner, Julius Schäffer, Albert Dietrich, not to mention that profound writer of religious music
C. F. Wilsing, with his devotion to the highest art. Niels W.
Gade, C. F. Mangold, Robert Franz, and Stephen Heller
should also be mentioned as active heralds of this new ten-
dency.) As I followed the career of these clever talents with
the greatest interest, I thought that, after such a prelude,
there must and would suddenly appear one whose destiny
should be to express the spirit of our age in the highest and
most ideal fashion, one who should not reveal his mastery by
a gradual development, but spring, like Minerva, fully armed
from the head of Jove. And now he has come, a young creature over whose cradle the Graces and heroes have kept
watch. His name is Johannes Brahms; he comes from Hamburg, where he has worked in quiet obscurity, though trained
in the most difficult rules of his art by the enthusiastic solicitude of an admirable master (Note: Eduard Marxsen of Hamburg), and recently introduced to me by a revered and well-
known artist. Even in his outward appearance he bore all the
distinguishing signs which proclaimed him one of the elect.
Sitting down to the piano, he began to open up regions of
wonder. We were drawn more and more into charmed circles.
Add to this a technique of absolute genius, which turned the
piano into an orchestra of wailing or exultant voices. There
were sonatas—which were rather veiled symphonies—songs

whose poetry one could have understood even without knowing the words, though a deep singing melody runs all through
them—many separate piano pieces, some of a demonic nature,
though most graceful in form—then sonatas for violin and
piano—quartets for stringed instruments—and all so different
from one another that each seemed to spring from a different
source. And then it seemed as though, rushing onward like a
river, they all merge as in a waterfall, with the rainbow of
peace playing on its downward streaming waters, while but-
terflies flutter round it on the banks, accompanied by the song
of nightingales.

If he would only point his magic wand to where the might
of mass, in chorus and orchestra, offers him its power, yet more
wondrous glimpses into the mysteries of the spiritual world
await us. May the highest genius give him strength for this!
And indeed there is every prospect of it, since another genius,
that of modesty, also dwells within him. His comrades hail
him on his first journey into the world, where wounds perhaps
await him, but laurels and palms besides. We welcome him
as a stout fighter.

Every age is dominated by a secret coalition of kindred
spirits. Do you who are its members draw the circle closer,
that the truth of art may shine ever more brightly, spreading
joy and blessing on every side.

Albert Dietrich

Brought to Light

Albert Dietrich (1829-1908) was a German composer, a pupil of
Schumann; his music always showed the latter's influence. He died in
Berlin as Royal Professor.

In his youth he was a member of the group of young musicians who
gathered around Schumann at Duesseldorf, in the Rhineland. He was on

intimate terms with Brahms in the years immediately following the
latter's introduction to the public, from 1853 to 1874.

His reminiscences give us a picture of the handsome young fellow.
Brahms has given his heart to his new friends, especially to Robert and
Clara Schumann. He has so far written three piano sonatas, a scherzo,
some songs and four ballads.

IN THE AUTUMN of 1851, having then attained my twenty-
second year, I went to live at Duesseldorf in order to be near
Schumann, for whom I had the deepest veneration. He and
his wife received me with great kindness, and I soon became
a daily visitor at their house.

Warm sympathy with the aspirations of young musicians
was a leading feature in Schumann's character, and this explains the enthusiasm with which, in 1853, he welcomed
young Brahms to Duesseldorf. Joachim had recommended
him most warmly, and had also drawn Schumann's attention
to the works of the young genius.

Soon after Brahms' arrival, in September of the same year,
Schumann came up to me at a rehearsal of our choral society
with an air of mystery, and with a happy smile said,

"One has come of whom we shall all hear great things; his
name is Johannes Brahms."

And then he led him up to me. The appearance, as original
as interesting, of the youthful, almost boyish-looking musician, with his high-pitched voice and long, fair hair, made a
most attractive impression upon me. I was particularly struck
by the characteristic energy of the mouth, and the serious
depths of his blue eyes.

Brahms (then twenty years of age) was soon at home in
Duesseldorf circles, especially amongst the artists and their
families, and he was a frequent guest at the houses of Sohn,
Lessing, Gude, and Schirmer, and also of the blind Fräulein
Leser, an intimate friend of the Schumanns, at whose house
many musical gatherings took place. His modest and winning
manner soon gained all hearts.

I have a particularly lively recollection of one evening party which took place, soon after Brahms' arrival, at the house of the hospitable and music-loving family Euler.

Brahms was asked to play, and executed Bach's Toccata in F Major, and his own Scherzo in E Flat Minor, with wonderful power and mastery; bending his head down over the keys, and, as was his wont, in his excitement humming the melody aloud as he played. He modestly deprecated the torrent of praise with which his performance was greeted. Everyone marveled at his remarkable talent, and above all, we young musicians were unanimous in our enthusiastic admiration of the supremely artistic qualities of his playing, at times so powerful, or, when occasion demanded it, so exquisitely tender, but always full of character; his wonderful compositions likewise took us by storm, so that there was a general desire to hear him again.

Soon after there was an excursion to the Grafenberg. Brahms was of the party, and showed himself here in all the amiable freshness and innocence of youth; pulling turnips up from the fields, and cleaning them carefully, he playfully offered them to the ladies as refreshment. On the homeward journey Brahms and I, the only musicians of the party, found ourselves alone together. In the course of conversation he told me how, when composing, he liked to think of the words of folk songs, these seeming to suggest musical themes to his mind. Thus, in the finale of his Sonata in C Major, the words "My heart's in the Highlands" had been in his mind; whilst in the Sonata in F sharp minor, Opus 2, he had built up the theme of the second movement on the words of an old German song: *"Mir ist leide, dass der Winter beide, Wald und auch die Haide, hat bemachet kahl."* ("I am sad at heart that the winter hath made both forest and heath bare.")

These two sonatas were already masterly productions, full of power and imagination, and perfect in construction. He presented me with the manuscript of the second sonata, very neatly written and with a dedication. As a rule Brahms never spoke of the works on which he was engaged, neither did he make plans for future compositions.

We spent the evening of that day at the hospitable house of Professor Sohn, whose pleasant music room soon resounded with melodious strains. Among the party were some young Swedish artists, whose charming singing of quartets rendered them most popular in Duesseldorf society. Then Brahms followed with the songs *O versenk* ("In the sea, In the sea . . .") and *Sie ist gegangen, die Wonnen versanken* ("Ah now she is gone"), at which the enthusiasm of his audience knew no bounds. Most interesting also was his playing of Schubert's tender and poetical Fantasia in G Major. He also played variations of his Sonata in C Major on the old song *Verstohlen geht der Mond auf* ("So slily does the moon hide"), with which he made a deep impression.

The young artist was of vigorous physique, even the severest mental work hardly seeming an exertion to him. He could sleep soundly at any hour of the day, if he wished to do so. In intercourse with his fellows he was lively, often even exuberant in spirits, occasionally blunt, and full of wild freaks. With the boisterousness of youth he would run up the stairs, knock at my door with both fists, and, without awaiting a reply, burst into the room. He tried to lower his strikingly high-pitched voice by speaking hoarsely, which gave it an unpleasant sound.

Max Kalbeck

How Brahms Worked

Max Kalbeck (1850-1921) was an eminent critic and writer on musical subjects. From 1880 on he lived in Vienna as music critic for the *Allgemeine Zeitung*, later for the *Neues Wiener Tagblatt*. Among Kalbeck's literary works, aside from his newspaper criticism, are studies on the *Nibelungen-Ring* and *Parsifal* and translations into German of many opera librettos. His most important book, however, is his *Life of Johannes Brahms* in eight volumes, published in 1914.

Kalbeck was an intimate friend of the master and firmly convinced that Brahms was absolutely Beethoven's equal as a composer.

THE GRUBER HOUSE had two levels, a double floor that made it admirable territory for hide and seek. Outside, next to the broad part of the house, was a long wooden stairway leading into the little fruit and vegetable garden; from here the initiated stepped directly into the entrance of the Brahms' first floor—whereas the ignorant stranger had to pass through the front door in the parterre opening to the street. Thus Brahms could evade unwelcome visitors; from his corner window he could see the approaching guest far off and could slip away in time. His front windows looked to the farther bank of the little river Ischl, which cuts through the valley. He had a charming view of the park of the royal villa running up the mountainside. Beyond the park . . . Brahms habitually took his morning rambles. There, long before the sleepers of the spa had risen from their beds, he would be out hunting noble game, the quarry of musical ideas. . . . He liked best to wander without apparent plan or goal, cross-country. . . .

In Ischl I later had a few unlooked for opportunities of overhearing Brahms at work. Like him, I was an early riser and a nature lover. One warm July morning I went outdoors very early. As I walked I suddenly caught sight of someone coming out of the woods, running toward me across the meadows; I thought it must be a peasant. My heart misgave me; I imagined I was trespassing and immediately started worrying in anticipation of all sorts of disagreeable developments. And then I saw that the supposed peasant was none other than my friend Brahms. But what a condition he was in—how the man looked! Bareheaded, in his shirtsleeves, no vest, no collar; he was swinging his hat in one hand, dragging his coat after him through the grass with the other, dashing ahead as if he had some invisible pursuer at his heels. Even from a distance I could hear him panting and groaning. As he came nearer I saw the sweat pouring down over his hot cheeks, flowing in streams from his hair, which had fallen over his brow. His eyes were staring straight ahead into nothingness; they flashed like the eyes of a beast of prey—he gave the impression of a man possessed.

Before I could recover from my fright he had shot past me, so close that we almost brushed each other. I realized at once that it would be stupid of me to call his name; he was glowing with the fire of creation. Never shall I forget the frightening sense of elemental power that apparition left with me.

There is another experience I can never forget: the one and only hour I was privileged to listen as a secret ear witness to certain inspirations he was confiding to his unbetraying walls—in all likelihood before he had written them down at all. On this occasion too the demonic blended strangely with the artistic. I was making a morning visit in the Salzburger-strasse; I had mounted the above-mentioned outside stairway and entered the garden. I was just about to pass through the wide open back door when I noticed that the door of the music room was also open. At the same moment I heard the strains of bewitching piano music that held me rooted to the threshold. It sounded like improvisation, but then I noticed that certain passages were repeated several times, with changes, and I realized that Brahms was going through a new composition he had finished in his head, improving and polishing it before committing it to paper. He repeated the piece several times, in sections, then finally played it all the way through without interruption. This rare delight alone would have sufficed me and my enjoyment would have overtopped my interest in the progress of his work, had not the solo suddenly turned into the strangest sort of duo. The more richly the composition developed, the more passionate the *cre-*

scendo, the louder rose an odd accompaniment: a continuous growling, whining, and groaning which at the peak of the musical climax degenerated into a loud howling. Was it possible that Brahms, quite against his inclinations, had got himself a dog? It seemed to me utterly inconceivable that he should tolerate the accursed beast in the room. After about half an hour the howling ceased along with the playing; the piano stool moved and I entered the room. There was no sign of a dog. Brahms seemed a little embarrassed; he wiped his eyes with the back of his hand like a bashful child. He must have been crying violently, the bright drops were still hanging on his beard and his voice sounded weak and uncertain. I acted as if I had just that moment come to the house and noticed nothing. He was soon very cheerful again and in the mood for joking, and he played me a fugue of Bach.

A third time I surprised him working on a score. I wanted to take myself off at once, but he went on writing calmly and said, "Stay here, you're not disturbing me in the least. . . . Tell me what's new in Rittendorf (a suburb of Ischl where I was living). I'll just finish this page and we can go to the Elisabet together."

When he didn't eat at the "Gasthof Zur Post," Brahms usually took his meals at the "Kaiserin Elisabet," a first-class inn situated right where the esplanade begins. Herr Koch, the attentive proprietor, was Buergermeister of Ischl, a respected personage; he knew how to value the honor Brahms did his establishment. He would have given just about anything to have his famous dinner guest adorn the table of his elegant main dining room. But this Brahms would consent to do only on exceptional occasions when distinguished friends invited him to dinner and so disrupted his regular daily schedule. He didn't like it even then, and he seldom failed to assure his companions that it was much nicer "downstairs." Downstairs, that is in the cellar, was not only the popular drinking tavern but also the *Beisel,* where you could eat as well but cheaper and in less exacting company. Here he had a big table reserved for him in the best spot, under the window, and here he would sit with his close friends and acquaintances afternoons and evenings, chatting at ease and at leisure, drinking and smoking. After dinner he regularly sipped his black coffee at the Café Walter, read the papers, surveyed through his pince nez the passing parade of elegant promenaders, listened to the latest jokes and risqué stories, engaged in conversation with one or another young musician, and was not troubled in the least by the glaring contrast between his own plain, sometimes rather insufficient attire and the patrician toilettes of the fashionable ladies and gentlemen about him. His short black lustring coat, shimmering into gray, and his coarse woollen shirt were smilingly tolerated by beautiful eyes; his full beard, which he had not permitted to be sheared since his fiftieth birthday, decently concealed the absence of the cravat he had forgotten to put on. When the "Herr Doktor" made his appearance among the chestnut trees of the esplanade, the café waiters would rush up to him, lead him with ceremony and obeisance to his little marble table, drag every possible periodical over to his seat, bring him what he wanted without orders, and in general treat him with the civility and kindness that even the common people show a man of merit in Austria. The Herr Doktor was soon one of the most popular personalities in Ischl, and he was naive enough to enjoy his popularity.

Andrew de Ternant

Debussy Visits Old Brahms

After his release from the regimen of the "Grand Prix de Rome" scholarship, young Debussy made up his mind to make the personal acquaintance of as many eminent foreign composers as possible. His biggest game was Brahms. He succeeded in meeting him in Vienna in 1887.

Years later the English music critic Andrew de Ternant, editor of the magazine *The Musical Times*, asked Debussy to dictate him an account of this remarkable meeting between the dean of German composers, now an old man, and the newest of French composers, still an unknown student.

There are few reminiscences of the aging Brahms that show him in so charming and magnanimous a mood.

IT WAS no easy task to approach "the lion in his den." He wrote a letter to him, and received no reply. He called twice at his house. On the first occasion he was informed that the master was unwell, and on the other that he was engaged. At last the wife of one of the secretaries of the French Embassy at Vienna promised to help him in his difficulty. She was a Hungarian by birth, though married to a French diplomat, and had been in her younger days to some extent a pupil of Brahms. The German master was no French scholar, and when he received a business letter from France or Belgium he always called on the lady to assist him in making out a draft in reply. It was not long before Debussy received an invitation to luncheon from the lady, and she stated there would be only three persons present, viz., the master, Claude Debussy, and "yours sincerely."

After the introduction, Brahms growled out, "Are you the Frenchman who wrote to me and called twice at my house?" Debussy bowed graciously. "Well, I will forgive you this time," exclaimed Brahms, "but don't do it again." During the luncheon, Brahms did not utter a single word, but after drinking several glasses of French champagne at the end, he said it was "the most glorious wine in the world," and quoted the lines from Goethe's Faust:

> One cannot always do without the Foreigner,
> But give him to me in the shape of wine.
> A true-born German hates with all his heart
> A Frenchman—but their wines are excellent.

Franco-German wars were inevitable, Brahms said, but French and German art would always flourish, and would be, until the Day of Judgment, the glory and wonder of the world. He was quite aware of the fact that the French musical public considered him the most German of contemporary composers. The brilliant French nation was correct in its judgment, and he was heartily thankful. He was proud to be a German composer. A musician who abandoned his nationality in art would never leave any permanent mark on the history of the music of his own country. There was no excuse for the imitation of foreign music. That was why he so much admired French literature, art and music. Auber's music was French all over, though the scenes of his operas take place in Italy, Spain, and Portugal. The Spaniards in Molière's comedies were in reality Frenchmen, and Racine's Greeks and Romans in his tragedies were French princes and noblemen at the Court of the great monarch Louis XIV. The greatest opera produced in Europe since the Franco-German war was undoubtedly Georges Bizet's *Carmen*. He (Brahms) had attended twenty performances of the work at the Vienna State Opera House, and was by no means tired of it. Bismarck—who was certainly the best amateur judge of music he had ever met—told him that he had witnessed twenty-seven performances. A Spanish countess once said to him that *Carmen* was not much appreciated by Spaniards: "It is too French in style." "That, Madame, is where its greatness lies," replied Brahms. "The French are the most cultured of the Latin countries, and this is reflected in their masterpieces of literature, art and music. Bizet did not paint Carmen as a low-bred follower of Spanish soldiers, but as a bewitching, cultured woman of his own nationality."

A few weeks before the production of *Carmen*, Brahms was informed by his old friend, Camille Saint-Saëns, that Georges Bizet had expressed a desire to meet him. He always regretted since he heard this, that the opportunity was now lost. He

would have gone to the end of the earth to embrace the composer of Carmen. But he hoped some day to meet this gifted
son of France in a better world. Bizet, unlike some of the great
composers, had not produced a brood of imitators. This curse
of the history of music had been responsible for some lamentable results. It was the avalanche of sickly imitations of
Mendelssohn which drove that great master's compositions
out of the concert room. Rossini would have had a longer
reign with his melodious operas if a crowd of his miserable
countrymen had not drowned the Italian theaters with imitations of his tricks and mannerisms, without even a spark of his
genius. Wagner might be annihilated by an idiot with a
twelve-night music drama embracing all the legends of Germany. Brahms had also suffered in a modest way. He had
been inundated with parcels of chamber music sent for in-
spection, which were mere pale imitations of his works of that
kind, and had even been asked to express an opinion on the
manuscripts submitted. The patent-medicine manufacturer
was legally protected from imitation in all countries by inter-
national law, but the composer who devoted much thought
and study to finding a new road for himself, evidently was not
considered worthy of protection.

Before they parted, Brahms invited his lady friend and
Debussy to dine with him on the following evening at a restaurant close to the State Opera House. After that there
"would be a treat in store for his new young French friend."
Brahms said he was sorry he could not entertain at his house,
because he was living with rather "homely people, who were
a bit ill at ease in their manners, and had not the slightest idea
of French politeness." The three met again on the evening
arranged, and during the dinner Brahms was crackling with
wit and repartee. At the conclusion Brahms said the "treat in
store" was a performance of Carmen. It would be the twenty-
first performance he had attended, and practically his "coming
of age" in connection with the work. He had secured a box,

and the title role was to be taken by the best actress-singer in Vienna. During the performance the German master followed every note with the closest attention, and in the intervals delivered quite a lecture on the principal numbers, and criticisms of the singers' performances of their respective parts.

Brahms subsequently devoted an entire day to conducting Debussy to places of musical interest in Vienna. They visited the graves of Beethoven and Schubert, the Conservatory, and inspected the famous collection of musical manuscripts and autographs in the Imperial Library. Before leaving Vienna, Debussy called at the house of Brahms. He was "at home" this time, and, wishing Claude bon voyage and a successful career, the great German master embraced the young Frenchman like a son. He said a "crusty" old bachelor had quite as much fatherly feeling as a more fortunate married man.

Guido Adler

The Personality of Brahms

Guido Adler (1855-1941)) was the most prominent and celebrated music professor of the University of Vienna at the beginning of our century. He was also editor in chief of the *Denkmäler der Tonkunst in Oesterreich*.

Adler knew Brahms very well. He is able to tell us not only about Brahms' work but about his personality and character as well.

BRAHMS' CHARACTER is not simple and straightforward like the character of the Viennese classicists Haydn and Mozart; more like Beethoven's, which presents all sorts of contradictions. Benevolence is his basic trait as it is theirs. Yet, unlike these representatives of an optimistic period, Brahms is not optimistic, even when he attains spiritual liberation in the last movements of his First Symphony and other cyclic works, following the precedent of Beethoven's Ninth. He is not pessimistic in the sense in which Schopenhauer uses the word, not egocentric like Wagner, not altruistic like Schumann, Liszt, and Mahler. His personality is complex, yet perfectly consistent. Fine traits of character are blended with harshness, rudeness, even coarseness, self-applause with self-criticism, modesty with self-esteem.

Work was the keynote of his life from his first compulsory servitude in the sailors' bars of Hamburg to his last *Ernste Gesaenge*. At the same time he realized Beethoven's lifelong ambition and, aside from the few short-lived appointments he held before his forty-second year, steered clear of permanent positions, traveling in winter to perform his works, visiting musical festivals in summer for the same purpose. Teaching was a burden to him. He shrank from publicity and only once allowed himself to be misled into a "declaration," that against the new German school.

Never married, Brahms was passionately fond of children, kind to those in distress, anxious to give and reluctant to receive, economical in his expenditures, charitable toward his family and toward needy artists whose talent he valued and whose advancement he sought. He was a fervent lover of nature and a faithful friend. Surly toward strangers, his attitude changed by slow degrees, growing more and more cordial until the tie became permanent. Friction was not infrequent, though it seldom marred the course of friendship; here too tenacity and perseverance asserted themselves. Sometimes, but not often, these disturbances had their humorous side; the same is true of his music, of his *Academic Festival Overture*, for example. Given to irony and sarcasm, he avoided shallow wit. In a circle of close friends his good nature got the upper hand, as it does sometimes in his works; at other times the gloomy side of his personality overpowered him, and he saw liberation only in "life after death."

Deeply religious, well versed in the Scriptures, Brahms was a Lutheran and a member of Protestant society, standing above denominations by reason of his dislike for dogmatically restricted sects, tolerant to the point of skepticism, independent, freethinking. While there is an affinity between his motets and the Protestant organ chorale, he touches, in passing, on Gregorian motives and resorts to psalmody in parts of his *German Requiem*. His *Marienlieder* and his sacred choruses are expressive of his individuality, prefigured like his other sacred works by historic prototypes, with Johann Sebastian Bach, the supreme ruler of his artistic heaven, at their head. Bach and Mozart were his musical gods; Beethoven's "gigantic footsteps" he followed deferently and devoutly. "To follow in Beethoven's footsteps transcends one's strength," he said.

It was Brahms' good fortune to win the friendship and, at the same time, the admiration of a select group of men and women. Flattery repelled him; he asked only for sincerity and honesty in thought and word, and offered dedications in return. Robert and Clara Schumann, with their children, head the list; the former had cleared the road to fame for Brahms with the article "New Paths," placing him at the same time under a heavy obligation to fulfill his promise. To mention Joseph and Amalie Joachim, Julius Stockhausen, Hans von Buelow, Max Klinger, Eduard Hanslick, Theodor Billroth and Philipp Spitta is to name only a few of the friends who received such dedications. The number of art-loving, highly cultured women who interested themselves in his music is not inconsiderable; prominent among these admirers were Elizabeth von Herzogenberg and Henriette Feuerbach, stepmother of the painter Anselm Feuerbach.

* * *

Every artist is subject to his time, the ground from which he rises, and even the greatest master is bound in this way, no matter how independent his development may be. Talented young artists, bent on discovering new territory quickly, sometimes try to tear themselves free. But for all the individuality of his gifts, Brahms was not the impetuous type. He stood on traditional ground, clinging to those things that strengthened and stimulated him artistically.

At the outset of his career, only two of the Viennese classicists—Haydn and Mozart—had achieved general recognition. The works of Beethoven's last period had not yet begun to count, and there were few who sought to promote their cultivation. Brahms was one of these pioneers. Yet he did not regard himself as bound by Beethoven's example to combine poetry and music in cyclic instrumental works; it was Berlioz who attempted this. Brahms kept aloof from Berlioz and his programmatic theories, at some distance, too, from the operatic production of his time, however much the idea of writing an opera himself attracted him. The romantic tendencies of Schubert, Weber, Mendelssohn, Chopin, and Schumann he understood perfectly. Not that he ever became completely converted to romanticism himself; his aim seems rather to have been a synthesis of the classic and romantic, and this ideal accompanied, or, more correctly, guided him throughout his life. In company with friends he approached the Liszt circle in Weimar, only to retire quickly and firmly. Many an artifice and superartifice he took over from the virtuosity of Liszt and, more especially, of Paganini, diverting their magic to his own uses, broadening Beethoven's piano technique to meet the demands of his music and to permit the free development of his individuality without ever succumbing to virtuosity as an end in itself.

Whatever else Brahms took over he owed to the music of Bach, so successfully revived during his youth—Bach's portrait hung over his bed like a patron saint's—to his study of Handel, and to the accessible vocal works of a few older masters, including compositions of the late fifteenth and early

sixteenth centuries, the dawn of the Reformation. It was in his
day that plans were formulated for the publication of the complete works of the great masters; Brahms was deeply interested and, on occasion, actively involved in this project.

*   *   *

A synthesis of North and South German elements took
place in Brahms' case very much as it had in Beethoven's.
Beethoven, when out of sorts, sometimes spoke critically of
Vienna, but as the third of the Viennese classicists he belonged to the city and was powerless to leave it. His development, to be sure, coincided with his thirty-six years of residence there; Brahms came to the city of his choice a fully
mature master. Making an exception here, I recall an episode
from our association together, a remark Brahms made to me
with a grimace worthy of Beethoven: "Vienna is for me a summer residence in winter!" Surprised, I parried by replying:
"Presumably because it is in summer that you do most of
your writing!" After having changed his summer address repeatedly, trying Baden-Baden, Thun in Switzerland, Ruegen,
Woerthersee, and Muerzzuschlag, Brahms finally settled on
Ischl in 1880, almost a Viennese suburb, the Emperor's summer residence. Here he visited with Johann Strauss, whom he
admired and respected, and with other Viennese artists and
writers. His fondness for Strauss is reflected in his own sets of
waltzes, his love for Hungarian music in his gypsy pieces.
   It was not easy for Brahms to establish himself in musical
Vienna. In one of his letters he boasts of "the Viennese public,
which stimulates one so differently from our own," but this
was written soon after his arrival, when he was winning an
audience as a pianist. His major works were at first more
warmly received in certain cities of Northern Germany than
in Vienna, where such opposition arose as real leaders have
always to contend with. Despite invitations addressed to him
from London, Paris, St. Petersburg, Rome, Milan, Brussels,

New York, and Boston, he never appeared in concerts abroad. That he never visited England and France is doubtless due in part to his not having mastered foreign languages. On the other hand he visited Italy repeatedly for recreation with his friends. Yet the impressions he received there, pleasant as they were, left no direct mark on his work, the opinions of others to the contrary.

MODESTE PETROVICH MUSORGSKY

Born: Karevo, Russia
March 21, 1839
Died: St. Petersburg, Russia
March 28, 1881

MODESTE PETROVICH MUSORGSKY, the greatest genius of Russian music, was born on the Pskov estate of his parents, near the village of Karevo, Toropetz County. When he was ten the family moved to St. Petersburg. After two years of secondary schooling, Modeste was transferred to an army preparatory school, and in August of 1852 he entered the School of the Guards Ensigns. No one would have suspected that this snobbish, superficial, typical czarist officer would within ten years be leader of the vanguard of Russian naturalistic music—"The Five" or the "Balakirev Circle," as these elite were called. Other members of the group, besides Mili Balakirev himself, were César Cui, Alexander Borodin, André Rimsky-Korsakoff, and Vladimir Stasov.

When he began studying composition at the age of nineteen, Musorgsky displayed no particular aptitude, no special interest in the technique of instrumental music. His early songs and piano pieces bear no trace of the personality that was to assert itself in later years.

He abandoned his army career to devote himself to music, but he was soon forced to accept a government clerkship. The opera *Boris Godunoff*, his masterpiece, was

completed in 1869, but remodeled in 1872. It aroused a
storm of reaction, but the truth is that only about a dozen
of his contemporaries really recognized Musorgsky's
greatness. He lost all confidence in himself and his destiny.
The latter part of his life was spent in sordid surroundings,
and at the end he ruined himself utterly by drunkenness
and addiction to drugs.

Nikolai Kompaneisky

Musorgsky as a Young Officer

Nikolai Ivanovitch Kompaneisky (1848-1910) was a musician who
for some time studied with Musorgsky and later wrote his reminiscences.
The first of the two pieces reprinted here describes the young composer
as a cadet, the second as an officer.

. . . HERR MUSORGSKY was still surrounded by the same atmosphere of serfdom as on the country estate where his
childhood had been spent. Every ensign had his own valet-
serf, who was flogged by the authorities if he failed to humor
his young master. There was also a serf-master relationship
between the junior and senior cadets, a relationship of blind
obedience to military superiors. The senior cadets called
themselves "Messrs. Cornets," and bore themselves haughtily
in the presence of their junior comrades, whom they called
"vandals." Each cornet had a vandal as well as a valet-serf
for his service, and bullied him in various ways by the right
of might; for example, the vandal was obliged to carry his
cornet on his shoulders to the washroom. Messrs. Cornets
considered it humiliating to prepare their own lessons. This
opinion was also shared by the school director, General
Sutgof.

All the dreams of Messrs. Cornets were concentrated on the grandeur and honor of a Guards uniform. All free time after drilling was dedicated by the cadets to dancing, amours, and drink. General Sutgof vigilantly saw to it that drunken cadets shouldn't return to school on foot, and that they shouldn't drink common vodka; for the sake of the school's honor he was proud when a cadet came back from leave drunk from champagne, sprawled in an open carriage drawn by his own trotters. This was the sort of institution in which the young Musorgsky was educated; he studied German philosophy enthusiastically, read historical works and translated foreign books, for all of which General Sutgof, who took a personal interest in him, scolded him, saying: "What sort of an officer will *you* make, mon cher?"

His piano lessons continued throughout the several years of Musorgsky's stay in the Guards school. Herke introduced the young Russian *virtuoso* to German piano literature exclusively. The *virtuoso* loved to improvise, guided only by his ear and his imagination, without the slightest idea of how to put down his thoughts on paper or of the most elementary rules of music. In the School of the Guards Ensigns the young pianist was compelled to bang out dances endlessly to humor the cadets, varying his repertoire with his own improvisations.

While still in school Musorgsky sang Italian opera arias with a fresh baritone. As to Russian composers, especially Glinka and Dargomizhsky, this well-mannered youth had not the faintest notion of them. Musorgsky never suspected the existence of any sort of musical theory or science . . . .

*   *   *

In the Preobrazhensky Regiment: training, marching, equestrian drill, making formal calls, dancing, cards, drinking, purposeful amours in search of a rich countess or, if it came to the worst, a merchant's daughter with a fat wallet.

Musorgsky acquired perfectly the external qualities of a
Preobrazhensky officer: he had elegant manners, walked
cockily on tiptoe, dressed like a dandy, spoke French beautifully, danced even better, played the piano splendidly and
sang wonderfully; he even learned how to drink, abandoned
his reprehensible study of German philosophy—in short, the
future smiled upon him.

But he didn't have a chance to scatter as much money as
did his comrades. He took part in carousal, he hammered out
polkas for whole nights at a time, and his comrades valued
these merits, but they weren't enough to support the honor
of a guardsman's uniform—one had to scatter riches . . . .
These unsuitable conditions eventually forced Musorgsky to
resign. But his three years in the milieu of a Guards officer
had a destructive influence on all his subsequent life . . . .

Nikolai Andreyevich Rimsky-Korsakoff

As Seen by an Old Friend

Rimsky-Korsakoff (1844-1908) is one of the most popular Russian
composers; in addition to many songs, three symphonies and some
chamber music, he has to his credit the celebrated operas *Maid of Pskof*
and *The Golden Cockerel*. He is known also as the man who finished
Musorgsky's works, which were all left uncompleted.

He was one of the master's oldest friends. In the autumn of 1874
they even decided to share lodgings. They took two rooms next to each
other; both were young and worked day and night.

Later Rimsky-Korsakoff became a prominent professor at the Petro-
grad Conservatory and conductor of the Symphony Concerts. It was
with great sadness that he watched the decline of his friend.

During the 1866-67 season I became more intimate with
Musorgsky. I used to visit him; he lived with his married

brother Filaret, near the Kashin Bridge. He played me many excerpts from his opera *Salammbo*, which much delighted me. Then also, I think he played me his fantasy *St. John's Eve*, for piano and orchestra, conceived under the influence of the *Totentanz*. Subsequently the music of this fantasy, having undergone many metamorphoses, was used as material for *A Night on Bald Mountain*. He also played me his delightful Jewish choruses, *The Rout of Sennacherib* and *Joshua*. The music of the latter he took from *Salammbo*. The theme of this chorus had been overheard by Musorgsky sung by Jews living in the same house as he and celebrating the Feast of Tabernacles. Musorgsky also played me the songs which had failed with Balakirev and Cui. Among these were *Kalistrat* and the beautiful fantasy *Night*, on a text by Pushkin. The song *Kalistrat* foreshadowed the realistic mode that Musorgsky later made his own while the song *Night* represented that ideal side of his talent which he subsequently trampled into the mire, though he still drew on its reserve stock in emergencies . . . .

His ideal style lacked a suitable crystal-clear finish and graceful form. This was because he had no knowledge of harmony or counterpoint. At first Balakirev's circle ridiculed these needless sciences, and then declared them beyond Musorgsky. And so he went through life without them and consoled himself by regarding his ignorance as a virtue and the technique of others as routine and conservatism. But whenever he did manage to obtain a beautiful and flowing succession of notes, how happy he was! I witnessed that more than once.

During my visits, Musorgsky and I used to talk freely, unmolested by Balakirev or Cui. I went into ecstasies over much that he played; he was delighted and freely communicated his plans to me. He had many more than I.

* * *

In general, after the production of *Boris Godunoff* Musorgsky appeared in our midst less frequently and a marked
change was to be observed in him: a certain mysteriousness,
nay, even haughtiness, if you like, became apparent. His self-
conceit grew enormously, and his obscure, involved manner
of expressing himself (which had been characteristic even
before) became worse and worse. It was now often impossible
to understand those of his stories, disquisitions and sallies
which laid claim to wit. This is approximately the period in
which he fell to loitering at the Maly Yaroslavyets and other
restaurants until early morning, sitting over cognac, alone or
with companions unknown to us. When he dined with us or
with other mutual friends, Musorgsky usually refused wine
flatly, but hardly had night come when something immediately drew him to the Maly Yaroslavyets. Subsequently one of
his boon companions of the period, a certain V-ki, whom I
had known from Tervajoki, told us that in the lingo of their
set there was a certain term—"to trans-cognac oneself"; this
they put into practice. With the production of *Boris,* the
gradual decadence of its highly gifted composer had begun.
Flashes of brilliant creativeness continued to appear for a
long time, but his mental powers were growing dim, slowly
and gradually. After his retirement from service, when he
became a professional composer, Musorgsky wrote more
slowly, by fits and starts, lost the connection between one
moment and the next, and jumped from subject to subject.

❋   ❋   ❋

What was the cause of our friend's spiritual and mental
decay? To a considerable degree it was due to the success of
Boris; later on it was due to its failure. Cuts were presently
made in the opera; the splendid scene Near Kromy was omitted. Some two years later, the Lord knows why, productions
of the opera ceased altogether, although it had enjoyed uninterrupted success, and the performances of Pyetroff had

been excellent. There were rumors abroad that the opera had displeased the Imperial Family; there was gossip that its subject was disagreeable to the censors; the result was—the opera was struck from the repertory.

On the one hand V. V. Stasov's delight in Musorgsky's brilliant flashes of creative genius and his improvisations had raised Musorgsky's self-conceit; on the other, the adulation of people incomparably inferior to him and yet his boon companions, and the approval of others who admired his virtuosity without being able to distinguish between its true flashes and its felicitous talent for pranks, both pleased and irritated his vanity. Even the barkeeper at the restaurant knew *Boris* and *Khovantchina* wellnigh by heart and honored Musorgsky's genius. Yet the Russian Musical Society denied him recognition; at the opera he had actually been betrayed, though on the surface he was still treated with affability. His friends and companions, Borodin, Cui and I, still loved him as before and admired whatever was good in his compositions, but we took critical measure of much else. The press berated him continually. Under these circumstances his craving for cognac and his longing to lounge about in taverns grew more intense from day to day. "Trans-cognacing oneself" was nothing serious for his cronies; but for his morbidly nervous temperament it was sheer poison.

Ilya Yefimovich Repin

Our Poor Musoryanin!

Ilya Repin (1844-1930) is regarded by many as the greatest painter of nineteenth-century Russia. He was a good and faithful friend to Musorgsky and painted the famous portrait of the dying master.

Vladimir Stasov (1824-1906) was the only member of the Balakirev circle who was not a musician; he was its ideologist, its adviser. He became one of the most intimate friends of Musorgsky; after the composer's death he organized the campaign to collect his manuscripts and to erect a monument over his grave in Alexander Nevsky cemetery.

By 1874 Musorgsky's situation had become precarious. He held an ill-paid government post, and had practically no money. *Boris Godunoff* had been performed in Moscow, but only a handful of people recognized it as a masterpiece. By this time he was succumbing more and more to the drinking habits he had formed at school.

STASOV was in an especially happy mood all this time in Paris. Only one sorrow gnawed at his heart: he was often desolate on Musorgsky's behalf. "Ah, what is happening to our poor Musoryanin!" More than once he attempted to rescue his genius friend, who in his absence sank to the depths. It was really incredible how that well-bred Guards officer, with his beautiful and polished manners, that witty conversationalist with the ladies, that inexhaustible punster, as soon as he was left without Stasov quickly sank, sold his belongings, even his elegant clothes, and before long descended to cheap saloons, where he personified the familiar type of the "has been"; the childishly happy, chubby boy, with his red potato-shaped nose, was already unrecognizable . . . . Was it really he? The once impeccably dressed, heel-clicking society man, scented, dainty, fastidious! How many times Stasov would return from Europe and find himself hardly able to dig his friend out of some basement establishment, nearly in rags, swollen with alcohol. Musorgsky would sit with shady characters until two in the morning, sometimes till daybreak. While still abroad, Stasov bombarded all his closest acquaintances with letters, asking for word of Musorgsky, now a mysterious stranger . . . . for no one knew where he had vanished to . . . .

D. Mikhailovna Leonova

The Desperate Last Years

Mikhailovna Leonova was one of the greatest Russian singers of the second half of the nineteenth century. Her triumphal road led her to Japan, America, to London and Vienna. She took the role of the hostess of the inn in *Boris* and made a tour with Musorgsky through southern Russia. The following piece is taken from her memoirs. Hers are the only written reminiscences of those last months before Musorgsky had to enter the hospital where he died soon afterward.

I HAD KNOWN Musorgsky even before the performance of *Boris*. I remarked in the man as in the artist—aside from a few odd traits—infinitely attractive qualities which inspired respect. I wanted to know more of him. I met him at the house of mutual friends and we drew closer to each other. Musorgsky was a man who hardly had his equal in the world— a stranger to intrigue of any sort, incapable of doing anyone an injury—in a word, an ideal personality. While he was working on his *Khovantchina* he visited me more often. He acquainted me with each new scene and with the way he wanted it to be interpreted. I sang, he waxed enthusiastic, and so the work went forward. I was planning a tour through south Russia and he was to accompany me. On this trip Musorgsky collected a lot of folk-song themes, especially in Little Russia . . . .

He spent his last summer in my country house, where he completed *Khovantchina* and many other compositions. At this time we were laying plans to give singing courses. He had hopes of financial gain from such courses; things were very bad with him indeed. Unfortunately we took in very little the first year, and this much discouraged him. Nonetheless we carried on diligently in the hope that the pupils would

come gradually. We tried an altogether new method of instruction. Musorgsky wrote duets, terzets or quartets in the
form of solfeggios, to be used by students who were technical-
ly on the same level. He was astonished at the progress made
thanks to this method. Everything looked bright for the
future of our enterprise . . . but before the season was out,
death overtook him . . . .

He lived in terrible misery, and one day he came to me in
a state of frightful nervous excitement. He told me he did
not know how he could go on; all his money was gone and
there was nothing for him to do but go and beg in the streets.
I implored him to be calm and told him how happy I would
be if I might be permitted to share with him the little I
possessed. As he listened to me he regained his composure.
That same evening we went to General Sokhansky, whose
daughter—my pupil—was to sing for the first time before a
rather large audience. Her delightful singing made a strong
impression on Musorgsky and I noticed how nervous he was
while accompanying her.

There was dancing later, and while it was in progress my
pupil suddenly came to me and asked me if Musorgsky was
subject to epileptic fits. I replied that I had seen nothing of
the kind so far. And then I learned that he had just had such
an attack. A doctor in the company had gone to attend him.
By the time the gathering broke up, Musorgsky was all right
again. We took a cab together. When we got to the neighborhood of my house, he implored me to let him stay with me;
he said his nervous condition was getting worse, he felt a fit
of anxiety coming on. I knew how alone he was in his apartment, with no help near, and I took him with me. I ordered
a little room prepared for him and instructed my maid to
keep watch over him all night and call me immediately if it
was necessary. He slept through the night in a sitting position.

While I was taking tea next morning he came in looking
very cheerful. I asked him how he was; he thanked me and

said he was fine. But even while he was saying this I saw him stagger, and suddenly he fell flat on the floor. My fears had not been groundless, it seemed; had he been left alone he would have died. We rushed to his aid and I sent for the doctor. In the course of the day he had two more attacks. In the evening I called our friends, particularly Stassowo and Filippow, and we took counsel. Since it was to be expected that he would continue to require medicines and special treatment, we decided on the hospital; we considered it the best thing for him. We explained to him the necessity for this step and promised him his own room. For a long time he wouldn't agree, he wanted to stay at my house; but finally he let himself be persuaded. The next day he was taken to the hospital in a carriage.

Serge Bertensson

Last Hours

Serge Bertensson was the son of the doctor Lev Bernardovich Bertensson, who was the personal physician of Musorgsky, Piotr Tchaikovsky, and Lev Tolstoy. The doctor and his wife Olga were faithful admirers of the unhappy composer.

Olga's operatic career was cut short two years after her début by her marriage to Dr. Lev Bertensson, but this was by no means the end of her musical activity. She and her husband maintained a famous literary and theatrical salon in St. Petersburg.

My father was one of the most prominent physicians of old Russia. Favorable circumstances connected with his profession, and an inborn love of the artistic, brought him into intimate and friendly association with the greatest musicians of his time, and especially with the progressive, talented group of Balakirev, Rimsky-Korsakoff and Cui. Of this group —which was known as "The Five" or "The Mighty Côterie," and whose ideals were trumpeted in the press by Cui and the art critic Stasov—Musorgsky was the greatest favorite.

During the last years of Musorgsky's life, my father gave freely of his professional services; and it was he who cared for the composer with infinite tenderness and devotion up until the moment of his passing away. For many years he was Musorgsky's personal friend, and he admired greatly the master's compositions when he heard them prior to their publication either at the home of some mutual friend, such as Glinka's sister, L. I. Shestakova, or at our home, where the composer was always a welcome guest.

My mother, too, likes to tell a little story about her first meeting with Musorgsky. It occurred during the years before her marriage, when she was a well-known singer under her maiden name of Olga Skalkovsky. She had a very beautiful voice and upon graduating from the St. Petersburg Conservatory of Music, was engaged by the Imperial Opera House as a leading soprano. Soon after her successful debut at this famed institution in 1875, the composer presented himself at the apartment where she was living with her mother. Without hesitation he introduced himself, engaged my mother in a brief conversation on current social topics, then asked if she would sing some of the songs of Dargomijsky for him. Dargomijsky was a very fine Russian composer famous for his vocal works but unfortunately quite unknown in this country. At the time, my mother was preparing a special program of his compositions for one of the symphony concerts at which she was to appear as soloist.

Musorgsky went directly to the piano and began to play, while my mother sang the songs he so deeply loved. The warmth and sincerity of his praise for her rendition has always remained one of her treasured memories. Being still a very young singer, she was deeply thrilled by the great

master's approval and took the opportunity to ask him for
suggestions on how to improve her performance. But this was
not the only time that the two of them met. A few years later
Musorgsky and his friend, the poet Count Golenistcheff-
Koutousoff, became frequent visitors in our home, and it was
here on many occasions that she had the privilege of singing
to his masterful accompaniment in the intimacy of her own
salon.

When Musorgsky gave up his job as a minor government
clerk, his compositions were bringing in very little money,
and he was living in the poorest surroundings. It was then
that he fell seriously ill, the result of heavy drinking for
many years. His most intimate friends, Stasov, Rimsky-Kor-
sakhoff, Cui, and Borodin, turned to my father for help. They
well knew his wholehearted interest and affection for all
musicians and artists. They asked him if he would find some
way to place Musorgsky in a hospital where he would get
the best possible care. But there was no money to pay for such
attention. My father was both worried and alarmed at this
request, because he could see no means of complying with it.
At that time he was connected with two hospitals, the Christmas City Hospital for laborers, with no private rooms, and
the Nikolai Military Hospital for army officers and soldiers.
At both institutions my father was then merely one of the
staff doctors—in other words, a man of little importance and
without executive power. He could act only in the capacity
of a humble petitioner.

At the City Hospital nothing could be done, even if His
Honor the Mayor of St. Petersburg himself were to intervene.
But the Nikolai Hospital offered a little hope because, in his
earlier years, Musorgsky had been an officer of the Imperial
Guard. Encouraged by this thought, my father hastened to
the superintendent, Dr. N. A. Viltchkovsky. The first attack
on this eminent personage not only was unsuccessful but
provoked an irritated remark to the effect that Dr. Bertens-

son requested the impossible. As my father, deeply grieved, was about to leave, Viltchkovsky suddenly offered a most unusual suggestion: to admit Musorgsky to the hospital as the "orderly of Dr. Bertensson," providing of course that such an "honorary rank" be accepted by the patient and his friends. This unexpected and happy solution to a difficult problem was joyously received.

It was not possible or necessary to obtain the consent of Musorgsky, whom a high fever had rendered unconscious, so with the approval of his friends my father moved the sick man to the Nikolai Hospital. He procured for his patient one of the best private rooms, spacious and sunny and located in a quiet, isolated part of the big building. He also organized the most careful attendance for him, consisting of two Red Cross nurses, two male hospital nurses and an assistant doctor. As for himself, he showed Musorgsky the most tender consideration not only as a close friend but as a physician who understood the historic importance of his patient. As Musorgsky began to recuperate, he repeatedly told his friends—especially Stasov—that the room he was given, his surroundings, the infinite care made him feel as though he were at home among his closest and dearest ones.

The weather was beautiful, and the room in which Musorgsky lay was filled with sunshine. Here the famous artist, Repin, drew his well-known portrait of the composer, which was completed in four days, March 2, 3, 4 and 5, 1881, while the invalid had strength enough to sit in an armchair.

To the many friends who visited him at the hospital Musorgsky kept saying that he had never felt better in his life. Unfortunately, this condition did not last long. His illness took a grave and unexpected turn, and despite all the efforts of the doctors to save him, he passed away.

PETER ILICH TCHAIKOVSKY

Born: Votkinsk, Russia
May 7, 1840
Died: St. Petersburg, Russia
November 6, 1893

PETER ILICH TCHAIKOVSKY had a life of strangely mingled success and failure. He was a man subject to alternating fits of elation and depression; he was constantly passing from abject gloom through frivolity to triumphant jubilation and back again. In every mood, however, he was extraordinarily sincere, candid, and honest.

His father was a mine inspector in Kamsko-Volinsk, in the Government of Vialka, a man moderately well off, with a fine house, a staff of servants and a number of human beings whom he more or less owned. Peter studied first at St. Petersburg, in the School of Jurisprudence; he even entered the Ministry of Justice at the age of twenty and worked there for four years. At this time he was no better than a gifted amateur of music. He was twenty-seven before he completed his First Symphony. He overstrained his too-delicate nerves working on this composition; the almost pathological condition that resulted was to recur at intervals throughout his life.

Tchaikovsky won fame in Russia in a comparatively short time. In Vienna, Paris, and Berlin his works at first evoked decided opposition. At the very beginning of his

career he married, out of pity, a stupid, empty-headed
girl; after several months of misery they separated.

His fame grew and spread. He was constantly besieged
with invitations to conduct in the principal cities of
Europe. In May of 1891 he visited America; they "tore
him to pieces" in an ecstasy of admiration. The four concerts he conducted in New York were arranged in connection with the dedication of Carnegie Hall.

Fanny Duerbach

The Indefinable Charm of the Child

Peter Ilich was four-and-a-half-years old when Fanny Duerbach was
taken on as governess to his brother Nicholas and his cousin Lydia. This
French girl influenced Peter more than anyone else in his life. She
spent only four years in the house of the Tchaikovskys, but Peter continued to write letters to her throughout his career.

The rest of her life she spent at Montbeillard, near Belfort, France.
Here are some of her recollections as told to Peter's brother Modeste.
At seventy-two she still considered the four years at Tchaikovsky's the
"happiest time of my life."

I TRAVELED from Petersburg with Madame Tchaikovsky and
her son Nicholas. The journey took three weeks, during which
time we became so friendly that we were quite intimate on
our arrival. All the same, I felt very shy. Had it only depended
upon Madame Tchaikovsky and her boy, all had been well;
but there was still the prospect of meeting strangers and
facing new conditions of life. The nearer we drew to the
journey's end, the more restless and anxious I became. On our
arrival, a single moment sufficed to dispel all my fears. A
number of people came out to meet us, and in the general

greeting and embracing it was difficult to distinguish relatives from servants. All fraternized in the sincerity of their joy. The head of the family kissed me without ceremony, as though I had been his daughter. It seemed less like a first arrival than a return home. The next morning I began my work without any misgivings for the future.

❊　　❊　　❊

At lessons no child was more industrious or quicker to understand; in playtime none was so full of fun. When we read together none listened so attentively as he did, and when on holidays I gathered my pupils around me in the twilight and let them tell tales in turn, no one could improvise so well as Peter Ilich. I shall never forget these precious hours of my life. In daily intercourse we all loved him, because we felt he loved us in return. His sensibility was extreme, therefore I had to be very careful how I treated him. A trifle wounded him deeply. He was brittle as porcelain. With him there could be no question of punishment; the least criticism or reproof, which would pass lightly over other children, would upset him alarmingly.

❊　　❊　　❊

Once during the recreation hour, he was turning over the pages of his atlas. Coming to the map of Europe, he smothered Russia with kisses and spat on all the rest of the world. When I told him he ought to be ashamed of such behavior, that it was wicked to hate his fellow men who said the same "Our Father" as he, only because they were not Russians, and reminded him that he was spitting upon his own Fanny, who was a Frenchwoman, he replied at once, "There is no need to scold me; didn't you see me cover France with my hand first?"

❊　　❊　　❊

I observed that music had a great effect upon his nervous system. After his music lesson, or after having improvised for any length of time, he was invariably overwrought and excited. One evening the Tchaikovskys gave a musical party at which the children were allowed to be present. At first Peter Ilich was very happy, but before the end of the evening he grew so tired that he went to bed before the others. When I visited his room I found him wide awake, sitting up in bed with bright, feverish eyes, and crying to himself. Asked what was the matter, he replied, although there was no music going on at the time: "Oh, this music, this music! Save me from it! It is here, here," pointing to his head, "and will not give me any peace."

Herman Augustovich Laroche

The Years at the Conservatory

Tchaikovsky was no child prodigy—on the contrary. As a youth he studied law and even became a petty clerk in the Ministry of Justice. It was not until his twenties that he grew tired of all the waltzes, polkas, and *Rêveries de Salon* he had so far produced.

He discovered his mission slowly. Along with the superficial amateur vanished the society man; he abandoned his frivolous mode of life— for good.

He threw himself into the study of music at the St. Petersburg Conservatory.

Herman Augustovich Laroche (1845-1904)—as a music critic—was an ardent champion of the great composer. He had attended the Conservatory with him, later held a professorship at the Moscow Conservatory. The extracts included here are from his Memoirs.

They picture the young man as he was then and as he remained: oversensitive, overshy, weak of will and frighteningly strong of feeling.

At the Conservatory, founded by Anton Rubinstein in 1861, under the patronage of the Grand Duchess Helen, the curriculum consisted of the following subjects: Choral Singing (Lomakin and Dütsch), Solo Singing (Frau Nissen-Soloman), Pianoforte (Leschetitzky and Beggrov), Violin (Wieniawsky), Violoncello (Schuberth), and Composition (Zaremba). Of all these subjects Tchaikovsky studied only the last.

Nicholas Ivanovich Zaremba was then forty years of age. A Pole by birth, he had studied law at the University of St. Petersburg, and had been a clerk in one of the Government offices . . . . Music—especially composition—he had studied in Berlin.

Zaremba had many of the qualities of an ideal teacher. Although, if I am not mistaken, teaching was somewhat new to him, he appeared fully equipped, with a course mapped out to the smallest details, firm in his esthetic views, and inventive in illustrating his subject . . . . Zaremba was a progressive liberal as regards music, believed in Beethoven (particularly in his latest period), detested the bondage of the schools, and was more disposed to leave his pupils to themselves than to restrict and hamper them with excessive severity.

I have spoken of Zaremba as progressive. He was actually an enthusiastic admirer of Beethoven's later period; but he stopped short at Beethoven, or rather at Mendelssohn. The later development of German music, which started from Schumann, was unknown to him. He knew nothing of Berlioz and ignored Glinka. With regard to the latter he showed very plainly his alienation from Russian soil. Tchaikovsky, who was more disposed toward empiricism, and by nature antagonistic to all abstractions, did not admire Zaremba's showy eloquence, nor yet that structure of superficial logic from the shelter of which he thundered forth his violent and arbitrary views. The misunderstanding between pupil and teacher was aggravated by the fact that Zaremba most frequently cited the authority of Beethoven, while, following the example of his master, Marx, he secretly—and sometimes openly—despised Mozart. Tchaikovsky, on the contrary, had more respect than enthusiasm for Beethoven, and never aimed at following in his footsteps. His judgment was always somewhat skeptical; his need of independence remarkable. During all the years I knew him, he never once submitted blindly to any influence, nor swore by anyone in *verba magistri*. His personal feelings sometimes colored his views. Zaremba, however, had no emotional fascination for him. Neither in Tchaikovsky the composer, nor in Tchaikovsky the professor, do we find any subsequent traces of Zaremba's teaching. This is the more remarkable because the composer went to him as a beginner to be grounded in the rudiments of musical theory, so that he had every opportunity of making a very deep and lasting impression. I must, however, relate one occurrence which partially contradicts my statement that Zaremba had no influence whatever upon his pupil. When in 1862, or the following year, I expressed my admiration for the energy and industry with which Tchaikovsky was working, he replied that when he first attended Zaremba's classes he had not been so zealous, but had worked in "a very superficial way, like a true amateur," until on one occasion Zaremba had drawn him aside and impressed upon him the necessity of being more earnest and industrious, because he possessed a fine talent. Deeply touched, Peter Ilich resolved to conquer his indolence, and from that moment worked with untiring zeal and energy.

From 1861-62 Tchaikovsky studied harmony, and from 1862-63 studied strict counterpoint and the church modes under Zaremba, with whom, in September 1863, he began also to study form; while at about the same time he passed into Rubinstein's class for instrumentation.

The great personality of Anton Rubinstein, the Director of the Conservatory, inspired us students with unbounded affection, mingled with not a little awe. In reality no teacher was more considerate and kindly, but his forbidding appearance, his hot temper and roughness, added to the glamor of his European fame, impressed us profoundly.

Besides directing the Conservatory, he taught the piano, and his class was the desired goal of every young pianist in the school, for although the other professors (Gerke, Dreyschock and Leschetitzky) had excellent reputations, they were overshadowed by Rubinstein's fame and by his wonderful playing. In his class, which then consisted of three male students and a host of women, Rubinstein would often set the most comical tasks. On one occasion, for instance, he made his pupils play Czerny's *Daily Studies* in every key, keeping precisely the same fingering throughout. His pupils were very proud of the ordeals they were made to undergo, and their narrations aroused the envy of all the other classes. As a teacher of theory Anton Rubinstein was just the opposite of Zaremba. While the latter was remarkably eloquent, the former was taciturn to the last degree. Rubinstein spoke a number of languages, but none quite correctly. In Russian he often expressed himself fluently and appropriately, but his grammar was sometimes faulty, which was very noticeable in his exposition of a theoretical problem, demanding logical sequence. Yet it was remarkable that this deficiency in no way spoiled his lectures. With Zaremba everything was systematic, each word had its own place. With Rubinstein a fascinating disorder reigned. I believe that ten minutes before the lesson he did not know what he was going to talk about, and left all to the inspiration of the moment. Although the literary form of his lectures suffered in consequence, and defied all criticism, they impressed us deeply, and we attended them with great interest. Rubinstein's extraordinary practical knowledge, his breadth of view, his experience as a composer—almost incredible for a man of thirty—invested his words with an authority of which we could not fail to be

sensible. Even the paradoxes he indulged in, which sometimes irritated and sometimes amused us, bore the stamp of
genius and thought. As I have said, Rubinstein had no system whatever. If he observed in the course of a lesson that
he was not in touch with his pupils, he was not discouraged,
and always discovered some new way—as also in his pianoforte class—by which to impart some of his original ideas.
On one occasion he set Tchaikovsky the task of orchestrating
Beethoven's D minor Sonata in four different ways. Peter
Ilich elaborated one of these arrangements, introducing the
English horn and all manner of unusual accessories, for which
the master reprimanded him severely. I must add that Rubinstein was sincerely attached to Tchaikovsky, although he
never valued his genius at its true worth. It is not difficult
to understand this, because Tchaikovsky's artistic growth
was perfectly normal and equal, and quite devoid of any
startling developments. His work, which was generally of
level excellence, lacked that brilliancy which rejoices the
astonished teacher.

The silent protest Tchaikovsky raised against Zaremba's
methods affected in a lesser degree his relations with Rubinstein. The latter had grown up in the period of Schubert,
Mendelssohn, and Schumann, and recognized only their
orchestra, that is, the orchestra of Beethoven, with the addition of three trombones—natural horns and trumpets being
replaced by chromatic ones. We young folk, however, were
enthusiastic about the most modern orchestra. Tchaikovsky
was familiar with this style of orchestration from the operas
of Meyerbeer and Glinka. He also heard it at the rehearsals
of the Musical Society (to which, as students, we had free
access), where Rubinstein conducted works by Meyerbeer,
Berlioz, Liszt and Wagner. Finally, in 1862, Wagner himself
visited Petersburg, and made us acquainted in a series of
concerts, not only with the most famous excerpts from his
earlier operas, but also with portions of the *Nibelungen Ring*.

It was not so much Wagner's music as his instrumentation which impressed Tchaikovsky. It is remarkable that, with all his love for Mozart, he never once attempted, even as a *tour de force*, to write for the classical orchestra. His medium of expression was the full modern orchestra, which came after Meyerbeer. He did not easily acquire the mastery of this orchestra, but his preference for it was already established. Rubinstein understood it admirably, and explained its resources scientifically to his pupils, in the hope that having once learned its secrets, they would lay it aside forever. In this respect he experienced a bitter disappointment in Tchaikovsky.

In spring the students were generally set an important task to be completed during the summer holidays. In the summer of 1864 Tchaikovsky was expected to write a long overture on the subject of Ostrovsky's drama, *The Storm*. This work he scored for the most "heretical" orchestra: tuba, English horn, harp, tremolo for violins *divisi*, etc. When the work was finished he sent it to me by post, with the request that I take it to Rubinstein (I cannot remember why he could not attend in person). I carried out his wish, and Rubinstein told me to return in a few days to hear his opinion. Never in the course of my life have I had to listen to such a homily on my own sins as I then endured vicariously (it was Sunday morning too!). With unconscious humor, Rubinstein asked, "How dared you bring me such a specimen of your own composition?" and proceeded to pour such vials of wrath upon my head that apparently he had nothing left for the real culprit; when Peter Ilich himself appeared a few days later, the Director received him amiably, and only made a few remarks upon the overture.

Nadejda Filaretova von Meck

Beloved Friend

It is impossible to speak of Tchaikovsky without reference to his strange romance with Nadejda von Meck (1831-1894), the widow of a wealthy railway engineer.

Early in 1877 she had grown interested in Tchaikovsky's work. She gave him several commissions, for which she sent him exorbitant fees. Finally she settled an annual allowance of 6,000 rubles on him for life to ensure his financial independence. Her one condition was that they should write each other as often as possible, but never meet. They kept to this arrangement. When they accidentally did come face to face they passed each other like total strangers. Yet their thirteen-year correspondence ranks among the immortal collections of love letters.

A romantic affair of this kind accords well with the character of the composer of the nineteenth century's most romantic music. Here are a few lines from Madame von Meck's first letters to Peter.

LET ME CONFESS that I am incapable of separating the musician from the man; and in him, servant of such a great art, more than in other people, I look for those human qualities I revere. My ideal man is a musician, but only when character equals talent does he make a deep and true impression. If, on the contrary, in the musician there is no man, the better his composition musically, the more he seems to me a living lie, a hypocrite, an exploiter of simple people. I think of a Musician-Man as one of the greatest creations of nature. Even after many mistakes and disappointments, I cannot change my opinion. That is why I feel such intense interest in musicians, and why I immediately wanted to know, after my first great joy in hearing your music, what the man was like who created such a thing. I began looking for opportunities to know more about you, never permitting any means of obtaining such news to escape me. I listened to general opinion, personal opinion, to any chance remark, and I can tell you that often enough, what others criticized made me very enthusiastic. Everyone to his taste! Recently in a chance conversation I heard one of your opinions quoted that excited me very much; it was so like me that it made you very near and dear. I think that, more than contact, similarity of opinion and feeling brings people together; two persons can thus be close though very far. I am interested in everything about you; I should like at all times to know where you are and approximately what you are doing. From all I have observed or heard about you, favorable and unfavorable, a sense of fellow feeling and enthusiasm has grown in me. I am happy that in you musician and man unite so beautifully, so harmoniously, that one can give oneself to the full charm of your music; it expresses fineness and truth. You have not written for the crowd but to express your own feelings and ideas. I am happy that my ideal can now be realized, that I need not abandon it and that, on the contrary, it constantly grows more precious and dearer. If only you knew what I feel, listening to your music, and how grateful I am for those feelings!

There was a time when I wanted to meet you. Now, the more I am charmed, the more I fear meeting. I could not talk to you. If somewhere, accidentally, we should come face to face, I could not look upon you as a stranger—I should give you my hand, but only to press yours wordlessly. At present I prefer to think about you at a distance, to hear you in your music and in it to feel with you. It is too bad that I have not yet heard your *Francesca da Rimini*. Impatiently I await the time of its publication for piano.

Forgive me, Peter Ilich, for saying all this—you do not need it—but do not regret giving to one who is drawing near the end of her life, who is indeed practically dead, the opportunity to feel alive, for a moment, in such a beautiful way.

*   *   *

As to my feelings toward you, my God! Peter Ilich, how can you think for a moment that I despise you when I not only understand all that has happened, but feel it as you feel it; I myself would have done the same, only I would surely have taken the step of separation earlier, because it isn't natural to me to make such a sacrifice as you have made. I live in your life and your sufferings; everything you feel and do is comprehensible and precious to me. Dear Peter Ilich, why do you vex and offend me by torturing yourself with the material side? Am I not close to you? You know how I love you, how I wish you well. I think that not blood and physical ties, but feeling and spiritual kinship give one the right to help, and you know what happy moments you give me, how deeply grateful I am for them, how indispensable you are to me, and how I need you, exactly as you are; therefore it is not you I help, but myself. Agonizing over it, you spoil my joy in taking care of you, making me seem no more than a stranger. Why do you do it? It hurts me. If I needed something from you, you would give it. . .? So then, we are quits, and please do not interfere with my taking care of your affairs, Peter Ilich.

P. V. Tchaikovsky

My Brother-In-Law

Madame P. V. was the wife of Tchaikovsky's brother Anatol. Anatol and Modeste were twins and much younger than Peter. He loved them more than anyone else in the world.

This lady describes the composer at the height of his career; his works are already being played and admired in Europe and America. He is one of the very few composers who gained full recognition during their lifetime.

Madame Tchaikovsky describes with delicate understanding the depth of his tenderness for mankind, his sense of loneliness, his shyness, and his inferiority complex. She also speaks frankly of his homosexuality, the tragedy of his life. As a young man he had married an extremely stupid girl—out of sheer pity. It was a short-lived relationship.

PETER ILICH, who had been abroad, returned to Moscow to be present at our wedding. I saw him at the door of the church just before the ceremony began. I could not believe my eyes. I could only think of another Tchaikovsky, pale, thin, bearing every mark of extreme suffering. I now saw an elegant, white-haired gentleman who greeted me with a smile from his magnificent blue eyes. He was then forty-two years old. After the ceremony he came up to me and spoke charmingly and with much affection. There was a great crowd at our wedding and I was much amazed at his ease of manner. He spoke to everyone and talked in the most amusing way.

Later I realized that society bored him and that he hated to be in a crowd. When I asked him why he took the trouble to pretend to be a "society darling," he answered that, as he was compelled to appear in public, he had no right to pester people with his moods.

From the year 1882 to his death in 1893 I saw him constantly. He visited us regularly wherever he lived and stayed with us for three or four months. During the first three years of my married life my husband had an appointment in Moscow. Every summer we took a house with Peter Ilich in the country. In these surroundings, as he himself admitted, he became the "real Petya." He was free. He loved his brother, and he only saw his closest friends. He adored nature and for that reason we always chose a house situated in beautiful country.

His capacity for labor was astonishing. There was even something pedantic in his manner of organizing his day's work. He rose at eight o'clock. At nine o'clock, after breakfast, he read Russian and foreign papers and wrote letters.

His correspondence was enormous, for it was his principle to answer every letter, whether from Russian or other sources. He read all newly published books and reviews and played the piano. This occupied his morning. He dined at one o'clock. Afterward he took long solitary walks in the woods and fields. During these walks he thought out his compositions, making notes in a little book he always carried with him. At half-past four he came back for the tea which he so much adored. At five he retired to his rooms to set to work upon the inspiration of his afternoon walk.

His generous nature laid him open to a kind of exploitation that he particularly disliked. Young students sought him out hoping for advice and encouragement in the self-chosen career of composer or executant. With all his sensitiveness Tchaikovsky had to choose between kindly insincerity and a frank counsel to look elsewhere for a life's occupation. He had, again and again, to advise his visitors to leave music for some more suitable career. On one occasion kindliness and integrity could meet. One interview and audition led him to interrupt the solitude of his late afternoon to proclaim in our presence the great name of Rachmaninov. "For him," he said, "I predict a great future."

After supper we used to go for a stroll. He would talk with much animation about all kinds of things. He loved to speak of his childhood and early days, of people whom he liked and disliked. His admiration for his mother was almost a cult. Although he had lost her at the age of twelve he still could not speak of her without tears coming to his eyes. On the anniversary of her birthday it was his custom to go to church, where prayers were offered in her memory.

Another favorite topic was his French governess, Fanny. Fanny had never tired of impressing his mother with her conviction that he was an exceptional child who would one day achieve great things. She kept all his copybooks, childish verses and drawings. When, after an interval of thirty-five years, she read in the press that he was coming to Paris, she wrote to him from Montbélliard, where she was then living. He lost no time in going to see her and thereafter, until her death, he never failed to visit her when he was in France.

Neither in town nor in the country did he work during the evening. He played whist or went to theaters and concerts. His favorite pastime was to go mushrooming. This was how he would spend his Sundays in the country. When he found a mushroom he gave vent to his feelings like a child. He could walk for miles and miles in search of them. On one of these expeditions I got so tired that I could not make my way back to the carriage. I had to be carried. Tchaikovsky said: "What made you marry this poor creature? You see what a nuisance she is to us now."

He adored strong tea, saying that he could not play his hand at whist without it. I had heard somewhere that if a pinch of soda were added to the teapot the tea would look much stronger than Russian tea usually does. I tried this one evening. At first sight he was delighted. He took one or two mouthfuls and then asked me what the concoction was. I did my best to reassure him. The next day I was up to the same trick. At the very moment when I was slipping the soda into the teapot someone sprang out from behind a curtain, shouting, "Petya has caught Panya out," and waltzed me furiously around the kitchen.

These exuberant outbursts were nearly always followed by periods of intense depression. He then seemed completely unaware of his surroundings and became extremely absentminded. One autumn day, when it was very cold and windy, he announced his intention of going to the chemist to buy some cotton wool to put in his ears. I asked him at the same time to buy me a pound of apples. To my great astonishment he returned with an enormous load of cotton wool. It appeared that the chemist had asked him whether a pound would be enough. This sufficed to make him forget his commission. He left his umbrella and the apples at the chemist's and was too shy to go and recover them.

He suffered to an almost incredible degree from an inferiority complex. He was nearly always dissatisfied with his compositions and thought that they won more applause than they deserved. In 1892, the year before his death, I went with him and his favorite nephew, Bob Davidov, for a cure to Vichy. We stopped in Paris on our way. Paris was mad about him at that time. His portrait was displayed in all the music shops and brochures with a biographical sketch were on sale everywhere. We read in the paper that they were going to perform his Fifth Symphony. This naturally gave him pleasure, but he did not want to have any ovation. We therefore booked seats in the cheapest row, right under the roof. He bought a huge pair of dark spectacles, in order not to be recognized. The applause was deafening, and we sat delighted at the top of the house. The next day we went to the Café de Paris, where we chose a quiet corner and conversed in low tones, my brother-in-law still wearing his dark spectacles. People at adjoining tables began to stare at us, among them a very well-known French composer with whom Peter Ilich was closely acquainted. My brother-in-law stared straight at the Frenchman without greeting him. At first the Frenchman seemed to be at a loss to know how to act. In the end he came to our table, saying, "Excuse me, are you not Tchaikovsky?" "No," said my brother-in-law, "I am Davidov." "What an extraordinary resemblance." "I know. We are closely related."

The next day we went to Vichy. When the cure was over Peter Ilich left for America. In St. Petersburg we learned through the press that his success was terrific. He was torn to pieces. He was carried shoulder-high. Poetry was written about him. But when he came back he only told us that his success was not deserved. That was his swan song. Six months later he died.

We had a special method of teasing each other. He used to

say that he would like to live until I was old enough to wear a cap. I used to tell him that he tried to conceal his age—actually he was only fifty-two—by lavish expenditure on clothes. And in fact in Paris he ordered far more clothes and hats than I did myself, and he had a special liking for expensive perfume.

In one of the recent biographies there occurs the statement that Peter Ilich loved money. This is not true. Certainly he liked to have it at his command, but only that he might be able to give lavishly, right and left. Even when he was badly off he used to give to those who had still less. In his days of affluence he was downright extravagant. I judge from my own experience, for he was constantly giving me unnecessary and very expensive presents. At the restaurants it was always he who paid. He lent money to anyone who asked and never demanded it back. In his presence nobody was allowed to take out his purse.

Another legend will have it that he was so nervous as to be constantly seen crying. It is true that he was extremely nervous. Sometimes in the middle of an animated conversation his expression would change completely, a look of suffering would spread over his features and he would relapse into silence. It is possible that he cried when he was alone. He even mentioned it in his diary. But he never gave away in the presence of others, even of those nearest to him. I never saw him cry.

            ✧   ✧   ✧

Was he ever in love? Yes, on a single occasion, at the beginning of his musical career. His love was inspired by Desirée Artôt, the famous singer. She was a highly talented and intelligent Belgian, unusually well educated. She came with her mother to Moscow, to sing at the Italian Opera. Peter Ilich was first attracted by the remarkable character of her voice. They soon became acquainted and he fell in love with her.

His love was reciprocated, and it was arranged that when he returned from abroad they should marry. Unhappily this marriage was not to take place, owing to the action of Nicolas Rubinstein, Anton's brother. Nicolas was then the idol of Moscow, Director of the Conservatory and conductor of the Symphony Concerts. He was the first to see Tchaikovsky's talent and predicted for him a glorious future. At the beginning of his career he gave him the most valuable assistance, drawing attention to his compositions and arranging for their performance. He regarded him as his own child. When he learned that Tchaikovsky was engaged to Desirée Artôt he at once decided that the marriage must not take place. He feared that the young composer would have to follow in the train of an already famous wife, that he would in fact become *le mari de la reine*. His career as a composer could not but suffer. Rubinstein accordingly called upon the singer's mother and told her that Peter Ilich was not fitted for the part of husband and that he could not make her daughter happy. Desirée Artôt immediately left Russia and shortly afterward married the well-known Spanish singer Padilla. Tchaikovsky never suspected the trick that Rubinstein had played him, and his grief and astonishment were profound when he learned of the marriage from the papers.

Was there any foundation of truth in what Rubinstein told the singer's mother? Unhappily there was, and it was a source of acute moral suffering to Tchaikovsky all his life. Those who knew him well were convinced that this marriage would have cured him, and that he would have been a different and a happier man. The woman whom he did marry he never loved. He only married her out of pity, and told her so quite frankly before the marriage. She was incredibly stupid and vulgar and drove him to the verge of madness.

During the last years of his life he was so much beset by visitors, while living alternately in Moscow and St. Petersburg, that he decided to rent a small estate situated between the

two towns. He found a suitable property lying amid beautiful surroundings near the little town of Klin in the Government of Moscow. In later years his twin brothers bought the
property and fitted up a museum in the house in his memory.
This museum still exists and has now been equipped by the
Soviet Government as a place of rest for musicians.

On one occasion I visited Klin with my husband to stay
with the composer, and I was again impressed by his extraordinary kindness. People came in great numbers from Klin and
the surrounding villages with all sorts of petitions for help,
which he never refused. I heard of a poor village woman who
had been taken ill and had no one to look after her. Peter Ilich
took care of her like a nurse for several days and nights. One
day when out for a walk we came upon a village which
seemed deserted. But no sooner had we entered it than we
were surrounded by people who fastened on the composer
like flies: old people and children all clamoring for something.
"I want some money"; "I want some sheets"; "I should like a
book." A little girl opened a window and called out: "My
mother is ill, Peter Ilich. Come in and see her," which he at
once did. It ended with his turning out his pockets to show
that he had nothing more.

At the same time even among those in close contact with
him there were some who irritated him intensely. He could
not endure boastful, self-satisfied people and he could not
conceal his dislikes. He was both erudite and versatile, unlike
some musicians who could only talk of their own subject. He
liked to speak on all sorts of topics and could not bear to discuss music with dilettanti.

A number of biographies have appeared lately, containing
the most extraordinary statements. Among these may be mentioned the legend that he did not die of cholera, but that he
poisoned himself. There is no truth in this. The famous doctor,
Professor Bertensson, who attended him during his last illness
published daily bulletins. These still exist. Peter Ilich was

terrified of death and often said, "I hope that vile sorceress will not come near me for a long time."

To me it seems that he had a dim presentiment of his approaching end. It appears in the tragic music of his last symphony, which he conducted in person in the Symphonic Hall of St. Petersburg. The next morning he fell ill after drinking a glass of unboiled water at lunch with his brother and Bob Davidov. The epidemic of cholera was practically over, but there were still a few isolated cases.

I saw my brother-in-law for the last time in September 1893, three weeks before his death. My husband was then Vice-Governor of Nizhni Novgorod. In the summer we took a house not far from the town on the magnificent estate of the Prince of Georgia. Peter came to stay with us. He enjoyed the beautiful walks in the country tremendously. I went for a long walk with him in the forest on the day he left us. He was in perfect health and full of plans for the future. He went straight from us to St. Petersburg to conduct the Sixth Symphony, staying in the flat shared by Modeste and Bob Davidov. He had promised to spend Christmas with us at Nizhni Novgorod and we greatly looked forward to this visit. Instead, it was we who went to St. Petersburg to be present at his funeral in October 1893.

SIR ARTHUR SULLIVAN

Born: London, England
May 13, 1842
Died: London, England
November 22, 1900

SIR ARTHUR SULLIVAN, one of the most successful comic-opera composers who ever lived, was born of English parents and educated in London. But it was in Germany, where he studied at the famous Leipzig Conservatory, that his musical destiny was molded. "I often try to think," he once wrote in a letter, "what would have become of me had I never come to Germany."

He began as a composer of symphonies, orchestral suites, concertos for violoncello and orchestra, and the like; he was immediately recognized as an exceptionally gifted young man. He was also organist in London and conductor of the Leeds Festival.

He made his first effort at operetta in 1867; with his acquisition of W. T. Gilbert as librettist he came fully into his own. One success followed on the heels of the other; the team became rich and famous.

Thomas Frederick Dunhill, analyzing Sir Arthur's operetta scores, finds these virtues: an absence of manufactured music, a total unpretentiousness, an unaffected simplicity, a sense of humor and satire almost always combined with a sense of beauty.

Christopher Vickry Bridgman

Arthur's Chapel Royal Days

Arthur Seymour Sullivan was the son of an army bandmaster and clarinet teacher at the Royal Military School of Music. He entered the Chapel Royal at twelve. Four years later he was sent on a scholarship to the Leipzig Conservatory, the most famous music school in Europe. Here he received his education as composer and conductor.

In the Chapel Royal, St. James's, Arthur met the two brothers Cellier as schoolfellows; they later collaborated with him successfully at the Savoy Opera. He also met the author of the following reminiscences and became his close friend.

IT WAS in April 1854, that Sullivan became a junior chorister, otherwise one of the fags, in the choir of the Chapel Royal, St. James's. We numbered ten and were boarded and educated at the residence of the Master, the late Rev. Thomas Helmore, at 6 Cheyne Walk, Chelsea. Clad in our heavy scarlet and gold-lace-adorned uniforms we used to walk twice each Sunday and saint's day to St. James's Palace, the total distance covered being ten miles. From the first, at the age of eleven, Sullivan furnished proof of much ability in all educational subjects, and he had not been a chorister many months before he showed extraordinary talent, both in singing and composing. He was speedily promoted to the ranks of the four senior boys, and, subsequently, became principal soloist.

His voice was a very pure high soprano—his top A or B flat used to ring out with brilliant effect and apparently without effort. The enunciation of his words was very distinct, and, moreover, he sang from his heart. This was early recognized by no less an authority than the late Sir Michael Costa. The occasion was the christening of the late Duke of Albany (Prince Leopold), for which Costa had composed, as an anthem, a setting of the words "Suffer little children to come unto Me." At the rehearsal, after having heard Sullivan sing the solo, Costa created much amusement among band and choir by saying to him: "Vell done Soolivan, very vell done. But you must put your accent as clear as your vords. Now, listen to me," and then Sir Michael sang: "Soofer leetle cheeldren to cume after me, and forbeed them not, and forbeed them not, for of sooch is the kengdom of Haven." So well did Sullivan sing on that Royal occasion that it pleased the Queen—whom we all so greatly mourn—to send him, through the Prince Consort, a special message of congratulation.

We were close companions. My home was then at Tavistock, in Devonshire, and Sullivan's at Sandhurst, where his father was Bandmaster at the Royal Military College. During the "parson's fortnight" of the Christmas holidays I went to Sandhurst with Sullivan and he used to pass the summer vacation with me at Tavistock. He became much attached to my mother, herself a sweet singer and gifted musician. He used to pass many hours of his holiday time at the pianoforte, singing to her and playing her accompaniments. Thus it was that, at the age of thirteen, his first published song (O Israel) was composed while he was visiting my home. It was dedicated to my mother and published by Novello. It was always very difficult to get Sullivan away from his composition absorption, even to join a picnic party—not that he failed to take delight in nature and the beauties of the country, but he was so enthusiastically devoted to his dear music—in fact, he was ever engrossed in it.

As a boy he possessed much droll fun and humor. We used to chaff him on his initials, A.S.S., and call him donkey; but he was anything but an ass. On a wet half-holiday nothing would delight him more than to get us boys to stand round the pianoforte, each with a comb covered with paper. He would compose impromptu pieces—waltzes, songs without words, etc.—and taking his baton, generally a ruler, he used to con-

duct his "band," as he called us. The combs were of various
sizes and each boy had his allotted part. Even with these
primitive "instruments" some excellent, although quaint
music was produced under Sullivan's clever manipulation. It
was a great delight to him to take some popular comic song,
or common tune of the day, and turn it into a psalm or hymn
tune. Some of his best hymn tunes, if played in appropriate
time and manner, will be found to have originated in this way.
He was very clever at fugue. He would frequently say to one
of us: "Now, like a good chap, hum or whistle me something,"
and his request being complied with, he would rush off to the
pianoforte and make a good fugue from the subject given
him. He used to say that one of his greatest enemies was a
consecutive fifth. We were often amused when, we at our
respective studies and Sullivan at his composition, he would
break the silence with "Oh, drat it!—consecutive fifths again!"

Ernest G. de Glehn

Twenty-Five Years Old

The following letter was written to Henry Saxe Wyndham (1867-
1940), a well-known music and theater historian, when he set about
writing Sullivan's biography. Wyndham tried to get in touch with almost
everyone who had known his hero personally. He worked especially
hard to find material on the years after Sullivan's return to England from
the Conservatory in Leipzig.

Glehn describes just this period. Sullivan was twenty-five years old,
had written symphonies, chamber music and oratorios—and now his
first little operetta, *Cox and Box*. It was an immediate success.

THANKS for your letter. I should be very glad to meet you and
have a talk about Arthur Sullivan, but I do not think that I

can contribute anything to your work that would repay you
for a journey to London. It is true that I knew Sullivan pretty
intimately in the sixties, but I have no letters of his, neither
can I produce any correspondence of his with members of my
family, none of whom survive of those who knew him well.
My memories of those early days are unfortunately very dim,
though some few relating to Sullivan survive in clear outline.
He was for some years an intimate in my old home, known as
"The Peak" to a wide circle of friends, and he was equally an
intimate in the house of George Grove, known and beloved as
"G," and also became a constant visitor at the house of John
Scott Russell, the well-known engineer, whose three beautiful and accomplished daughters were on the closest terms of
intimacy with my sisters; indeed, with all of us, including the
beloved "G." Sullivan was in and out of these three houses
an ever-welcome guest, for he had a charm that was irresistible. I think the first time he came to our house was very soon
after his return from Leipzig; and with him came his fellow
student, Franklin Taylor. Henry Chorley, the critic, an old
friend of my mother's, was there, and Taylor was invited to
play. He announced that he would like to play us some new
works of Schumann—on which Chorley burst out that nothing
would induce him to listen to Schumann, and when the rest
of those there insisted, he went out and sat in the hall while
Taylor played. I often think of this when we early Victorians
cry out against the ultramodernists of today. It was at this
time that Sullivan's music to the *Tempest* was produced at
the Crystal Palace, and I well recollect the first performance,
but can tell you nothing about it that you will not be able to
get better from other sources.

At my own house we used to indulge a good deal in private
theatricals, greatly helped by a schoolfellow of mine, Lionel
Lewin, who became very intimate with Sullivan and wrote
words for some of his songs. He was in many ways an extraordinary personality, a born comedian, clever versifier, irre-

sponsible and irrepressible, but irresistible. Sullivan was very fond of him, put up with his eccentricities, and often helped him in difficulties—at a time when he was casting about for a libretto, he had hopes that Lewin might produce what he wanted, but nothing materialized. In these theatricals Lewin always took the lead both as author and actor, and on a few occasions Sullivan would act with us—but the memorable occasion was the first (or nearly the first) performance of *Cox and Box* at our house, in which Sullivan played Box; Fred Clay, Cox; and Norman Scott Russell, Bouncer; while Franklin Taylor officiated as orchestra. Both Sullivan and Clay had voices of great beauty, and this delightful little operetta went with a charm and go which I don't think has been equaled by any other performance since. . . . Clay and Sullivan were great friends, and it was a delight to us to get the two of them to the piano, and set to improvising *à quatre mains*—this they could do with something like reciprocal intuition, as if the four hands were worked by one brain (Mendelssohn and Moscheles used to do the same thing, so the latter's daughter told me).

In later years I saw less and less of Sullivan, but retained an affection for him which he returned in memory of those early days.

François Cellier

How Author and Composer Worked Together

François Cellier (1849-1914) was musical director of the Savoy Opera and a long-time friend of Sullivan and Gilbert. He held his post, which was a responsible and arduous one, for over thirty-five years and faithfully maintained the high standard set by the librettist and composer.

Sir William Schwenck Gilbert (1836-1911) was an English dramatist and author of the popular *Bab Ballads*. In 1871 he began his collaboration with Sir Arthur Sullivan: *Trial by Jury, The Pirates of Penzance, H.M.S. Pinafore, The Mikado, The Gondoliers, Patience*—were some of the delightful fruits of that partnership.

A special company, the Opera Comique, was formed by d'Oyly Carte to play Gilbert and Sullivan. The first work they put on was *The Sorcerer*, the second *H.M.S. Pinafore*. Their success induced d'Oyly Carte to build the Savoy Theater.

To THOSE unversed in the inner workings of the operatic stage it may sometimes be a subject of wonder how it is, when the selection of principal artists takes place, the author and composer do not find their personal views running counter. Such an undesirable situation may occasionally arise, but it is generally so when the collaborators have not learned to know each other well enough to make it easy to dovetail their respective interests and requirements, each giving and taking for the sake of the ensemble.

But as regards Gilbert and Sullivan it may honestly be affirmed that, from first to last, throughout their long association, they seldom found occasion for any serious controversy concerning the suitability of an artist for the part to be assigned.

During the process of building, like wise architects, our author and composer held continued conference over every detail of the structure in hand. From basement to roof every Sullivanesque bar and every Gilbertian bolt was jointly tested and mutually approved, and then, they being of one and the same refined artistic taste, the style of decorations was found easy to decide upon. Sullivan, perhaps, held some advantage as a judge of the requisite matériel. He knew to what extent he could rely upon finding actors and actresses who could at once be depended upon to speak the lines to the author's satisfaction, and, at the same time, be able to sing effectively and at least without actually murdering the music—in short,

be capable of satisfying librettist and composer alike. Gilbert,
on the other hand, confessed to some lurking dread of singers as actors—especially so of tenors; but then it was ever
his boast that he did not know a note of music, that he had not
the ear to distinguish *God Save the King* from *Rule Britannia*.
This, however, his Savoy associates were inclined to accept as
half-truth, seasoned with a considerable amount of Gilbertian
sarcasm. Anyway, our unmusical genius, the writer of lyrics
that compelled melody, was often heard during rehearsals
humming to himself some of the latest musical numbers. True,
he generally jumbled ballads, bravuras, and patter songs into
a strange potpourri wonderful to listen to, and in none of his
renderings was he precise to Sullivan's original key; nevertheless, it was not always impossible to identify the tune or tunes
intended, and certainly his efforts were good enough to raise
speculation as to the limit of Gilbert's aural capacity.

* * *

Author and composer alike, having taken the measure of
their respective capabilities and personal characteristics, had
succeeded in finding each performer a part which fit like a
glove.

The perfect state of preparedness in which *H.M.S. Pinafore* was launched showed Gilbert to be the master absolute
of stagecraft. From rise to fall of curtain, there was evidence
that every situation and grouping, every entrance and exit,
had been studied, directed, and drilled to the minutest point.

Gilbert was a clever draughtsman, as witness his delightful
thumbnail illustrations of *Bab Ballads* and *The Songs of a
Savoyard;* and so he always designed his own stage sets. For
the purpose of obtaining a perfectly correct model of a British
man-of-war, he, accompanied by Arthur Sullivan, paid a visit
to Portsmouth and went on board Nelson's famous old flag-
ship, the *Victory*. There, by permission of the naval authori-

ties, he made sketches of every detail of the quarter-deck to the minutest ring, bolt, thole pin, or halyard. From these sketches he was able to prepare a complete model of the *Pinafore's* deck. With the aid of this model, with varied, colored blocks to represent principals and chorus, the author, like an experienced general, worked out his plan of campaign in the retirement of his studio, and so came to the theater ready prepared to marshal his company.

Gilbert was by no means a severe martinet, but he was at all times an extremely strict man of business in all stage matters. His word was law. He never for a moment adopted the methods and language of a bullying taskmaster. Whenever any member of the company, principal or chorister, either through carelessness, inattention, or density of intellect, failed to satisfy him, he vented his displeasure with the keen shaft of satire which, whilst wounding where it fell, invariably had the effect of driving home and impressing the intended lesson. It was, in fact, a gilded pill that our physician administered to his patients, for his bitterest sarcasm was always wrapped in such rich humor as to take the nasty taste away.

As an instance of Gilbert's humorous instinct, let me recall how, during a rehearsal of *Pinafore,* when the piece was revived at the Savoy, our author was instructing the crew and the visiting sisters, cousins, and aunts as to their grouping in twos. When they had paired off, one sailor was found with two girls. Gilbert, impatient at what he thought was some irregularity, shouted out, "No—no—go back—I said *twos.*" They went back with the same result, simply because one male chorister was absent from rehearsal. When, accordingly, Gilbert discovered he had been too hasty, he promptly turned the situation into a joke. "Ah, now I see; it is evident you have just come off a long voyage"; then, turning to our stage manager, remarked that if the ship's crew remained incomplete the only thing to do was to employ a press gang.

Most remarkable was Gilbert's faculty for inventing comic

business. He would leave nothing to the initiative care of the
comedians. Not only was a gag disallowed, being looked upon
as profanation, but the slightest sign of clowning was promptly nipped in the bud, and the too daring actor was generally
made to look foolish under the lash of the author's sarcasm.

*   *   *

Whilst on the subject of rehearsals, it must not be supposed
that an opera was presented to the public precisely in the
state in which it was brought to the theater from the desks of
the author and the composer. Far from it. The main hull of
the ship, so to speak, was made ready for the launch, but there
yet remained the fitting and rigging to render it seaworthy.
Both libretto and music were subjected to scissors and spoke-
shave until every rough edge had been removed.

When the opera was placed in rehearsal, after Gilbert had
read his book to the assembled company, the teaching of the
choral music was first taken in hand. This occupied many
days, after which came the principal singers in concert with
the chorus. The trial of the solo numbers followed later in
order. Then, if any song appeared to the composer to miss
fire, Sullivan would never hesitate to rewrite it, and in some
instances an entirely new lyric was supplied by Gilbert.

The author invariably attended the music rehearsals in
order to make mental notes of the style and rhythm of the
songs and concerted numbers to assist him in the invention of
the stage business to accompany each number.

Like his colleague, Arthur Sullivan was most strict and exacting as regards the rendering of his music. There must be
nothing slipshod about it. If an individual departed from the
vocal score to the point of a demiquaver or chose his own
tempo, the chorus was at once pulled up and the defaulter
brought to book. It was sometimes ludicrous to see some
nervous chorister, whose ear was not sensitive and whose

reading ability was limited, called upon to repeat again and again, as a solo, the note or two upon which he had broken down. It was a trying ordeal, but the desired end was always attained. Thereupon the blushing chorister thanked the smiling composer for having taken such pains to perfect his singing.

Long and trying as were those rehearsals, there was seldom a sign of tedium or impatience on the part of any member of the company. They loved their work, and, whenever Sullivan came to the theater with a fresh batch of music, everyone appeared eager to hear it and hungry for more study. As with the chorus, so with the principals. There were occasions when a singer would, with full assurance of his own perfection, give forth some song hardly recognizable by the composer, whereupon Sullivan would humorously commend the singer on his capital tune and then he would add—"and now, my friend, might I trouble you to try mine?"

I remember one instance when a tenor, as tenors are wont to do, lingered unconscionably on a high note. Sullivan interrupted him with the remark, "Yes, that's a fine note—a very fine note—but please do not mistake your voice for my composition."

"How rude!" I fancy I hear some amateur remark. Yes, but Arthur Sullivan's rudeness was more winsome than many a lesser man's courtesy. His reproach was always so gentle that the most conceited, self-opinionated artist could not but accept it with good grace.

Sir Arthur Lawrence

How the Operas Were Produced

Lawrence (1842-1900), the best of Sullivan's biographers, enjoyed the advantage of close contact with his hero. Every word he wrote about the composer carries the unique authority of Sullivan's own approval.

THE DESCRIPTION of the way in which Sir Arthur Sullivan's compositions are written will form, I hope, not the least interesting part of this book. To many who picture every composer as compelled to sit at a piano, running his fingers over the keys, seeking after inspiration, it will be almost a shock to discover that, in this instance, at all events, the composer handles nothing but pen, ink, and paper.

"Of course the use of the piano," Sir Arthur remarks, when discussing the subject, "would limit me terribly, and as to the inspirational theory, although I admit that sometimes a happy phrase will occur to one quite unexpectedly rather than as the result of any definite reasoning process, musical composition, like everything else, is the outcome of hard work, and there is really nothing speculative or spasmodic about it. Moreover, the happy thoughts which seem to come to one only occur after hard work and steady persistence. It will always happen that one is better ready for work needing inventiveness at one time than another. One day work is hard and another day it is easy, but if I had waited for inspiration I am afraid I should have done nothing. The miner does not sit at the top of the shaft waiting for the coal to come bubbling up to the surface. One must go deep down and work out every vein carefully."

Sir Arthur's methods would certainly seem to be distinguishable from those of many composers in two directions—

his insistence upon rhythm before everything, and the extreme rapidity of his work.

Referring more particularly to the famous comic operas, to quote his own words:

"The first thing I have to decide upon is the rhythm, and I arrange the rhythm before I come to the question of melody. As an instance let us take

> Were I thy bride,
>   Then all the world beside
>   Were not too wide
>   To hold my wealth of love
> Were I thy bride!

> Upon thy breast
>   My loving head would rest,
>   As on her nest
>   The tender turtledove—
> Were I thy bride!

You will see that as far as the rhythm is concerned, and quite apart from the unlimited possibilities of melody, there are a good many ways of treating those words," and that I might not be unconvinced Sir Arthur sat down at his table and worked out the little exercises in rhythm, in the form of dummy bars. This essay of rhythm will be of interest to musicians, and it will be seen that that rhythm given last, as being the one ultimately selected, is best suited to the sentiment and construction of the lines.

"You see that five out of six methods were commonplace, and my first aim has always been to get as much originality as possible in the rhythm, approaching the question of melody afterward. Of course, melody may come before rhythm with other composers, but it is not so with me. If I feel that I cannot get the accent right in any other way, I mark out the meter in dots and dashes, and it is only after I have decided the rhythm that I proceed to notation.

"My first work—the jotting down of the melodies—I term 'sketches.' They are hieroglyphics which, possibly, would seem undecipherable. It is my musical shorthand. When I have finished these sketches the creative part of my work is completed. After that comes the orchestration, which is, of course, a very essential part of the whole work, and entails some severe manual labor. Apart from getting into the swing of composition, it is often an hour before my hand is steady enough to shape the notes well and with sufficient rapidity. When I have made a beginning, however, I work very rapidly."

To carry on the description of the method of work adopted for the operas, Sir Arthur continues:

"When the 'sketch' is completed, which means writing, rewriting, and alterations of every description, the work is drawn out in so-called 'skeleton score,' that is, with all the vocal parts, rests for symphonies, etc., completed, but without a note of accompaniment or instrumental work of any kind, although, naturally, I have all that in mind.

"Then the voice parts are written out by the copyist, and the rehearsals begin. On those occasions I vamp an accompaniment, or, in my absence, the accompanist of the theater does so. It is not until the music has been thoroughly learned, and the rehearsals on the stage, with the necessary action and 'business,' are well advanced, that I begin orchestration.

"As soon as the orchestration is finished, the band parts are copied, two or three rehearsals of the orchestra only are held, then the orchestra and the voices together without any stage business or action; and, finally, three or four full rehearsals of the complete work on the stage are enough to prepare the work for presentation to the public."

Sullivan deferred writing the accompaniment from week to week, from day to day, until the very last week had arrived, and the performance was announced for the following Saturday afternoon. Up to the previous Monday evening not a note for the orchestra had been written. On that night he began to score, and finished two numbers before going to bed. On the Thursday evening two more had been completed and sent to the copyist, so that on Friday evening, at eight o'clock, when he sat down to work, there were still five longish numbers to be scored, and the parts to be copied. Then began the tug of war. Two copyists were sent for, and as fast as a sheet of score was completed by the composer, the copyists in another room copied the parts. Throughout the night they kept it up, until at somewhere about seven in the morning Sullivan, on going into the other room, found them both fast asleep. He was in despair. A moment's thought, however, decided him. One thing was certain—there was no time to score. There was then but one alternative—to orchestrate the remaining numbers in parts. This he did, and at eleven in the morning all was finished, and at twelve the piece was rehearsed.

What the achievement of a feat of this kind means, the strain on the memory and the application required, only a musician can fully realize. But in this respect he is, at all events in England, unique. For rapidity of work Mr. Willeby writes, "he may have been equaled in the history of music, but I do not think that he has been surpassed."

Contrabandista was composed, scored, and rehearsed within sixteen days from the time he received the MS libretto. The Overture to *Iolanthe* was begun at nine in the morning and finished at seven the next morning. That to *The Yeoman of the Guard* was composed and scored in twelve hours, while the magnificent Epilogue to *The Golden Legend* was composed and scored within twenty-four hours.

CLAUDE DEBUSSY

> Born: St.-Germain-en-Laye, France
> August 22, 1862
> Died: Paris, France
> March 26, 1918

CLAUDE ACHILLE DEBUSSY began to study the piano at a very early age. When he was eleven he entered the Paris Conservatoire. He worked carefully, from start to finish, and won his recognition and honors slowly, step by step.

After finishing school he took a trip to Russia, then to Rome, for he had won the famous *Grand Prix de Rome*. In that city he wrote the first compositions which show his rare personal qualities—his sublime delight in beauty, his exquisite sensibility to all the vague and shifting moods of nature. By temperament and interest he was in sympathy with the impressionistic school of art; he used sounds as the painter uses and blends colors.

In 1892 he wrote his most famous work, *Prélude à l'après-midi d'un faune;* this was followed by three nocturnes for orchestra, two books of preludes, his G Minor Quartet, the songs of *Bilitis, La Mer,* and others. Then came his one supreme creation in lyric drama, *Pélleas et Mélisande.* Produced in Paris at the Opéra Comique in April 1902, it was a sensation. America soon heard of it and the first American performance was given in New York in 1907; Mary Garden was the unforgettable heroine.

With the years Debussy became established as the renewer of French music, the leader of impressionism in
music, the *musicien français par excellence*. He died of
cancer in 1918, after a painful and useless operation. Paris
was within range of German guns; he was given a hasty
funeral amid wartime confusion.

Camille Bellaigue

A Short Sketch of the Student

In October 1873, when Debussy was eleven years old, he entered the
Conservatoire, the most famous music school of France. He was already
such a remarkable pianist that he was permitted to enter one of the
two advanced piano classes. He was a poor boy, timid and awkward,
dressed like a child of the working classes.

One of his fellow students, his senior by four years, was Camille
Bellaigue (1858-1930), who early in his career became music critic
for the *Revue de Deux Mondes*.

AMONG the rank and file of Marmontel's class, there was one
pupil about whom his comrades had few illusions. Or rather,
they had many, all of them unflattering. Time was to unde-
ceive them markedly to his advantage—to his glory, indeed,
and their discomfiture. "Here you are at last, my boy," Marmontel would say, as a small, sickly-looking lad came in,
generally late. He wore a belted tunic and carried in his hand
a kind of cap. Nothing about him suggested the artist, present or future; neither his face, nor his speech, nor his playing.
His only remarkable feature was his forehead. He was one
of the youngest of the pianists, but by no means one of the
best. I remember, in particular, the nervous habit he had of
emphasizing the strong beats by a kind of panting or raucous

breathing. This exaggerated marking of the rhythm was certainly the very last thing of which he could have been accused later on, as a composer, even if it applied to him as a pianist. You will agree with me when you hear his name. He was Claude Debussy. A very reserved, rather sullen boy, he was not popular with his fellow students.

Gabriel Pierné

Debussy in His Teens

Gabriel Pierné (1863-1937) was one of the foremost French composers at the dawn of the twentieth century. As students at the Paris Conservatoire, he, Debussy and Paul Vidal formed a triumvirate of revolutionaries opposed to the other boys, who kept strictly to the academic line.

By about 1879 Debussy had already composed his first songs. His friends admired him without envy and the more difficulty he had with his teachers, the more important this admiration became for Debussy.

I KNEW Debussy in Lavignac's solfeggio class at the Conservatoire around 1873. He was a big boy of ten or twelve, short, heavy, thickset; he wore a black jacket, enlivened by a flowing cravat, and velvet breeches. At this time he was living in a fourth-floor apartment Rue Clapeyron. He was extraordinarily clumsy and awkward, at once timid and almost savage.

In Marmontel's piano class he astonished us with his bizarre mode of playing. Whether it was natural clumsiness or timidity I don't know, but he literally charged down on the piano and forced all his effects. He seemed in a frenzy of rage against the instrument; he attacked it with brusque, precipitate strokes, puffed noisily while executing difficult passages. Then at times these defects were less in evidence and he could even achieve an amazing mellowness and sweetness. With its mixture of faults and virtues, his playing was altogether singular.

He was a gourmet, not a gourmand. He adored good things but the quantity mattered little to him. I still remember well how he used to relish the cup of chocolate my mother treated him to at Prévost's on our way home from the Conservatoire. I remember how he used to choose at Bourbonneux's in the little show window reserved for luxury items: he would pick out some miniature sandwich or exotic dainty instead of contenting himself like his comrades with more solid chunks of cake. A poor child, from the most commonplace environment, he yet had aristocratic tastes in everything.

He displayed a special predilection for tiny objects, fine and delicate. My father had a collection of the *Monde Illustré,* carefully bound. When Achille came to the house (such was his first name during this period) we had a wonderful time looking through the pictures. Debussy preferred those that took up only a little space and left a vast margin all around. One day he persuaded me to cut out the illustrations with him to decorate our rooms. The crime was speedily perpetrated, and I remember that Debussy carried off some reproductions of famous paintings, particularly Meissonnier, with enormous margins. I need not describe the fury of my parents!

I lost sight of him in the higher classes. I was with Massenet, he was with Guiraud. But I was still in Rome when he arrived at the Villa Medici in 1885. The students lived together, but there was no real intimacy between him and the other boys. He remained very solitary and fled our company. He went out frequently, browsed around the antique shops and practically cleaned them out of the diminutive Japanese pieces that captivated him. He was hardly to be seen except at mealtimes.

It was not until many years later than we renewed our close friendship.

Marguerite Vasnier

The Eighteen-Year-Old

Debussy was eighteen or nineteen when he met the Vasniers, an elderly architect and his beautiful singing wife. Debussy became enamored of her and spent much of his time at the Vasnier home at Ville-d'Avray. Whether Madame Vasnier ever actually became his mistress is harder to prove than that she sang his songs and inspired them. He dedicated to her the first of his *Fêtes Galantes*.

His winning of the Prix de Rome meant his separation from the Vasniers.

The little idyl is told by Marguerite Vasnier, daughter of the family. She gives a vivid picture of the egocentric adolescent, his moods and his dynamic creative force.

AT EIGHTEEN Debussy was a big beardless boy with strongly marked features and thick black curls, which he wore flattened down on his forehead. With his hair disheveled at the end of the day (which became him much better) he was, in the words of my parents, an original type of the medieval Florentine. His was a highly interesting physiognomy; the eyes attracted your attention first, and you sensed a personality. His hands were strong, bony, his fingers square; he played the piano with sonorous emphasis, as if hammering out the notes, and then sometimes he played very sweetly, singingly.

He came of a most ordinary family and had no fortune, so he was obliged to earn his living. He was accompanist at Madame Moreau-Sainti's singing course and there he met my mother, who had a delightful voice and sang admirably.

It was for her he made his first melodies and everything he wrote before he went to Rome was for her and dedicated to her. She had the originals and he did not publish them until he had obtained her authorization. He accompanied her when she sang at musicales; once he had her sing a rondel *chinois* not yet published. I have kept two of these programs; they betray the fact that he once toyed for a moment with the idea of calling himself Ach. de Bussy. But a petty vanity like that could not last long with a spirit of such scope.

He was not happy with his family—a pretentious father of small intelligence, a mother of narrow, niggardly ideas. Little encouraged, inadequately cared for, ill understood, he asked my parents for permission to come and work at our home. From that day forth the door was open to him as to a child of the house.

I see a picture, distant and a little dimmed: He is in the little salon again, No. 5 Rue de Constantinople. There he produced most of his compositions during five years of his life. He came almost every evening, often in the afternoon as well. He would leave behind the pages he had started and as soon as he was back they took their place on a little table.

He composed at the piano, an old Blondel of bizarre construction which I still have. Or sometimes he walked about while he worked. He would improvise for a long time, then start pacing to and fro, humming the while, with his eternal cigarette butt in his mouth, or he would roll paper and tobacco between his fingers. When he had found, he wrote. He erased little but searched a long time in his head or at the piano before putting anything down. He was not easily satisfied with his own work.

In the summer my parents rented a little villa in Ville-d'-Avray. Debussy came every day in the morning and left in the evening by the last train, since the singing course was over.

He worked a great deal, but sometimes we took long

walks in the park of St. Cloud or played interminable games of croquet. He was skillful but a poor player.

In the country sometimes he was carefree and full of fun as a child again. When we went out in the woods he would not hear of a straw hat; he put on a big blue felt, which he turned up on the side. One day the eternal cigarette burned the brim a little and we hid the hole by sewing a piece of blue velvet over it. The incident delighted him.

On such outings he would make his cane into a guitar, strike the attitude of a Florentine singer and improvise little songs and serenades or parody the Italian music he disliked.

One day some street singers stopped in front of the house. He began accompanying them on the piano and singing with them, then he asked them to come in and made them play, adding his own clowneries until we all nearly died laughing. Such moments of high gaiety he had, but then came the hours of sadness and discouragement.

In the evening my mother used to sing, accompanied by him. Usually they contented themselves with his music, which they practiced together. When I left my games and came to lean my elbows on the piano and listen, he said, "This little one is going to love music, I'll make her work hard." But that enterprise was to have a lamentable issue. Sometimes on rainy days we played cards. He was always a very poor player and when he lost his mood was murderous, the more so because he often counted on the winnings to pay for the train trip that brought him to us every day. To restore his good humor we would slip a package of tobacco under his napkin just as we were sitting down to table. How happy that made him! Let me add, he was between eighteen and twenty.

He had singular, set tastes in everything. He liked blue very much; he chose everything he wore with care and was much pleased when someone asked his advice. He would read a volume of poetry and engage in long debate about the choice of a piece to set to music. These were the good times, when we called him Achille, a name he found supremely ridiculous.

He was a mistrustful nature, very touchy, extremely impressionable; a trifle could put him in good humor, but a trifle could also make him sulk or throw him into a rage. Barbarian that he was, he did not hide his displeasure when my parents received guests and thereby prevented him from coming, since he often refused to be with strangers. If by chance he did come and the favored visitors had the good fortune to please him, he knew how to make himself agreeable. He played and sang Wagner, he imitated and parodied some modern composer . . . . But let him take a dislike to someone and he knew how to show that too. In short, an original character, a bit corroded but altogether charming with people he was fond of.

He was deplorably ignorant and too intelligent not to take himself to task. During the long days of summer when he could not always be composing or walking, he read a great deal. I often saw him looking among my schoolbooks for a dictionary, which he studied conscientiously. "I love to read the dictionary," he told me, "you learn a lot of interesting things."

He had an inborn taste that enabled him to judge anything in the domain of art, even paintings and engravings, which at this period anyway, interested him little. My father, a great lover of art, would sometimes get him talking on the subject and discovered in him quite remarkable judgment, clear, definite and altogether individual.

He made preparations to compete for the *Prix de Rome*, which did not tempt him in the least. Had it not been for my father, it is possible that he would never have entered the competition at all, but in any case I am quite sure that he would later have withdrawn and his fear of my father's disapproval was the only thing that deterred him. For the rest, although the influence of my parents at this time is undeniable, it probably did not importantly affect his future. Spirits like his always attain their goal, no matter what their initial gropings and hesitations.

So then, he competed for the *Grand Prix* twice. The first time was with *Le Gladiateur;* he received only second prize, and certainly the joy of staying in Paris must have more than compensated him for his disappointment, if he felt any. The mere prospect of being closed in for weeks on end filled him with horror. While he was *en loge* we often went of an evening to pay him a visit at the Conservatoire. The *logistes* received their parents and friends in a garden court, where we stayed as long as we possibly could to comfort him. He showed us where the window of his room was, and when I asked him why there were bars, he said, "Doubtless because we're regarded as wild beasts."

Finally, the second time, he got his prize—but then some months passed and he had to leave. What despair, what heartrending letters of desolation! He had a wretched struggle serving out his time (which did not pass without a little festive interlude in Paris); but when he came back for good the old intimacy was over. He had developed, so had we. We had moved, made new acquaintances. Untamed, suspicious, this creature of habit never felt at home with us again.

Nevertheless he still came often in the evening to play us what he had written when he was far away. On setting out for Rome he had left with us the bulk of his manuscripts; later on he took back a good many that he needed. But he still came to ask advice and counsel, even material aid. He was no longer living with his parents and was not yet well known, but he had to eat. It was at this time, wishing to please my parents, that he got started on his vague project of giving me piano and harmony lessons. What a wretched teacher! Not a shadow of patience, and he was incapable of adapting his explanations to the very young intelligence before him;

it was necessary to understand him before he had finished speaking. We had to give it up. He too made new acquaintances, and little by little he stopped coming, and we never saw him again. Shortly before the war I thought to write him under the pretext that I wanted to see *Pelléas et Mélisande*. Through negligence I failed to do so. This I deeply regretted when I later learned of his death. I sincerely believe he would have found pleasure in seeing again a witness of those good years that he could not have forgotten, if only because they were the years of youth, of health and of hope. Now all three have vanished and no one will ever again hear my mother sing the melodies of Debussy while he plays for her.

J. G. Prodhomme

An Intolerant Critic

Debussy liked to write music criticisms. They were published in *Revue Blanche, Gil Blas, Renaissance Latine,* where his mocking tone and paradoxical opinions served to confirm his reputation as a disagreeable artist. His criticism is always interesting, hyper-individualistic, passionate, and formless, and he does not hesitate to find fault with great masters like Beethoven and Berlioz.

The words here published were spoken to J. G. Prodhomme, a distinguished French musicologist and translator of Richard Wagner.

"I LOVE MUSIC too much," he proclaimed once, "to speak of it otherwise than passionately." So we must not be surprised at the bold, disrespectful judgments which he passed equally on the gods of music—universally (and conventionally) adored—and on the consecrated reputations of his own time. We heard him just now making some concession to the "worthy man" Sebastian Bach, for whom he was, I really think, full of a certain respect. But Gluck was for him only a "pedant," not less than Wagner; he called the Tetralogie *bottin* and found Wagner's masterpieces "manufactured." Of songs of Schubert he cries, "They are inoffensive; they have the odor of bureau drawers of provincial old maids— ends of faded ribbon—flowers forever faded and withered— out-of-date photographs! Only they repeat the same effect for interminable stanzas and at the end of the third one wonders if one could not set to music our national Paul Del- met." In Schumann's *Faust,* "one stumbles on Mendelssohn," Beethoven is "a deaf old man," Berlioz a "monster," César Franck "a Belgian" . . . . Of the new Italian school and the performance of *I Pagliacci* at the Opera in 1903, Debussy wrote: "There are jokes on which it is bad taste to insist"; elsewhere one finds in Puccini and Leoncavallo "an almost complete imitation of the manias of our most notorious mas- ter"—that is, Massenet, for whom Debussy has nowhere else a cruel word.

These attacks in the style of a Paris street urchin, which express aloud what many others, artists or critics are silent- ly thinking, have contributed, at least as much as his music, to Debussy's fame as an iconoclast. But on the other hand— in what terms were his own productions described! While he found critics, enthusiastic biographers, for whom music be- gan with him, Debussy always had against him—I mean against his art, for I do not think a man as happy as he was had many enemies besides his *confrères*—he always had against him a large group, a majority spirit of unconquerable hostility.

Pasteur Vallery-Radot

Le Maître Toujours Insatisfait

Pasteur Vallery-Radot (born 1886) was one of the great physicians of France. He was professor at the Faculté de Médicine de Paris, Chevalier de la Légion d'Honneur, an eminent scientist—and in addition an ardent advocate of modern music.

No one has given such an excellent description of Debussy at the height of his career. The battle for *Pelléas et Mélisande* is won and Debussy is planning to write operas based on Poe's short stories. With the outbreak of World War I his creative career comes to a sudden end. His illness (cancer) turns out to be fatal.

IT WAS around this time that I became intimate with Claude Debussy. On April 30, 1910 I had ventured to send him a line and a few flowers in memory of the première of *Pelléas*. He answered the next day:

"No one but you, dear sir, remembered the 30th of April, 1902! . . . Please believe that I was deeply touched at your delicate perfuming of the memory, and please believe also in my warm and genuine response.

CLAUDE DEBUSSY"

At the end of October of that year he wrote me asking me to come and see him. On Wednesday, November 2nd I stood in agitation before No. 80 Avenue de Bois de Boulogne. At the end of a long blind alley lined with tree-enveloped villas was the house where he lived. An iron gate. You walked up some steps and found yourself in a rather dark vestibule. Then came a room full of light; the trees of a little garden seemed to lean right into the room. The atmosphere was restful, everything on a sombre note; rather uniform, despite the disparity between the furnishings. At the other end of the room was a big worktable, at the right a very small piano of black wood, a Buddha, some Japanese drawings on the wall, roses. Here in his study he received me that first day and here he was to receive me later, all during our friendship, which ended with the last day of his life.

Seeing him for the first time you were astonished at the immense, protuberant forehead. His hair was black, a little curly, his beard fine, his cheeks rather heavy. His dark eyes were full of sweetness and malice. His gestures were all curves. He spoke in a soft voice, without the slightest affectation, slowly, searching for the *mot juste* to convey the image. Sometimes he would stop in the middle of a phrase as a horse hesitates before an obstacle: he could not find the term that was the proper clothing for his thought. He expressed himself graphically as one who sees and is always able to pick out the salient feature. His phraseology was often purposely imprecise so as to give the vagueness of an idea or an impression, and then a word exploded suddenly, vibrant. You were always under the spell of his sensibility, and at the same time you were afraid he would be irritated by an unexpected noise, a too harsh light, a misplaced word.

He had a delightful taste, a delightful sense of proportion in all things. He loved luxury but refined luxury, without gaudiness or glitter. Rare and precious objects were his passion. This love for everything beautiful made him prodigal to excess; but you forgave him, he had such charming spontaneities.

His wife enveloped him in tenderness, understanding that he had in him the caprices of a child and that it was necessary to clear from his path all the stumbling blocks of life. One of his most genuine delights was to listen to his adorable daughter Chouchou reciting, singing, playing or dancing to one of the rhythmic pieces he had invented for her.

His fastidious, cultivated mind, his perennially agitated sensitivity, led him to seek in everything the measure and proportion so dear to the French spirit. He loved order, clarity. In literature and in art he had a predilection for everything subtle, delicate, consummate. His literary preference ran to Mallarmé, Verlaine, Jules Laforgue, P. J. Toulet; his musical favorites were Bach and Rameau.

His concern with measure and moderation made him detest publicity and intrigue. He had a horror of anything that smacked of condescension. Nor did he seek either honors or official functions. He cherished above all his independence: "I love my liberty too much and what is mine!" he wrote when he was only twenty-three years old.

He was indifferent to success, and the approbation of the public moved him little. He reacted to the diatribes of his enemies with shoulder-shrugging; the immoderate enthusiasms of his admirers rather annoyed him, for he hated excess of any kind. "I make music," he wrote, "to serve the art as best I possibly can; I have no other concern."

Like nearly all artists who have been influenced by symbolism, he despised the mob, "to which," he said, "art is absolutely useless."

You might have thought him arrogant; he was not. "Personally," he wrote to his publisher, M. Jaques Durand, in January 1912, "I am in a fever to find everything I lack, I am in an agony to finish no matter what, at any price! It is a curious malady that Leonardo da Vinci suffered from. Only he had genius at the same time. That makes up for a lot of things. I am satisfied to have untiring patience—it has been said that patience will sometimes take the place of genius." Some months later he wrote again to M. Jacques Durand: "The title of 'great innovator' goes a bit beyond what I deserve, but I do not thank you any the less for giving me this encouragement for the future!" He regarded himself simply as one carrying on the French musical tradition of the eighteenth century, too long forgotten.

✧   ✧   ✧

His longing for perfection sometimes forced him to labor for weeks, for months on one page—which he then destroyed. "After my death," he often remarked to me, "they won't find a note of mine left. I destroy everything that doesn't satisfy me." It took him ten years to write the score of *Pelléas et Mélisande*. I have in front of me four pages written by Debussy to his friend Ernest Chausson on October 2, 1893. The handwriting is small and labored; every letter, traced like a design, expresses his delicate sensitivity.

"I was too much in a hurry," he says, "to shout in triumph for *Pelléas et Mélisande*. After one white night, which gave me counsel, I had to confess to myself that it was nothing of what I had believed, nothing at all!. . .So I tore the whole thing up and set off again in search of a little chemical solution of more personal phrases. I strove to be *Pelléas* as well as *Mélisande*. I went looking for music behind all the many veils she wraps round herself even against her most ardent devotees. I brought away something you may like; as for the others, I don't care. I made use—quite spontaneously too—of a device that seems to me rather rare, that is, silence (don't laugh!) as an agent of expression—perhaps the only way to convey the full emotion of a phrase. If Wagner used it I think he did so only for purely dramatic purposes, rather in imitation of other dubious dramas like Bouchard, d'Ennery, and so on."

"Oh, if only the times were not so miserable, if you could ask people to interest themselves in something else than a new kind of bicycle! I don't know why I say that though, I have no intention whatever of reigning over the spirits of my contemporaries—but still and all it would be nice to found a school of neo-musicians where you could endeavor to keep intact the noble symbols of music—in a word, where you could restore respect for an art sullied by so many. The crowd might learn to temper its enthusiasms a bit and to distinguish between a Franck and a Massenet. . . .For the rest, we owe this state of affairs to the slogan inscribed on our monuments: *"Liberté, Egalité, Fraternité!"* Good words for coachmen maybe—that's all!"

❀   ❊   ❀

The many works he planned and never executed—because he was always dissatisfied! The many times he spoke to me of Tristan! He dreamed of writing a libretto based on Bedier's novel and composing the score. "Something altogether different from *Tristan and Isolde,*" he told me, "something in the French spirit."

With what a fluent facility he could have written if he had just let himself go with the stream of his fancy! But instead he labored, painfully, to express what he had perceived in the dark depths of his consciousness. When I entered his study I often found him nervous, staring at a white page before him. At such times I knew that any word spoken would irritate him; I did not address a syllable to him. Then later he would turn around and say to me, with a friendly smile, "I like you very much, you don't 'disturb' my atmosphere." Other times, when he had found the "formula" he was looking for, he received me joyfully. "This time I think I've got it!" And he would sit down at the piano and ask my opinion. "I like to gauge the impression," he told me, "on an ignoramus of music like you who *feels* what I'm doing without in the least being able to analyze the technique. That's always the important thing—never learn your notes!"

RICHARD STRAUSS

Born: Munich, Germany
June 11, 1864
Died: Garmisch-Partenkirchen, Germany
September 8, 1949

RICHARD STRAUSS was, throughout his lifetime, the representative musician of our time; his fame was matched only by Stravinsky's. His was a rich, genuine talent, imaginative, humorous, life-affirming. He composed with the fluent ease of the old masters; if he had any inhibitions, they were few. His development moves from the purely classic—with a strong rejection of Wagner—to Liszt and Berlioz and on to a passionate "Neuwagnertum" ("Neo-Wagnerism"). With that it stopped. He went on producing work after work, but with no new element or insight; his astounding skill was now applied almost mechanically.

Several of his first works were performed when he was still a pupil in the Gymnasium. In 1884, a year after he finished his university course, his F minor Symphony was performed in New York. Thereafter his works reached the American public as quickly as the European.

The years just before World War I were his most fertile and his most famous: *Elektra* (1908), *Der Rosenkavalier* (1910), *Ariadne auf Naxos* (1912), *Deutsche Motette* (1913), *Alpensinfonie* (1915).

Franz Trenner

Richard's Start in Life

Franz Trenner (born 1915) is a schoolteacher in Munich, Germany. He studied musicology at the University of Munich and obtained his doctor's degree with a thesis on the collaboration between Hugo von Hofmannsthal and Richard Strauss.

To find out details of the early years of the master's career, he looked around for people who had personally known Strauss' father. He found two old musicians, and received much valuable information from them.

Richard Strauss was the son of Franz Strauss, first hornist at the Munich Court Opera, who had married into the wealthy Pschorr family of brewers. At five, before Richard had even entered elementary school, the boy began to show great aptitude for music; at six he composd a funny *Schneiderpolka* for piano.

Franz Strauss made his young son a member of the Dilettantenorchester Wilde Gungl, which he conducted. The milieu is genuine Bavarian.

THE BIRTH YEAR of Richard Strauss, 1864, is also the year in which the Munich amateur orchestra "Wilde Gungl" was organized. As the name indicates, this was to be nothing like the Kapelle of the professional musician and composer Gungl but simply a group of music lovers come together to make music for their own amusement. The year 1875 turned out to be a decisive one for the repute and standing of the orchestra society; chamber musician Franz Strauss, father of Richard Strauss, became conductor. This famous hornist of the Hoforchester—only a year later he was made honorary member of the society—significantly raised the level of the programs. The "musical entertainments," as the Wilde Gungl concerts were called, henceforth fell into three parts: first came overtures and slighter pieces of noted composers, in the middle a symphony, and at the end lighter music. Father Strauss also stepped forward here as composer of gavottes, quadrilles and the like, and as arranger.

On the occasion of one such musical entertainment on May 29, 1880, Franz Strauss offered a rich program with something special added, a surprise. The *Sueddeutsche Presse* and *Muenchner Nachrichten* report: "The program included a gavotte by Richard Strauss marked with a sign indicating a first performance and it was favorably received. After repeated calls the composer was led in by the President of the Society; it was the fourteen-year-old son of Conductor Strauss. He will certainly bring honor to the name, that is assured by his indisputable talent and his great love for music. . . ." This gavotte seems to have been the first work of Richard Strauss to be publicly performed.

. . .In March 1881, three more works of the young composer received their première . . . Franz Strauss opened a concert of the Wilde Gungl with his son's *Festmarsch* in E Flat Major, which had been written back in 1876, the same year as the gavotte, and was later published as Opus 1 . . . . In this march you feel clearly that the young Strauss handles orchestral composition with perfect ease. It is hardly at all reminiscent of other masters . . . . He was only twelve years old when he wrote it and his musical impressions were necessarily limited; but the natural facility with which he makes music at such an age plainly foretokens the effortless skill he will command in later years.

At twenty the boy was already esteemed in Munich musical circles; of this we have evidence in a dialogue printed by the *Bayrische Landeszeitung* on January 17, 1884, in the *Muenchner Wochenchronik*. Under the title "What they're talking about these days in concert intermissions," we find: ". . . 'As far as I know young Richard Strauss is in Berlin now.' Is he really! Very definite talent there. Of course the new wine has to clear, but he's got the stuff in him. His last concert overture showed marked progress."

Having baptized two of his son's works with the Wilde Gungl, Father Strauss decided that after Richard's graduation from the Gymnasium in 1882 it was time to make him an active member of the orchestra, which then numbered thirty players. The membership list for 1883-84 puts him third in the first violins. But during the next year he seems to have been moved up to first place, and apparently he even conducted sometimes at rehearsals. Steinitzer tells us something he learned from one of the musicians playing in the orchestra at the time: "The older gentlemen took a liking to their very modest comrade and also took considerable delight in his 'boners'—when he played a difficult passage for the first time, or when he was tuning up his violin with a soft *pizzicato,* one eye on the old man to see if he could hear it, and his father suddenly 'Sshhd!' down angrily at him from the conductor's podium . . . . "

*   *   *

The year 1884 brought the twentieth anniversary of the founding of the Wilde Gungl, which was celebrated with a festival in Tegersee. We learn from the circumstantial report in the *Bayrische Landeszeitung* that ". . . In particular the performance of a splendid piano work by the composer Richard Strauss (club member) evoked stormy applause and made the hours vanish all too quickly." Strauss had just passed his first winter in Berlin; the sojourn had given him a wealth of musical and general artistic impressions. His Cello Sonata, his Violin and Horn Concerto and his First Songs (Opus 10) had already been performed. Buelow had accepted his Serenade for Winds for a concert tour with the Meininger Hofkapelle. In the months following Strauss worked on his Piano Quartet, his Suite for Winds and his *Wanderers Sturm-*

lied. Shortly after making his debut as conductor of his Serenade for Winds, Strauss gained renown in even wider circles
through his F Minor Symphony, which received its first performance in New York.

All the more impressive is the fact that he continued to
attend the "Wilde Gungl" rehearsals conscientiously. Early
in 1885 Father Strauss conducted a program which included
the *Festmarsch* No. 2 in D Major; this had probably been
written earlier but was now heard for the first time. . . . That
was the last performance of his own work by the Wilde
Gungl in which Richard Strauss participated. In September
of the same year he wrote to the founder of the society, Herr
von Rutz, stating that he must leave, and he then took up his
post as Herzoglicher Hofmusikdirektor in Meiningen.

William Armstrong

Interview with Richard Strauss

It was in 1903 that William Armstrong, editor of the American magazine *The Étude,* went to London to see Strauss and talk with him. The
master had already achieved world fame with his tone poems—*Till
Eulenspiegels Lustige Streiche, Also sprach Zarathustra, Don Quixote,*
and others. His operas, except for *Feuersnot,* were still to come.

The interview in *The Étude* was written to introduce Strauss on his
first visit to America. He came twice: in 1904, when he conducted the
first performance of the *Sinfonia Domestica* with Wetzler's orchestra,
and again in 1922.

THE FACE of Richard Strauss is a combination of strength and
weakness. The strength lies in the noble development of the
forehead, and the weakness in the chin and jaw, quite feminine in outline and curious by contrast with the upper part

of the face. His eyes are full of the poetry of his mind. Large, grayish blue in color, and set far apart, they show high development of the imaginative faculties. They are absolutely frank, and there is an expression of the ideal in them that nothing would have the power to disturb.

It was six o'clock in the evening, and at the house of Mr. Speyer, the London banker, which had been placed at his disposal during his stay in the metropolis to conduct the Strauss festival, that I met him, for *The Étude*. The day had been spent in rehearsal; it would presently be time to dress for the concert. With an active, springy step he came down the stairs, hurrying into the room. Tall and angular, his clothes hang on him in a characterless way. His brown hair is thin to the point of baldness, his manner is of a simple dignity that impresses itself.

Of his compositions he spoke reluctantly; on that subject his staunch advocate, Mr. Willem Mengelberg, conductor of the Amsterdam orchestra, and his assistant in the festival, spoke at length to me later, and as a student enthusiastic on his theme.

"My composing is done in the afternoon and evening," said Mr. Strauss, "and I keep it up until one or two o'clock in the morning. But it never leaves me nervous; that is a strange thing about it. When I finish, my mind seems absolutely free from a thought of it, and I go to sleep immediately.

"But I need the calm and quiet of the country to write in, so the major part of my work is done in the summertime. In Berlin I have too much else to do; the stress is too great to make it possible to compose; I score my work there, but I cannot compose. That would be impossible.

"My work in composition means not revolution but evolution, and evolution built on the classics which must be the foundation of all musical composition.

"My compositions are built on classical lines; all real music must be. I believe in the old masters; for Mozart especially I have a great love.

"We have composers in Germany today," Strauss asserted, "but the difficulty is that the picture of Wagner is so great that it dwarfs all others. His breadth, his power, and his forcefulness overshadow by contrast. But we have our smaller composers, nevertheless. There are Mahler, Schilling, von Hausegger, Pfitzner, Humperdinck, and others."

In his interest to have mention made of some of his colleagues; he took my notebook and himself wrote their names.

"Where do I think the chief difficulty in interpreting my compositions lies? In this—lack of sense of humor. Humor is generally the last quality an orchestral conductor has. Look at Beethoven, how full of humor he is in his Fourth and Eighth Symphonies! But how few conductors look for humor in Beethoven, and yet he is so full of humor!

"Shall I follow my plan of setting other poems to music for recitation as I have done in *Enoch Arden?* No, scarcely. That was merely a side issue. Such things can be done with a piano or very small orchestra. The theory that Madame Bernhardt has advanced, for instance, that an entire play be scored with the speaking voice is impossible, nor could any such revolution come, for the reason that no speaking voice could be sustained against an orchestra. Only the singing voice will accomplish that.

"The first of my compositions to be played in America, my First Symphony, was done from the manuscript by Mr. Theodore Thomas in New York. I was seventeen years old at the time. I have never seen him since that meeting in Munich, when my father took me to see him, and he accepted the work; but I know that he has generously given my compositions a hearing."

As he talked, the impression of his simplicity and sincerity deepened. In one sense he is, apparently, among the few—he recognizes thoroughly the place he holds in musical art, his value he knows fully and completely, but as a man associating with other men he is as other men are.

His manner toward an orchestra in rehearsal is calculated to be particularly grateful to the men. If a thing is well done he gives his recognition as soon as the final chord is sounded. If a player does a solo well, even though it be a short one, he steps down from the desk and shakes hands with him when the piece is ended.

Turning presently to his songs, Strauss, in reply to a question as to the sequence in which they should be taken up in study, said: "Even the easiest are difficult; they are for singers already accomplished."

Sidney S. Bloch

The Greatest Conductor of his Time

Sidney S. Bloch (born 1895 in New York) studied music in Berlin for the career of a conductor. For some years he was violinist at the Royal Opera of Berlin. He now lives in New York.

IN MY JUDGMENT Richard Strauss was the most important conductor with whom I ever worked. There was absolutely nothing of the showman about him—and therein he distinguished himself from very nearly all his colleagues.

An elegant grand seigneur of uncommonly tall and slender figure would come in and make the public a short bow. He stood before the orchestra with his legs close together, a giant of a man, and conducted with the greatest economy of motion. He never behaved like a star. He was a creative musician who also knew how to conduct—more he never pretended to be.

But the astounding thing, the mystery of it was that this

unassuming, matter-of-fact craftsman was in fact a true magician. I shall never in my life forget the first time I played under him; it is one of my great experiences. I had known all the great conductors of my time—but the effect of this man was something altogether different. The moment Strauss walked in some kind of power radiated from him, so strong that not a single member of the orchestra could resist it. We instantly fell silent. He did not have to ask us to quiet down. With Furtwaengler, Walter, or other conductors the orchestra generally subsided gradually when the "teacher" came in. With Strauss a kind of high tension set in, an excitement that concentrated itself on him alone. This never diminished through the years. Even musicians who had played for him hundreds of times later confessed to me that every time he appeared they felt that same strange sensation.

Outwardly there was nothing of sorcery to be observed. He used a short little stick, amazingly abbreviated motions; his mouth was partly open, as if he were half-asleep. Only at certain particular spots he would launch into big, broad gestures. There was not a suggestion of the customary conductorial gymnastics, when the sweat pours from brow and armpit and the body writhes in ecstasy. This was a kind of hypnosis. No other conductor—and here I am thinking only of the greatest—could evoke with the most violent gesticulation the ineffably tender *pianissimo subito* that Strauss achieved with a little movement of his left hand and a slight bend of the knees.

Because he was a magician, he needed a minimum of rehearsals. As a young novice I attended rehearsal for a concert tour he was to make with a Berlin symphony orchestra through various German cities. I had expected that he would drill the men from ten in the morning to five in the afternoon. To my astonishment all the rehearsing for the tour—an important one—was finished in barely one hour. He began each composition, a Mozart symphony or something of his own, and then after five minutes broke it off. "All right, that'll do," he said each time in his rough Bavarian, "now give me the next, please. . . ."

And the tour actually turned out a sensational success. That hypnotic power seemed to flow out of him and guide the musicians, as if they were playing in a trance.

I have never before or since heard the Prelude to *Tristan and Isolde* as interpreted by him; he attained the highest conceivable tension. He made it an absolutely new work of art. His relation to Richard Wagner had always been a close one, immediate, almost personal. This was the more remarkable because he had grown up in an atmosphere fiercely hostile to Wagner. His father, Franz Strauss, a highly gifted musician—one of the best hornists in Germany—had been a member of the notorious Munich clique that fought Wagner. Under its influence the young Richard was also anti-Wagner, then later swung over to the opposite camp.

His undisputed favorite, all his life, was Mozart. Mozart was for him "the" consummate achievement. His was the perfect form, untouched by earthly sentimentality, the same clear, spotless, transparent form we find in the last paintings of Raphael. Strauss' interpretation of the *Jupiter* Symphony, *Figaro, Idomeneo* showed not the slightest trace of romanticism, not the faintest emotional retardation.

I can recall countless little details of the Berlin Staatsoper concerts that I attended. Our surprise, for instance, at Franz Schubert's C Major Symphony. In the last movement there is a famous passage where the horn comes in, followed by two oboes. This passage—quite naturally—is always played in whole measures. Strauss, however, covered four measures with one stroke of the baton. What he created was a harmony, a unity of such unearthly power as had never before been heard. I am convinced that such inspirations were not born of previous deliberation; they came on the spur of the moment.

I well remember also how he handled Beethoven's *Turkish March* from the *Ruins of Athens*. It was as if he had summoned out of some land strange and remote a host of oriental soldiers who marched before us with exotic movement and gesture and then vanished into the distance again. The public was absolutely delighted. Strauss, who never gave encores, was forced to play the piece three times over.

He was not the man to work out every little detail of a composition with the members of his orchestra; he relied on their artistic skill. He was concerned only with the spirit of the work to be performed. He expected his orchestra to follow him even when he did not give them their cues. If he succeeded somehow in conveying to the orchestra and to the audience his artistic intention—he was satisfied.

Likewise unique was the finesse with which he handled witty or humorous compositions. Cornelius' *Barber of Bagdad* became under his baton a triumph of humor over all human weakness. Strauss' *Fledermaus* and Rossini's *Barber of Seville* fairly turned somersaults of joy. Even singers who had never displayed the slightest sense of humor now suddenly developed one. But then a few days later, when the same opera was done by some other conductor, these temporarily inspired performers became once more the dry and insipid and unwitty creatures they had always been.

Richard Strauss could be devilishly rude on occasion—in this he was like many Bavarians. He could go purple in the face and he could bluster. But as a general rule he was on comradely terms with his orchestra. And all the members were convinced that as an important composer he understood the essential meaning of the music he was playing better than most conductors. Certain composers he seldom played, only when he was obliged to. I believe he had little feeling for Brahms, or for Bruckner, still less for Tchaikovsky.

In a sense he took over Mozart, Beethoven, and Wagner. His personality was so overpowering that he could not avoid

turning them a little into Richard Strauss. Such has been the
case, however, with all important composers who were also
important conductors—Wagner, Berlioz, Liszt, Mahler.

Max Marschalk

Revelations of His Working Methods

Max Marschalk (1863-1940) was one of the leading music critics of
Berlin during the years when it was the world's music center. He wrote
for the *Vossische Zeitung*, a highly influential newspaper. He was also
something of a composer in his own right; he wrote charming little
operas and set to music the plays of Gerhart Hauptmann and Maeter-
linck. His is the most revealing interview with Strauss ever recorded.

I STAND at the door and pull the bell. A voice comes to me
through a speaking tube, and after I have given my name
the magic door opens and I enter the garden. As I slowly
make my way up the walk, I hear steps approaching from
the left; Strauss greets me and leads me to a side entrance
of the villa, where a maid receives me and forthwith sets to
work on my boots. This is a rule of the house. First the boots
are wiped off with a damp cloth, then with a dry one. Strauss
stands by smiling and remarks with satisfaction and humorous importance: "The damp cloth is *my* invention."

I am familiar with this procedure from years back; as I
then appreciated its deep significance in the aftertaste, so do
I now in the foretaste, since I already know Frau Pauline's
strict and meticulous insistence upon the spotless cleanliness
of her house. We take our tea in the comfortable loggia,
inveigh against the unscrupulous hoarders who are ruining
prices for the "natives," and then we betake ourselves to the
study. Frau Pauline leaves us to our fate.

First I am permitted to hear twelve new *Lieder*. I should

like to make some remark about their character, but I have
been obliged to take an oath of silence. The moods of this
sovereign master of his art find vent and utterance in the
songs. . . . After this bright intermezzo our conversation
returns to the subject we had already touched on briefly in
Munich. "You want to know something about my methods
of work. . . . I work very long on melodies; it's a far road
from the first flash of the idea to the final melodic figure.
Yes—the melodic form; in the conservatories they teach
everything only not how to construct melodies with the proper thoroughness—which seems to me the most important
thing. The motif is a matter of inspiration; it is the idea, and
most composers content themselves with the idea, whereas
true art manifests itself only in the development of the idea.
The important thing is not the beginning of the melody but
its continuation, its development into a fully completed melodic form. Meyerbeer, for instance, has brilliant ideas; in
the first few measures of a melody he fascinates you—and
then he loses his effect. It is the same thing with Brahms.
His melodies are not worked through to the end either; they
swing up in bold flight and then immediately droop their
wings as if they were weary. The most consummate building
of melody we find in Mozart; he has the lightness, the ease
that is really the goal. With Beethoven the melody is heavier;
you can clearly feel the effort in it. Listen to the wonderful
expansion of a Mozart melody." He sits down at the piano and
plays Cherubim's canzone *Ihr, die Ihr Triebe*. He interrupts
himself and says, "You think it's finished and it goes on, it
goes on and on."

"Yes, the melody. In my younger years, after Brahms had
heard my F Major Symphony in Weimar and declared that
my handling of counterpoint was too facile, he advised me
to study the Schubert dances from the point of view of melody construction and to devote myself perseveringly to the
invention of eight-bar melodies. This advice I followed. Here

is one of my exercise books. For example, I take the first two measures of a lovely old folk song and develop it in my way into a large, complex formation." Once again he sits down at the piano and gives a few samples. "Of course building the melodic structure is a matter of talent; but it involves also one of the most difficult technical problems. Our brains are no longer fresh; we already have much development behind us, too much, and therefore we must be extremely careful in our work. Two bars of a melody occur to me spontaneously; now I spin on and write a few more bars, but already I begin to feel defects and insufficiencies; I set one stone upon another until the final composition is achieved. Sometimes it takes a long while, a very long while. A melody that seems to have been born of the moment is almost always the product of laborious effort. And incidentally—work is also a matter of talent. The song *Stern* with the text of Achim von Arnim—you heard it recently—and also the song *Traum durch die Daemmerung*—they were born of the moment. But they are rarities."

"What else shall I tell you? It all depends on self-criticism, on how far you can educate yourself to it and how strong it is in you. As I said, melody gives me a lot of trouble; what Wagner calls Melos. The harmony is part of it too—the disposition of the harmonies over a movement or an act. I give most attention of all to the choice of keys. I decide on the keys for a long stretch in advance, and the way I move from one to another often takes a great deal of work. As you already know, the instrumentation generally goes along rather rapidly with me. Commencing a new work presents me with very special difficulties because usually—think of *Salome,* for instance— it means deciding on the new style I shall write in. I am growing more and more cautious how I begin a work so as not to forfeit in advance the possibility of *Steigerung.* Take Wagner's *Meistersinger* overture; it is so powerful that only a genius like Wagner can still evoke strong effects after

that opening. The *Leonore* overture is too tremendous for
Fidelio; Beethoven does not reach his summit until the Mar-
zelline aria."

Frau Pauline entered the room, served real Black Forest
cherry brandy and informed "Richard" that she had reserved
a table at an inn for the evening and had ordered a supper.
My time had run out; I had to catch the last Mittenwald
train. Strauss accompanied me to the station.

Rudolf Hartmann

Last Visit to Richard Strauss

Rudolf Hartmann (born 1900) is one of the prominent opera stage
directors of Europe. Until 1945 he was at the Staatsoper in Munich;
later he was invited as guest by opera houses in Zurich, Vienna, Paris,
Naples, Salzburg. He is a specialist in all of Richard Strauss' operatic
works.

. . . ALL THE more shocking was the news that reached Zurich: his general condition was worse. On August 28th I returned from Zurich, immediately got in touch with Garmisch
and received confirmation of the report: since August 13th
Richard Strauss had been bedridden. The day before he had
still been able to work a few hours at his desk. Even the signature he put to a sketch of *Daphne* (which he sent me in Zurich
through his grandson Richard, as a gift) had been written on
the 12th; the beautiful words of this dedication were the last
ever written by his hand.

On August 29th I called up and was told that Richard
Strauss wished to see me. In the early afternoon of the day
following, Dr. Franz Strauss, his son, and Christian, his second
grandson, came to call for me in Ebenhausen. We rode rather

silently through country radiant with sun. Dr. Strauss gave me a brief history of his father's grave illness, told me the opinion of the doctors, who gave the sick man only a few days, perhaps only a few hours, to live. I knew now that this would be my last visit. Memories of my meetings with Richard Strauss began to rise and pass before me in a stream of constantly shifting scenes. I did not see much of what was around me, the ride was half-unconscious; the Bavarian landscape before Garmisch unrolled itself past me like a carpet. Once, when we were already beyond Murnau, Dr. Strauss broke the silence and said smiling, "He's looking forward to seeing you, very much. Since morning he's been worrying about your getting picked up on time."

We glide over the moor between two rows of birch trees, then a short way close beside the swift-flowing Loisach, and a few minutes later we drive into the familiar garden path. After a brief but hearty welcome from young Richard and Alice, whose face shows visibly the strain of devoted sick nursing, we all go in to the little sitting room on the first floor. I learn that Richard Strauss suffered severe attacks two days ago, that his wife, Frau Pauline, is unwell and in the hospital. At the moment the sick man is sleeping a little; Frau Alice tells us that about an hour ago he said, "Now I'll sleep a bit more so I'll be wide awake later." We carry on a halting conversation in an undertone. All faces are grave and tense. My glances keep wandering to the white door at the other end of the little parlor. Frau Alice finally rises to go and see. I arrange with Dr. Franz Strauss that after about twenty minutes with the patient I will leave, so as not to overtire him. Then I am called and Frau Alice opens the bedroom door for me, I go in. The room seems very light; the bed is white, with its foot facing the entrance. Richard Strauss has his head slightly turned, reaches me his hand and greets me: "It's nice that you're here. Sit down here next to me." As I move the chair over to the bed, my glance falls on the big oxygen apparatus standing ready near us. I think with anguish of what I have just heard about his sufferings these past few days. I put a cautious, groping question—how does he feel? He answers only with a slight, speaking gesture. He is silent and I would like to say something to him, to comfort him, but in the agitation of this tense moment I do not find the right words. He gives me a long look and I am mute under the knowing, bright, untroubled eyes. Then he says, "Death has dealt me the first hard blow, given me the first sign."

But then he immediately changes his tone, inquires about personal matters—warmly interested as always. The look of his face has changed little; only the deep pallor is unusual and the languor. Gradually his thoughts shift to the things that always move him. He lies there quietly, propped up rather high, and his hands slide over the covers in short, emphatic gestures. I hear the deep, rather hoarse voice speak again of his recurring anxiety as to the progress of the European theater. Then after a slight pause he says, "Just think, a hundred and forty years ago Goethe and Napoleon shook hands in Erfurt! What a world that would have been—Napoleon ruler of a united Europe, Goethe his first Minister of Education—and those other three could have vanished into limbo, Friedrich Wilhelm, Alexander and Franz—the world would have been spared much." He continues this line of thought, tells me that he is composing a long letter to an important political figure of present-day France, François-Poncet, he has half-finished dictating the first draft. He talks in a more lively tone now, utterly engrossed in the topic he has chosen, and he does not notice when the door softly opens. Frau Alice gives me a brief look of understanding, goes to the other side of the bed and tries to hand the sick man some food. He jerks back, a little frightened, when he sees the plate, and refuses it almost violently. But then at once he says a few loving and appeasing words to his patient nurse and turns to me, half apologetic: "I'm supposed to eat all the time, I can't—my stomach isn't quite right any more." Frau Alice leaves us again. . . .

I see from the constantly changing expression of the eyes in the motionless face before me that his mind is working with an undiminished vivacity in his wasted body. Then the voice comes again: "I never had so much to do before as I have now—but still I think a lot of the things I tried for and initiated will bear fruit." He looks over at me, half-questioning. When I agree with him, he speaks of that afternoon visit in July and the plans for Munich laid by Alois Johannes Lippl. Obviously he has been doing a lot of thinking about things; names come up, little memories of great personalities—Buelow, Wagner—but his talk keeps coming back to the present and the future. He speaks warmly of recent fine interpretations of his work by important opera conductors—he mentions Klemens Krauss' unforgettably lovely world première of *Capriccio*, he names Karl Boehm and others. Drawing on his many years' experience, he explains the principles of a classical repertoire, which includes his own work. He talks fluently, with animation, and in his face I see nothing more of illness or exhaustion. I have a commission to discharge: I ask him for precise instructions with respect to the coming first performance of his opera *Die Liebe der Danae*. He is instantly concentrated on the question; he states unequivocally that the work should first be performed in Salzburg, and he fixes the date, just as decisively, that seems right to him. (These instructions he later repeated to his son.)

Meanwhile more time has passed than I intended. The door opens again, grandson Richard comes in to remind me that my train leaves at such and such. Richard Strauss pricks up his ears; he wants to go on with our talk and once again he orders the car for my return trip. I am afraid he is overexerting himself, but he insists vehemently on having his own way. "Who knows when we shall be able to have a talk like this again?" The interruption has upset him. He draws a few heavy

breaths, rather like gasps, and I am suddenly filled with anxiety. It is nothing—he quiets down again when I have helped him a little. Once more he begins talking, tries to recapture the lost thread of his discourse, but is again distracted, this time by me. A quick movement has pulled a button off my jacket, I look for it with an irritated glance. "What is it?" Richard Strauss asks, watching me intently, and when he learns the trouble he is all at once the practical-minded father of a family: "Stand up and it will fall on the floor and you can keep it." It works just that way, and he looks on attentively while I stick the renegade button carefully in my pocket. He nods in satisfaction, then turns and stares straight before him, trying to get back the train of his thought. After a while he has it: "I believe I conducted the works of Wagner well. With Wagner a lot depends on the orchestra conductor, he really has to hold the whole thing together, and he has to move forward at the decisive moment. For example, in *Siegfried*. After the idyl there has to be an animated spirit till the end— all the slow tempi are meant to be only relatively slow— but very few understand that. Especially in the big final scene with Bruennhilde, when the erotic emotion overwhelms the young Siegfried for the first time, this is infinitely important." He grows very lively now, sits way up in bed: "You know which spot I mean, after the idyl?" Without waiting for an answer he raises his arms and starts conducting and singing, in a loud voice, the orchestra melody. His face is slightly flushed, his shining eyes look far, far beyond the walls of the room. Fascinated, I follow the expressive movements of his long, narrow hands until they sink down on the cover. He leans back against the pillows, his eyes moist with tears. "For-
so many things to think about—you get a little overemotional."
give me," he says, "when you lie alone like this and you have
I cannot answer, overcome as I am by my sense of the terrible nearness of his artistic nature revealing its last threads and fibers. I am almost relieved when he starts talking again. He

returns to the present-day theater personalities with whom he is familiar, inquires about the artistic activities of each. I tell him what I know. He is sad about all the theater houses that have been destroyed, speaks of the inner and outer reconstruction going on, enthusiastically makes plans and more plans. He would like to see this or the other talent properly placed; he carefully weighs the possibilities of the great opera houses still in existence; and finally he says with a smile, "We would have divided up and apportioned the world nicely— *our* world!" Then he is silent for a long time, pursuing thoughts almost palpable to me. A while later his voice, completely altered, softly says, *"Gruess mir die Welt"* ("Remember me to the world"). He stops, asks, "Where is that from?" I think hastily of similar words from the *Walkuere,* mention them, but he shakes his head. "No, no, that's not it, that part comes somewhere else," and he repeats, *"Gruess mir die Welt. . . ."* He is silent for a long while and I see that his face shows signs of fatigue; I feel it is time to leave him. But it is terribly hard for me to bring out the first word of farewell. Richard Strauss lies there quite still. As I gaze at him, taking in his face and look, names flash through my mind, the external stages of his triumphantly successful life: Weimar, Munich, Berlin, Vienna, Salzburg, Bayreuth. . . . He turns his eyes back to me. With a great effort I remain composed. Meanwhile more than two and a half hours have elapsed since my arrival. I tell him that I must leave. He looks long at me. "Yes, I'm tired now. Stay another ten minutes, we can talk a little more, and then I'll sleep."

Once again he pulls all the threads together, reviews what he has confided to me during this visit about what he wants done with his work, what he hopes for the future of his grandson Richard. His eyes hold mine fast with a penetrating force. At last he grows calmer and in the charming conversational tone peculiar to him, he inquires further about my next works. I mention Switzerland and Zurich, and Richard Strauss speaks with warmth and gratitude of his biographer Willi Schuh's fine work.

It is time to go. I rise to take my leave. He reaches me his hand, thanks me for the visit, making a visible effort to free this farewell of its sadness and significance. Somewhat hesitant, I turn away. Then he reaches for my right hand once more with both of his, holds me fast: "Maybe we'll see each other again—if not, you know everything." A last violent pressure, his hands release me and I leave the room quickly. As I go out I hear Richard Strauss give a muffled sob and then call loudly to his son. . . .

Meanwhile it has grown dark outside. Grandson Richard drives me home. We do not speak. I look out into the landscape of the night, listening still to the words whose soft, penetrating sound will never leave me: *Gruess mir die Welt.*

GUSTAV MAHLER

Born: Kalischt, Bohemia
July 7, 1860
Died: Vienna, Austria
May 18, 1911

GUSTAV MAHLER was the son of a struggling Jewish tradesman who pinched and saved in order to give the boy a good education. By the time he entered the Conservatory of Vienna, in 1875, he was already a fine pianist and a bold composer. His first works were failures, however, and he turned to conducting to make his living.

After years at the opera houses of Prague, Hamburg, and other music centers, he received the directorship of the Imperial Opera in Vienna—then the most famous of its kind in the world. Now began Mahler's years of glory. He was fiercely fought by the powerful conservative clique, but passionately loved by the young and progressive. Within a few years he had revolutionized modern opera production. During his vacations he composed nine symphonies and a wealth of other compositions which include his moving choral work *Das Lied von der Erde* ("Song of the Earth").

Mahler was the symphonic representative of a romanticism fast vanishing. His theme was always the same, the expression ever developing, ever more monumental: a new world-brotherhood of man. But through all runs another cry—the desolate individual lost on earth, the lonely wanderer whom only the winds, the birds and the grass will ever know.

When Mahler finally gave up his post in Vienna, he accepted despite his ill-health an invitation to conduct the Philharmonic Orchestra in New York. The venture was not successful; neither public nor critics could understand the misanthropic little conductor who flouted every tradition of his craft that the Americans had been taught to revere. His exalted symphonies, with their strange orchestration, found even less understanding. He was brought back to Vienna, where he died soon afterward.

Bruno Walter

The Young Kapellmeister

In the year 1894 Bruno Walter (born 1876) was engaged as coach at the Opera in Hamburg. Gustav Mahler was Erster Kapellmeister. Mahler was thirty-four years old, Walter eighteen. All his life Walter has emphatically maintained that these years of his early friendship with Mahler were the most decisive of his career. Even as a young man Gustav Mahler clearly displayed the chief traits of his character: fanatical sincerity of purpose, tyrannical obstinacy in his relations with co-workers, deep-rooted melancholy.

FROM the depths of memory I call up the picture of Gustav Mahler as he first appeared to me, then a youth of eighteen. A shout of indignation had resounded through the musical press in June 1894, an echo of the performance of the First Symphony—called at that time *Titan*—on the occasion of the Musicians' Festival of the Allgemeiner Deutscher Musikve-

rein, in Weimar. To judge by the criticisms, the work had justified indignation by sterility, triviality, and an accumulation
of extravagances. It was, above all, the *Funeral March in the
Manner of Callot* which was rejected with anger and scorn. I
recall distinctly with what excitement I devoured the newspaper reports on the subject. I admired the daring author of so
strange a funeral march and felt a burning desire to know this
extravagant man and his extravagant work.

It was but a few months later that a letter of introduction
to Pollini, the theatrical manager, took me as coach to the
Hamburg Opera, whose first conductor was the same Gustav
Mahler. And there he stood in person, in the office of the
theater, when I left Pollini's sanctum after my first call on
him: pale, thin, small of stature, with longish features, a steep
forehead framed by intensely black hair, remarkable eyes behind spectacles, lines of sorrow and humor; his face, when he
spoke, showed the most astonishing change of expression—the
very incarnation of Kapellmeister Kreisler—interesting, demoniac, intimidating—as he would appear to the imagination
of youthful readers of E. T. A. Hoffmann's fantastic tales.
Pleasantly and kindly he inquired as to my musical abilities
and knowledge; I replied, to his visible satisfaction, with
mingled modesty and self-reliance—and he left me in a sort
of stupor, deeply moved.

My next recollection shows him to me at one of the early
rehearsals of *Haensel und Gretel,* a new work then in preparation at the Hamburg Opera. Never before had I seen such
an intense person, never dreamed that a terse word, a commanding gesture, a will concentrated on a clear goal could
frighten and alarm others and force them into blind obedience. An unsatisfactory piano accompanist tried Mahler's
patience; suddenly—what luck—he saw me, a fascinated onlooker, standing in the wings, and asked me if I dared accompany the opera, which was unknown to me, at sight. My proud
"Of course!" elicited an amused smile and the request that I

replace the unfortunate colleague who had been removed by a motion of the hand. The oft-repeated echo sung out in the forest scene was unsatisfactorily shaded; Mahler turned to me with words to this effect: "I trust that you know how things happen in a forest—go and rehearse the echo for me." Thus, one of the very first rehearsals furnished me with a thorough impression of Mahler's manner as a conductor: guiding and commanding, possessed by the music, sure of his goal, irritable and harsh when confronted with an inadequate performance, kind, trusting, sympathetic when he thought he sensed ability and enthusiasm.

The third recollection: In company with Mahler I left the building by the stage door and was about to take leave of him when he detained me with the words, "Come with me for a bit." What I recall of our conversation is merely that I started making a remark concerning the Humperdinck work, which he said was "fashioned in masterly manner, but not really fairy-tale-like." From explaining what fairy-tale-like meant he moved to other subjects, and again I was fascinated to observe how the same intensity, the same spiritual tenseness that he had just revealed during rehearsal was now manifested in his conversation. The vehemence with which he objected whenever I said something unsatisfactory to him—and how timidly I said it!—his sudden submersion in pensive silence, the kind glance with which he received an understanding word on my part, the unexpected, convulsive expression of secret sorrow and, added to all, the strange irregularity of his gait: a stamping of the feet, a sudden halting and rushing ahead again—everything confirmed and strengthened the impression of demoniac obsession; and I should hardly have been surprised if, after saying good-by, he had started moving faster and faster and had finally flown away from me in the shape of a vulture, as Archivarious Lindhorst leaves the student Anselmus in Hoffmann's *Golden Pot.*

*   *   *

Nothing in his life—as I quickly realized—was systematic; his style of living resembled a river with cataracts, like the Nile in its middle course, and not a uniformly flowing stream. In the judgments of his personality, therefore, no epithet appeared even at that time more frequently than "desultory." He impressed me, too, as being desultory, but not in the sense of unthorough; he was ready for the next mental leap only when his cataracts of thought and feeling had rushed forth and all had come to rest again. The period of rest, to be sure, lasted only until he effervesced again under a new impulse.

Hardly ever, therefore, did he give me deliberate instruction; but I gained immeasurably through my living experience of a personality that spent itself freely in word and music without premeditation, from sheer inner superabundance. Mahler's impulsive outbursts are a possible explanation of the agitation I observed in almost all who came in contact with him. They included those nearest to him, but especially, of course, singers and members of the orchestra. He spread about himself an atmosphere of high tension, which produced performances filled with his intent and pulsing with the fervor of his enthusiasm—performances which gained for the Hamburg Opera its leading position in the musical life of Germany. While those of higher caliber were attached to him by profound admiration, the less gifted and the arrogant were filled with bitterness and hate, felt themselves maltreated by the stern taskmaster. But willingly or unwillingly, they all bowed to his will.

His inner vitality at that time gave him a certain outer violence and agility. I can still see him at an orchestra rehearsal of *Goetterdaemmerung*: rushing toward the trumpets and trombones in a far corner of the orchestra pit to impress upon them the significance of some passage in the *Funeral Music;* or quickly climbing up via a double-bass stool to the stage, since issuing directions from the conductor's desk would have been less convenient or would have entailed a loss of time—as, for instance, in connection with the shading of a distant chorus or of music on the stage. The orchestra meanwhile, sat in hypnotic silence, under the spell of the master. And he himself, spellbound by the intrinsic conception of the work under his hand, seemed compelled by some driving force to make his co-workers comply with the irresistible dictates of his innermost self.

To balance such utter concentration there was inevitably a proportionate absentmindedness in all things that lay outside his momentary sphere of interest. Many were the comic occurrences resulting from this absent-mindedness. One day, for example, at a stage rehearsal with orchestra, the stage manager asked him to have a little patience, certain matters on the stage needed his immediate attention. Impatient at first, Mahler soon sank into deep thought, while the stage manager toiled to put things right. When this was done, however, repeated shouts that everything was ready and he might continue quite failed to awaken the conductor. Then suddenly, aroused by the general quiet and expectancy, he looked about in bewilderment, tapped his desk with the baton and called out *"Zahlen!"* ("Check, please!"). Peals of laughter resounded from all sides, and he finally joined in heartily himself.

When he had gradually become convinced of my passionate interest in his creative work, he began to enjoy familiarizing me with it at the piano. I still have in my ears the grotesquely-quaint sounds as he sang to me *St. Anthony's Sermon to the Fish*, and I recall his high spirits in the rendition of *To Make Naughty Children Be Good* and *Self-Reliance*, and his passion and sorrow in the *Songs of a Traveling Fellow;* I still feel the strong emotion that shook me when I at last became acquainted through him with the anxiously awaited First Symphony. More and more his creative work came to occupy the foreground of our relations and conversation. In the course of my study of his works, of our discussions about them and

about the books he read, the poets and philosophers he loved,
as I gained a deeper view of his soul, my initial impression of
Mahler as a fanatic-demoniac nature belonging to the world
of E. Th. A. Hoffmann broadened into a more correct and in-
clusive picture, though one more difficult to understand.

Guido Adler

Personality of Mahler

We have met Guido Adler as a friend of Brahms. He was also a
friend of Mahler, from boyhood days, and remained faithful until the
grave. He knew the most secret corners of the great master's heart.

He describes Mahler as a passionate worker, a great pioneer in those
glorious years when he directed the Imperial and Royal Opera House
in Vienna. His work there was decisive for the development of the
European theater. He was the animating spirit of the whole institution—
conductor, stage director, producer, designer—though he was assisted
in the nonmusical departments by eminent experts.

IF WE ARE properly to understand Mahler's way of producing
and reproducing, we must form a clear conception of his character—as with every artist. Creation and rendition are reflected images of the psychic life of the artist; more, his works
are his offspring, they are the stamp and seal of his personality; insofar as it is not mechanical, his interpretation of a
musical work is a fragment of his own life. Mahler's was a
nature founded on goodness and energy. His strength of will
was fanatic, alike in the divine mania of the artist and in his
inexorable drive toward truth in all the manifestations of his
life. Like a child, he let the moment carry him away; at such
times he seemed a creature utterly free and unfettered. Yet
his actions were in fact ultimately governed by a clear intelli-

gence. His will showed itself inflexible, yet his temper was
mild, his heart soft. He was generous; like a child he felt with
his fellow men, with great and small, with grownups and with
the young. He was touching in his friendship, in his attachment; he was open, unreserved to the point of self-abnegation.
He could enjoy everything—and he could lose his temper over
the merest trifle that did not match his mood of the moment.
Extremely sensitive and irritable, he could yet bear the most
acute pain without complaint—and the next moment show
annoyance at the slightest discomfort. He was communicative
and confiding toward friends whom he won and recognized
as such, mistrustful and reserved with disagreeable people in
whom he found no understanding—and he was capable of
striking out with the harshest home truths, so that now and
then he hurt. This explains the enmities that not infrequently
arose from wounded vanity. He wanted to grasp life in all its
heights and depths. Tragedy and joyous serenity in all its
manifestations drew from him an inward echo and response.
Thus it is that in his symphonies we find extreme simplicity
and unpretentiousness following immediately upon exalta-
tion. . . .

*   *   *

When he conducted his own and others' works, both his
own personality and that of the composition found expression.
He plunged into the work of art, it drew him to itself, he surrendered himself utterly. Subject and object became one.
When he was recreating a work of art, he exerted an irresistible power of suggestion on those who labored with him,
those he led, his companions; he magnetized them to his conception. He permitted every coworker the maximum freedom
possible without detriment to the unity of the rendition. He
drew from his players the very best they had to give, and all
resources he placed at the service of the composition he was
interpreting. The musicians were thus made subject to his

will; with a general's eye he disposed his troops in accordance
with the strategic plan inherent in the music itself, adapting
it to the situation and to the capacities of the players. At rehearsals you could watch how the terrain was taken step by
step, how he kept his eye on the cohesion of the whole, even
during the punctilious polishing of the most minute detail.
First he would give some comparison by way of explanation,
then he would blow or fiddle a motif or a passage with his
throat and lips, his arm and hand would draw the lines, show
the kind of movement he wanted; he would stab at the air,
grow to giant size with the *crescendo,* shrink to a dwarf with
the *decrescendo;* his facial expressions—the lowering brows,
the pleading corners of his mouth, the creased forehead—
called forth the most inward response, evoked the highest
tension from pppp to ffff. He encouraged his men with humor,
rebuked them with sarcasm—always and only in an effort to
spur the player or the singer on to new deeds. He would tell a
little story to reanimate the imagination. The softest middle
register in a many-voiced composition had only to sing a
wrong note—he caught it and delivered his reprimand; in the
midst of a raging storm he waves back the note of an instrument that has not come in properly, in a great choir he notices
a singer who has sung too low, a violinist who has played the
right note in the *tutti* but on the wrong string. With a few rehearsals he forged a unified instrumental body out of a perfect
jumble, an orchestra thrown together solely for special performances of his symphonies and other works. At piano,
opera, and concert rehearsals he displayed a consummate mastery of the instrument, accompanying the singers himself. He
was able to create the illusion of an orchestra, and yet he kept
within the boundaries that must be respected in relation to
the singing voices. In the chamber-music ensemble he showed
himself a partner of delicate sensibilities; he traced with fine
lines within the frame of the miniature. He had a predilection
for chamber music. When he accompanied songs he was able

to adapt himself to the singer and at the same time to guide
him without letting this guidance be felt. When he rehearsed
the winds and strings separately he sought to maintain their
tonal relation to the entire orchestra, and every player felt a
little like a soloist. . . .

❊   ❊   ❊

When the little man with the lively movements approached
the podium, silence fell. In a clear, friendly, pleasant voice he
greeted the musicians. The instant he raised his baton they
yielded to the fascination of his glance, surrendered themselves to his will. His face speaks earnestness and holy zeal;
the flashing eyes cast forth brilliant light; at mystic passages
they gaze dreamily before them. The vigorous chin expresses
an energetic will, as do the dilated nostrils of his sharp-cut
nose and the high forehead, which makes furrows at the first
rise of doubt or anger—but then there are the fine narrow lips
that can smile gently. Thoughtful and superior in everything
he does, he gives free rein to the movements of his body, which
sometimes become grotesque, with nervous twitchings and
tapping of the foot. But in his years of maturity his gestures became more and more concentrated. His arms seemed inclined
then to content themselves with the necessary indication of
beat and *tempo;* his eyes and the whole expression of his face
bored into the consciousness of the men looking up at him
attentively; wrist and fingertips achieved more than arms and
feet had achieved before. Mahler's conducting grew more and
more spiritual, and his will communicated itself like an elec-
trical discharge, remaining invisible to the observer's eye. His
work in conducting and composing became ever more inward. . . .

Ugo Giardini

Mahler in New York

Ugo Giardini (1888-1944) was an Italian musicologist and journalist who lived for some years, during his twenties, in the United States. He obtained permission from Mahler to attend his rehearsals of the Philharmonic Orchestra; later on Giardini wrote a series of articles on his impressions of four music seasons in New York for Italian newspapers.

IT WAS generally known that Mahler had frequent conflicts with the women managers of the Philharmonic Orchestra who raised the large funds necessary to cover the deficits of the organization. One of these busybodies attended the rehearsal of one of Mahler's own symphonies and then went to the composer's room to congratulate him. She could not refrain from remarking that she thought he had played the first movement much too slowly. I could hardly believe my own ears. It was plain to see that Mahler had to struggle with himself not to give her the answer she deserved; but he won. The little man, ghastly pale, utterly exhausted from the long, grueling rehearsal, simply turned away from her in silence.

New York made him frightfully nervous. A sea of meaningless stone, he called the city; he found it intolerable. Every hour he spent here he longed for the wide green parks of his Vienna, for his country house in the Alps. He considered that in making the short journey from his hotel to Carnegie Hall he was performing an act of self-sacrifice for which he was being paid. "I can't breathe between these eternal walls," he complained to me. "They're crushing me, slowly but surely."

When he had accepted the New York offer, it had been on

condition that he have an absolutely free hand, full authority in the arrangement of all the Philharmonic programs—just as he had had full authority in Vienna, where his word was law. The promise was not kept. He was in constant battle with the ladies. They knew far better than he what was good music and what was not. One of them raised violent protest against the performance of any work by Franz Schubert. She informed Mahler that she had once read a book entitled *History of Music* which had clearly established that Schubert was a rank amateur.

Toward the end Mahler was little more than a quivering bundle of nerves. In Vienna he was a man who jumped out of bed mornings full of high expectancy, a man who asked himself what new musical delights the day would bring. In New York he had to drag himself out from under the covers. "I feel like an old steer making up his own mind to go to the slaughterhouse," he told me. He stood at the open window and listened to the swelling thunder of traffic from the streets below.

"A strange life," he sighed. "A life in noise—noise—noise. I wonder when the modern world will produce the artist to mirror it in music . . . The symphony of the skyscrapers . . . It must come, of course . . . And such monster cities are nature too . . . perhaps they are beautiful nature. . . ."

When it came to his ears that the Philharmonic subscription list was steadily shrinking, he seemed not to care very much. I had the impression that he had already, long since, come to understand that he and New York would never meet; he was resigned. The audience felt he was insulting their musical intelligence by editing the works of the masters—by multiplying parts in a Beethoven symphony—adding a kettle-drum in the *Pastorale*, for instance—or cutting down the strings and doubling the flutes in Mozart's G Minor. . . .

Alma Mahler

The End

When Mahler came to the United States he was already a sick man without knowing it. During the forty-seventh concert of his third season with the New York Philharmonic Society (1910-11) he collapsed. He was rushed back to Europe for medical treatment—and died in his beloved Vienna.

He had married Alma Maria Schindler in 1902. Her book on the great master contains a moving account of her years of pain and joy with him.

WE NOW ENDEAVORED to get in touch with the doctors whose names Fränkel had written down for us, but it was just before Easter and not one was available. The only bacteriologist we could get hold of was Chantemesse. When he came he insisted on instant removal to a nursing home of Dr. Dupres' in Rue Dupont. This was the best and most up to date of all the clinics in Paris at that time, but somewhat primitive compared with our hospitals in Vienna. There were wonderful rooms looking onto a garden, but no nursing to speak of. However, my mother and I needed no help in our devoted care of him.

There was no shutting our eyes now to the unmistakable signs. His growing weakness was arrested only by a feverish excitement. Yet he was glad to talk and he talked a great deal. He read works of philosophy all through his illness and up to the very end. The last book he read was *The Philosophy of Life* by Eduard von Hartmann. By the end it was in fragments. He tore the pages from the binding, because he had not the strength to hold more than a few pages at a time. Chantemesse, who was a celebrated bacteriologist, now

made a culture from Mahler's blood and after a few days
he came to us in great delight with a microscope in his hand.
I thought some miracle had happened. He placed the microscope on the table. "Now, Madame Mahler, come and look.
Even I—myself—have never seen streptococci in such a marvelous state of development. Just look at these threads—it's
like seaweed." He was eager to explain, to cast his light
abroad. But I could not listen. Dumb with horror, I turned
and left him. The shock it gave my mother did her serious
harm.

Once when Mahler was feeling better I sat on his bed and
we discussed what we should do when he recovered. "We'll
go to Egypt and see nothing but blue sky," he said.

"Once you are well again," I said, "I shall have had enough
of suffering. Do you remember, when you first got to know me
you thought I was too happy. I've suffered enough now. I
don't need any more chastening. We'll live a careless, happy
life."

He smiled tenderly and stroked my hair. "Yes, you're right.
God grant I get better and then we can still be happy."

But he got worse, and in my anguish I telegraphed to
Professor Chvostek, the most celebrated doctor in Vienna,
asking him to come at once. He arrived next morning. I told
him first how to behave with Mahler and then he went into
the sickroom and began in a loud jovial voice: "Now then,
Mahler, what's all this about? Working too hard, that's what
it is. You'll have to knock off for six months or a year. You've
brought it on yourself—you can't treat your nerves that way,
you know."

Mahler gazed at him with growing astonishment.

"Shall I be able to work again then?" he asked, his face
lighting up with joy.

"Of course. Why not? Keep your heart up, that's all. This
evening we'll be off to Vienna together."

Chvostek told me to make preparations for leaving as soon

as possible. Anything might happen and then it might be too late to move him. All the same, I did not lose all heart, and when I went back into Mahler's room the joy in his face was such as I had never seen. He cried out again and again: "Oh, the lovely man, the lovely Chvostek! Oh, for tonight—how soon can we start?"

And it seemed that his overwhelming joy made a new man of him. He could not endure delay. We packed madly. Moll hurried out to reserve sleepers. Mama was to follow us to Vienna with her granddaughter. Mahler was dressed long before it was time to start, blissful, transfigured.

Chvostek and I accompanied him in the ambulance and then he was carried to the train on a stretcher. His traveling cap was awry—so helpless he was. I took it off; his beautiful face showed he understood. It was horrible to see him manipulated into the train on a stretcher along the narrow corridor. He went straight to bed, and Moll, Chvostek, and I took turns watching through the night. "Are you there? You're an angel," he said, and after a pause: "We're coming home in poor trim this time. But we'll soon be on our feet again." I was sitting on a suitcase beside him. I laid my head on his hand and kissed it.

Chvostek called me out in the middle of the night and made Moll take my place.

"No hope," he said solemnly. "And may the end come quickly. If he did pull through, which is not likely, he'd be condemned to a bath chair for the rest of his life."

"Better that than nothing," I said. "I can't face life without him."

"Yes, but then the whole nervous system will go too and you don't want to wheel a senile idiot about."

I refused to submit and asked Moll to let me return to my post. Journalists came to the door at every station in Germany and Austria for the latest bulletin; his last journey was like that of a dying king. They all knew his importance and had to find out how he was at half-past ten, at eleven, at twelve. Mahler asked who each of them was and what paper he represented, and it seemed to do him good. He said to me over and over again, "My madly adored Almschi."

Vienna—and by ambulance to the Löw nursing home, where an enormous room with a verandah was ready for him. Not only the room but the corridor too were wreathed in flowers, and Mahler was obviously delighted. More and more flowers arrived. I had to bring them all for him to see and to arrange them with care. A white basket of flowers arrived with a card: "From the Philharmonic." "*My* Philharmonic," he said again and again.

After a time he lay completely still. His mind was becoming confused. Justine paid him another visit and at the sight of her his eyes dilated unnaturally.

"Who is this lady?" he stammered. She fled.

Berliner arrived from Berlin, true to their old friendship, and Mahler recognized him and grasped his hand. "My dear friend," he said, and then turned to the wall, perhaps to hide his emotion.

During his last days he cried out: "My Almschi!" hundreds of times, in a voice, a tone I had never heard before and have never heard since. "My Almschi!" As I write it down now, I cannot keep back my tears.

When Gucki came to his bedside he put his arms round her. "Be a good girl, my child."

Did he know? Or not? It was impossible to tell. He lay there groaning. A large swelling came up on his knee, then on his leg. Radium was applied and the swelling immediately went down. On the evening after, he was washed and his bed made. Two attendants lifted his naked emaciated body. It was a taking down from the cross. This was the thought that came to all of us.

He had difficulty in breathing and was given oxygen. Then uremia—and the end. Chvostek was summoned. Mahler lay with dazed eyes; one finger was conducting on the quilt. There was a smile on his lips and twice he said: "Mozart!" His eyes were very big. I begged Chvostek to give him a large dose of morphia that he might feel nothing more. He replied in a loud voice. I seized his hands: "Talk softly, he might hear you." "He hears nothing now."

How terrible the callousness of doctors is at such moments! And how did he know that he could not hear? Perhaps he was only incapable of movement?

The death agony began. I was sent into the next room. The death rattle lasted several hours.

The ghastly sound ceased suddenly at midnight of the 18th of May during a tremendous thunderstorm. With that last, last breath his beloved and beautiful soul had fled, and the silence was more deathly than all else. As long as he breathed he was there still. But now all was over.

GEORGE GERSHWIN

Born: Brooklyn, New York
September 26, 1898
Died: Hollywood, California
July 11, 1937

GEORGE GERSHWIN came of a poor Brooklyn family. Despite his unpropitious surroundings, he early gave signs of talent and his relatives did their best to help him study music. Although he had, at various times, well-known teachers, his gifts were largely self-developed. His first important success was his musical comedy *La, La, Lucille* (1919). In the same year he wrote his *Swanee*, which was introduced by Al Jolson.

Gershwin wrote thirty musicals for the stage and screen, most of them to his brother Ira's lyrics. Then he discovered that jazz could be serious music too. Paul Whiteman, whose dream was to bring jazz into the concert hall, invited George to Aeolian Hall on February 12, 1924. He played his *Rhapsody in Blue* and American music was revolutionized. Out of the European tradition a genuine American idiom had emerged. There followed Gershwin's Concerto in F, *An American in Paris*, the *Cuban* Overture, and, finally, his opera *Porgy and Bess*.

He spent 1936 in Hollywood and turned out the Astaire-Rogers picture *Shall We Dance?* He began suffering from severe headaches; three weeks later a brain tumor was discovered. He died after an unsuccessful operation in a Los Angeles hospital.

Ira Gershwin

My Brother's Childhood

Ira Gershwin (born 1896), the elder brother of the composer, wrote the words for most of George's songs.

MY BROTHER, born in Brooklyn, New York, September 26, 1898, was the second of four children of Morris and Rose Bruskin Gershwin. I was the oldest, then came George, then Arthur and last, our sister, Frances. Most of our early boyhood was spent on the lower East Side of Manhattan where my father engaged in various activities: restaurants, Russian and Turkish baths, bakeries, a cigar store and pool parlor on the 42nd Street side of what is now Grand Central Station, bookmaking at the Brighton Beach Race Track for three exciting but disastrous weeks. We were always moving. When my father sold a business and started another we would inevitably move to the new neighborhood. George and I once counted over twenty-five different flats and apartments we remembered having lived in during those days.

It was when we were living on Second Avenue that my mother added a piano to our home. George was about twelve at this time. No sooner had the upright been lifted through the window to the "front-room" floor than George sat down and played a popular tune of the day. I remember being particularly impressed by his left hand. I had had no idea he could play and found out that despite his roller-skating activities, the kid parties he attended, the many street games he participated in (with an occasional resultant bloody nose) he had found time to experiment on a player-piano at the home of a friend on Seventh Street. Although our piano was purchased with my taking lessons in mind, it was decided that George might prove the brighter pupil.

His first teacher was a Miss Green. She was succeeded by a Hungarian band leader, impressively mustached, who was down on his uppers and condescended to take an occasional pupil. Composer of a *Theodore Roosevelt March*, his fancy ran to band and orchestra literature and George was studying a piano version of the *William Tell Overture* when he was brought to Charles Hambitzer, a talented pianist and composer of light music. Hambitzer, quick to recognize his ability, encouraged his harmonies and introduced him to the works of the masters, with special emphasis on Chopin and Debussy. George attended the High School of Commerce for a short period. During that time he was pianist for the morning assembly exercises.

At the age of fifteen and for a consideration of fifteen dollars a week George became a pianist in the "professional department" of Jerome H. Remick and Co., publishers of popular music. He was probably the youngest piano pounder ever employed in Tin Pan Alley. He played all day, traveled to nearby cities to accompany the song pluggers, was sent to vaudeville houses to report which acts were using Remick songs, wrote a tune now and then and, whenever he could, attended concerts. Several of his confreres looked askance at this side of his activities. A song plugger was quite indignant: "I went to a recital once. What's the idea? Why, they only had a piano on the stage!"

One day George submitted a song of his own to the professional manager. He was told: "You're here as a pianist, not a writer. We've got plenty of writers under contract." Shortly after, he gave up his job. Soon, at another house, a song of his was accepted. This was in 1916 and the song was called *When You Want 'Em You Can't Get 'Em, When You've*

Got 'Em You Don't Want 'Em. George received an advance of five dollars. Murray Roth, who wrote the lyric, was more persuasive and received fifteen. The next published song, written with Sigmund Romberg and Harold Atteridge, was sung in *The Passing Show of 1916*. This also had an arresting title—*Making of a Girl*—and proved pretty conclusively a girlie's looks were greatly dependent on her wearing the proper clothes. As the returns on this song were somewhat less than seven dollars George decided he couldn't live on royalties.

At this stage he became rehearsal pianist for the Dillingham-Ziegfeld production *Miss 1917*. During a Sunday night "concert" at the Century Theater where *Miss 1917* was playing, Miss Vivienne Segal introduced two of his numbers. These brought him to the attention of Max Dreyfus, then head of Harms, Inc., music publishers. He signed with Dreyfus at thirty-five dollars a week. Although he had many more financially flattering offers he decided his place was with Dreyfus, who was not only a publisher of musical comedies and operettas but also a fine musician and student of the classics. During this time he continued his studies with Edward Kilenyi and then Rubin Goldmark. There was rarely a period in his life when he was not studying. His last teacher was Dr. Joseph Shillinger. I find among the notes of his lessons with Schillinger strange graphs with headings such as "Rhythmic Groups Resulting From the Interference of Several Synchronized Periodicities" and "Groups With the Fractioning Around the Axis of Symmetry."

George began interpolating in various shows. His lyrics were mostly by Irving Caesar. He also began to accept lyrics by Arthur Francis (a pseudonym I concocted from the names of my other brother and my sister) and our first joint effort was a song called *The Real American Folk Song Is a Rag*, which Nora Bayes sang for a while in *Ladies First*. As this piece was more of an essay than a song it didn't get very far.

Finally George got a chance to do a show where he was to be sole composer. It was called *Half Past Eight* and advertised a Broadway Beauty Chorus which was nonexistent. With just a few second-hand curtains and sets for production, it opened in Syracuse and was so bad that one critic headed his next morning's review with "*Half Past Eight* Not Worth Price of War Tax."

A young producer, Alex Aarons, had great faith in George and in 1919 had him do the complete score for *La, La, Lucille*. This was a smartly conceived musical comedy and the result was quite successful. I recall Victor Jacobi, the light opera composer, telling George, in the Harms elevator, how much he liked its musical subtleties. Jerome Kern also predicted a great future. That same year, 1919, Caesar and George wrote *Swanee*, which, when subsequently introduced by Al Jolson in *Sinbad*, was widely played and purchased.

Beginning in 1920 he wrote, among other things, the music for *George White's Scandals* for five consecutive years. It was for the fourth of this series that he and B. G. DeSylva turned out in six days a short one-act opera called *135th Street*. Lasting only one night it was eliminated not because it was ineffective artistically but because it changed the mood of the audience and the tragic note it injected in the proceedings handicapped the gayer numbers that followed. Intimations of the musical paths George was later to follow, especially in recitative, may be found in *135th Street*. It was also in 1923 that Eva Gauthier, with George at the piano, introduced a group of popular and musical comedy songs at an Aeolian Hall recital. It included numbers by George, Kern, Berlin, and Donaldson. Needless to say, this concert caused quite a commotion in musical circles.

Early in 1924, Paul Whiteman announced a concert with new works by Deems Taylor, Victor Herbert, and George Gershwin. The newspaper item was the first inkling George had that Whiteman was serious when he had once casually mentioned that some day he expected to do such a concert and hoped for a contribution from George. Finding in his notebooks a theme (the clarinet glissando) which he thought might make an appropriate opening for a more extended work than he had been accustomed to writing, he decided to chance it. Three weeks later, with an orchestration by Ferde Grofé, Whiteman was rehearsing *Rhapsody in Blue* in the night club Palais Royal. A week later when it was presented at Aeolian Hall with the composer at the piano, the response was immediate. Soon it was being played all over the world.

Rouben Mamoulian

Gershwin Liked Being Gershwin

Rouben Mamoulian (born 1897), Russian-born stage director and movie producer, was at the height of his Broadway career in the thirties when he knew Gershwin. He was famous for his staging of grand operas, operettas and musicals, including the world première of *Porgy and Bess*.

THE FIRST TIME I met George Gershwin was in late 1923 in Rochester, New York, where I had recently arrived from Europe to direct operas at the Eastman Theater. One evening I was asked to join some friends at a little place called the Corner Club. Among them I found Gene Goossens, the English conductor, Artur Rubinstein, the pianist, and a slim young man whom I had never met before. He was introduced as George Gershwin, the song writer. After an interlude of conversation, sandwiches and beer, Artur Rubinstein played the piano. He played brilliantly some of the great classic composers. When he finished we asked Gershwin to play for us. He willingly agreed and played several of his popular melodies with that sparkling vitality and fascinating rhythmic punctuations, the secret of which he knew so well. Among the songs he played was that humorous ditty *Misha, Yasha, Tasha, Sasha,* which always remained one of his favorites in spite of the fact that it had never been generally published. (Curious that the first time I met George he played this ditty and he played it again the last time I saw him, which was a few days before his death.) After having played his popular songs to our great enjoyment, Gershwin said that he had been working on something that he hoped would reach the concert stage. He was a little shy about playing it in front of Artur Rubinstein. However, we insisted, so he played parts of that new composition. I will never forget the novelty and freshness of that music—its marvelous colors and rhythmic variations and the strength and authority that underlined it. After he had finished playing, I asked him, "What are you going to call this, Mr. Gershwin?" He said, "I thought I'd call it *Rhapsody in Blue. . . .*"

A few months later he played it to a sensational reception in Carnegie Hall.

My first impression of Gershwin during that evening was that of a rather worried and anxious young man—very ambitious and not very happy. Rather reserved and self-centered and in some curious way suspicious of the world, looking not unlike a child with more apples than he can comfortably hold in his hands and afraid that someone would take them away from him.

I did not see Gershwin again until years later when I started working on *Porgy and Bess.* I was in Hollywood directing motion pictures when I heard that George was going to use *Porgy* as a libretto for his first opera. At first I was shocked. I felt that the play was so pure and complete in its form, had such a direct simplicity and strength, that any attempt to translate it into operatic form might spoil it. However, my second thought was that if there was a composer in the whole world equipped by the quality of his talent to achieve this task, George was that composer.

When the score was completed I was still on the Coast. The Theater Guild and George asked me to come back to New York and direct the opera. The score couldn't be sent to me in Hollywood because George was busy orchestrating it, but I felt so sure that it would be exciting and beautiful, that I signed a contract with the Guild without having heard a single note of what I was to direct.

George was particularly keen to orchestrate the score all by himself. He worked very long and hard at it. He wrote me in a letter, "I am orchestrating the opera at the present time and have about five months' work left. It is really a tremendous task scoring three hours of music." It was, and he did it. (And his was such a beautiful-looking manuscript!)

I finally arrived in New York and on the first evening I was to hear George's score, I met George and Ira in the Gershwin apartment. All three of us were very excited. George and Ira were obviously anxious for me to like the music. As for me, I was even more anxious. You see, I loved the story of *Porgy* and every single character in it; I loved its changing moods, its sadness and its gaiety, its passion and its tenderness, and all the emotional richness of the Negro soul expressed in it.

Porgy, the play, having been my very first production in New York, meant a great deal to me. I felt about it the way I imagine a mother feels about her first-born. If it were to be "clothed" in music I was jealously anxious for that music to be good. It had to be good!

It was rather amusing how all three of us were trying to be nonchalant and poised that evening, yet we were trembling with excitement. The brothers handed me a tall highball and put me in a comfortable leather armchair. George sat down at the piano while Ira stood over him like a guardian angel. George's hands went up in the air about to strike the shining keys. Halfway down, he changed his mind, turned to me and said, "Of course, Rouben, you must understand it's very difficult to play this score. As a matter of fact, it's really impossible! Can you play Wagner on the piano? Well, this is just like Wagner!" I assured George that I understood. Up went his nervous hands again and the next second I was listening to the opening "piano music" of the opera. I found it so exciting, so full of color and so provocative in its rhythm that after this first piano section was over, I jumped out of my armchair and interrupted George to tell him how much I liked it. Both brothers were as happy as children to hear words of praise, though heaven knows, they should have been used to them by then. When my explosion was over and they went back to the piano, they both blissfully closed their eyes before they continued with the lovely *Summertime* song. George played with the most beatific smile on his face. He seemed to float on the waves of his own music with the southern sun shining on him. Ira sang—he threw his head back with abandon, his eyes closed, and sang like a nightingale! In the middle of the song George couldn't bear it any longer and took over the singing from him. To describe George's face while he sang *Summertime* is something that is beyond my capacity as a writer. "Nirvana" might be the word! So it went on. George was the orchestra and sang half of the parts, Ira sang the other half. Ira was also frequently the audience. It was touching to see how he, while singing, would become so overwhelmed with admiration for his brother, that he would look from him to me with half-open eyes and pantomime with a soft gesture of his hand, as if saying, "*He* did it. Isn't it wonderful? Isn't *he* wonderful?" George would frequently take his eyes away from the score and covertly watch me and my reaction to the music while pretending that he wasn't really doing it at all. It was very late into the night before we finished with the opera and sometimes I think that in a way that was the best performance

of it I ever heard. We all felt exultantly happy. The next
morning both George and Ira had completely lost their
voices. For two days they couldn't talk, they only whispered.
I shall never forget that evening—the enthusiasm of the two
brothers about the music, their anxiety to do it justice, their
joy at its being appreciated and with it all their touching
devotion for each other. It is one of those rare tender memories one so cherishes in life.

The first day of rehearsing a play is always difficult. It is
like breaking mountains of ice. The end of it leaves one completely exhausted and usually a little depressed. Everything
seems awkward, disorganized, almost hopeless. That's the
way I felt after the first day of *Porgy and Bess*. I lay in my
bed in my apartment at the Navarro and was indulging in
rather melancholy and misanthropic thoughts. Suddenly the
phone rang and George Gershwin was announced. This delighted me as I felt in need of encouragement and kind words.
I picked up the receiver and said "Hello" with eager anticipation. George's voice came glowing with enthusiasm: "Rouben,
I couldn't help calling you . . . I just had to call you and
tell you how I feel. I am so thrilled and delighted over the
rehearsal today." (My heart started warming up and already
I began to feel better!) "Of course," he went on, "I always
knew that *Porgy and Bess* was wonderful, but I never thought
I'd feel the way I feel now. I tell you, after listening to that rehearsal today, I think the music is so marvelous—I really don't
believe I wrote it!"

George's attitude toward himself and his work was apt
to be misunderstood by people who did not know him well.
Because he liked his own music and praised himself, some
of them thought he was conceited. This was not so, as I myself discovered. Conceit is made of much sterner stuff—it was
not that with George. It was his faculty to look at himself
and his work in just as detached a manner as if he were looking at somebody else. George had a tremendous capacity for

appreciation and enthusiasm and always gave it generous expression in words. Whatever he liked, he praised. He happened to like his own music too, so he praised it without any self-consciousness or false modesty.

George was so completely naive and innocent in his liking of his own work that it actually became one of the endearing qualities of his nature. Some little expressions that would seem arrogant coming from other men were touching and lovable when coming from George. I remember once I had to meet George and several other friends for dinner in a restaurant across the street from the Guild Theatre. I was late, so I went there unshaven and rather haggard-looking. I apologized to the company for my appearance. George said, "Rouben, don't apologize. Personally, I love you when you're unshaven." "Why, George?" I asked. "Because," said he, "when you're unshaven, you look like me."

Another time we were having lunch at Lindy's after a morning's rehearsal which George had attended. As we sat there, I started, for some unknown reason, humming an air out of Rimsky-Korsakoff. George stopped eating, turned to me with a very shocked expression on his face and said, "Rouben, I think this is terrible! You have just been rehearsing my music and here you are humming some Russian melodies. Why do you do that?" At first, I thought George was joking, but then I saw the hurt look in his eyes and knew he was in dead earnest. So I said, "George, I am very sorry. I don't know why I did it." The lunch went on, but George didn't touch his food for quite a while, looking very depressed. Then suddenly his face lighted up with a smile, he turned to me and said with a triumphant ring in his voice: "I know why you were humming that Russian music." "Why?" I asked. "Because my parents were Russian," he said.

All artists need appreciation of their work from other people. It was especially so with George. With him it was a very vital need—he loved it and was hungry for it the way a flower is hungry for water. His talent thrived on success.

George loved playing the piano for people and would do it at the slightest provocation. At any gathering of friends, if there was a piano in the room, George would play it. I am sure that most of his friends in thinking of George at his best, think of George at the piano. I've heard many pianists and composers play for informal gatherings, but I know of no one who did it with such genuine delight and verve. Just as the few chosen people are blessed with *joie de vivre,* so was George blessed with the joy of playing the piano. George at the piano was George happy. He would draw a lovely melody out of the keyboard like a golden thread, then he would play with it and juggle it, twist it and toss it around mischievously, weave it into unexpected intricate patterns, tie it in knots and untie it and hurl it into a cascade of ever-changing rhythms and counterpoints. George at the piano was like a gay sorcerer celebrating his Sabbath.

He enjoyed his playing as much as his listeners did. Nor did he ever get tired of a melody. He could play *I've Got Rhythm* for the thousandth time, yet do it with such freshness and exuberance as if he had written it the night before. Through the whole period of *Porgy* rehearsals, whenever we got together for an evening of relaxation, George would go to the piano and play *Porgy and Bess* again. I remember once during the rehearsals he invited me to spend a week-end with him and some friends in Long Beach. "You must come out, Rouben, to relax and forget about *Porgy and Bess* and my music for a while," he said. I couldn't go, but on Monday morning I asked Alexander Steinert, who was in the party, what did they do over the week-end at George's. Alex replied, "We played *Porgy and Bess* Saturday and Sunday—all day and all night."

Oscar Levant

The Last Months

Gershwin was commissioned to write the score for the movie *Shall We Dance?* with Astaire and Rogers. He welcomed the opportunity to go to California; there he fell sick. It was a brain tumor, which turned out to be fatal.

Oscar Levant (born 1906), pianist, has appeared as soloist on all-Gershwin programs at the Lewisohn Stadium in New York and the Hollywood Bowl in California. His recording of the *Rhapsody in Blue* is still the most widely known and is regarded as an authentic interpretation.

ONE OF THE MOST memorable experiences I have ever had in music occurred during that California visit, when Mrs. Elizabeth Coolidge sponsored the performance of the four Schoenberg Quartets and the last group of Beethoven, played by the Kolisch ensemble. George, Ira, and I were overjoyed by this opportunity, and all of the music impressed us deeply.

We were all together on the tennis court one morning when the talk turned to the concert of the previous day.

"I'd like to write a quartet some day," said George. "But it will be something simple, like Mozart."

Schoenberg mistakenly interpreted Gershwin's typically irrelevant reflection as a comment on his work and answered, somewhat nettled.

"I'm not a simple man—and, anyway, Mozart was considered far from simple in his day."

Though George's acquaintance with formal music was a rather scattered one he had pronounced likings both in classic and contemporary works. A rather curious discernment—since it was so opposed to the characteristics of his own work—was his perception of the quality in Alban Berg's music. He first became acquainted with the *Lyrische Suite* by this most famous of Schoenberg's pupils in 1927 during a visit to Vienna. This, of course, was several years before Berg was known even as a name in America. Gershwin treasured the piano score of *Wozzeck* and was deeply impressed by the opera when he journeyed to Philadelphia for the performance under Stokowski in 1931.

Like many another musician, George found that he could get even more from phonograph records of his favorite works than he could from their scattered performances in public. Among the albums I recall which gave him particular pleasure were Stravinsky's *Symphonie des Psaumes*, the First Symphony of Shostakovitch, the Milhaud Violin Concerto, the *Lyrische Suite* of Berg and the complete Schoenberg Quartets privately recorded by the Kolisches in California. Somewhere, somehow, he had acquired a liking for the records of Honegger's lively operetta *Les Aventures du Roi Pausole*. On the other hand, he admired greatly certain records of Duke Ellington's orchestra for their rich effects and fine tonal originality—mood pieces like the *Creole Love Song*, *Swanee Rhapsody*, and *Daybreak Express*.

Among modern works he studied in score were Stravinsky's *Les Noces*, the Third Piano Concerto of Prokofieff, the Debussy piano preludes—for which he had great fondness—and various orchestral works by this composer and Ravel. During the period of work on *Porgy* he referred constantly to the score of *Die Meistersinger* as a guide to the plotting of the choral parts and for general precepts in vocal writing. Curiously, however, he refused throughout his career to study orchestration with a teacher, preferring his pragmatic approach, bulwarked by Cecil Forsyth's *Orchestration*, which he regarded almost as a Bible. . . .

So far as a partiality in older music was concerned, George leaned particularly toward certain expansive moods of

Brahms, whose string quartets we frequently played four-handed at the piano. It was the long line and free development of melodic material in Brahms that attracted him.

As a corollary, he identified certain expressions of his own with this composer, referring to the second theme of the *Second Rhapsody*—a swelling *legato* subject in A Major—as a Brahms theme. Also, one of his last songs to be published, *Love Walked In,* was always associated in his mind as a "Brahms strain" . . . .

One of his favorite chamber-music works was the great C Major Quintet (with two cellos) of Schubert, with which he first became acquainted during the period when he was writing *Of Thee I Sing* and *Let 'Em Eat Cake.* As a matter of fact, there is a slight influence of the beautiful second theme of the quintet's first movement in the tune he wrote for *Let 'Em Eat Cake, Two Hearts Are in Communion,* in the *Union Square* number.

George played little concert music at the piano, with the exception of certain Chopin preludes, for which he had no pronounced interpretative feeling. For technical purposes, when he was preparing to play his own music in public, endless repetitions of the first Cramer study sufficed.

❖   ❖   ❖

It was during the period of work on the *Goldwyn Follies* that the first evidence of George's illness asserted itself. All during his residence in California he had devoted himself recurrently to making public appearances as a pianist, even in cities as remote as St. Louis, Seattle, Portland and Detroit, making overnight trips by plane. One would see George on a certain day and return the next day to discover he was in the middle of a tour. This series culminated with his first appearance in Los Angeles, as soloist at a concert conducted by Smallens. The chorus and soloists of *Porgy and Bess* also appeared.

Though he had played the *Concerto* dozens of times in public with great fluency I noticed that he stumbled on an easy passage in the first movement. Then, in the *andante,* in playing the four simple octaves that conclude the movement above the sustained orchestral chords, he blundered again. When I went backstage he greeted me with the curious remark,

"When I made those mistakes I was thinking of you, you . . .", concluding with some gruffly uncomplimentary characterization.

At the second concert of the series, on the following night, he afterward remarked that he had experienced a curious odor of some undefinable burning smell in his nostrils as he was conducting one number, and a sudden dizzy headache. Nobody considered it to be anything of moment, including George himself. He was so completely the personification of vitality and resonant health that a physical or mental break-down seemed altogether unthinkable, particularly to George. The care of his physical being was almost a mania with him, a pursuit which he cultivated with considerable success. In the hills near his Hollywood home he had staked out a six-mile walk, whose daily execution seemed to me not only a feat in physical endurance but also an action traitorous to everything for which I stood.

I have no taste for annotating the next—and last—six months of George's life. There are, however, certain things which I would like to say briefly. The recurrence with in-creasing frequency of the headaches disturbed his friends, but not because they associated it with any organic disorder. The spells were interpreted as a neurotic manifestation of his dissatisfaction with working conditions in Hollywood, an expresson of his yearning to be elsewhere.

This, however, was plainly fallacious, for George's interests at this time continued to expand, his work went well and his mental outlook was altogether healthy. He took a great interest in the contemporary music that was being played in Los Angeles at the time, where, contrary to the usual opinion, the musical atmosphere was a sharp and bracing one. Stravinsky made a guest appearance with the Los Angeles Orchestra, conducting his own works; there were the Schoenberg Quartet concerts; the WPA Schoenberg-and-pupils concert; the presence of Ernest Toch and Aaron Copland on the coast—all these things interested and stimulated him.

The freshness of these contacts, indeed, aroused George to the contemplation of renewed work in large forms, which had not engaged his attention since *Porgy* more than two years before. From his conversation I believe this would have been in the field of ballet or, possibly, a string quartet.

As the weeks went on the headaches George suffered did not arouse anything more than quizzical comment until several months after their first occurrence, when a particularly severe attack prompted Leonore and Ira to insist that George submit to a thorough physical checkup.

This finally occurred on a Sunday morning, some six or seven weeks before his last Sunday. The doctor and neurologist arrived, and we went outside in the garden to have lunch. There was no ominous strain or tension in the air, for there had been no suspicion on which to base such feelings.

When George came down and shuffled over in his beach robe and sandals I called to him facetiously,

'What did the doctors say?"

He laughed, as if in relief, and said,

"Well, before they told me anything they wanted to rule out the possibility of a brain tumor."

With this final irony—in retrospect as in actuality—I reject the association of George with anything but life.

NOTES

Bach

Johann Sebastian's father, Johann Ambrosius, came from Erfurt to Eisenach in 1671, having been appointed town musician. He succeeded another member of the Bach tribe in that post. He married twice. Johann Sebastian was the eighth and last child of the first marriage.

The principal instruments for which Bach composed were: clavichord and harpsichord (the 48 preludes and fugues of his Well-Tempered Clavichord, the 32 Goldberg-Variations, etc), violin, organ, violoncello, violoncello piccolo, double bass, flute, clarinet.

Some biographers maintain that old Bach's blindness was the result of note-reading and manuscript copying which strained his eyes in early youth. An eye operation performed in 1750 by the famous English oculist John Taylor gave brief promise of success. But shortly thereafter Bach suffered a paralytic stroke.

Tibia=Flute.
Citharoedist "one who sings to the accompaniment of the cithara or lyre (the ancient guitar)." The reference here is to the ancient Greek musicians of this type.

Handel

We spell the name "Handel" in English fashion. There are documents in existence which indicate that the composer spelled his name variously—: Haendel, Hendel, Handel. The form "Hendel" was generally used by his relatives. In England, however, the composer always kept to "Handel."

At the beginning of February 1726 Handel applied for his English naturalization. On 14 February he went to the House of Lords and took the oath of allegiance. Six days later the King put his signature to the Bill that made him a British subject.

Beethoven

During his first epoch Beethoven was well on the way to becoming the first piano virtuoso of his time. A noted rival once burst out in exasperation: "He's no man—he's a devil. He will play me and all of us to death." As a composer he evolved slowly. Had he died as young as Mozart, he would not now be famous.

Clavecin = a French form of the clavichord. The clavichord (*clavis* key plus *chorda* string) is a keyed stringed instrument, the real forerunner of our pianoforte.

Beethoven's brother Johann, often called "unnatural," was a brute type. He was originally an apothecary at Linz, Upper Austria, but made a considerable fortune by taking army contracts in 1809. He acquired the estate of Gneixendorf near Krems, on the Danube. His matrimonial relations were so utterly disgusting that Beethoven had hitherto always refused to visit him.

Schubert

The cause of Schubert's death was officially recorded as "nervous fever." More precisely, it was typhus, typhus abdominalis. His obesity, a certain inclination towards alcoholism, and the bad water of the Neue Wieden district—all contributed to his contraction of the disease.

Berlioz

The last years of Berlioz's life are mainly a record of hard blows, one after the other. His son Louis died of yellow fever in Havana, at the age of thirty-three. His old journalistic colleague d'Ortigue died of apoplexy. At Monte Carlo, in March 1868, Berlioz suffered an attack of cerebral congestion; he was picked up by some workmen, dazed and bleeding. Eaten away by his incessant intestinal neuralgia, he could find relief from his pain only in opium.

Schumann

After Robert's death Clara Schumann became one of the most cele-brated pianists in the world. She combined feminine grace with mascu-line energy, and was equally at home with the works of Bach, Mozart, Beethoven, Chopin, and, of course, Schumann and Brahms. In her old age she was famous as a piano teacher. She died May 20, 1896.

Verdi

In private life Blanche Roosevelt was the Marchesa d'Alligri. Before her marriage she was Blanche Roosevelt Tucker, daughter of W. H. Tucker of Virginia, and was related to Theodore Roosevelt. Her bond to Verdi was the platonic admiration of a music fanatic and an opera-singer for a great maestro.

Debussy

Solfeggio, French: solfège = a vocal exercise using single syllables—do, re, mi, fa, sol, la, si.

SOURCES

Whenever the original source as well as the English translation are known to me, both are listed. In cases where I have not been able to ascertain the precise original source, I have cited only the work in which the item was found.

Wherever it was found advisable, Phoebe Rogoff Cave has edited and amended the material here compiled, both original and translated.

Johann Sebastian Bach

1) JOHANN FRIEDRICH AGRICOLA:
   Musikalische Bibliothek oder Gruendliche Nachricht nebst unpartheyischem Urtheil von alten and neuen musikalischen Schriften und Buechern. Band 1–4 (herausgegeben von Lorenz Mizler) Leipzig 1736-54.

   In English:
   The Bach Reader. A life of Johann Sebastian Bach in Letters and Documents. Edited by Hans T. David and Arthur Mendel. W. W. Norton & Company, New York, 1945.

2) JOHANN MATHIAS GESNER:
   See the Bach Reader.

3) CONSTANTIN BELLERMANN:
   Programma in quo Parnassus Musarum etc., von Constantin Bellerman, Minden, 1743.

   In English:
   See the Bach Reader.

4) JOHANN NIKOLAUS FORKEL:
Life of Johann Sebastian Bach. With a Critical View of his Compositions, by J. N. Forkel, Translated from the German by Mr. Stephenson, London, 1820.

5) HEINRICH NIKOLAUS GERBER:
Historisch-Biographisches Lexicon der Tonkuenstler Vol. I. Leipzig 1790-1792.

In English:
The Bach Reader.

6) PHILIP EMANUEL BACH:
See Forkel.

Ludwig van Beethoven

1) KARL CZERNY:
Beethoven. Depicted by his Contemporaries by Ludwig Nohl. Translated from the German by Emily Hill. London, William Reeves 188-.

2) BETTINA VON ARNIM:
See Nohl.

3) LUDWIG SPOHR:
See Nohl.

4) KARL GOTTLIEB FREUDENBERG:
See Nohl.

5) FRANZ GRILLPARZER:
Recollections of Beethoven by Franz Grillparzer. Translated by Mary Katherine Horgan. Music and Letters, January 1923, Volume IV, Number 1, London.

6) Dr. L.:
   "Beethoven in Gneixendorf" von Dr. L. Deutsche Musikzeitung,
   1862. Wien, Wessely und Buesing.

   In English:
   See Nohl.

7) ANSELM HÜTTENBRENNER:
   Music and Manners in the Classical Period by Henry Edward
   Krehbiel. New York 1898. The book contains Hüttenbrenner's letter
   to Thayer.

Hector Berlioz

1) ERNEST LEGOUVÉ:
   Sixty Years of Recollections by Ernest Legouvé, of the Académie-
   Française. Translated with notes by Albert D. Vandam. In two
   volumes, Vol. I, London and Sydney 1893.

2) FERDINAND HILLER:
   Hector Berlioz, von Ferdinand Hiller. Westermann's Monatshefte,
   45. Band. Braunschweig, Georg Westermann 1879. Translated by
   Phoebe Rogoff Cave.

3) RICHARD WAGNER:
   My Life by Richard Wagner. In two volumes. New York, Dodd,
   Mead and Company, 1911.

4) SIR CHARLES HALLÉ:
   Life and Letters of Sir Charles Hallé. Being an Autobiography with
   Correspondence and Diaries. Edited by His Son, C. H. Hallé and
   His Daughter, Marie Hallé. London, Smith, Elder & Co., 1896.

5) CAMILLE SAINT-SAËNS:
   Hector Berlioz. From the French of Camille Saint-Saëns, The Musical World, Vol. III, January 1903. Boston, Leipzig, New York.

Johannes Brahms

1) Eduard Marxsen:
Johannes Brahms von LaMara. Neubearbeiteter Einzeldruck aus den Musikalischen Studienkoepfen. Leipzig. Breitkopf & Haertel 1911. Translated by Phoebe Rogoff Cave.

2) Robert Schumann:
"Neue Zeitschrift fuer Musik" 1853, October 23, Leipzig, J. A. Barth.
In English:
Brahms by Walter Niemann. Translated from the German by Catherine Alison Phillips. 1929. Alfred A. Knopf, New York.

3) Albert Dietrich:
Recollections of Johannes Brahms by Albert Dietrich and J. V. Widmann. Translated by Dora E. Hecht. London, Seeley and Co. Limited, 1899.

4) Max Kalbeck:
Johannes Brahms von Max Kalbeck, Berlin 1904-14, Deutsche Brahmsgesellschaft. Translated by Phoebe Rogoff Cave.

5) Andrew de Ternant:
Debussy and Brahms. By Andrew de Ternant. The Musical Times, July 1, 1924. London, Novello and Company, 1924.

6) Guido Adler:
Johannes Brahms. His Achievement, His Personality and His Position, by Guido Adler. The Musical Quarterly, Vol. XIX, No. 2, April 1933. Georg Schirmer, New York—Boston.

Frederic François Chopin

1) FELIX MENDELSSOHN:
   Briefe aus den Jahren 1830 bis 1847 von Felix Mendelssohn-
   Bartholdy. Herausgegeben von Paul Mendelssohn-Bartholdy und
   Prof. Dr. Carl Mendelssohn-Bartholdy. Vierte Auflage. Leipzig,
   Hermann Mendelssohn, 1878.

   In English:
   Robert Schumann, by Frederick Niecks, Edited by Christina Niecks,
   J. M. Dent & Sons LTD, London, New York: E. P. Dutton.

2) ALFRED JAMES HIPKINS:
   How Chopin Played. From Contemporary Impressions collected
   from the Diaries and Note-books of the late A. J. Hipkins by Edith
   J. Hipkins. London, J. M. Dent and Sons, LTD, 1937.

3) FRANZ LISZT:
   Life of Chopin by F. Liszt. Translated from the French by Martha
   Walker Cook. Boston, Oliver Ditson & Co., 1863.

4) GEORGE SAND:
   Histoire de ma vie, par George Sand. 3 volumes. Paris, L. Schnauss,
   1855.
   In English:
   Frederick Niecks: Frederick Chopin as a Man and Musician. Lon-
   don & New York, Novello, Ewer & Co., 1888.

5) ANNE RICHMOND RICHIE:
   See A. J. Hipkins.

6) MORITZ KARASOWSKI:
   Frederic Chopin. His Life, Letters and Works by Moritz Karasowski.
   Translated from the German by Emily Hill. Vol. II. London: Wil-
   liam Reeves, 1879.

Claude Debussy

1) CAMILLE BELLAIGUE:
Souvenirs de Musique et de Musiciens. Nouvelle Librairie Nationale,
Paris, 1921.

In English:
Léon Vallas, Claude Debussy. His Life and Works. Translated from
the French by Maire and Grace O'Brien. Oxford, University Press,
London, 1933.

2) GABRIEL PIERNÉ:
Souvenirs d'Achille Debussy par Gabriel Pierné. Revue Musicale, 1er
Mai, 1926. Editions de la Nouvelle Revue Française, Paris. Trans-
lated by Phoebe Rogoff Cave.

3) MARGUERITE VASNIER:
Debussy à dix-huit ans par M. Vasnier. See Revue Musicale. Translated by Phoebe Rogoff Cave.

4) J. G. PRODHOMME:
Claude Achille Debussy by J. G. Prodhomme. The Musical Quarterly, vol. 4, No. 4, October 1918. Georg Schirmer, New York–Boston.

5) PASTEUR VALLERY-RADOT:
Claude Debussy, Souvenirs par Pasteur Vallery-Radot. Revue des
Deux Mondes, CVIIIe Année, 1938, 15 Mai, Paris. Translated by
Phoebe Rogoff Cave.

George Gershwin

1) IRA GERSHWIN:
George Gershwin. Edited and designed by Merle Armitage. Longmans, Green & Co., London, New York, Toronto. 1938.

2) ROUBEN MAMOULIAN:
See Merle Armitage.

3) OSCAR LEVANT:
Oscar Levant, A Smattering of Ignorance. Doubleday, Doran & Co. New York, 1940.

Christoph Willibald von Gluck

1) KARL DITTERS VON DITTERSDORF:
   The Autobiography of Karl von Dittersdorf. Dictated to his Son.
   Translated from the German by A. D. Coleridge. London, Richard
   Bentley and Son, 1896.

2) CHARLES BURNEY:
   The Present State of Music in Germany, the Netherlands, and
   United Provinces. Or, the Journal of a tour through those countries,
   undertaken to collect materials for a general history of music by
   Charles Burney, vol. I. London, T. Becket and Co., 1773.

3) OLIVIER DE CORANCEZ:
   Gluck, by Martin Cooper. With a preface by Edward J. Dent. New
   York, Oxford University Press, 1935.

4) CLAUDE JOSEPH DORAT:
   Coup. d'oeil sur la littérature, Neuchatel 1780, Partie 1. Translated
   by Phoebe Rogoff Cave.

5) MICHAEL KELLY:
   Reminiscences of Michael Kelly of the King's Theatre and Theatre
   Royal Drury Lane, vol. I. London, Henry Colburn, 1826.

6) JOHANN FRIEDRICH REICHARDT:
   Allegemeine Musikalische Zeitung, 1813, No. 41. Leipzig. Translated by Phoebe Rogoff Cave.

Georg Friedrich Handel

1) JOHN MAINWARING:
Memoirs of the Life of the Late George Frederic Handel. To which
is added a catalogue of his works and observations upon them.
London. Printed for R. and J. Dodsley, 1760.

2) RICHARD CLARK:
Reminiscences of Handel, His Grace the Duke of Chandos, Powells
the Harpers, The Harmonious Blacksmith and others with a list of
the Anthems etc. By Richard Clark. London. Published for the
Editor 1836.

3) FREDERIC BONNET:
Frederic Bonnet, Brandenburg envoy to the English Court. Report
in the Berlin Archives, July 19, 1717.
In English:
George Frederic Handel. His Personality and His Times by New-
man Flower. New York, Charles Scribner's Sons, 1948.

4) CHARLES BURNEY:
An Account of the Musical Performances in Westminster Abbey and
the Pantheon Commemoration of Handel. By Charles Burney. London, 1785.

5) SIR JOHN HAWKINS:
General History of the Science and Practice of Music by Sir John
Hawkins. Volume the Second. London, J. Alfredo Novello, 1853.

Franz Joseph Haydn

1) JOSEPH CARPANI:
   The Life of Haydn in a series of Letters written at Vienna. Followed
   by the Life of Mozart with observations on Metastasio by L. A. C.
   Bombet. With Notes by William Gardiner. Boston: J. H. Wilkins
   and R. B. Carter. Philadelphia, 1839.

2) ANONYMOUS:
   Haydn. A Creative Life in Music by Karl Geiringer. W. W. Norton
   & Company. New York, 1846.

3) GEORG AUGUST GRIESINGER:
   Biographische Notizen ueber Joseph Haydn. Von Georg August
   Greisinger. Leipzig, bey Breitkopf und Haertel. 1810. Translated by
   Phoebe Rogoff Cave.

4) ALBERT CHRISTOPH DIES:
   Biographische Nachrichten von Joseph Haydn. Nach muendlichen
   Erzaehlungen desselben entworfen und herausgegeben von Albert
   Christoph Dies, Landschaftsmaler. Wien 1810. Camesinaische
   Buchhandlung. Translated by Phoebe Rogoff Cave.

5) STENDHAL:
   See L. A. C. Bombet.

Franz Liszt

1) ADAM LISZT:
Life of Liszt by Ludwig Nohl. Translated from the German by George P. Upton. Chicago. A. C. McClurg & Company, 1887.

2) MARIE COUNTESS D'AGOULT:
Countess d'Agoult (Daniel Stern), Memoires, 1833-1854, une introduction de Daniel Ollivier, Paris, 1927.
In English:
The Man Liszt, A Study of the Tragi-Comedy of a Soul Divided against Itself, by Ernest Newman. Cassell and Company Limited, London, Toronto, Melbourne, Sydney, 1934.

3) JOSEPH FISCHHOFF:
Liszt in Wien. (Aus einem Privatbriefe vom 13ten). Neue Zeitschrift fuer Musik. Herausgegeben von Robert Schumann. Achter Band, No. 34, den 27. April 1838. Leipzig, bei Robert Friese.
In English:
Franz Liszt. Artist and Man 1811-1840 by L. Ramann. Translated from the German by Miss E. Cowdery. Vol. II. London: W. H. Allen & Co. 1882.

4) RICHARD WAGNER:
My Life, by Richard Wagner. In two volumes. Vol. I. New York, Dodd, Mead and Company, 1911.

5) AMY FAY:
Music-Study in Germany from the Home Correspondence of Amy Fay. Edited by Mrs. Fay Peirce. Eighteenth Edition. New York, The Macmillan Company 1905.

6) THE REVEREND HUGH R. HAWEIS:
Hugh Reginald Haweis: Memories of a Musical Life. New York, C. Fisher; Boston, J. White, 1909.

Gustav Mahler

1) BRUNO WALTER:
   Bruno Walter: Gustav Mahler. Translated by James Galston. With a
   Biographical Essay by Ernst Krenek. The Greystone Press, New
   York 1941.

2) GUIDO ADLER:
   Gustav Mahler von Guido Adler. Universal Edition A.–S. Leipzig–
   Wien 1916.

3) UGO GIARDINI:
   Gustav Mahler in New York by Ugo Giardini. Corriere de la Sera,
   1912, Milano.

4) ALMA MAHLER:
   Gustav Mahler. Memories and Letters by Alma Mahler. Translated
   by Basil Creighton. John Murray. London 1946.

Felix Mendelssohn-Bartholdy

1) LUDWIG RELLSTAB:
   Life of Felix Mendelssohn-Bartholdy. From the German of W. A.
   Lampadius. With Supplementary Sketches by Julius Benedict,
   Henry F. Charley, Ludwig Rellstab, Bayard Taylor, R. S. Willis, and
   J. G. Dwight. Edited and translated by William Leonhard Gage.
   New York & Philadelphia. Frederick Leypoldt, 1865.

2) WILLIAM SMYTH ROCKSTRO:
   Mendelssohn by W. S. Rockstro. New York, Scribner and Welford,
   1884.

3) EDUARD PHILLIPP DEVRIENT:
   My Recollections of Felix Mendelssohn-Bartholdy and his Letters
   to me by Eduard Devrient. Translated from the German by Natalia
   Macfarren. London. Richard Bentley, 1869.

Wolfgang Amadäus Mozart

1) JOHANN ANDREAS SCHACHTNER:
Life of Mozart by Otto Jahn. Translated from the German by Pauline D. Townsend. With a preface by George Grove. In three volumes. London 1891.

2) FRIEDRICH MELCHIOR GRIMM:
Friedrich Melchior Grimm: Correspondence littéraire, philosophique et critique, Paris 1813, III. Translated by Phoebe Rogoff Cave.

3) JOHANN GEORG LEOPOLD MOZART:
The Letters of Mozart and His Family. Chronologically Arranged, Translated and Edited with an Introduction by Emily Anderson. With extracts from the letters of Constance Mozart to Johann Anton André translated and edited by C. B. Oldman. Volume II. Macmillan and Co. London 1938.

4) MICHAEL KELLY:
Reminiscences of Michael Kelly of the King's Theatre and Theatre Royal Drury Lane. Vol. I. London, Henry Colburn 1826.

5) ADOLPH HEINRICH VON SCHLICHTEGROLL:
The Life of Haydn in a series of Letters written at Vienna. Followed by The Life of Mozart with observations on Metastasio by L. A. C. Bombet. With Notes by William Gardiner. Boston: J. H. Wilkins and R. B. Carter. Philadelphia 1839.

6) FRANZ NĚMETSCHEK:
Franz Němetschek, Leben des K. K. Kapellmeisters Wolfgang Gottlieb Mozart, nach Originalquellen beschrieben. Prag 1798. Translated by Phoebe Rogoff Cave.

7) JOSEPH DEINER:
Mozarts Persoenlichkeit; Urteile der Zeitgenossen, gesammelt und erlaeutert von Albert Leitzmann. Leipzig, Insel-Verlag, 1914. Translated by Phoebe Rogoff Cave.

Modeste Petrovich Musorgsky

1) NIKOLAI KOMPANEISKY:
The Musorgsky Reader. A Life of Modeste Petrovich Musorgsky in Letters and Documents. Edited and Translated by Jay Leyda and Sergei Bertensson. W. W. Norton & Company, New York.

2) NIKOLAI ANDREYEVICH RIMSKY-KORSAKOFF:
My Musical Life. Translated by Judah A. Joffe. Edited with an introduction by Carl Van Vechten. Alfred A. Knopf, New York, 1925.

3) D. MIKHAILOVNA LEONOVA:
Neues ueber Musorgsky. Von Helene Orthmann—Berlin. Die Musik. XV. Jahrgang, Heft 7, April 1923. Deutsche Verlagsanstalt in Stuttgart.
Translated by Phoebe Rogoff Cave.

4) ILYA REPIN:
The Musorgsky Reader.

5) SERGE BERTENSSON:
Modeste Musorgsky's Last Hours. (Short pages from family memoirs) by Serge Bertensson. The Etude (Music Magazine) July 1941, Philadelphia, Pa.

Henry Purcell

1) LORD CHAMBERLAIN:
   Purcell by J. A. Westrup. The Master Musicians. London, J. M. Dent and Sons. New York, E. P. Dutton and Co., 1937.

2) SIR JOHN HAWKINS:
   General History of the Science and Practice of Music by Sir John Hawkins. Volume the Second. London, J. Alfredo Novello, 1853.

3) CHARLES BURNEY:
   A General History of Music. From the Earliest Ages to the Present Period (1789) by Charles Burney. Volume the Second. With Critical and Historical Notes by Frank Mercer. London 1935. G. T. Fouls & Co.

Jean Philippe Rameau

1) THE ARCHIVES OF CLERMONT EN AUVERGNE:
Les années de jeunesse de J. P. Rameau par Henri Quittard. Reprint in Revue d'Histoire et de Critique Musicale, 1902. Translated by Phoebe Rogoff Cave.

2) HUGUES MARET:
La jeunesse de Rameau par Michel Brenet. Rivista Musicale Italiana. Volume IX, Anno 1902. Fratelli Bocca Editori, Torino, 1902. Translated by Phoebe Rogoff Cave.

3) EMILE DACIER:
L'Opéra au XVIIIe siècle. Les premières représentations du "Dardanus" de Rameau, par Emile Dacier. La Revue Musicale, No. 4, Avril 1903, Paris. Translated by Phoebe Rogoff Cave.

4) CHARLES COLLÉ:
Lionel de la Laurencie, quelques Documents sur J. P. Rameau et sa famille. Paris, Impressions Artistiques L. M. Fortin, 1907. Translated by Phoebe Rogoff Cave.

5) FRIEDRICH MELCHOIR GRIMM:
Friedrich Melchior Grimm: Correspondence littéraire, philosophique et critique. Paris 1813, VI. Translated by Phoebe Rogoff Cave.

6) MICHEL-PAUL-GUIDE CHABANON:
Eloge de M. Rameau par M. Chabanon de l'Academie Royale des Inscriptions & Belles Lettres. Paris, de l'Imprimerie de M. Lambert, 1764. Translated by Phoebe Rogoff Cave.

Franz Schubert

1) FERDINAND SCHUBERT:
   Aus Franz Schubert's Leben, von Ferdinand Schubert. Neue Zeitschrift fuer Musik. 23. April und 3. Mai 1839, Leipzig, J. A. Barth.

   In English:
   The Schubert Reader, by Otto Erich Deutsch, Translated by Eric Blom. W. W. Norton & Co. New York, 1947.

2) ANTON HOLZAPFEL:
   Zwei Briefe an Ferdinand Luib ueber Schubert von Anton Holzapfel, 1858. Jarbuch der Grillparzer-Gesellschaft, Wien 1901.

   In English:
   Franz Schubert. The Man and His Circle by Newman Flower. Cassell and Co. London, Toronto, Melbourne and Sydney, 1928.

3) JOSEF FREIHERR VON SPAUN:
   Aufzeichnungen des Josef Freiherr von Spaun ueber Franz Schubert. Mitgeteilt von A. Fellner. Der Merker, 2. Jahrgang, Heft 10/11. Wien. Translated by Phoebe Rogoff Cave.

4) ANSELM HÜTTENBRENNER:
   Erinnerungen an Schubert von Anselm Hüttenbrenner. Jahrbuch der Grillparzer-Gesellschaft, Wien, 1906.

   In English:
   See Newman Flower.

5) FRANZ AND FRITZ VON HARTMANN:
   See The Schubert Reader.

6) FRANZ VON SCHOBER:
   The Life of Franz Schubert by Heinrich Kreissle von Hellborn. Translated by Arthur Duke Coleridge. With an appendix by George Grove. Vol. II. London, 1869.

Robert Schumann

1) FRIEDRICH WIECK:
Der Musikpaedagoge Friedrich Wieck und seine Familie. Mit
besonderer Beruecksichtigung seines Schwiegersohnes Robert Schumann von Dr. Victor Joss. Dresden, Verlag von Oscar Damm, 1902.

In English:
Schumann by Joan Chissell. London, J. M. Dent and Sons. 1948.

2) F. GUSTAV JANSEN:
Die Davidsbuendler. Aus Robert Schumann's Sturm-und-Drang-
Periode. Ein Beitrag zur Biographie R. Schumann's nebst unge-
druckten Briefen, Aufsaetzen und Portraetskizzen aus seinem
Freundeskreise. Von F. Gustav Jansen. Leipzig, Verlag von Breit-
kopf und Haertel 1883. Translated by Phoebe Rogoff Cave.

3) FRIEDRICH NIECKS:
Schumanniana: Reminiscences, Anecdotes, and Discussions by Fr.
Niecks. The Monthly Musical Record. Vol. XIV—1884. London.

4) WILHELM JOSEF VON WASIELEWSKI:
Robert Schumann. Eine Biographie von Wilhelm Joseph von
Wasielewski. Dresden: R. Kunze, 1858.
In English:
Life of Robert Schumann by Wilhelm Joseph von Wasielewski.
Translated by A. L. Alger. Boston: O. Ditson & Co. 1871.

5) CLARA SCHUMANN:
Clara Schumann. An Artist's Life, based on Material Found in
Diaries and Letters by Berthold Litzmann. Translated and abridged
from The Fourth Edition by Grace E. Hadow. With a preface by
W. H. Hadow. Vol. II. Macmillan & Co., London, 1913.

Richard Strauss

1) FRANZ TRENNER:
Schweizerische Musikzeitung. Revue Musicale Suisse. 90. Jahrgang,
No. 8/9. 1. September, 1950. Zuerich. Translated by Phoebe Rogoff
Cave.

2) WILLIAM ARMSTRONG:
Richard Strauss and His Works. A Talk with the Composer by
William Armstrong. The Etude. 1903, Vol. 21, No. 12, Philadelphia,
Pa.

3) MAX MARSCHALK:
From an interview with Richard Strauss by Max Marschalk. Berliner
Tageblatt. Clipping. (Year and date unknown). Translated by
Phoebe Rogoff Cave.

4) SIDNEY S. BLOCH:
Interview with Sidney S. Bloch by Otto Zoff. Translated by Phoebe
Rogoff Cave.

5) RUDOLF HARTMANN:
See Schweizerische Musikzeitung.

Sir Arthur Sullivan

1) CHRISTOPHER VICKRY BRIDGMAN:
   The Chapel Royal Days of Arthur Sullivan, by an Old Fellow-
   Chorister (Christopher Vickry Bridgman). The Musical Times.
   Vol. XLII, London, 1901.

2) ERNEST G. DE GLEHN:
   Arthur Seymour Sullivan by Henry Saxe Wyndham. London, Kegan
   Paul, Trench, Trubner & Co., J. Curwen & Sons. 1926.

3) FRANÇOIS CELLIER:
   Gilbert, Sullivan and d'Oyly Carte. Reminiscences of the Savoy and
   the Savoyards, by François Cellier & Cunningham Bridgeman.
   London, Sir Isaac Pitman & Sons. 1927.

4) SIR ARTHUR LAWRENCE:
   Sir Arthur Sullivan. Life Story, Letters and Reminiscences by Arthur
   Lawrence. With critique by B. W. Findon and Bibliography by
   Wilfrid Bendall. Herbert S. Stone and Company, Chicago and New
   York, 1900.

Peter Ilich Tchaikovsky

1) FANNY DUERBACH:
The Life and Letters of Peter Ilich Tschaikovsky by Modeste Tschaikovsky. Edited from the Russian with an Introduction by Rose Newmarch. London: John Lane The Brodley Head. New York: John Lane Company, 1906.

2) HERMAN AUGUSTOVICH LAROCHE:
See Modeste Tschaikovsky.

3) NADEJDA FILARETOVNA VON MECK:
Beloved Friend. The Story of Tchaikovsky and Nadejda von Meck. By Catherine Drinker Bowen and Barbara von Meck. New York, Random House 1937.

4) P. V. TCHAIKOVSKY:
Recollections of Tchaikovsky by Mme. Anatol Tchaikovsky. Music and Letters, April 1940. Vol. XXI, No. 2. Sussex.

Giuseppe Verdi

1) FRANCIS TOYE:
   Giuseppe Verdi. His Life and Works by Francis Toye. Introduction
   by Herbert Weinstock. Alfred A. Knopf, New York, 1946.

2) GIULIO RICARDI:
   Verdi. An Anecdotic History of His Life and Works by Arthur
   Pougin. Translated from the French by James E. Matthew. London,
   H. Grevel & Co. 1887.

3) MARIANA BARBIERI-NINI:
   Gino Monaldi, Verdi. Torino 1926, Fratelli Bocca, Biblioteca artistica
   vol. 16.

4) BLANCHE ROOSEVELT:
   Verdi: Milan and Othello. Being a Short Life of Verdi, with Letters
   written about Milan and the New Opera of Othello by Blanche
   Roosevelt. Ward and Downey, London, 1887.

5) ANTONIO GHISLANZONI:
   Antonio Ghislanzoni: Reminiscenze artistiche ed artisti di teatro.
   Milano, 1871–80.
   In English:
   See Pougin.

6) ARRIGO BOITO:
   See Toye.

Richard Wagner

1) FERDINAND PRAEGER:
Wagner as I knew Him, by Ferdinand Praeger. New York, Longmans, Green & Co. 1892.

2) FRIEDRICH PECHT:
Life of Richard Wagner of C. F. Glasenapp. Authorised English Version by Wm. Ashton Ellis, vol. I. London, Kegan Paul, Trench, Trubner & Co., 1900.

3) MALWIDA VON MEYSENBUG:
Memoirs of Malwida von Meysenbug. Rebel in Bombazine. Edited by Mildred Adams from the translation of Elsa von Meysenbug Lyons. New York, W. W. Norton & Co. 1936.

4) ELIZA WILLE:
Fuenfzehn Briefe von Richard Wagner. Nebst Erinnerungen und Erlaeuterungen von Eliza Wille. Berlin. Verlag von Gebrueder Paetel 1894. Translated by Phoebe Rogoff Cave.

5) COSIMA WAGNER:
Eberhard Kretschmar, Richard Wagner, Sein Leben in Selbsteugnissen, Briefen und Berichten. Im Propylaeen-Verlag Berlin 1939. Translated by Phoebe Rogoff Cave.

6) SOPHIE RÜTZOW:
Sophie Rützow, Richard Wagner und Bayreuth. Ausschnitte und Erinnerungen; 1943. Verlag Knorr & Hirth, Muenchen. Translated by Phoebe Rogoff Cave.

7) PAUL VON JOUKOWSKY:
Richard Wagner. Der deutsche Musiker und Mensch. Selbstzeugnisse und Zeitberichte, eingeleitet und biographisch gestaltet von Paul Alfred Merbach. Robert Lutz Nachfolger, Otto Schramm, Stuttgart 1933. Translated by Phoebe Rogoff Cave.

INDEX

DE